MAN AND SOCIETY

MAN AND SOCIETY

In an Age of Reconstruction

STUDIES IN MODERN SOCIAL STRUCTURE

BY

KARL MANNHEIM

With a Bibliographical Guide to the Study of Modern Society

A Harvest Book

NEW YORK

HARCOURT, BRACE & WORLD, INC.

Based on
Mensch und Gesellschaft im Zeiltalter im des Umbaus
Leiden (Holland) 1935

Translated from the German
by
Edward Shils
Revised and considerably enlarged by the Author
London, 1940

TABLE OF CONTENTS

CONTENTS

PART I

RATIONAL AND IRRATIONAL ELEMENTS IN CONTEMPORARY SOCIETY

I

II

III

IV

V

II

III

IV

V

VI

VII

VIII

IX

X

PART III

CRISIS, DICTATORSHIP, WAR

I

PART IV

THOUGHT AT THE LEVEL OF PLANNING

I

II

III

IV

V

VI

of and of lagging behind one's age. Realistic thinking
must always take into account the factors of uncertainty.
Two dangers: rationalist dogmatism and the mental
indolence which sometimes terms itself irrationalism . 199

PART V

PLANNING FOR FREEDOM

I

1. *Our ambivalent attitude towards planning.* Antagonism
   between the traditionalist and functionalist modes of
   thinking. Meaning of the Romanticists' rebellion
   against the dehumanizing effect of the application of
   science to social relationships. The technical approach
   to society goes hand in hand with a corresponding
   type of social philosophy.
2. *Preliminary Classification of Social Techniques.* Their
   definition. Marx's approach as contrasted with the
   multidimensional conception of society. Three main
   hypotheses suggested in this book for characterizing
   the basic trends in modern society.

II

1. *Their change from the craftsmanship level to mass
   organization.* Tribal and medieval society. Liberal
   age. The army of the absolute state as the first experiment in applying social techniques on a large scale.
   The different meaning of social techniques in American
   society, in Soviet Russia, in Fascism.
2. *Lessons democracy could learn from the use of social
   techniques in totalitarian states.* The distorted and the
   true meanings of co-ordination. Difference between
   planning for conformity and planning for freedom.

III

Planning as the rational mastery of the irrational. Transformation of society in terms of the transformation of social
controls. Simpler forms of social control. The difference
between immediate influencing and anonymous pressure.
The transmutation of social energy. Analysis of an historical

PART VI

FREEDOM AT THE LEVEL OF PLANNING

CONTENTS

ACKNOWLEDGMENTS

As this book has been in the making for the past five or six years, certain parts of it have already appeared in various forms : Parts I, II, and IV were published in an abridged form in German as *Mensch und Gesellschaft im Zeitalter des Umbaus* (A. W. Sijthoff's Uitgeversmaatschappij N.V., Leiden, 1935). In English the preliminary drafts of some of the chapters have appeared either as lectures or articles. Part I was given, 1934, as a *Hobhouse Memorial Lecture* at Bedford College, University of London, under its present title, and was published as a lecture by the Oxford University Press. A sketch of the second part was published by the *Sociological Review*, vol. 26, No. 2, London, 1934. The body of Part III corresponds to a lecture given at the London School of Economics, and published as one chapter of the book *Peaceful Change : An International Problem*, edited by C. A. W. Manning (London, Macmillan and Co., 1937). A brief section of Part V was published in the volume *Human Affairs*, edited by R. B. Cattell, J. Cohen, and R. M. W. Travers under the title " Present Trends in the Building of Society " (London, Macmillan and Co., 1937). I wish to express my gratitude to the Trustee of the *Hobhouse Memorial Lectures*, the editorial board of the *Sociological Review*, and to the publishers, A. W. Sijthoff, and the Macmillan Company for allowing me to use these parts again.

It may also be worth while to point out the differences between the parts in relation to the time they were published, because the German book especially, which appeared in 1935, forecast certain recent trends of our present society in their initial stage, forecasts which then appeared rather bewildering. Since that time not only have events moved in the direction it suggested, but also the methods of thinking and research it diagnosed as promising new trends seem to be gaining in validity. This is perhaps worth mentioning in a period when we are discussing whether forecasts in the social sciences are possible at all. Small as it is, this apparent corroboration of certain hypotheses is encouraging to an author who is only groping his way to the understanding of some of the present changes in our society.

The new parts, which represent more than half of the present volume, reflect, as the introduction points out, the recent developments of the author's thinking.

The present book would not have been possible without the devoted help of my friends and students. In the German edition I have already expressed my gratitude to my wife, who has always taken an active part in my fundamental interests, and to Adolf Löwe, whose similar background and experiences helped in discussions to clarify many of the issues. In this English edition I have first to give my thanks to Edward Shils (University of Chicago), who has not only prepared the translation of those chapters which coincide with the German book, but who has also supplemented the bibliography which I have been collecting for many years with some kindred items. His very valuable understanding and broad knowledge meant not only responsiveness, but new stimulus. I owe very many stimulating suggestions to Dr. Hans Gerth. The new parts were written originally in English, but a more or less adequate expression of my ideas in a new language would not have been possible without a thorough discussion of nearly all the items with Miss Joan Tracey, B.A. (Oxon.), Mrs. Jane Floud, B.Sc.Econ. (London), and Miss Helen Hiett, B.A. (Chicago). For their help in reading the manuscript I have to thank Mr. O. Dick, B.A. (London) and Mr. Gilbert Parr. I owe many thanks to Dr. A. Schwarzschild who has given me devoted assistance, especially in preparing the index and in checking the references of the bibliography.

MAN AND SOCIETY

INTRODUCTION

THE SIGNIFICANCE OF THE AGE OF SOCIAL
RECONSTRUCTION

The Crisis of Liberalism and Democracy as seen from the Continental and Anglo-Saxon Points of View

The German edition of this book was dedicated to " My Masters and Pupils in Germany ". Thus it was originally dedicated to those who had experienced in their own lives the tremendous changes of an age of transformation. If this book appears in English, its function alters automatically. It is no longer an attempt at self-enlightenment, made for the benefit of those who have actually lived through these experiences ; it attempts to explain the standpoint of these people to a world which has only hearsay knowledge of such changes and is still wrapped in an illusion of traditional stability.

We should not try to belittle or conceal the difference between these points of view. It is most clearly expressed in the fact that to the Western countries the collapse of liberalism and democracy and the adoption of a totalitarian system seem to be the passing symptoms of a crisis which is confined to a few nations, while those who live within the danger zone experience this transition as a change in the very structure of modern society.

For those who are spared these convulsions it is consoling to think that the world is still suffering from the effects of the War. They are glad to soothe themselves with the reflection that dictatorships have often been established in the course of history as temporary solutions in an emergency. On the other hand those who have had first-hand knowledge of the crisis, even if they are keen opponents of dictatorship, are united in the belief that both the social order and the psychology of human beings are changing through and through, and that if this is an evil it is an evil which sooner or later is bound to spread. They are convinced moreover that we should not let ourselves be duped by this momentary lull, but should use it to acquire the new techniques, without which it is impossible to face the new situation. The difference in experience is irreconcilable ; it colours both the interpretation of isolated facts and the diagnosis of the position as a whole. Where human and social problems are concerned there ought to be a continuous exchange of ideas between different countries and groups. It is only too easy for a nation to drug itself with false assumptions or to distort the meaning of events to fit a frame of reference which is justified, not so much by the facts themselves as by the mood prevailing in the country. Here exaggerated pessimism can be just as dangerous as exaggerated optimism. The task of those to whom destiny has given the opportunity of living in many different countries and of identifying themselves with various points of view has always been to consider this conflict of attitudes and to work it out for themselves, in a form where differences of opinion can either be diametrically opposed or blended in a new synthesis.

The author has derived the greatest profit from learning to think about this very matter both from the German and the English points of view. This book in its present form has been influenced first by his experiences in Germany and later by the English way of thinking, and is an attempt at reconciling the two.

To this book the old saying, " *Habent sua fata libelli* " can be truly applied. When the different chapters of this book were written its author was completely under the influence of experiences bred by the disintegrating tendencies of liberal democratic society. His attention was primarily directed to the failure of the liberal democratic machinery in the Weimar Republic ; he had witnessed its impotence to solve the problems of modern mass society. He saw how, under certain social conditions, the planlessness of the liberal order turned into anarchy, how the principle of *laissez-faire*, which once maintained the balance of the social process, at this stage of development resulted in chaos, both in political and in cultural life.

Owing to these experiences he realized that *laissez-faire* in the old sense would no longer work ; but that at the present stage of industrial society planning in some form or other was inevitable. He was not at all clear what form this planning ought to take, if it were not to do violence to the spontaneous forces of society. He had not at that time much hope of learning anything from a study of the liberal and democratic countries, for he involuntarily shared the feeling prevalent in Central Europe that the democratic system had already run its course.

This sceptical outlook was not in keeping with his private inclinations. This book was written, even then, from the point of view of a man for whom freedom and personal responsibility were the highest of all values. But he, and those like him, were anxious to guard against self-deception. A realistic description and a theoretical analysis of what was happening in the crisis of liberal democracy seemed to him more important than a mere ideological assertion of the merits of freedom and self-determination.

The concrete analysis of this failure would—he thought—at least draw attention to the cause of the evil. The social organism cannot be cured by pure enthusiasm, but only by a sober investigation of the causes of the disease.

The German edition of this book is in this sense complete in itself, and represents a stage in the writer's attempt to explain the working of modern society. The English edition, compared with the German, is almost a new work ; partly because it contains new chapters, but also because the original sections have been redocumented and further elaborated. The most important difference in outlook—as already indicated—is that recently the writer has been living in a country where liberal democracy functions almost undisturbed. This gave him the opportunity of studying the effects of its principles at close range. Although it helped him to enlarge the framework of his experience and to free himself from his deep-rooted scepticism as to the vitality of democracy in our age, in the new surroundings he encountered certain facts which he did not wish to face in the spirit of a mere inquirer. He was constantly tempted, owing to the temporary security of this country, to give way to an optimism which could make him forget that we all are sitting on a volcano, and that those who have actually experienced the eruption have a greater knowledge of the nature and depths of the crater which is yawning beneath our Western society.

II

The Clash of the Principles of Laissez-faire and Planless Regulation as the Main Cause of Maladjustment in Modern Society

He feels it is important to remember that our society is faced, not with brief unrest, but with a radical change of structure ; for this realization is the only guarantee of preventive measures. Only if we know why Western society in the crisis zone is passing through a phase of disintegration, is there any hope that the countries which still enjoy comparative peace will learn to control the future trend of events by democratic planning, and so avoid the negative aspects of the process : dictatorship, conformity, and barbarism. It seems to the writer that after studying the matter from many angles and weighing the different interpretations of the changes of the last decade, we are bound to come to the conclusion that in the period before us, planning will be inevitable. We naturally hope it will take a very different form from that conceived by the dictatorships. Neither the nature nor the function of a planned social system demands the sacrifice of our real liberties or of the idea of democratic self-determination.

Naturally one is enough of a realist to see that planning can easily be corrupted into dictatorship and the suppression of all freedom. But it is just this realistic attitude that prevents the writer from rejecting the thought of planning out of hand. An accurate analysis of the changes in the structure of society and in the modern technique of government leaves us—as this book attempts to show—with no other alternative. Thus agreement with the diagnosis of this book depends on whether the reader will concede that the technical and structural foundations of modern society have been completely transformed. Given this assumption there is no longer any choice between planning and *laisser-faire*, but only between good planning and bad. The author himself would rather live in a period in which the social order and the techniques of control did not allow one group of people to force its conception of " the good life " upon another. But we have no power to choose the social order and its techniques of control. They are already in existence, and the most we can do is to combine and mould them to the best advantage.

In these circumstances every theoretical contribution which throws some light upon the question whether there is any form of planning which is in itself a guarantee against despotic abuse, every investigation which distinguishes between the valuable modern elements in planning and the retrograde conception of dictatorship, is of more than theoretical importance. We must not forget that up to the present history has not produced genuine attempts at planning, since the experiments of which we know are blended with the spirit either of oriental despotism or military dictatorial traditions. Thus a naïve study and description of the existing totalitarian states is quite inadequate ; only a theoretical analysis of the facts in the light of the concrete experiences of the last decade can separate the grain from the chaff.

Realism prevents one from prophesying a Utopian future. It must be said in all seriousness that there is only a chance that the Western states with their deep-rooted democratic traditions will grasp the position in time, and will be enthusiastic enough to revitalize their ancient heritage to meet the new situation. But to-day this regeneration cannot be simply a question of mood. The new policy must also be accompanied by a process of theoretical interpretation, so that a form of planning can be found which will allow a maximum of freedom and self-determination. At the present stage of development the successful organization of society cannot be left to chance. Prevailing trends cannot be successfully influenced or even deflected in the spirit of " muddling through ". There is no reason why, as the pressure of circumstances increases and the menace to democratic civilization becomes more and more evident, our habits of thought should not be transformed.

If we are to direct the social forces effectively we must not remain absorbed in the continued pursuit of short-run interests. The new form of policy can only succeed at a much higher level of consciousness, a consciousness with a taste for experiment.

If we want to control the situation which confronts us in this phase of history instead of letting it control us, we must turn all our available scientific energies to studying the causes of the crisis and the wreckage of the democratic system. At the same time we must try to understand without prejudice that the pyschological changes and the development of institutional organization in the dictatorial states are different ways of reacting to the same basic situation— a situation which has become universal in the late industrial age.

In these circumstances our investigations must be pervaded by the feeling that *tua res agitur* ; though not in the sense that we ought to imitate dictatorial solutions. On the contrary, we must devote ourselves to studying them, so that when similar crises occur in our midst we can face them in our own way, in the spirit of the Western democratic tradition. We must never forget that the totalitarian solutions were often only bewildered attempts to deal with the concrete difficulties in which these countries were suddenly involved. Even in private life the individual reacts aggressively, and tries to place dictatorial restrictions on other people's freedom, when he is not in theoretical and practical control of a situation. Spiritual cramp is often due to the helplessness of ignorance and to fear of the unknown. Thus it is important both to understand the difficulties of liberal, democratic society and its failure in times of crisis and to study the forced solutions called dictatorship.

This is the only way in which there is any hope that the dictatorial elements will be divorced from planning. Perhaps in the next phase of political history social mechanisms can be found which will unite the principles of freedom and planning, so as on the one hand to avoid the chaos which must arise in unplanned social processes, and on the other to ensure that power and totalitarian expansion shall not be treated as ends in themselves. This can only be achieved by thought, experiment, and political action. The more one gets into the habit of regarding political problems as questions partly of power and partly of successful or unsuccessful social organization, the less utopian it seems that one should not only stress the former aspect but also the latter. This makes it important to use all our intellectual energy towards finding a combination of social controls which would determine how far individual liberties should be left unrestricted in order to preserve both the freedom of the individual and the efficiency of the community.

The method of vindicating democracy and liberalism adopted in this book differs from the usual method in that it does not regard the problem merely as ideological but tries to explain by means of a concrete sociological analysis what sort of freedom, democracy, and culture would be possible under an altered social system. The usual vindication of freedom, democracy, and culture can be described as ideological because the discussion generally terminates in showing that freedom in itself is better than regimentation, self-determination better than dictatorship, and spontaneous culture better than censorship of self-expression. No reasonable man will deny this as long as the question arises in an abstract form. But it seems to the writer that this is too cheap a victory. We are not concerned to-day whether any abstract form of freedom is better than any abstract form of regimentation. The problem is rather to discover what structural changes in the different countries led to the downfall of the type of freedom, culture, and democracy which prevailed in the nineteenth century. The disastrous situation in which we find ourselves cannot be diagnosed, let alone remedied, merely by repeating the classic liberal arguments, with their relatively undeveloped sociology, and applying analyses which were only valid at a former stage of social development and for a completely different structure.

It is clear that these urgent problems cannot be solved as long as freedom and democracy are regarded merely as ideological postulates, or abstract principles of universal application. We really begin to grapple with them only when we are in a position to analyse them sociologically, just as a natural scientist investigates a zoological species, studying it in relation to the sole surroundings in which it can survive. In the same way the relevance of principles of political organization can only be discovered by empirical means, that is by recognizing the social processes which either allow a mechanism to function in a society or else annihilate it.

But it is not enough to rely upon the empirical analysis of society alone. Empiricism only answers theoretical questions if the theory is framed to fit new problems and enlarged experience. The hypothetical question, whether the once irreconcilable conceptions of freedom and planning are not really incongruous, cannot be answered unless we are willing to revise the traditional interpretations of democracy and freedom and to reach a new level of thinking. Those who do not draw a clear distinction between blind regulation and well considered planning, just because both interfere with a hypothetical natural order of things, will never be able to understand the difference between a judiciously planned society and the selfish manœuvres of a monopolistic group. The people who still use terms which were useful as a defence against an absolutist bureaucracy will never understand why planning to-day should mean something different from what bureaucratic interference meant in the age when liberalism was fighting against state interference. The word planning, if it includes every kind of regulation, without making a distinction between haphazard interference and co-ordinated control, is too vague to provide any clue why it should be precisely in this generation that planning begins to be of real significance.

One can demonstrate by this example that all political thinking automatically formulates its fundamental terms *ad hoc* according to the special circumstances of the time. A more thoroughgoing analysis of these basic concepts will always reveal an unconscious tendency to take the peculiar characteristics of social and spiritual experiences of one's age as absolute and so to include them in the general definition of an idea.

Thus, for instance, the nineteenth century inevitably meant by freedom those forms of freedom which were possible and customary in its own social order. When this order changed new situations arose, and it gradually became evident that the old definition was based on examples that were too limited in scope, and these fundamental terms had to be revised to embrace the new empirical material and the wider aspects of the problem.[1] This seems to be the reason why every new epoch begins by redefining its terms. State, sovereignty, authority, property, law, and so on are constantly redefined in the course of history. But it is not only political ideas in the narrow sense that are liable to take on a wider meaning. All the ideas that must be described as historical, since they are essentially embedded in

---

[1] Cf. Part VI. "Freedom at the level of Planning."

the cultural setting of the age, change with the changing conception of human nature, and with the ethics and psychology which go with it. It would be wrong to suppose that these historical terms change because political, moral, and psychological thought is less scientific than that of the natural sciences. Every age defines these terms afresh, for in the historical sciences the new empirical material can only be obtained during the changing course of history. The natural sciences are always redefining their terms in order to keep pace with the growth of knowledge. They enlarge their definitions as soon as new facts compel them to revise the current labelling of phenomena. But while the natural scientist can increase that range of new empirical facts at any time to cover more and more data, the sociologist very often has to wait for the appearance of a new social order in which facts appear in a new setting. In the historical sciences the variability of the social order only reveals itself in the course of history, and only the changing social situation shows how wide the range of variability is.

Countries in which social disorganization and recon-struction are not yet far advanced will be the first to reject this reinterpretation of familiar terms, such as freedom and planning. They are not yet in a position to realize that the former state of affairs was only one possible form of existence, and that the old habits of thought were limited in their conceptions, i.e. could only serve to interpret the funda-mental relationships of their own epoch. But in spite of such opposition we must emphasize the fact that the fundamental problems of our age cannot be grasped until we realize that the process of transformation embraces thought itself.

For this reason parallel with the empirical analysis of the essential changes in our society, an attempt is being made to think about thought itself, and to interpret methods of thought which are now in conflict as a part of the social process. We hope that this sociological interpretation may help to show why the problems of the present time cannot be solved within the framework of former problems or with the old equipment of ideas.

If one looks at the changes in the Western world from the point of view of an observer haunted by a sense of crisis, it is clear that these changes do not consist of a series of disagreeable incidents and isolated disturbances, but of a slow or sometimes a swift dissolution of the old social order, a dissolution in which the first traces of reconstruction are already visible. We know to-day that the tendency to conceive the course of history as a dramatic change from one kind of social order to another and to speak of a radical reconstruction, reflects the mood of revolutionary groups, and unconsciously lays all the stress upon a few spectacular events. This is to overlook the fact that even in so-called revolutionary periods the old and the new are blended. In these periods, too, the crucial changes are to be found in the too often unheeded processes of social adjustment. The blaze of revolution lights up only a few of the more conspicuous phases in this continuous change in human conduct and social organization. Revolutionary fervour could not spread its reforms far and wide without quiet preparation, and for this reason, if the revolutionary goes too far and decrees too many changes, in the course of time reaction follows, or the new institutions are fused with the old through the continuous adjustment of the various factors at work in the process as a whole. Figuratively speaking, reconstructing a changing society is like replacing the wheels of a train while it is in motion, rather than rebuilding a house on new foundations.

This study of the social process, which lays but little emphasis on glamour and incident and thinks in terms of transition rather than of absolute antithesis, must not overlook the fact that entirely new principles of construction can often be found even in trivial microscopic processes, provided they are integrated in a certain manner. Thus major principles are not infrequently concealed behind the mask of petty details. If the attention is concentrated not on the contrast between evolution and revolution but on the content of the changes themselves, it is obvious that all highly industrialized states to-day are in course of transformation. They all are suffering from the same dislocation of their normal existence, and the fact that some show obvious symptoms of the crisis and others are experiencing similar changes at slower speed under cover of social peace, is due merely to an uneven distribution of pressure on the different states, and to the existence of greater mental and material resources in certain countries.

None of us can clearly prophesy to-day what form the society of the future will take. But we know from history that even what is radically new in the contemporary situation is usually only one factor in the later reality, for history always has more forces at work than reformers who look for a single panacea are willing to admit. Recent years especially have taught us that even revolutionary systems have abandoned much of their original framework, while the apparently peaceful states have been reluctantly compelled to adjust themselves more and more to the opposing system. Under the veneer of social peace they have become at least semi-totalitarian, while on the other hand the totalitarian states have had to give up many of their former plans. Owing to regulation and state intervention in the democracies, the alterations made in Russian communism, the silent exclusion of capitalist influence in several vital economic spheres in Germany, a great many tendencies in these states, with their widely different outlooks, are beginning to converge. All this leads us to suspect that the deeper forces, which were present in the late industrial age, but which only the transformation of modern society has brought to light, sooner or later are bound to break through. In all these states there are tensions and difficulties which inevitably arise when the old *laissez-faire* and the new principle of regulation are allowed to exist side by side without control. In the international sphere the effect of this antagonism is to be seen in the fact that production in every country is logically moving towards international economic exchange. Instead of accepting this we create national economic self-sufficiency through the subtle medium of protection. Technical progress, together with modern currency and credit economy shows every promise of increasing the common good, but nevertheless the masses are being steadily pauperized by the crises, and increased production is faced with dwindling markets. We are centralizing the powers and resources of state sovereignty and destroying the last remnants of self-government, the last chances of resistance within the national boundaries. But this process of social integration into ever larger units is counteracted by the autarchic claims of despotic states, great and small, which, fortified by the latest devices of military technique, are working not for world order, but for world destruction.

Even as far as the internal order of these states is concerned, we find antagonistic social forces at work not only in the dictatorships but also in the democracies. In the latter the tendencies which regulate internal organization are at loggerheads without the public realizing the fact or seeing any theoretical necessity for it. Statesmen and theorists still think in terms of liberalism, while the number of institutions and decrees which pave the way for a planned state increases day by day. Owing to a rift in consciousness which sets a gulf between men's principles and their real actions, these decrees and regulations are working underground. But this in no way lessens their significance ; on the contrary they do all the more harm since no one has stopped to consider the consequences. Thus they clash with the freer system at every turn and paralyse its working.

On the other hand, in the totalitarian states the factors which make for greater flexibility are struggling for expression. Dictatorship, which in its mania for regulation regards planning as a kind of strait-waistcoat for the body politic, is not in a position to suppress criticism and the urge for self-reform. Its social system is like a steam-kettle on the verge of explosion. As no institution is provided to act as a safety-valve, there is always the danger that it may burst. Purges are a very inadequate substitute for intelligent reconstruction. All these symptoms go to prove that every country alike is groping for a new way of organizing industrial society. The democracies have not yet found a formula to determine which aspects of the social process can be controlled by regulation, and the dictatorships cannot see that interfering with everything is not planning. For planning can only have a positive value if it is based on the creative tendencies in society ; i.e. if it controls living forces without suppressing them.

Processes are at work both in national and international affairs, which can only find fulfilment in a new form of planning. As long as the social forces are left to themselves, conflict breaks out just when they are on the point of reaching a solution. But it is due to human inadequacy, and not merely to the social forces themselves, that men fail at the eleventh hour to build these latent tendencies into a workable system. At a certain stage of social development it is not enough to leave external trends to themselves ;

we need a new type of man who can see the right thing to do, and new political groups which will do it.

While hitherto the major changes of history have very often been incomprehensible both to individuals and to sectional groups, the evolution of society has now reached a point at which these processes cannot be adjusted without adequate insight on the part of the actors. Moreover, while hitherto no particular group has had the responsibility of creating social integration—for anything that happened was the result of haphazard compromise between conflicting tendencies—to-day there are indications that if the groups engaged in politics still refuse to look beyond their own immediate interests, society will be doomed. At the present stage of events we need a new kind of foresight, a new technique for managing conflicts, together with a psychology, morality, and plan of action in many ways completely different from those which have obtained in the past. It is only by remaking man himself that the reconstruction of society is possible. The reinterpretation of human aims, the transformation of human capacities, the reconstruction of our moral code are not a subject for edifying sermons or visionary utopias. They are vital to us all, and the only question is what can reasonably be done in this direction.

III

THE NEED FOR A PSYCHOLOGY WHICH WOULD BE SOCIALLY AND HISTORICALLY RELEVANT

Faced with this demand, we come to the problems which form the central theme of this book ; the problem of how psychological, intellectual, and moral developments are related to the social process, and the problem of discovering the various sociological factors which could explain why civilization is collapsing before our eyes.

Economic theory, though beset with controversies, is able to explain many symptoms of the present crisis by maladjustment in the system of production and distribution. But if we ask why our psychological, moral, and cultural life is showing the same traces of breakdown, we are hardly in a position to offer a connected scientific explanation. Here and there we find attempts to give a descriptive summary of the symptoms. From the point of view of a genuine explanation they are no more than a lament.[1] It is impossible to indicate a single work which shows the connection between the rapid change in human beings—the abrupt alteration in their behaviour—and the great contemporary changes in the social system.

The main reason for our failure in this branch of human studies is that up till now we have had no historical or sociological psychology. We have a laboratory psychology for an experimental study of the general laws of human conduct, and an older psychology, based on introspection, for working out the general characteristics of the human mind by means of self-observation. But this type of psychology deals with man in the abstract, while the understanding of history and contemporary action would imply a different psychology, which could explain how particular historical types were derived from the general faculties of man. Why did the Middle Ages and the Renaissance produce entirely different types of men? Why do certain definite changes take place in human behaviour when war and revolution succeed times of peace ?

From another point of view, it is high time that a link were forged between psychology and the social sciences. Economics and social science are based on certain psychological premises, which are taken on trust by the sciences concerned, without asking whether the data have been checked, or whether highly problematical assumptions as to the uniformity of human behaviour may not unconsciously have crept into studies of economic and political events. There is no economic study, and no economic history in particular, that does not imply some conception of the constancy or variability of the profit motive and its relation to other human incentives, no political science that does not involve unconscious theories about the nature of power and the desire for prestige.

In all these fields it is always an unsolved problem whether

---

[1] J. Huizinga's *In the Shadow of To-morrow*, transl. by J. H. Huizinga, London, Toronto, 1936, and J. Ortega y Gasset's *The Revolt of the Masses*, London, 1932, are valuable collections of symptoms, but do not analyse the causes and structure of events from the sociological point of view.

human nature is eternal as far as that particular branch of science is concerned, or whether its basic attitudes change with the changing social system. In times of slow transformation there is a tendency to regard human nature as constant in its essentials, for every one involuntarily regards the historical form of human nature which is current in his own epoch as eternal. In revolutionary times, therefore, the problem of the variability of human nature always appears in a new light. To-day both the rapid movement of events and the accumulated knowledge as to the range of this variability make it essential to study the question once more, both from the theoretical and the empirical point of view, with special reference to historical changes. We still have no contemporary thinker who could summarize the many new discoveries about human psychology which are to be found in experiments and monographs, and who could try to interpret the great changes of our time upon this basis. Instead the most important politicians and historians are content with a kind of vulgarized psychology, long since out of date, and cannot even understand the superficial, let alone the deeper causes of events.

Of course it is not easy to bring scientific psychology to bear in analysing historical experiences and in diagnosing the symptoms of the present time. The main difficulty is that we are not yet accustomed to studying the human mind in relation to the changes in the social situation. For reasons which it is difficult to gauge, there is already a tendency in everyday life to concentrate almost exclusively either on the individual and his character or on the outside world, which by a typical simplification, is interpreted as a combination of a few vaguely apprehended factors. What we really need is a stubborn observation which never fails to perceive the social aspect of every psychological phenomenon, and to interpret it in terms of a continual interaction between the individual and society.

The very same method of approach, which in our everyday experiences isolates psychology from the social situation, pervades our thinking when we turn to the scientific study of events. Thus it will only be possible to look at history from a new angle when we can study the changes of the human mind in a historical setting, in close connection with the changes in the social structure.

Marxism took an important step in this direction when, unlike the idealistic philosophy of evolution, which studied each phase of the human mind individually, it regarded the development of consciousness, not as an autonomous process, but as bound up with the whole course of social history. It thus created a valuable pattern of thought for investigating the larger context of social events. The natural sciences—physics especially—work with such patterns of thought when they have to reduce a complicated process to its essential elements, and are anxious not to lose their way in a tangle of causes of minor importance. A hypothetical scheme, which allows us to see the intermediate links between economic, political, and psychological processes, leads to a great economy in thought. When this advantage has been pointed out it must at once be added that as soon as a pattern of thought is used, not as a tool with which to study reality, nor as a working hypothesis, but as a dogma, there is a danger that it may lead the observer to become too set in his ideas, and may prevent him in a given instance from using other models either as a substitute or as a supplement. Each system of thought can only be applied to a certain kind of process. A hypothetical interpretation only serves its proper purpose as long as it is able to order facts in a certain limited field of experience without distorting their inner nature. That is the reason why this sort of system cannot be immediately generalized. It may work in one sphere and not in another, or only with modifications. This is equally true, *mutatis mutandis*, of the systems used by physicists and sociologists. It applies, for instance, to the Marxian system for the economic interpretation of history. In certain epochs the onward course of events, the sequence of cause and effect, may fit in with the scheme, because the mainsprings of the age are technical and economic. But there can be other epochs in which vital changes with powerful repercussions arise in spheres other than that of economic technique, or spring from violent shocks to human consciousness.

To trace all the effects of economic influences, direct or indirect, upon our mental life would be a very important piece of research. Thus it is, of course, important to realize that under capitalism, which is centred on exchange and marketing, everything tends to be regarded as a commodity. Moreover, it is undoubtedly true that certain men who have grown up under this system will tend to look at every relationship through a tradesman's eyes. They will tend more and more to picture natural objects as commodities and look at personal relationships from a mercenary point of view. In this process those much-discussed psychological phenomena, self-estrangement and dehumanization, will develop and a type of man is born for whom a tree is not a tree, but timber. Moreover, it is possible to show, as Simmel [1] has done, that the institution of a money economy has developed our capacity for abstract thought and experience, not only in economic matters but in every sphere of life ; so that money forms not only our economic thought but our whole consciousness as well.

But this method of contemplating our inner life in the light of economic processes does not exhaust all the possibilities of interpreting the mind in its relation to contemporary history. In our opinion there are many relationships which have nothing to do with economics and yet are social. These have quite as much effect on the content and development of psychological and cultural processes as the economic elements we have just discussed. In order to realize the existence of these non-economic, but sociological relationships, we have only to consider the simple fact that a small child behaves quite differently in the nursery and in the drawing-room and that an adult leads one kind of life in his family circle and another at the club. In the nursery and its sociological surroundings hundreds of things are allowed that are forbidden in another sociological setting. In psychological terms this means that inhibition and the lack of it are at work in different groups, to different degrees, and in different forms. The forms of self-expression and ultimately the cultural conditions are thus constantly related to the different types of social groups and to the processes which take place in them. No one will assert that the nursery or drawing-room, the family or club, are economic groups, governed by economic relationships, even if some economic factors enter in. Thus there are an infinite number of relationships and processes, like authority and subordination, distancing and isolation, prestige and leadership, and

[1] Simmel, G., *Philosophie des Geldes*. Leipzig, 1900.

their effect on psychological expression and culture may be sensed in different social settings.

In this book we shall concentrate mainly on studying the effect of these genuine sociological relations and processes on the inner life and on civilization, on many aspects of the sociological conditioning of mental life which are usually disregarded. Apart from this we believe that it is only possible to understand the real extent of sociological influence on civilization as a whole if we call attention also to the psychological effects of the elementary social processes. It is not only the economic framework of society which is reflected in the vicissitudes of the human mind, but changes in the other surroundings, wide and narrow, in which men struggle or co-operate. How and where and why people meet, how power and influence, risk and responsibility are distributed, whether men act spontaneously or under orders, what social controls are possible ; all these things, taken individually and collectively, decide what is said, how it is said, what is consciously suppressed, or repressed into the unconscious, and within what limits the dictates of public morality are regarded as binding for all or as valid only within certain groups. Anyone who has noticed how a *tête-à-tête* conversation changes both in subject and tone when an onlooker arrives, will realize how every change in the structure of society, in the function of social groups, and in the major social processes has a corresponding effect on the forms of self-expression and ultimately on the state of civilization.

The study of these influences, which are not economic but are nevertheless sociological, must be very significant even to a Marxist if he has a genuine understanding of his problem and comes to it with an open mind. He cannot by empirical means, establish his contention that psychological changes are ultimately due to changes in the technical processes of production, until he has reconstructed all the links in social history through which the original technical impulse was transmitted. Thus, if in analysing the transformations of an epoch he would like to take the changes in the division of labour and class stratification as the first intermediate links in the chain of cause and effect, followed by the change in the conception of property and in the administration of justice, and then by the change in government organization and the class hierarchy, at about this point he would have to discuss those intermediate social links of which we have just spoken. But Marxist research bars the way, for by regarding the economic and political factors as absolute, it makes it impossible to proceed to the sociological factors proper. Thus these relationships, which are neither economic nor political but social, form the real centre of the drama, in which social changes are directly transformed into psychological changes. Rightly understood, these non-economic yet social factors are the answer to the much-discussed problem of " mediation " (*Vermittlung*), for they represent transmission belts which act as a vehicle by which the basic principles underlying our society (among which the economic are undoubtedly very important) are transformed into psychological processes.

In our opinion the number of sociological relationships and processes which effect the psychology of man is much greater than is usually supposed. We are even inclined to think that on principle the smallest change in the social configuration cannot take place without being immediately converted into a change in psychological and cultural expression. Owing to a faulty technique of observation we do not always realize this. Most of us are still sociologically blind and so not in a position to notice what is happening in our society, to say nothing of studying it systematically. Now all these social but non-economic relationships are not of equal importance. Anyone who wants to approach a systematic study of the whole course of social history in its psychological aspects must naturally begin with the most important points.

Among this variety of social relationships one pair of opposites is of outstanding importance in the present age of transformation : the conflicting principles of competition and regulation. One of the most urgent tasks in this book is to trace a large proportion of the changes in the mental outlook and culture of our society to the effects of these principles, and to show that not only in economics, but in every sphere of life the principle of regulation is replacing the principle of competition.

The objection might be raised that we have just contradicted the statement that important psychological changes always arise in the economic sphere, and yet competition and regulation are economic principles. But this objection would be ill-founded. For these are universal sociological principles, which are equally operative in any province of society. There is competition for success in love, in art, in religion, in politics and so on, and in all these spheres the social aspect of the problem is reflected in the intellectual achievement. It was only because of the particular trend of thought prevailing in those social sciences which reflected the rise of industry, that the principle of competition was first discovered in the economic field, and that its economic effects were described in greater detail. That is why the universal validity of the principle was only gradually recognized, for no one looked beyond this particular instance of it, and its psychological and cultural effects were never explicitly stated. The change from competition to regulation in any sphere—as in politics, science, or art—may in certain cases be due to economic causes, but it cannot be denied that it has a significance of its own, for its influence is felt in every kind of social activity.

If these problems are dealt with in this way, the next task in a sociological study of culture will be to work out, if possible, the social changes underlying the psychological and cultural changes to the last detail. This kind of empiricism is not as simple as the observation of society is popularly supposed to be. To-day there are even some scientists who think that if they devote themselves to a branch of social research and catalogue, enumerate, and describe everything they find, establishing a few correlations, they have made a scientific contribution to our knowledge of society and of civilization. Yet even a slightly deeper study of social phenomena would prove that naïve observations of facts do not suffice because sociological conditions mostly appear in a distorted form, and it requires theoretical knowledge and trained observation to unmask them, and interpret their vicissitudes as a function of the underlying processes. Perhaps it will not be considered an unnecessary digression if we give a few examples in a simpler setting to prove that the sociological meaning of psychological and cultural processes is almost always obscure to the untrained observer, and that sociology consists in analysing the social factors working beneath the surface.

We may begin with an example in which the process of

social selection is at work behind the psychological changes. To the layman every opinion seems to originate with a definite person and is then adopted by others.   On the contrary, in everyday life we very rarely think out a situation logically from the beginning.   We usually deal with fragmentary sections of it and only the most popular and conventional aspects of those.   If this is true every individual opinion is the result of a long process of social selection.   Hundreds and thousands of people in similar circumstances have made individual attempts to formulate the problem with which we are concerned.   We have unconsciously absorbed fragmentary definitions of the various situations which are likely to occur.   From these similar but varying individual interpretations we compile the opinions which seem to express our own view of the case. If the situation changes, we consider the modifications which we had previously rejected and another version of the same opinion will again become current.   The speaker, of course, knows nothing of this process of selection and honestly thinks he has formed his own opinion, although he has only adapted a popular variation to meet his own needs.   This is the only way in which the gradual changes in political ideology (Conservatism, Liberalism, or Socialism) can be explained.   People repeat the same argument with infinite variations, and in spite of the apparent imitation, a change in the trend of opinion, closely corresponding to the changing situation, makes itself felt.   These facts, together with the tremendous part played by the revival of former habits of thought, if recurrent situations re-vitalize them prove that selection takes place in the realm of mind as well as in the realm of nature.

To take another example, the layman again misinterprets psychological trends when he speaks of a sudden change in national character.   How often in the last few years has one heard the remark that it is quite inexplicable how the Germans could have changed so completely in so short a time.   The most serious mistake which the layman, and even the psychologist who has had no sociological training, is apt to make is to select a single man as his criterion, and then to regard him as the incarnation of all the changes that have taken place.   If the different phases of the psychological changes which have been diffused throughout a large community are projected on to a single individual, one has only to multiply this figure a millionfold in order to pride oneself on being a social psychologist. In this case it is clear that the cardinal mistake was in creating the fiction of a uniform change passing steadily over an entire nation, instead of making a concrete analysis of social mechanisms. If we are to avoid mistakes of this kind we must divide this complex transformation into its successive phases, with a different social mechanism at work in each.

First we must correct the phrase " the Germans ", which implies that " the German " in the abstract has evolved a new form of thought and experience. This abstract talk about the genus " man " displays the layman's ignorance of sociology in its most primitive form. Everyone who has studied the origins of the National Socialist movement knows that not all Germans have changed, and that even at the time of the Weimar Republic the first signs of this new outlook, this storm trooper's philosophy, were already visible in unrepresentative fringes and groups. By the process of social ascendancy in a revolutionary society the once despised ideals of the classes then rising to power came to represent the standards of the whole community. But this in its turn could not have happened had not two other sociological laws come into play.

First there was the rule, usually justified by experience, that people tend to imitate the actions and opinions of the ruling classes. National character in this sense is really the behaviour which is characteristic of the ruling classes and is gradually adopted by their subordinates. To-day this is reinforced by another mechanism. At the present stage of centralized propaganda new patterns of thought and behaviour can be popularized in a much shorter time and on a much larger scale than was formerly possible. Once centuries passed before the customs and conventions of the ruling classes became general ; now they can be taken over in a few years. Thus we ought to study the rôle of three sociological mechanisms in order to see how these psychological changes fit in with one another. These mechanisms are the rise of lower groups, the spontaneous imitation of the ruling classes, and the modern devices for propagating new standards of thought and behaviour.

We will give a further instance of the foreshortened

perspective which inevitably misleads the naïve observer. It is well known that the lives and writings of eighteenth-century thinkers and politicians show a remarkable optimism and belief in progress. This attitude can either be explained by tracing the causes of this optimism to events in their private lives, or by making a historical study of the psychological tendencies of the age, groping in the past for the first traces of this confident belief in progress. But neither method is really convincing as a final explanation of the universal mood which can only be explained by interpreting the optimism of individuals in terms of the common social situation.

In the second half of the eighteenth century, France, as far as the intellectuals and the bourgeoisie were concerned, was in a very favourable position, owing to the development in economic processes and in the political sphere. Whole groups within these classes were given opportunities of rising in the social scale. The universal delight in progress, the belief in action and reform, sprang from the common experience. This was the origin of the general inclination to take an optimistic view of history itself or to believe in such interpretations. The pessimistic tendency, so widespread in Germany after losing the War, has the same sociological significance, although confidence has been replaced by despair. This tendency is reflected in the popularity of Spengler's book *The Decline of the West*. The specialized research which concentrates on the lives of individual authors, ignoring the sociological conditions which formed the common background of experience and gave rise to this progressive spirit, is necessarily incapable of understanding what really happened to these individual men. The student who confines himself to one section of reality becomes the victim of a kind of foreshortened perspective, in which he involuntarily treats these isolated individual careers as though they were complete in themselves.

If we look at material production we all know that every process is only one element in a division of labour covering the whole of society. But when we study the life of the mind and trace the development of moods, attitudes, and outlook, we are apt to forget that here too we only see a section of its collective history, and the individual's point of view, e.g. his private optimistic philosophy is very often only a single reaction in a uniform social and psychological development.

Genuine sociological empiricism can never consist of piecemeal observation but must always include theoretical reconstruction of the nature of the whole process as well as an emphasis on petty details. This can be done in two ways : very often a single wisely chosen representative incident tells more about the very structure of society than a mass of unanalysed material. But in other cases, it might also be very useful to start with the principle and find the facts through which it expressed itself. But whatever procedure we might choose, facts and structure are continuously related to each other and facts only become more than data if their function in the whole mechanism is adequately realized, for it is the total structure of society alone which reveals the real function and meaning of the parts.

We must always begin by assembling the pieces, taking account of all their different aspects, so that they can be seen as phases of the underlying social processes. If the facts are to be studied scientifically they must be grasped in all their sociological bearings. Newton's achievement in seeing the falling apple not as an apple but as an expression of the laws of gravity, has only exceptionally been rivalled in the sociological or cultural spheres. These phenomena have not as yet been properly analysed or related to other events, so that the sociological principles governing their changes and developments have too seldom been treated as a coherent theme. We are still at a stage in which we talk about the apple and rarely mention the laws of gravity. Just as no theory of money could be formulated as long as money was regarded as the concrete commonplace thing it appeared to be, and it only became really intelligible when its changes and the processes they involved were translated into terms of its economic and social functions, so we must translate the other phenomena of human and social history into terms of functional and structural analysis. It is high time that everything which the classical economists have done for economic behaviour should also be done for social behaviour.

This does not mean that we refuse to admit the validity of psychology, æsthetics, jurisprudence, or any science of man or civilization other than sociology. We only mean that as long as all these separate sciences are unable to translate their individual conclusions into sociological terms, they are ignoring one of the most important aspects of their subject. To-day it is impossible to make a systematic and historical study of religion, art, or law, without considering their social implications, or to investigate the history of psychology and of the inner life without relating the reactions of the individual psyche in its dealings with its fellows to the social situation as a whole.

IV

LIMITATIONS AND SHORTCOMINGS OF THE PRESENT BOOK

It is perhaps too ambitious to provide so many justifications for a few sociological essays. Had not the writer learnt by experience that every new science has similar difficulties in gaining acceptance, he would have preferred to let his researches speak for themselves. But as these very difficulties teach us so much about the processes which govern the dissemination of ideas, we must dwell a little longer on this theme.

Directly a new science appears questions of method are bound to arise, for the established sciences unconsciously try to belittle the newcomer, or when that is impossible, to translate its discoveries in terms of their own habits of thought and their own frame of reference.

Of course in theory the only aim of research is to establish the facts of the case and get at the truth, and the forum in which the merits of every achievement must be judged is scientific publicity. In fact, from the sociological point of view, there is no scientific publicity as such. There are only the scientific publics of historians, psychologists, anthropologists, economists, and so on, which inherit many of the characteristics of human groups, and very often betray all the symptoms of sectarian thinking. But a careful analysis of this collective attitude shows that every branch of science is expert, not merely at devising methods of studying certain provinces of life, but also at creating inhibitions and defence mechanisms which bar the way to a complete and adequate knowledge of society.

The historian is all too often inclined to impress upon his pupils that nothing that is excluded from documents and archives deserves to rank as a fact, and that the whole of contemporary history is, therefore, unworthy of scientific treatment, for it has no access to the arcanum reserved for documents. Everyone knows how superior an archivist feels and it is difficult not to ascribe this hauteur and the methods that go with it to an exaggerated estimate of the importance of his work and a kind of compensation for the sacrifice involved in collecting facts for archives.

The same extravagant emphasis on a particular approach to the facts can often be observed in the anthropological and sociological field-worker, though it appears in a different form. He only describes an analysis as " realistic " when it is obtained by the method of direct observation, if possible without the aid of theoretical reasoning. The same also frequently applies to the statistician except that he makes a fetish of measuring and tends to regard only measurable elements as the genuine substance of knowledge.

Turning to the psychologist or psychiatrist who has the opportunity while at work in his consulting room of probing into hidden motives by sympathetic intuition, or sounding the depths of the unconscious, one senses a new kind of self-satisfaction, which regards the proud methods of the archivists and field-workers as superficial dabbling. In his opinion these men touch only the institutional surface of human history, a mere façade which hides the living spirit. For psychologists and psychiatrists only the personal aspect of experience matters ; the hidden motives of individuals are the mainspring of events.

But all these students of social history have to face the opposition of the theorists, who sometimes as economists, sometimes as sociologists, raise the methodological objection that all these forms of approach give us nothing but frag-ments, unnaturally torn out of their context, and that their real meaning can only be revealed by imagining a kind of working model of society, designed to include every aspect of its functions.

The theorist considers that from the standpoint of genuine

empiricism, the greater accuracy obtained by a meticulous attention to detail is outweighed by the loss of perspective, the failure to see the wood for the trees. Once a single branch of knowledge is studied in isolation it becomes unreal, and paradoxical as it may sound, the only person who is acting realistically is the theorist, who pieces these fragmentary observations together to form a coherent scheme. The stronger his theoretical powers are, the clearer his realization that the only perceptions worthy of the name of reality are those which have passed the stage of survey and statistical researches and are able to interpret events in all their different aspects as fragments of a complete social order, the outlines of which can be drawn through carefully stated inference. Economic theorists are used to working with hypothetical models of thought in which deductive reasoning plays a great role. This very often makes them think that a higher scientific dignity is attached to such thought processes, whereas everyone knows that these deductions are no better implements for grasping reality than any other tool which does justice to the special sphere of reality with which it has to deal.

So this unprofitable wrangle between the so-called conceptualists and the empiricists continues, although the conflict of opinions is really only imaginary, for there can be no empiricism without carefully defined concepts, and no realistic concepts without empiricism.

The contempt the sciences so often feel for one another, the defence mechanisms they devise to shield themselves against each other's methods, are a kind of professional ideology, current among specialists, which has a double origin. Every specialist is acting in good faith when he believes that his own method is the right one, for he unconsciously confuses the section of reality on which he is working with reality itself, and if a method is the best means of dealing with his own subject, he urges its adoption in every field. Apart from this more or less comprehensible illusion as to the value of familiar methods, this mutual aversion has a purely sociological origin, even more primitive in form. It is impossible to deny that there is a battle for prestige between the different faculties in the universities, and the bitterness with which this conflict of methods is waged is very often due to the fact that a faculty which is supported by an older academic tradition or is able to claim a greater accuracy of method raises its academic prestige.

There are, however, no methods which are more accurate in themselves ; mathematics are no more to be revered than a knowledge of hidden motives, concrete description is no nearer to reality than constructive inference ; their value is determined by the nature of the province they have to explore. Measurement can only be applied to something that is adequately measurable ; it becomes inaccurate when it is used to investigate motives. Description is only more realistic than constructive inference when it is dealing with subjects and relationships which by their immediate appearance convey what they really are, whereas if we were to deal with sociological facts, the meaning of which can only be discovered by reconstructing the whole social context of which they form a part, theoretical inference will be more accurate in its results than an insistence upon tangible detail.

To-day we see more and more clearly that defence mechanisms are at work in every province of thought ; and just as international co-operation is only possible when the disastrous effects of the defence mechanisms which the nations employ against each other have been traced to their true source, so the necessary co-operation between the different social sciences is equally impossible until these methodological defence mechanisms have been revealed.

It would be a tremendous step forward if social scientists realized that not only the collection and description of facts but the theoretical formulation of new problems must keep pace with the changing social process. In the social sciences the questions involved do not reveal themselves in bare facts but in a series of conflicts and crises which can only be illuminated by adequate analysis.

Owing to the contemporary mania for what are called facts, we are apt to forget that an age can only learn to know itself if the different methods of approach, the power of formulation, and the analysis of complex phenomena, do not lag behind the collection of data. It is not enough that our age should be rich in a knowledge of fundamental facts, which gives it ample scope for new experiences ; it must also frame its questions adequately. This it can only do if the tradition of theoretical formulation is held in the same esteem as the technique of sheer fact finding.

Now it cannot be denied that owing to the defence mechanisms created by this period of specialized fact finding, even our best sociologists have avoided the greatest themes. But as some interest in the nature and trend of the social process is indispensable in every society, the constructive themes of sociology are left to laymen. Without belittling their services as guardians of a vital interest, it must be admitted that the situation is serious, for these amateur theorists ignore the valuable results obtained by the scientific testing of facts and empirical analysis. Consequently at a further stage their work of synthesis is not based on a discriminating analytical knowledge, but consists mainly of a speculative elaboration of a few elementary assumptions, which, even if they once had a meaning are now out of date. In these circumstances it is clear that this period of mere fact finding has lasted long enough. We must try to create a period of theoretical integration, an integration that must be carried out with the same sense of responsibility which the specialists always feel in approaching their particular problems. Synthetic hypotheses are only valuable as long as they formulate the changes they set out to interpret with the aid of a comprehensive knowledge of detail.

I am convinced that the meagreness of our sociological knowledge in regard to essential issues can be traced to the fact that the specialized social sciences have been absorbed in details and have shut themselves off from the essential problems, which were involuntarily thrust upon the other professions. The solution of these vital questions fell into the hands of political dogmatists and literary essayists, who, of course, are not unimportant as a kind of social élite, but rarely have had the benefit of the tradition and training that is needed for the responsible elaboration of scientific facts. The political dogmatist is concerned with sociological questions, not from disinterested love of knowledge but in order to justify his party. The literary essayist tries to achieve a kind of private synthesis, the key to which lies in the chance biographies of individual writers, rather than in the evidence of scientifically studied material. The philosopher, who often tries to interpret political life on a speculative basis has no access to social empiricism owing to his aloofness from actual fact, and is usually content to justify a few metaphysical dogmas held by his own school of thought. It is this unprofitable division of labour and not the scarcity of material which makes it difficult to raise our knowledge of society to the level of a science.

Sociology will continue to ignore the essential questions as long as specialists refuse to see their problems as a whole and leave the synthesis to phraseologists. As long as scientific knowledge is scattered among the different specialists no one is responsible for considering the problem as a whole, and it passes into the hands of those who have a speculative axe to grind. If the social scientists wish to acquire a genuine knowledge they must think out the problem of scientific integration just as thoroughly as the problems of scientific specialization. If this problem is taken seriously the inhibitions caused by obsolete defence mechanisms will be overcome and the synthesis of results will be entrusted, not to the irresponsible layman, but to the scientist himself.

The following inquiries represent an attempt to explain in terms of sociological processes a great number of isolated events which have occurred in our age. A time will probably come when it will be easy to describe the events in our own lives or in the life of the community, not in narrative form, but as a series of sociological problems and conflicts. To try to translate them into these terms to-day is like exploring a new country, so that the writer feels it is better to confess that he is only groping his way rather than to create an illusion of finality or absolute proof. This incompleteness—in every sense of the word—has influenced the form of this book. It is a series of essays which were written at different times around the same theme ; an attempt to diagnose the changes in the social structure from the symptoms of this critical period. Since this book grew, as it were, out of the events themselves it had from the outset no uniform plan, but tried to reach the same centre from different points at the periphery. Thus a certain amount of repetition is inevitable ; here and there contradictory statements have not been reconciled where they seem to express the genuine predicament of our thought, as in general I feel that we should not aim at absolute consistency at too early a stage, when our main task is rather to break the old habits of thought and to find the new keys to the understanding of the changing world. The writer, when looking at the fragmentary nature of his contributions, sometimes consoles himself with the reflection that perhaps no one is to-day in a position to form a complete picture at a moment's notice, unless he satisfies himself with the repetition of older teachings in a dogmatic form. Textbooks, closed systems, philosophies of history mostly marshal the fragments of a knowledge which is already achieved and even this is usually done in a conventional way, while our immediate problem is not only to record the new kinds of facts emerging from the rapid changes of our time, but wherever possible to look below the surface of our cherished ideas. This disregard of the traditional methods of approach, now sociologically necessary, is of course only possible by fits and starts and is in itself unfamiliar, because, as we have seen, we must form a clear idea, not only of the things themselves, but of the way in which we think about them. Every system of thought tends only too quickly to become habitual in a certain group, whereas anyone who wants to understand the new element in events must be able to show why the former principles of investigation conceal the very facts he is anxious to discover and must also be able to explain what the new method of approach is really like. Yet every author who is trying to do this to-day will have felt the pressure of particular groups all wanting to influence by their special hypotheses the frame of reference for which he is groping. Very often it is only natural that these pressure groups in the sphere of the mind should exert all the power at their disposal to gain their own ends, since their professional task is not to seek for truth but to put through certain schemes. The politician, if he is to gain a following is forced to draw up a clear and definite pro-gramme. He must behave as though he had an answer to everything. But if there is to be a science of politics and of society there must be no obligation to find a definite solution before the time is ripe. The sociologist must be able to say : " Thus far have I come and no further : the rest I leave to my successors."

These studies are not intended to lead to the conception

of the world encouraged by political propaganda, but to offer a contribution, however small, to a synthetic study of the social sciences. It is becoming more and more obvious that this synthesis can never be achieved simply by pooling the results obtained by the special sciences, but only by learning to think without keeping one's thoughts in water-tight compartments. Later on we shall have more to say about the nature of this interdependent thought.[1] The technique of synthesis can only be worked out by starting with individual concrete problems and pursuing all the further questions which arise out of them at every turn without an undue respect for the boundaries of the specialized sciences. In this way it is possible to obtain a multi-dimensional view of social conditions, a view which is certainly not equivalent to a comprehensive conception of the social structure but only a first step towards this end. Every chapter in this book accordingly begins with a definite problem which is complete in itself, and gradually tries to proceed to the central problem of our time and to contribute something to the creation of a coherent picture of contemporary society.

In the first two studies we are concerned with the negative phenomena of disintegration and the psychological crises of mass society ; that is with problems that are bound up with the most recent changes in our civilization. In the third we investigate the more radical consequences of spiritual decay and the drift towards war. Only in the fourth is there a deliberate discussion whether, side by side with the destructive forces which are breaking up the present system, other processes are at work which give us cause to hope that they may bring about a transformation of man and of society. It is clear in this connection that a radical change is taking place, not only in our thought [2] but in our very nature. In taking stock of modern times one cannot fail to notice that new sociological and psychological methods of influencing human behaviour are being discovered and play an increasingly important role. Considered in this context the social significance of the different schools of

[1] Cf. Part IV of this book.
[2] Readers who are not particularly interested in epistemological questions should perhaps pass over those pages which might seem too technical for them.

psychology becomes clear. In the final study we shall suggest how the problem of the new social order may possibly be solved. Although the most we can do is to sketch the broad outlines of a solution, this is worth attempting, for we ought at least to have a clear idea of the essentials. Only the future can supply the details of such a diagnosis.

We hope that this book may be of use to those who are trying to gain a scientific knowledge of the present time. Thus both the educated layman and the expert may welcome the bibliographical notes which have been added at critical stages in the argument, and may appreciate the even more comprehensive systematic bibliography at the end of the book. The aim of these bibliographies is to encourage further research in various directions, and enable the student to follow up on his own account the inter-dependence of the factors operating in various fields. In this we are mainly hampered by the fact that bibliographies are usually compiled from the point of view of specialized branches of knowledge, and only very seldom bring together those investigations which would help us to understand the real, that is to say, the multi-dimensional nature of social events. The mere fact that books and characteristic articles which otherwise could only be found in widely scattered sources, are here mentioned in the same bibliography, might in itself facilitate the new type of exploitation of existing knowledge. It is needless to say that such a bibliography does not even suggest the idea of completeness, and will very often disclose the limitations of the author's knowledge.

PART I

RATIONAL AND IRRATIONAL ELEMENTS IN
CONTEMPORARY SOCIETY

I

THE PROBLEMS OF ENLIGHTENMENT

The crisis has its lessons and we must learn them. For many of us the problem of human nature and the possibility of changing it has only been raised through the events of the last few years. Two prejudices seem to have collapsed simultaneously: first, the belief in a permanent " national character ", secondly, the belief in the " gradual progress of Reason in history ".

It has suddenly become evident that our everyday, and often our scientific psychology as well, was unconsciously based on assumptions which implied a well integrated and stable society. It has become clear that even the most careful study of individuals and masses produces a false picture when it neglects the total situation of the society in which they exist. An enduring national character and slowly changing customs are only to be found in stationary or slowly changing societies. Reason progresses, and chaotic forces are suppressed only as long as the social structure fulfils certain conditions of harmonious growth as, for instance, when the psychological development of society keeps pace with its technical development.

Of these two widely held theories the latter seems to us to be the more relevant. We are much more interested in the share rational and irrational elements have in the formation of our personalities and of society than in the maintenance of the doctrine concerning the unchangeability of national character. In any case the doctrine of national character was always cherished by those who desired to maintain the *status quo*. Belief in progress, on the other hand, has chiefly been associated with a positive attitude towards the changeability of man and society.

Certain groups in society we always knew to be animated by latent irrational impulses. The most disastrous effect of events in recent years is by no means merely that these groups have abandoned themselves to irrationalism. Far worse is the way in which events have nonplussed those other groups from whom we had expected some resistance to an exaggerated irrationality and which now, overnight, have lost their belief in the powers of reason in society.

This sudden impotence of groups which have hitherto ruled society and which, at least since the Age of Reason have given our culture its special tone, has once again shown how important it is to have faith in one's mission.[1] It has demonstrated that it is by no means unimportant how social groups conceive the general course of history and their function in it. We must on that account revise our view of the main features of the historical process.

To begin with we must include in our picture of historical development our recent experience of the power of the irrational, which has really brought about the present confusion. It may well be true that belief in the progress of reason in history was merely a delusion. It may also be, however, that when people prophesied a continuous growth of reason in history, they took account only of one element in the whole process, and only recently have we been able to feel the full force of other factors which were latent.

Obviously such questions lead us back to problems raised by the Age of Reason—more comprehensive problems which we tended to lose sight of in our attempts at specialization, but which alone have given meaning to the partial observations of the specialist. But we must not be afraid to go back to the sources of our Weltanschauung and to revive certain fundamental questions. The questions raised in the Age of Reason—as to how far history is directed by rational reflection and how far by irrational forces, how far moral conduct can be realized in society, or how far blind impulsive reactions are decisive at the turning points of history—all these are now called in question again under the impact of present day events. To-day it is possible for

---

[1] The best treatment of this question is still Sorel's *Réflexions sur la violence*, Paris, 1912 (English translation, " Reflections on Violence," New York, 1912). More recently Harold D. Lasswell has undertaken to elaborate the social function of myths in *World Politics and Personal Insecurity*, New York, 1935, and *Politics : Who Gets What, When, and How*, New York, 1936. Cf. also K. Mannheim, *Ideology and Utopia. An Introduction to the Sociology of Knowledge*, London, New York, 1936, ch. iii and iv and bibliography.

us to formulate these questions much more precisely than before. For us they are no longer mere speculative themes in the philosophy of history. Since the Age of Reason we have gained a great deal of psychological and sociological insight, and what we really need now is a comprehensive framework in which the new knowledge in the various fields of learning can be fitted into place.

II

THE THREE POINTS OF DEPARTURE OF THIS STUDY

Let us begin the following inquiry with an illustration which will make clear the three main theses of this study. Let us imagine ourselves standing at a busy street corner in a large city. Everything about us is in motion. On the left a man is laboriously pushing a barrow, on the right a horse and cart passes at a steady trot. From different directions cars and buses roll by. Somewhere in the air the hum of an aeroplane can be heard. There is nothing unusual in all this, nothing that to-day would call forth surprise or astonishment. It is only when detailed analysis has revealed the unexpected implications of the most obvious things in life that we discover sociological problems underlying these everyday phenomena. Barrows, drays, motor cars, and aeroplanes all represent typical means of transportation in different historical epochs and accordingly in a different historical phase of technological development. In spite of their different historical derivation, in spite of the fact that they arose in different periods, they all fit in with one another as in the scene above. Their simultaneous operation does not lead to serious friction. This " contemporaneity of the non-contemporaneous " was first noticed by the art historian W. Pinder, in the course of his studies in his own field.[1] And, indeed, in art the co-existence of forms and influences which are very different in their origins does not necessarily lead to serious tensions or crises. Thus in an old cathedral, for instance, Romanesque walls, Gothic

[1] Pinder, W., *Das Problem der Generation in der Kunstgeschichte Europas,* Berlin, 1926.

pillars, and Baroque decorations can exist side by side in unbroken peace.

But although the inventions of various epochs may exist alongside one another in many spheres of social and intellectual life with very little friction, there are situations in which this non-contemporaneity may lead to a catastrophe. We need only imagine certain modifications in the scene portrayed above in order to see at once the tensions which would arise and the disastrous consequences they would have. Let us suppose that the aviator who was just flying above us so peacefully and harmlessly suddenly drops a load of bombs. In a single moment everything below him is demolished, everything living killed. All of us must admit that in our present situation this development is by no means a fantastic hallucination, but is rather to be classed with those terrors which may at any time be realized.

In face of this horrible sight our unlimited enthusiasm for human progress, which was the basic dogma of earlier generations, involuntarily decreases. To be sure, as regards technological scientific knowledge, men have accomplished great things since the invention of the barrow. But—we ask ourselves—is the human mind in other fields actually very different to-day from what it was in the days when the barrow was the chief means of transport? Do our motives and impulses really operate on another or indeed on a higher plane than those of our forefathers?

What is the significance of the aviator dropping the bombs? It is that human beings are able to make use of the most modern products of inventive genius to satisfy primitive impulses and motives. Thus, when a city is destroyed by means of the technique of modern military science, it must be attributed to the fact that the development of the modern technical mastery over nature is miles ahead of the development of the moral powers of man and of his knowledge of the social order and social control. The phenomenon suggested by this whole analogy can now be described in sociological terms : it is the phenomenon of a *disproportionate development* of human faculties. Individuals as well as historical and social groups may, under certain circumstances, suffer from the danger of disintegration because their capacities fail to develop equally and harmoniously. We know very well in the field of child psychology that a child may develop intellectually with extreme rapidity while his moral judgment and his temperament remain on an infantile level, and the same is equally possible in the life of social groups. If such an unevenness in total development is dangerous for the individual, in society it must sooner or later lead to a catastrophe.

Hence, our first thesis is as follows : the contemporary social order must collapse if rational social control and the individual's mastery over his own impulses do not keep step with technological development.

This disproportion in the development of human capacities has a twofold meaning. In so far as it refers to the fact that in a given society technological and natural scientific knowledge has advanced beyond moral powers and insight into the working of social forces, we will speak of a " *general disproportion in the development of human capacities* ". Likewise in none of the more complex societies is the good judgment and morality necessary for mastering social and economic problems equally distributed among all groups and classes. This second type of disproportion we will call " *social disproportion* " in the distribution of rational and moral capacities in human society.

Our second thesis is that the unfolding of reason, the ordering of impulses and the form taken by morality, are by no means an accident, nor do they involve primarily only single individuals and the characteristics they happen to have. On the contrary, it depends on the problems set by the existing order of society.

If we turn our attention to this order, we shall discover that it is primarily the existing division of functions in society which determines a man's social position and creates different kinds of opportunities for forming intellectual and emotional élites. It is the social structure which in this sense favours certain groups and condemns others to passivity since to one it assigns tasks which require certain acts of thinking and deciding, while the others can adjust themselves to their position only by renouncing all insight or initiative. In India, for example, this functional distribution of intellectual and emotional qualities took on a caste-like form, with the priestly caste concentrating in itself all intellectual and psychological culture and achievement, while the warrior caste practically monopolized the psychological capacity for the exercise of power. Similar to this, though not so crude, was the social distribution of psychological and intellectual functions between the nobility and clergy in the Middle Ages.

As a third thesis let us take the following : societies which existed in earlier epochs could afford a certain disproportion in the distribution of rationality and moral power, because they were themselves based on precisely this social disproportion between rational and moral elements. A society ruled by a despot—citing an extreme case so that we can observe the phenomenon in a pure form— exists by virtue of the fact that the insight and initiative necessary for ruling over a society is found at its maximum in the despot himself, while the others, slaves and subjects, cannot see things as a whole and have no initiative. In contrast with this, the novel element in modern society is the ultimate incompatibility of these two forms of disproportion with the continued existence of this society. Neither the general lack of rationality and morality in the control of the total process, nor their unequal social distribution will allow it to go on.

The reason why this double lack of proportion is in the long run incompatible with our type of society becomes clear when we consider two groups of facts which are essential to its working. On the one hand modern industrial society stirs into action those classes which formerly only played a passive part in political life. Let us call this new and far-reaching activity of the masses the *fundamental democratization of society*. On the other hand, another factor is at work in our society which we will call the process of *growing interdependence*. This is the ever-increasing degree in which individual activities are being linked up with one another into larger wholes.

We will now concern ourselves with a more exact analysis of these two processes.

III

THE PRINCIPLE OF FUNDAMENTAL DEMOCRATIZATION

To-day a growing number of social groups strive for a share in social and political control and demand that their own interests be represented. The fact that these social groups come from the intellectually backward masses is a threat to those élites which formerly sought to keep the masses at a low intellectual level. It was worth while for these ruling classes to keep down the masses intellectually, as long as they could assume that the ignorance of the masses would keep them away from politics. Even to-day dictators, after they have come to power, try to deaden the will to action of those very masses by whose newly mobilized energies they have risen to their present position. This may, of course, succeed for a time, but in the long run the industrial system leads to a way of life which constantly puts new vigour into the masses, and as soon as they enter in one way or another into politics, their intellectual short-comings and more especially their political shortcomings are of general concern and even threaten the élites themselves. If to-day we often have the impression that in times of crisis mass-psychoses rule the world, it is not because in the past there was less irrationality, but rather because hitherto it has found an outlet in narrower social circles and in private life; only to-day, as a result of the general momentum brought about by industrial society, is it forcing its way into the arena of public life and even at times dominating that arena.

As long as democracy was only a pseudo-democracy, in the sense that it granted political power at first only to a small propertied and educated group and only gradually to the proletariat, it led to the growth of rationality even when in fact this amounted to no more than the rational representation of its own interests. But since democracy became effective, i.e. since all classes played an active part in it, it has been increasingly transformed into what Max Scheler called a " democracy of emotions " (*Stimmungs-demokratie*). As such, it leads less to the expression of the interests of the various social groups and more to sudden emotional eruptions among the masses. It once looked as if the intensifying conflict of interests in the world to-day might culminate in an integration of interests which, although originally antagonistic, could be led to a rational compromise or fitted into a rational form of organization. But now it seems as though the irrational is to prevail after all. In the tumultuous periods of recent revolutions, such mass energies have forced their way to the top with increasing vigour. Any dominant group which has been naïve enough to believe that it will make use of these energies will soon find itself in the awkward position of being pushed instead of doing the pushing.

Here we see one of the reasons why a society in which rational habits of thought are unevenly distributed is bound to be unstable. As the democratizing process becomes general it is increasingly difficult to let the masses remain in their former state of ignorance. Either one desires democracy, in which case one must attempt to bring everyone to more or less similar levels of understanding, or one must reverse the democratizing process, which indeed the dictatorial parties are, of necessity, attempting to do.

The only way in which dictatorial solutions to social crises can be permanently successful is by centralizing the control of individual wills. The real problem, however, is to know how far these attempts are counteracted by the conditions of life in modern industrial society. It is difficult to-day to draw up a balance of the forces working for and against the progress of this democratizing process. Every step in the concentration of the control of the material apparatus of society, as described by Karl Marx and Max Weber—the concentration of the means of production, as well as that of political and military weapons—is a growing threat to the dynamic principles of democratization and brings about the dominance of small minorities under capitalism as well as under communism. In the former, it is apt to lead to political, economic, and cultural feudalism ; in the latter the intellectual and executive functions tend to become bureaucratic to the last degree.[1]

---

[1] On the possibilities of forming a new aristocracy under capitalism, cf. Carl Brinkmann, " Die Aristokratie im kapitalistischen Zeitalter " im *Grundriss der Sozialökonomik*, section ix, vol, i, pp. 22 seqq. (Tübingen, 1931).

The material concerning the situation in the U.S.S.R. is by no means clear or always trustworthy. Among recent writers, Eugene Lyon, *Assignment in Utopia* (New York, 1937), and Albert Rhys Williams, *The Soviets* (New York, 1937), contain considerable data. Cf. also the Webbs, S. and B., *Soviet Communism*, 2 vols., new edition (London, 1937). All these works must be consulted with much caution. Max Weber's essay, " Der Sozialismus," in *Gesammelte Aufsätze zur Soziologie und Sozialpolitik* (Tübingen, 1924), is still very much worth reading with respect to the problems of bureaucracy under socialism.

In America, in addition to the excellent older work of Gustavus Myers,

Apart from the concentration and centralization of capital, there are, above all, three ways in which positions of social power are monopolized, and all of them are in conflict with the process of fundamental democratization.

(*a*) Whereas the controlling élite formerly based their decisions on a general conception of life which was accessible to broad and inclusive groups, the process of rationalization heightens (as we shall later have occasion to show in more detail) the significance of the specialized expert who is highly trained within a limited sphere. Therewith, *social knowledge* and the power of making decisions become more and more concentrated for purely practical reasons in a limited number of politicians, economic leaders, administrators, and jurists.

(*b*) Hand in hand with this monopolization of knowledge goes concentration of administrative activity in a bureaucracy which is becoming increasingly separated from the other social strata.[1]

The great difference between the individualistic organization of the liberal epoch and the organization of the present and immediate future is not primarily to be found in the greater efficiency of the modern division of labour and in the formation of new interest groups. These factors are undoubtedly very important, but in its consequences the creation of an almost caste-like bureaucratic order will in the long run be more important and more penetrating than any of these factors. As a mediator between conflicting social groups or as the ally of certain classes the bureaucracy as an indispensable new functional unit will know how to

---

The History of the Great American Fortunes (new ed., New York, 1936), there have recently appeared several works containing much valuable material on the formation and functions of the American plutocracy. These are Anna Rochester, *Rulers of America* (New York, 1935) ; Dixon Wector, *The Saga of American Society* (New York, 1936) ; E. C. Lindeman, *Wealth and Culture ;* and Ferdinand Lundberg, *America's Sixty Families* (New York, 1937) ; Harry Laidler, *Concentration of Control in American Industry* (New York, 1931) ; and M. Berle and Gardner Means, *The Modern Corporation and Private Property* (New York, 1932). Cf. also the bibliography on " Social Control " at the end of this book.

[1] Cf. concerning the following, the chapter on bureaucracy in Max Weber's " Wirtschaft und Gesellschaft" in *Grundriss der Sozialoekonomik*, section iii, vol. 2, part 3, chap. 6, pp. 650–678 (Tübingen, 1925). Cf. also Gablentz, O. H. von der, " Industriebureaukratie," in *Schmollers Jahrbücher*, vol. 50, 1926, pp. 539–572. Cf. also in the Bibliography III, 4 a and b.

establish its monopoly of control. In the course of time it will also try to close its ranks to outsiders even to the point of making its offices hereditary.

(c) In the decisive political conflicts of the near future, however, the greatest significance must be attached to the *concentration of the instruments of military power*. Even in earlier social orders, this sphere offered a special opportunity for a monopoly of power to those minorities which succeeded in gaining control of it. The concentration of the instruments of warfare now in progress renders it probable that new dictators of the right and of the left will organize a sort of janissary troop of military technicians and specialists.[1] Like the army which upheld the Turkish power, a military force may be so isolated socially from the general population that it can always be used against it. The concentration of military instruments lessens the chances of every type of insurrection and revolution, as well as of the execution of the democratic mass will.

The secret of the democratization which took place in the eighteenth and nineteenth centuries lay in the simple fact that one man meant one gun, the resistance of one thousand individuals one thousand guns. To-day the relative strength of the opposed forces is not to be measured by counting heads but by the number of people who can be killed or held in terror by a single bomb. The guarantee of the general democratization of the preceding century lay not only in industrialization but also in the fact of universal conscription which, especially after a lost war, could become the means of a general insurrection. For the future every-thing will depend on the extent to which the military technique will require the support of the general population as well as of a relatively small professional army.

In spite of these powerful counter tendencies, the outlook for the advancement of fundamental democratization is not entirely hopeless. The forces which have created it and which maintain it are among the indispensable elements of an industrial society and can be destroyed only if it, too, is destroyed. The fact that in forming public opinion and in

[1] Cf. Silas Bent McKinley, *Democracy and Military Power*, New York, 1934, and Alfred Vogt's *History of Militarism*, New York, 1937, which contain a vast amount of information on this and cognate subjects and copious references to the literature.

various spheres of conduct increasingly violent methods must be used against it is the best proof that the fundamental democratic trend is still at work and is continuously being created anew out of the intricately spun texture of the modern social fabric. This society is in its very nature based on an increasing internal differentiation, so that its lesser units cannot all be controlled by the central body. Therefore in these lesser units there is always the possibility of escape for the individual who wants to resist, and a constant drive towards the creation of new forms of activity.[1] Suppressed elements learn to adapt their tactics to all manner of threats, including even military ones.[2] Thus, the political as well as the economic bureaucracy will only be able to cope with the complicated machinery of society as long as it can be sure to a certain degree at least, of the acquiescence of small personal groups and those which collect around industrial plants or are voluntarily organized for the pursuit of some common interest.

IV

THE PRINCIPLE OF INCREASING INTERDEPENDENCE

The second danger in the disproportionate development of intellectual and moral capacities is to be found in the

---

[1] Cf. the chapter on " situations ", pp. 299–306.

[2] It is predictable that the concentration of military technique and the creation of special guards will be followed by a new kind of revolutionary strategy aiming at the disorganization of the military forces. It has already been observed that quite ludicrously armed revolutionary troops can triumph with the aid of propaganda. For example, Lasswell, in this connection, mentions that in the Canton uprising 2,000 storm troops had no more than 200 bombs and 27 revolvers. In Shanghai 6,000 men had only 150 weapons. The Petrograd garrison had been worked on by propaganda before it allied itself with the Bolsheviks in 1917, cf. H. D. Lasswell, " The Strategy of Revolutionary and War Propaganda," *Public Opinion and World Politics*, ed. by Quincy Wright (Chicago, 1935), p. 215. Regarding the technique of the modern *coup d'état*, cf. C. Malaperte, *The Technique of the Coup d'État* (New York, 1933), and more recently R. Postgate, *How to Make a Revolution* (London, 1934). Leon Trotsky's *History of the Russian Revolution* (new one vol. edition, New York, 1936), contains many brilliant remarks on *coup d'états* in general as well as a shrewd analysis of the Bolshevik insurrection of November, 1917. A. Neuberg, *Der bewaffnete Aufstand : Versuch einer theoretischen Darstellung*, Zürich, 1928. Cf. also in the Bibliography V, 4 " Forms of Social Change."

fact that modern society, as a result of the great inter-dependence of its parts, can absorb these irrational, emotional shocks much less easily than earlier social orders. In many respects, it is true, modern society is much more flexible than earlier societies since, owing to technological advances, it has greater reserves at its disposal. Thus, for example, certain critics of capitalism never thought that it could possibly support such gigantic armies of unemployed for so many years. On the other hand, the interdependence of all its parts makes the modern order much more sensitive than a simpler form of economic organization. Indeed, the more minutely the individual parts of a large mechanism fit into one another, and the more closely the single elements are bound up together, the more serious are the repercussions of even the slightest disturbance. In a well-organized railway, for instance, the effects of an accident are more far-reaching than they were in the stage coach system of transport, where accidents and dislocation were taken for granted from the very beginning. In the more or less simple economy of pre-War Russia hundreds of thousands and even millions could die of starvation without causing maladjustments in the rest of the world. In contrast with this, in the world economy of the present day over-production in one market becomes the misfortune of other markets. The political insanity of one country determines the fate of others, and the brutal, impulsive, emotional outbursts of the masses in action signify a catastrophe for a whole society and even for the entire world, since the interdependence of the modern social organism transmits the effects of every maladjustment with increased intensity.[1]

If in a short time we cannot reach the same stage of reason and morality in the control of society and of our own natures that we have reached in technology, the social order will collapse. We should be neither sociologists nor even scientists if we were willing to let the matter rest with such a general diagnosis and vague prophecy. The problems which we have raised here concerning the growth of rational elements in our society and their relation to the irrational elements can only be cleared up by sociological research, as it is apparent that definite relation-

---

[1] On the principle of interdependence, cf. R. Muir, *The Interdependent World and Its Problems* (London, 1932).

ships exist between the development of these forces and certain social situations. Philosophers and sociologists once thought that there was a tendency towards rational and moral progress inherent in the human mind. That this is untrue is clear to everyone who knows what is happening in the contemporary world, for it can be asserted with confidence that in the last decades we have receded rather than advanced as far as moral and rational progress is concerned. We see ever more clearly that the human mind, when suddenly brought into unfavourable circumstances, can relapse quite directly into earlier stages of its development. When, however, we state the problem sociologically and not in terms of a philosophical theory of social progress—which can be no more than a philosophical faith in a mind independent of circumstances—we must ask ourselves above all which situations favour certain forms of egoism and recklessness, and which have the opposite effect of creating a capacity for responsibility. If we state our problems in this way, we break up the general philosophical problem into specific relationships which can be concretely observed. In this way, perhaps, it becomes possible to make significant statements about the broad and many-sided problems which concern us. There is, of course, one question which we can never answer scientifically, namely : What are the unique and individual paths which a given person must follow to attain a rational and moral way of life ? We can, however, easily diagnose the typical situations which lead to rational and irrational conduct.

V

CLARIFICATION OF THE VARIOUS MEANINGS OF THE WORD " RATIONALITY "

Before turning to the central question concerning the typical situations in industrial society from which certain forms of rationality or irrationality arise, we must first make certain observations about the general nature and species of rationality and irrationality. Few words are used in so many contradictory ways. For this very reason we will have to limit ourselves to explaining two of the most important uses of the words " rational " and " irrational ", which, in our opinion, are indispensable in sociological analysis.

Sociologists use the words " rational " and " irrational " in two senses, which we will call " substantial " and " functional " rationality or irrationality.[1]

It is not very difficult to explain the nature of

---

[1] It would take us too far afield if we were even to cite only the most important literature on " rationality " and " irrationality ", to say nothing of attempting to work out the various standpoints involved in this statement of the problem. We will therefore limit ourselves to references to those theories which are most useful to the sociologist. German sociology has placed the concepts " rational ", " irrational " at the very centre of its interests.

In this connection Georg Simmel and Max Weber are most important. The former's *Philosophie des Geldes* (Leipzig, 1900), attempts to determine the sociological consequences of the rationalization of life brought about by the use of money. Max Weber's whole work is in the last analysis directed towards the problem : " Which social factors have brought about the rationalization characteristic of Western civilization ? " In his works he uses the concept " rational " in many senses of which the type " purposeful rational behaviour " (Zweckrationales Handeln) is the best known. Although we have H. J. Grab's little book : *Der Begriff des Rationalen in der Soziologie Max Webers* (Karlsruhe, 1927), we still need further exploration and illumination of this theme. Cf. also A. von Schelting, *Max Webers Wissenschaftslehre* (Tübingen, 1934, sections i and ii).

In addition to Max Weber's use of " rational ", we should refer to Pareto's distinction between " logical " and " non-logical " conduct, as well as to his distinction between " derivations " and " residues ", all of which are important guides to the sociological analysis of political thinking. Cf. his *Traité de Sociology générale* (Paris and Lausanne, 1917) (English translation *Mind and Society*, New York, 1935, by Andrew Bongiorno and Arthur Livingstone), his *Les systèmes socialistes* (Paris, 1926), and the brief résumé of his work by Bousquet, G. H., *Précis de sociologie d'apres Vilfredo Pareto* (Paris, 1925). Also Borkenau, Franz, *Pareto* (London–New York, 1936).

In Anglo-Saxon literature, John Dewey's various writings, which seek to define the concept of thinking, seem to be the most fruitful for the sociologist. Here we will mention only his *How we Think* (Boston, 1933) (new edition) and *Human Nature and Conduct* (New York, 1922). George H. Mead's posthumously published *Mind, Self, and Society* (Chicago, 1934), is of the greatest importance for our understanding of this problem. Attention should also be given to G. Santayana's *Reason in Society* (London, 1937, 3rd edition). These theories deal with relationships between knowledge and conduct, a problem which, incidentally, is exhaustively treated in the German literature, though in a somewhat different manner, within the framework of the " theory of ideology " and the " sociology of knowledge ". Talcott Parsons's *The Structure of Social Action* (New York–London, 1937), also deals with this problem. For further references see pp. 82 and 206.

In addition to these, the theories of L. T. Hobhouse should be taken into account. Cf. among others his *The Rational Good : A Study in the Logic of Practice* (London, 1921). Among English students of the subject Morris Ginsberg has dealt with the problem in his *Psychology of Society* (London, 1928, 3rd ed.), chapter iii, " The Rôle of Reason."

" substantial " rationality. We understand as substantially rational an act of thought which reveals intelligent insight into the inter-relations of events in a given situation. Thus the intelligent act of thought itself will be described as " substantially rational ", whereas everything else which either is false or not an act of thought at all (as for example drives, impulses, wishes, and feelings, both conscious and unconscious) will be called " substantially irrational ".

But in sociology as well as in everyday language, we also use the word " rational " in still another sense when we say, for instance, that this or that industry or administration staff has been " rationalized ". In such cases we do not at all understand by the term " rational " the fact that a person carries out acts of thinking and knowing, but rather that a series of actions is organized in such a way that it leads to a previously defined goal, every element in this series of actions receiving a functional position and rôle. Such a functional organization of a series of actions will, moreover, be at its best when, in order to attain the given goal, it co-ordinates the means most efficiently.[1] It is by no means characteristic, however, of functional organization in our sense that this optimum be attained or even that the goal itself be considered rational as measured by a certain standard. One may strive to attain an irrational eschatological goal, such as salvation, by so organizing one's ascetic behaviour that it will lead to this goal or, at any rate, to a state of irrational ecstasy. Nevertheless, we should call this behaviour rational because it is organized, since every action has a functional rôle to play in achieving the ultimate aim. Whether a series of actions is functionally rational or not is determined by two criteria : (a) Functional organization with reference to a definite goal ; and (b) a consequent calculability when viewed from the standpoint of an observer or a third person seeking to adjust himself to it.

At first sight the distinction between substantial and functional rationality does not seem to be so important. One may object that a functionally rational series of actions must in imagination be planned out by somebody and

---

[1] In the following we are not concerned with *optimal* functional rationality because it is not of particular importance for the central theme of this investigation.

during its execution it must be also thought out by the person executing it, consequently both forms are only different aspects of the same type of rationality. This, however, is by no means, or at least not always, true. And in order to recognize this one need only think of an army. The common soldier, for example, carries out an entire series of functionally rational actions accurately without having any idea as to the ultimate end of his actions or the functional rôle of each individual act within the framework of the whole. Nevertheless each act is functionally rational since both criteria apply to it, (*a*) it is organized with reference to a definite goal, and (*b*) one can adjust oneself to it in calculating one's own actions. We shall, however, speak of the functional rationality of conduct not only when the organization, as in an army, depends in the last analysis on the plans of certain authorities far removed from the actors, but also when this organization and calculability can be traced back to traditionally inherited regulations. Even societies which are held together by tradition are rational in the functional sense since their activities are definitely calculable and individual actions derive their meaning from the part they play in achieving the goal of the whole course of actions. The most that one can say about them is that very often they are as yet not perfectly organized.

If, therefore, in the definition of functional rationality, emphasis is laid on the co-ordination of action with reference to a definite goal, everything which breaks through and disrupts this functional ordering is functionally irrational. Such disruption can be brought about not only through substantial irrationalities such as daydreams and the violent outbursts of unruly individuals, to mention the most extreme cases, but also through completely intellectual actions which do not harmonize with the series of actions on which attention is focused. An illuminating example of the disturbance which can arise from substantial irrationality may be seen, where, for example, the diplomatic staff of a state has carefully thought out a series of actions and has agreed on certain steps, when suddenly one of its members falls prey to a nervous collapse and then acts contrary to the plan, thereby destroying it. The functional rationality of the conduct of the diplomatic corps can also be disturbed, however, when it is opposed and rendered impotent by certain actions of the war ministry which have also been organized with the same amount of care and thoroughness. In this case the rationalization of the war ministry can be described as functionally irrational from the standpoint of the diplomatic staff.[1] It therefore becomes clear that the term " functional irrationality " never characterizes an act in itself but only with reference to its position in the entire complex of conduct of which it is a part.

Now that we have made these distinctions, we can safely make the following statement. The more industrialized a society is and the more advanced its division of labour and organization, the greater will be the number of spheres of human activity which will be functionally rational and hence also calculable in advance. Whereas the individual in earlier societies acted only occasionally and in limited spheres in a functionally rational manner, in contemporary society he is compelled to act in this way in more and more spheres of life. This leads us directly to the description of a particular type of rationalization which is most intimately connected with the functional rationalization of conduct, namely the phenomenon of self-rationalization.

By self-rationalization we understand the individual's systematic control of his impulses—a control which is always the first step to be taken, if an individual wants to plan his life so that every action is guided by principle and is directed towards the goal he has in mind. My mode of conduct, my control over and my regulation of my impulses will obviously be quite different when I am a member of a far-reaching organization, in which every action must be carefully adjusted to all the others, from what it is when I am more or less isolated and independent and can do whatever I think right.[2] As a factory worker, I should have to control

[1] One of the most striking examples is offered by the conflict between political leaders and the general staff represented by Ludendorff and Hindenburg during the last years of the Great War, a continuous conflict which always resulted in the thwarting of plans the politicians had made by the grumbling and disapproving generals, a conflict which in its most striking phases has been analysed by Bernhard Schwertfeger, *Das Weltkriegsende. Gedanken über die deutsche Kriegsführung, 1918.* (Potsdam, 1937), pp. 35–41, 119–142.

[2] The subordination of all actions to a single goal is excellently treated by Max Weber, op. cit. Another notable treatment of this process in history is Schücking, L., *Die Familie im Puritanismus* (Leipzig and Berlin, 1929).

my impulses and wishes far more completely than as an independent craftsman, where my professional activities would be so loosely organized that I could from time to time satisfy wishes which were not always immediately connected with the work in hand. Modern society attains perhaps its highest stage of functional rationalization in its administrative staff, in which the individuals who take part not only have their specific actions prescribed—this sort of rationalization of tasks may possibly be more advanced in the Taylorization of workers in an industrial plant—but in addition have their life-plan to a large extent imposed in the form of a " career ", in which the individual stages are specified in advance.[1] Concern with a career requires a maximum of self-mastery since it involves not only the actual processes of work but also the prescriptive regulation both of the ideas and feelings that one is permitted to have and of one's leisure time.

Thus we see that the different forms of functional rationalization are closely linked up with each other : the functional rationalization of objective activities ultimately evokes self-rationalization. But self-rationalization as we have met it so far does not represent the most radical form of the rationalization of the acting subject. Reflection and self-observation, as distinguished from sheer self-rationalization, are an even more radical form of it.

It is an example of self-rationalization if I adjust my spontaneous wishes or sudden impulses so as to attain a given end : thus if I obey the laws of a technique of thought or keep to the motions prescribed by the technique of a particular type of manual work, I am, by a process of mental training, subordinating my inner motives to an external aim. Self-observation, on the other hand, is more than such a

---

[1] Cf. K. Mannheim, " Wesen und Bedeutung des Erfolgsstrebens " in *Archiv für Sozialwissenschaft und Sozialpolitik*, vol. 63 (1930). The concept of " career " which is one of the most important in social psychology and sociology has not been treated to any considerable extent by modern sociology. There are numerous worth-while remarks in Max Weber's *Protestant Ethic* and *Wirtschaft und Gesellschaft* (esp. under " Bürokratie "). Cf. also Charles H. Cooley, " Personal Competition " in *Sociological Theory and Social Research* (New York, 1930), pp. 163–228. M. Lazarsfeld-Yahoda and H. Zeisl, *Die Arbeitslosen von Marienthal*, Leipzig, 1933. Harold D. Lasswell, *World Politics and Personal Insecurity*, New York, 1935. One of the more explicit analyses of this phenomenon is " Institutional Office and the Person ", by E. C. Hughes, *Amer. Journ. of Sociology*, vol. xliii (November, 1937), pp. 404–413.

form of mental training. Self-observation aims primarily
at an inner self-transformation. Man reflects about himself
and his actions mostly for the sake of remoulding or transforming himself more radically. Normally man's attention
is directed not towards himself but towards things which
he wishes to manipulate, to change, and to form. He
usually does not observe how he himself functions. He
lives in immediate acts of experience ; he is absorbed
in them without ordinarily comprehending them. He
reflects, and sees himself for the first time when he fails
to carry through some projected action and, as a result
of this failure, is thrown, so to speak, back upon himself.
" Reflection," " self-observation," " taking account
of one's own situation " assume, in such moments, the
functions of self-reorganization. It is clear that persons
who are confronted more frequently with situations in
which they cannot act habitually and without thinking and
in which they must always organize themselves anew will
have more occasion to reflect on themselves and on situations
than persons who have adapted themselves once and for all.
The impulses and drives of the latter have been organized
as far as a few situations which are important for them are
concerned, they function, so to speak, without friction.[1] On
that account mobile types of persons—among them the
Jews—tend more frequently to be abstract and reflective
than the so-called " stable " and deeply rooted types. At
the same time it becomes apparent that a society which
must carry out more complicated processes based upon
thinking and acting with a purpose in view, will, in certain
situations, necessarily tend to produce the reflective type
of person. From this point of view it is clearly fallacious to
regard reflectiveness—as many romantic thinkers do—as
being under all circumstances a life-extinguishing force.
On the contrary, in most cases, reflectiveness preserves life
by helping us to adjust ourselves to new situations so
complex that in them the naïve and unreflective man would
be utterly at a loss.

[1] W. I. Thomas's distinction between the Creative Philistine and
Bohemian types represents a recognition of this phenomenon from a
different point of view. Thomas studies the differential reactions to
change of three personality types, while we are interested in the types
of personalities created by changing or relatively static conditions. Cf.
Thomas, W. I., and Znaniecki, F., *The Polish Peasant in Europe and
America*, New York, 1927, vol. ii, pp. 1853 seqq.

VI

FUNCTIONAL RATIONALIZATION BY NO MEANS INCREASES SUBSTANTIAL RATIONALITY

Thus here, too, we see that the social source of rationalization can be clearly determined and that indeed the force which creates in our society the various forms of rationality springs from industrialization as a specific form of social organization. Increasing industrialization, to be sure, implies functional rationality, i.e. the organization of the activity of the members of society with reference to objective ends. It does not to the same extent promote " substantial rationality ", i.e. the capacity to act intelligently in a given situation on the basis of one's own insight into the inter-relations of events. Whoever predicted that the further industrialization of society would raise the average capacity for independent judgment must have learned his mistake from the events of the past few years. The violent shocks of crises and revolutions have uncovered a tendency which has hitherto been working under the surface, namely the paralysing effect of functional rationalization on the capacity for rational judgment.[1]

If, in analysing the changes of recent years, people had kept in mind the distinction between various types of rationality, they would have seen clearly that industrial rationalization served to increase functional rationality but that it offered far less scope for the development of substantial rationality in the sense of the capacity for independent judgment. Moreover, if the distinction between the two types of rationality which emerges from this explanation had been thought out, people would have been forced to the conclusion that functional rationalization is, in its very nature, bound to deprive the average individual of thought, insight, and responsibility and to transfer these capacities to the individuals who direct the process of rationalization.

The fact that in a functionally rationalized society the thinking out of a complex series of actions is confined to a

---

[1] Cf. Veblen, Th. B., *The Vested Interests and the Common Man* (New York, 1920), for an exposition of a divergent interpretation of the influence of industrialization on the possibilities of substantial rationality.

few organizers, assures these men of a key position in society. A few people can see things more and more clearly over an ever-widening field, while the average man's capacity for rational judgment steadily declines once he has turned over to the organizer the responsibility for making decisions. In modern society not only is the ownership of the means of production concentrated in fewer hands, but as we have just shown, there are far fewer positions from which the major structural connections between different activities can be perceived, and fewer men can reach these vantage points.

This is the state of affairs which has led to the growing distance between the élite and the masses, and to the "appeal to the leader" which has recently become so widespread. The average person surrenders part of his own cultural individuality with every new act of integration into a functionally rationalized complex of activities. He becomes increasingly accustomed to being led by others and gradually gives up his own interpretation of events for those which others give him.[1] When the rationalized mechanism of social life collapses in times of crisis, the individual cannot repair it by his own insight. Instead his own impotence reduces him to a state of terrified helplessness. In the social crisis he allows the exertion and the energy needed for intelligent decision to run to waste. Just as nature was unintelligible to primitive man, and his deepest feelings of anxiety arose from the incalculability of the forces of nature, so for modern industrialized man the incalculability of the forces at work in the social system under which he lives, with its economic crises, inflation, and so on, has become a source of equally pervading fears.

The liberal social order offered a much better chance of psychological preparation for the growth of substantial rationality. Based on relatively small economic units and on moderate individual property holdings, this first stage in the epoch of industrialization produced a relatively larger élite whose members were rather independent in their judgments and who had to direct and organize economic units according to their own more or less rational interpretation of the course of events. Side by side with these independent entrepreneurs with their intelligent self-interest,

[1] Cf. in the Bibliography IV, 4, "Leadership"

a relatively independent intelligentsia grew up. Together they guaranteed the existence of substantial rationality.

VII

CAN THE SOCIAL CAUSES OF IRRATIONALITY IN SOCIAL LIFE BE TRACED?

The fundamental question now arises whether we can discover the origins of the rational as well as the irrational elements in modern society. Modern society, which in the course of its industrialization rationalizes larger and larger numbers of persons and ever more spheres of human life, crowds together great masses of people in huge urban centres. Now we know, thanks to a psychology absorbed in social problems, that life among the masses of a large town tends to make people much more subject to suggestions, uncontrolled outbursts of impulses and psychic regressions than those who are organically integrated and held firm in the smaller type of group. Thus industrialized mass society tends to produce the most self-contradictory behaviour not only in society but also in the personal life of the individual.[1]

[1] Concerning the problems of mass-irrationality in modern society, cf., in addition to the bibliography cited on p. 107 n., Pareto, *Les systèmes socialistes* (Paris, 1904), and notice particularly the following headings in the index : " Raisonnements par associations des idées," " raisonnements et sentiments comme motifs determinants des actions humaines," " sentiment," " sentiments humanitaires," etc. Also Lasswell, H. D., *World Politics and Personal Insecurity* (New York, 1935), and Ghent, W. J., *Mass and Class : A Survey of Social Division* (New York, 1904) ; R. Balbêze, *La neurasthénie rurale* (Paris, 1911) ; Clarence Marsh Case, " Instinctive and Cultural Factors in Group Conflicts " in *American Journal of Sociology*, xxviii (July, 1922) ; W. Trotter, *Instincts of Herd in Peace and War* (London, 1915) ; Graham Wallas, *Human Nature in Politics* (London, 1915) ; H. D. Lasswell, *Psychopathology and Politics* (Chicago, 1930) ; R. Michels, " Psychologie der antikapitalistischen Massenbewegungen," *Grundriss der Sozialökonomik*, ix (Tübingen, 1926) ; i, pp. 241–359 ; K. Baschwitz, *Der Massenwahn* (München, 1913) ; W. Moede, *Experimentelle Massenpsychologie* (Leipzig, 1930) ; Th. Geiger, *Die Masse und ihre Aktion* (Stuttgart, 1926) ; G. Colm, " Die Masse," *Arch. für Sozialwissenschaft*, vol. 54 (1924) ; E. Gothein, " Soziologie der Panik " in *Verhandlungen des ersten deutschen Soziologentages* (Tübingen, 1911) ; Robert E. Park and E. W. Burgess, *Introduction to the Science of Sociology* (Chicago, 1921), chap. xiii, " Collective Behaviour," to which a valuable bibliography of concrete works is appended. And more recently, J. Ortega y Gasset, *The Revolt of the Masses* (London, 1932), and E. Glover, *War, Sadism, and Pacifism* (London, 1933).

As a large scale industrial society, it creates a whole series of actions which are rationally calculable to the highest degree and which depend on a whole series of repressions and renunciations of impulsive satisfactions. As a mass society, on the other hand, it produces all the irrationalities and emotional outbreaks which are characteristic of amorphous human agglomerations. As an industrial society, it so refines the social mechanism that the slightest irrational disturbance can have the most far-reaching effects, and as a mass society it favours a great number of irrational impulses and suggestions and produces an accumulation of unsublimated psychic energies which, at every moment, threatens to smash the whole subtle machinery of social life. Max Weber had already recognized many of these antinomies, but obviously he could not foresee the most recent crises which have arisen from them. It would be false, however, to believe that this process must *unconditionally* and *under all circumstances* lead to the catastrophes which it so often produces to-day.

In reply to the simplified mass psychology of a writer like Le Bon we must insist that although persons who are agglomerated into a mass (i.e. a crowd, or any undifferentiated, shapeless aggregate) are subject to suggestions and contagions, large numbers in themselves do not necessarily constitute a mass and that further, irrationality need not necessarily disintegrate society. To-day we can indicate quite definitely which social conditions tend to produce outbursts of irrationality among the masses, and under which conditions these outbursts are harmful to society. We can offer only a few comments here.

In the first place, as we have already said, great numbers in themselves by no means necessarily produce ecstasy and irrationality. As long as society as a whole persists in its old well-integrated form—as for instance in France or England—it shows no symptoms of chaotic mass reactions.[1]

---

[1] Adolf Löwe's *The Price of Liberty* (London, 1936), presents many suggestive ideas about the articulation of the English social structure. Cf. on the same subject also W. Dibelius, *England* (London, 1930). C. Wildhagen, *Die politische Struktur des englischen Menschen, und der deutsche Geist*. Festrede, etc. Breslau, 1932, and his *Der englische Volkscharakter seine natürlichen und historischen Grundlagen*, Leipzig, 1925.

From the psychological standpoint the key to the understanding of well integrated organic societies is to be found
in the fact that in these societies the collective impulses
and wishes are absorbed by the smaller groups of which
they are composed. These smaller groups then canalize and
direct these energies towards their own particular ends. In
the realm of the impulses, too, the sociological law of *divide
et impera* obtains. The secret of taboo and the collective
formation of symbols in primitive societies is mainly that
the free expression of impulses is held in check by the various
mechanisms of social control and directed towards certain
objects and actions which benefit the group. Only the
impulsive energies which have been set free by the
disintegration of society and are seeking integration about
a new object have those eruptive destructive qualities
which are customarily and vaguely regarded as characteristic
of every type of mass behaviour. What the dictatorships in
certain contemporary mass-societies are striving to do is
to co-ordinate through organizations the impulses which
the revolutionary period unchained and to direct them
towards prescribed wish-objects. The consciously guided
fixation of mass impulses upon new objectives takes the
place of earlier forms of wish fixation which found their
objectives organically, that is to say, through a slow
selective process. So, for instance, the attempt is made to
create a new religion, the function of which is first to
destroy the old emotional setting, and then to make these
disintegrated impulses more subservient to one's own aim
through the use of new symbols. It is not impossible,
indeed it is even highly probable, that these processes were
already at work during the Reformation and that after the
dissolution of medieval feudal society, the political powers
which were establishing themselves at that time found it
necessary, like some of our dictators, to use the new religious
feeling to regain their power and to curb and control the
irrational elements which had been set free.

We must, moreover, realize, that the irrational is not
always harmful but that, on the contrary, it is among the
most valuable powers in man's possession when it acts as a
driving force towards rational and objective ends or when
it creates cultural values through sublimation, or when, as
pure élan, it heightens the joy of living without breaking

up the social order by lack of planning.[1] In fact, even a correctly organized mass society takes into account all these possibilities for the moulding of impulses. It must, indeed, create an outlet for an abreaction of impulses since the matter-of-factness of everyday life which is due to widespread rationalization means a constant repression of impulses. It is in these offices that the function of "sports" and "celebrations" in mass society as well as that of the more general cultural aims of the society is to be found. All the great civilizations in history have hitherto been able to use sublimations to canalize and give form to irrational psychic energies.

We are now in a position to clarify what constitutes the specific danger of irrationality. In a society in which the masses tend to dominate, irrationalities which have not been integrated into the social structure may force their way into political life. This situation is dangerous because the selective apparatus of mass democracy opens the door to irrationalities in those places where rational direction is indispensable. Thus, democracy itself produces its own antithesis and even provides its enemies with their weapons. Here we are confronted once more with the process which elsewhere [2] we describe more precisely as "negative democratization".

The fact that the irrational elements in mass society force their way more and more into the sphere of politics is to be explained not psychologically but sociologically. It is a problem for psychology to show which irrationalities, which distortions of impulses in the form of neuroses are to be found in general in the human mind. It is the task of sociology to show at which points in a given society these irrationalities are expressed and which social functions and forms they assume. A psychology which ignores the

[1] Under the influence of Durkheim, Halbwachs, and others, this phenomenon has recently been made the object of a number of interesting investigations. Cf. Elton Mayo, *The Human Problems of an Industrial Civilization* (New York, 1933) ; F. J. Roethlisberger, W. J. Dickson, *Managment and the Worker* (Cambridge, Mass., 1934) ; and T. N. Whitehead, *Leadership in a Free Society* (Cambridge, Mass., 1936). Cf. also Henri de Man, *Joy in Work*, New York, 1931. Unfortunately, the fundamentally important problems of social stability which are involved in the use of leisure time and recreation have not received much attention from social scientists.

[2] Cf. p. 85 of the book.

sociological point of view believes that after it has discovered certain destructive psychological forces, such as sadism, it can describe their effect and significances in purely psychological terms, whereas the real question is the function these vices have in a given society. It must be recognized that in this sense modern industrial society in its present form is itself not entirely rationalized. It admits political irrationality in the form of violence. The irrational impulses which exist in the human mind could be diverted into other spheres in order either to abreact or to create cultural values, if the weak spots in the political ordering of society, in which violence can find a footing, did not always attract them, so that they can be mobilized for violent ends.[1]

Behind the huge organization of modern society and the comparatively smooth working of the industrial system lies the lurking possibility of a resort to violence. It is difficult to determine just when and where, in the sphere of foreign policy or of the inner struggle for mastery, bloody violence will take the place of peaceful compromise. This still unharnessed irrationality is always present in the actual working of modern society, and, from time to time, mobilizes the impulses of the masses. The same persons who, in their working life in the sphere of industrial organization are extensively rationalized, can at any moment turn into " machine-wreckers " and ruthless warriors.

The roots of this unharmonious growth go right back to prehistory. Thanks to the investigations of ethnologists and sociologists, we know that all highly developed cultures in history have arisen from the violent conquest by nomadic

---

[1] Contemporary social science has unfortunately not been very much concerned with the theoretical or systematical analysis of the rôle of violence and the conditions of its emergence. Of course, there are exceptions, notably with regard to war (cf. Ph. Q. Wright, *The Causes of War and the Conditions of Peace* (New York and London, 1935), S. R. Steinmetz, *Soziologie des Krieges* (Leipzig, 1929), and certain types of individual crime. The significance of violence in politics has not been dealt with to any serious extent except by Harold D. Lasswell, *Politics : Who Gets What, When, and How* (New York, 1936), chapter iii, " Violence," and *World Politics and Personal Insecurity* (New York, 1935, *passim*). H. Speier's article " Social Stratification " in *Political and Economic Democracy*, ed. by F. Lehmann and M. Ascoli (New York, 1937), has some interesting remarks on the conditions under which violence between social classes occurs. Cf. also Part III of the present volume and the bibliography therein.

groups of primitive communities, usually of peaceful agricultural peoples.[1] This element of force penetrated so deeply into the relatively peaceful small agrarian societies, that it left a permanent impression on their structure and influenced their further development. Even to the present day this contradiction has not been solved. Industrial society grew up within this political order which was regulated by force and was finally amalgamated with it. The processes of production and distribution are governed by means of calculation and compromise, embodied in the various techniques of exchange, but violence is the " ultima ratio ", the last word in wisdom in foreign and domestic politics.

To the extent that they observe the single individual and disregard his relations with society psychologists are, as we have mentioned, inclined to think that the continued existence of this tragic irrationality is due to the " eternally evil " elements in human nature—the sadistic impulses. They forget, however, that society has always found work for these irrational forces since the age of nomadic conquests. For this very reason it is one of the main objects of this discussion to show that behind every rational and irrational force in human society there is a social mechanism which determines when it is to appear and what forms it is to take. This social mechanism also regulates the growth and the repression of the rational and irrational elements in the life of the individual. From this it follows that the scientific treatment of this problem demands a much closer collaboration between psychologists, historians, and sociologists,[2] but the man in the street must also learn to

[1] Cf. Franz Oppenheimer, *Der Staat*, vol. ii of *System der Soziologie* (Jena, 1926), and W. C. MacLeod, *The Origin and History of Politics* (New York, 1931).

[2] Concerning the problem of the interdependence between culture and personality there are similar and very valuable trends to be found in the sociological literature of the U.S.A. Among the works of the older generation, cf. above all Cooley, Mead, Thomas, Park, Burgess, Faris, and others. The views of these authors are summarized in F. B. Karpf, *American Social Psychology*. Cf. K. Young, (ed.) *Social Attitudes* (New York, 1931), which contains in addition to essays by Faris, Park, *et al.*, bibliographies referring to research along these lines. In the past few years a new tendency with the same thesis but more influenced by psychoanalysis has emerged in the work of H. D. Lasswell, John Dollard, Erich Fromm, Karen Horney, and others. For several years the Social Science Research

see the connection between sociological and psychological problems. War as well as social revolution hover constantly in the shadow of even the most rational and calculating types of behaviour ; and it is not because of their unchanging human nature but because they are driven, now in one direction, now in another by the dual nature of the social structure that certain human beings are now calculating creatures who work out their actions to the very last detail, and now volcanic ones who think it right that at a given time they should reveal the worst depths of human brutality and sadism.

VIII

Can the Social Causes of the Rational and Irrational Elements in Morality be Traced ?

There is a complete parallel between the factors making for the growth and collapse of rationality in the intellectual sphere and those making for the growth and collapse of morality. Here, too, we find that on the one hand modern industrial society is a splendid means of education which has brought about a greatly increased capacity for responsibility. On the other hand, violence in our own form of society stimulates irresponsibility which works like an electrical short circuit. Here, too, it cannot be said that man in himself has ambivalent impulses and carries with him both evil and good in the same measure, as a psychological heritage. Here, too, we can show exactly at what point the prevailing social apparatus can at one time demand one kind of behaviour from its citizens and another at some other time. We should like, therefore, to follow up both these clues and to see which social mechanism leads to one kind of moral behaviour and which to the breakdown of that behaviour.

Council has had a special " Committee on Personality and Culture." For similar tendencies in England, cf. *Human Affairs*, ed. by R. B. Cattell, R. M. W. Travers, and J. Cohen, London, 1937, and my article, " Mass Education and Group Analysis," in *Educating for Democracy*, ed. by J. Cohen, R. M. W. Travers, London, 1939. Cf. also III, 1, f. " The Sociological Aspects of Psychology etc." in the Bibliography.

To describe the history of human morality even in its broadest outlines, human conduct at the various stages of its development must be dealt with from two points of view. These may conveniently be summed up by the following questions : How far did man's *range of vision*, conscious understanding and foresight extend into the sphere of his social behaviour in any given age ? To what extent was the representative individual of a particular era able to shoulder *responsibilities ?* Obviously these two questions do not exhaust all the issues relevant to a sociological understanding of morality, but here we are concerned only with that aspect which is important for the present discussion.

In the sphere of moral discipline, too, we can make use of the functional and substantial points of view, with certain modifications. The functional aspect of a given type of moral discipline consists in those standards which, when realized in conduct, guarantee the smooth working of society. There are many types of these and they vary with the social structure.

Substantial morality consists of certain concrete values, such as dictates of faith and different kinds of feeling, standards which may be completely irrational in quality. In the entire range of history from the most primitive times to the present day we can distinguish two forms of prohibitions or taboos, namely those which guarantee the functioning of the society in question and those which express the particular emotional attitudes, traditions, or even idiosyncrasies of a group.[1]

The more modern mass-society is functionally rationalized the more it tends to neutralize substantial morality or to sidetrack it into the " private " sphere. In public matters it seeks to confine itself to universal standards which have a purely functional significance. The idea of tolerance is nothing more than the philosophical formulation of the tendency to exclude all subjective or sectarian belief from public discussion, i.e. to do away with substantial irrationality, retaining merely those customs which facilitate the smooth working of social relations.

It is only when, through the mechanism of mass-society

[1] Cf. R. Briffault, " Taboos on Human Nature " in *The New Generation*, ed. by V. F. Calverton and S. D. Schmalhausen (London, 1930).

as we have described in the first part of this study, substantial irrationalities triumph also in the other spheres of social life and overthrow reason and rationalization, that doctrinal disputes and fights for intrinsic values make their appearance in the ethical sphere as well. As previously stated there are two main criteria by which we can judge changes in morality and their effects on practical affairs—the range of people's foresight and the range of their sense of responsibility.

Three essential historical stages [1] can be distinguished here: (1) man at the stage of horde solidarity : (2) man at the stage of individual competition ; (3) man at the stage of superindividual group solidarity.

(1) The early history of human morals begins in a certain sense at the level of what Durkheim called the mechanical solidarity of horde morals.   Think for example of the Germanic hordes which burst in upon Europe towards the end of Antiquity, whose members were all held together by inescapable solidarity and submissiveness.   The actions of the group were the result of a relatively *homogeneous* behaviour ultimately enforced by tradition and fear. From the standpoint of morals, range of foresight, consciousness, and capacity to shoulder responsibility, this stage is characterized by the fact that the individual had not yet been roused to a consciousness of his existence as a separate being.   He was still incapable of looking at life from an independent standpoint and of assuming individual responsibility. The sociological explanation of this kind of social behaviour is that the *entire* group adapts itself to the conditions and circumstances of collective life, the individual, therefore, can save himself only as part and parcel of this collective process of adaptation : he must stand or fall with his group.

(2) *In contrast with this world* of mechanical solidarity, *the world of individual competition* which arose from it represents in part a tremendous advance.   In it for the first

---

[1] It goes without saying, of course, that, first, these stages are by no means exhaustive, and could be still further differentiated, and secondly that we do not imply that all societies must necessarily pass through every stage.   We use the word simply as a rough means of classifying historical societies from the point of view of the problem which concerns us in this book.

time an individual is born—a man can see the world through other eyes than those of group convention and tradition, and who is not afraid of personal responsibility. Everyone who takes part in individual competition is compelled to make an individual adaptation. He must adjust himself to events in the way which will best serve his own interests. The chief stimulus to the growth of personal responsibility was the system of small property holdings. In this system the individual had to decide every step in his course of action in advance if he did not wish to go down in the competitive struggle. Thus individual competition led to the emergence of subjective rationality, i.e. the ability to calculate chances from one's own point of view and to foresee the immediate results of one's actions (but not necessarily the fundamental relationships between cause and effect in society as a whole). This subjective rationality was a kind of competitive thinking. Society was not the result of a preconceived plan but developed from a chance integration of many antagonistic activities. Every man was for himself against the others, without caring what sort of society was being formed out of the chaos of these conflicting activities and limited personal responsibilities.

Though this system may have made many people acutely aware of their own interests and of the immediate consequences of their actions, they still remained blind to the connections of this network of individual activities with the course of events as a whole.

(3) Our contemporary world is one of the large groups in which individuals who until now have been increasingly separated from one another are compelled to renounce their private interests and to subordinate themselves to the interests of the larger social units. On the one hand the technique of large-scale industry compels individual property owners to give up their competitive attitudes towards one another, to combine their capital and to form larger and larger enterprises and industrial organizations. These are pitted like large armies against other mammoth industrial concerns, themselves already in part the product of the renunciation of conflict and reciprocal opposition. On the other hand, the workers, organized in trade unions, learn solidarity and co-operative action even if they learn it from conflict with the employers' organizations. In other

words, the attitude produced by competitive action between antagonistic individuals is transformed into a new attitude of group solidarity, though the groups from which it derives are not all-inclusive. It should be noted, however, that this solidarity is no longer the mechanical horde solidarity which distinguished mankind at the level which both theoretically and historically precedes individualization and the growth of individual responsibility. The individual who to-day is learning, however painfully, to subordinate himself is urged to do so by his slowly awakening insight into the nature of social tendencies and by his own more or less considered judgment. He is gradually realizing that by resigning partial advantages, he helps to save the social and economic system, and thereby also his own interests. This means that the very process which at first brought men into competition with one another, so that their range of foresight extended only to isolated parts of the social process, is now causing them to understand the inter-dependence of events and helping them to gain an insight into the whole social mechanism. In short the highest level of reason and morality awakens in the members of society, even if only dimly, a consciousness of the need for *planning*. The individual is beginning to realize that he must plan the whole of his society and not merely parts of it ; that, further, in the course of this planning, he must show a certain concern for the fate of the whole. At present, it is true, we are only in that stage of development where each of the dominant social groups is intent on capturing for itself the chance of planning and controlling society in order to turn this power against rival groups. Though it may well be that the present generation is destined to experience nothing more than such a struggle for a *biased-planning*, these conflicts are the last remnant of the period when every man acted in his own .interests and against those of his neighbour. To-day the individual thinks not in terms of the welfare of the community or mankind as a whole, but in terms of that of his own particular group. Yet this whole process tends to train the individual to take a progressively longer view : it tends at the same time to inculcate in him the faculty of considered judgment and to fit him for sharing responsibility in planning the whole course of events in the society in which he moves.

IX

IRRATIONAL TENDENCIES IN MORALITY

The tremendous progress in the development of mankind from the stage of mechanical group-solidarity to that of free competition, and the complete and fundamental change in social relationships which was implied in the transition from the one stage to the other goes to prove that far-reaching changes in the life of the mind and in conduct *can* arise through adaptation, and that, therefore, such wholesale transformations of man are not impossible. This, then, is one aspect of the development brought about by industrialization and democratization, and this aspect, despite the difficulties with which it contends, is a promising one. Here, too, the modern integration of the masses and certain implications of the process of democratization are a danger to the slow but continuous growth of the moral forces which we have just discussed. Democratization is similar, in this regard, to the other achievements of modern technique, the radio and the press, in that it can produce destructive as well as constructive results, according to the direction in which it is guided. Just as science can be used to invent more and more cures for illness or to produce larger quantities of poison gas, so the modern achievements of democracy can also serve to further the power of socially destructive elements. Democracy in this sense is a means of radiating social influences which can work in a morally destructive, as well as in a constructive way. We might cite another instance of this.

Friedrich Meinecke in his *Die Idee der Staatsräson* [1] has produced ample evidence to show how a terrifying moral disquiet arose in the minds of many thinkers when they discovered that Christian and bourgeois morality did not obtain in international politics. What we ordinarily call "Machiavellianism" has a long history and consists in the fact that the ruling classes gradually had to persuade themselves that in the attainment as well as in the maintenance of power, all means were legitimate, even those that might be considered

---

[1] Cf. Friedrich Meinecke, *Die Idee der Staatsräson in der neueren Geschichte*, 2nd ed. (Berlin, 1925).

immoral in other contexts. There thus arose very early a dual morality for the ruling class—the princes and their advisers : the slowly emerging Christian-bourgeois morality mentioned above, obtained in private life, while in all those activities which can be included in the category of *raison d'état*, the morality of violence was regarded as valid. In the course of history the number of authors who discussed this contradiction increased but they did not settle the problem. Meinecke describes these theories very carefully, but since he does not use sociological methods, he fails to see that this growth of Machiavellian literature is nothing but a theoretical expression of the general political mobilization which was drawing more and more classes into the arena of active political life. As the problem of governing grew, the conflict between the two codes of morality grew with it. Whereas earlier, so to speak, there was a social and moral division of labour through which the lesser citizen could preserve his respectable morality and only the ruling classes were subject to these conditions of conflict, as a result of this democratic trend, the problem gradually became acute even for the least important persons. Whereas hitherto robber morality had consciously been regarded as valid only in extreme cases and for the ruling groups, with the democratization of society this element of violence not only did not diminish but (quite contrary to expectations) actually became publicly and generally acknowledged. It is impossible to foresee the fate that awaits public morality if once the mob gets hold of the secret which formerly overwhelmed the intellectual powers of even small sophisticated leading groups. If it becomes clear to the broad masses that robbery is the historical origin as well as the present basis of the state and of the relations between states, and that also through robberies and plundering success and social status can be gained for entire groups, the gradual educative influence of industrialization and a rise in the social scale will have been in vain. Once the acceptance of violence becomes the general principle of social morality, the fruits of a long moral training in the sphere of labour and of competition will be destroyed almost automatically.

The principle of democracy, which is that all social classes shall be politically active, thus acquires a peculiar dual function. In the conflict between functionally rational behaviour and mass psychosis—to which we alluded before—the democratizing process acted as a kind of social elevator. Every now and again it raised the pent-up irrationalities and uncontrolled impulses of the crowd to the level of the more individualized, reserved, and rational élites of society, e.g. in its attitude to war. Now, in the tensions between honesty in everyday life and the dual morality of " reason of state "—the democratizing process is like a lift which brings down from the upper to the lower social layers the cynicism with which, in extreme cases, the former defended the immorality of war.

Whereas, however, cynicism and irony were originally sublimated forms of embarrassment or the escape mechanisms of a complicated psyche, which sought to be responsible for acts with which it was in ultimate disagreement, once this cynicism penetrates to the mob in a mass-society, it becomes a formula which encourages the open expression of a natural brutality. This is, indeed, the fate of the older theories of race and violence as they were represented for the élite by Houston Stewart Chamberlain and Pareto : they have become the everyday morality of the lesser citizen who to-day practises a diplomacy of violence such as formerly was to be found only in the secret negotiations of leading statesmen. Here, too, the democratic principle of " publicity " makes public deeds and thoughts which in the past were allowed only in secret.

To sum up : on the one hand we see that human reason and moral discipline are able to attain the level of planning and self-responsibility ; on the other hand, we see how with the same dynamic drive the will to destruction becomes a public force. But this is by no means all. The worst aspect of this development is that the human type with the " handcart mind " which we portrayed as a symbol of the disproportion between intellectual and spiritual development, has learned how to use the press, the radio, and all the other techniques which democratic society places at his disposal for the manipulation of the mass mind. As a result, he is able to form human beings according to his own ideas and in this manner multiplies his own human type a million-fold.[1]

[1] Concerning the bibliography of the modern technique of propaganda, cf. Harold D. Lasswell, R. D. Casey, and B. L. Smith, *Propaganda and*

With this, a new factor has entered into the moulding of human nature. Up till now we could believe that relatively free competition between different forms of education and propaganda would, by natural selection, allow the rational, educated type of man, best fitted for modern conditions, to rise to the top. But when the instruments of propaganda are concentrated in a few hands, they may be monopolized by the more primitive type, and then the spiritual regression which has already appeared, becomes permanent. These are, in fact, new problems which arose only when mankind began to regulate its affairs for itself, instead of allowing history to follow its own unplanned course as before.

Let us conclude this discussion with a question which actually arose in the form of a personal experience. We were discussing briefly among friends the immense possibilities available to man for planning his social life. Someone said : " We have progressed so far as to be able to plan society and even to plan man himself. Who plans those who are to do the planning ? " The longer I reflect on this question, the more it haunts me. One thing, however, seems clear to me : the question has a two-fold meaning—a religious and quietistic one, and a realistic and political one. In the first place it seems that we may indeed behave as if we were acting according to our own plan, but in reality we are acting according to a law which is imposed on us and which lies beyond us. We can indeed direct and control the rational and irrational forces in certain spheres, but after a certain point they are beyond our reach and dominate us.

But in its realistic and political sense, the question implies that no one has planned the planners. Hence it follows that the planners can recruit themselves only from already exist-

Promotional Activities. An *Annotated Bibliography* (Minneapolis, 1935) ; Childs, H. L., *Propaganda and Dictatorship* (Princeton, 1936) ; Harold D. Lasswell, *Propaganda Technique in the World War* (London, 1927) ; Stern-Rubarth, E., *Die Propaganda als politisches Instrument* (Berlin, 1921) ; J. Rassak, *Psychologie de l'opinion et de la propaganda politique* (Paris, 1927, 1921) ; F. E. Lumley, *The Propaganda Menace* (New York, London, 1933) ; Aiken-Sneath, F. B., " The Press in Modern Germany," *German Life and Letters*, 1 (October, 1936), 53–68 ; Nelson, R. B., " Hitler's Propaganda Machine," *Current History*, 39 (1933), 287 ; " Propaganda Techniques of German Fascism," *Propaganda Analysis*, 1 (1938), 37–53.   Cf. also K. Young and R. D. Lawrence, *Bibliography on Censorship and Propaganda* (University of Oregon, Journalism Series No. 1, Eugene, Oregon, 1928), and Doob, L., *Propaganda* (New York, 1936) ; also Riegel, O. W., *Mobilizing for Chaos* (New Haven, 1934).

ing groups. Everything will, therefore, depend on which of these groups with their existing outlooks will produce the energy, the decisiveness, and the capacity to master the vast social machinery of modern life. Is it to be those human groups in which traces of primitiveness—the " old Adam "—operate without restraint or those which have, through gradual education, developed their rational and moral capacities so far that they can act not only for a limited group, but also for the whole of society, and bear the responsibility for it ? It is true that such groups are only small minorities to-day. But this conflict, too, like all the conflicts of history, will be decided by a small minority, for the masses always take the form which the creative minorities controlling societies choose to give them. We live in a world of unsolved problems, so it will, perhaps, be less useful to give an optimistic answer than to conclude with an open question. Let each decide for himself whether he prefers the question in its religious and quietistic form, " Who plans the planner ? " or in its political and realistic form : " Which of the existing groups shall plan us ? "

Part II

SOCIAL CAUSES OF THE CONTEMPORARY CRISIS IN CULTURE

I

Obstacles to the Discovery of the Rôle of Social Factors in Intellectual Life

So far we have discussed the symptoms of contemporary social disintegration and transformation as reflected in the psychological crises of our time. Now we must analyse the effects of social disintegration upon the development of culture. Until now too little attention has been paid to the fact that the production of culture depends upon the working of certain well-defined social factors, and that, further, the complementary process—the use made of culture, its consumption, as it were, and the selection of a public —also depends on certain conditions, and if these remain unfulfilled, disturbances and upheavals occur.

If indeed the scientist is the last to discover the relationships between cultural life and the social structure, it is because in peaceful periods, on the advanced level of social differentiation at which we find ourselves, the two spheres seem to operate independently of one another. In every society of a certain degree of complexity, cultural life not only develops its own institutions but even seems to exist in a world apart which does, indeed, in many respects have a continuity all its own.

In a stable and highly differentiated society, author and public become so rooted in the fixity of their institutions and the independence of their traditions that they tend to miss the real significance of the earthquake which we are all experiencing to-day. When the whole structure trembles they still pin their faith to the delusion that this is merely the temporary effect of the so-called social forces. But social forces always find expression in culture, even when they work unseen, and the problem is stated falsely if culture and society are torn apart from one another and are regarded as fully independent spheres which, as such, react upon one another. The social process is contained in the very structure of cultural life itself, so that it is never for one moment free from its influence.[1]

It is, therefore, false to think exclusively of economics and politics when we speak of society (basic structure) and to speak of the sociology of culture only when these spheres impinge upon culture.

In what follows we intend to substantiate the thesis which was merely indicated in the Introduction, i.e. that the same tensions which are causing such distress in economic life are also at work in the cultural sphere.[2] In just the same way as the two great mutually antagonistic principles of liberal *laisser-faire* and regulation do battle in the economic sphere, so our cultural life is being threatened from two sides : it is exposed to certain definite dangers, as long as democratic mass society in the liberal sense is allowed to function without guidance or control ; but it encounters still greater dangers when dictatorial supplant liberal forms. To these two facts, therefore, a third should be added, namely that these same social causes which bring about cultural disintegration in a liberal society, themselves prepare the way for dictatorship.

These three points, which we have placed at the forefront of our discussions, acquire, however, scientific validity (and are of practical value to those who direct our culture) when we do not merely speak about threats to culture and the decline of culture in general, as Spengler, for instance, did, but are able instead to reveal and analyse in detail these social forces and causes which bring about the disintegration of culture.

It is, therefore, not our task to make prophecies, but rather to seek out a clue which will help us to observe the effect of the most essential social factors influencing culture.

[1] We are used to formulating our problems in such a way that we speak of the influence of society on culture. This is the wrong term to use if one conceives of " society " as a self-contained province detached from the cultural province. It is, however, justified if one considers it as the sum of certain factors and principles (which regulate the social life and conduct of men), and in this sense investigates its influence upon culture. When we speak of the effect of social life upon culture, we take it in this latter sense, i.e. how the various principles of social organization influence the form and content of culture.

[2] Cf. pp 13 ff. of this book.

II

Two Ways of Analysing the Impact of Society on Culture

The social sphere consists of two completely different parts each of which affects the cultural process in its own way.

(a) First, we have the free, unregulated part of social life, which, in its spontaneous forms, moulds intellectual and cultural life.

(b) Secondly, we have those social organizations which, in the cultural sphere, take the shape of institutions. We are thinking here of the influence which churches, schools, universities, research institutes, press, radio, and all types of organized propaganda exert upon intellectual and cultural life.

Cultural life in modern, liberal mass-society is ruled mainly by the laws peculiar to an unregulated social order, whereas in a dictatorially governed mass-society it is the institutions which have the greatest influence on social life. We shall try, therefore, in the first part of this chapter to investigate more precisely the unregulated, uncontrolled effects of liberal *laisser-faire* society upon culture. In the second part we shall describe the chief consequences flowing from an institutional organization of cultural life.

We will start then with a sociological description of the type of liberal society in which there is a minimum of formal regulation, and will attempt to trace the process of cultural growth in it. At first sight such an unorganized type of social life appears as a haphazard, unarticulated whole. Upon closer examination, however, it can be seen that similar kinds of processes are at work in the non-economic spheres of society of the liberal social type, as are to be found e.g. in the freely competitive market, except that, where we are dealing with culture, we find that these processes work in a different way and are to be studied by other methods. At any rate, a sociological investigation of culture in liberal society must begin with the life of those who create culture, i.e. the intelligentsia and their position within society as a whole.

The problem of a sociology of the intelligentsia is, in spite of the fact that much energy has been devoted to it, still in a preliminary stage.[1]

From our standpoint the task of the intellectual élites is to inspire the life of culture and to lend it form, create a living culture in the different spheres of social life. We may distinguish the following main types of élites : the political, the organizing,[2] the intellectual, the artistic,

---

[1] There is an extensive literature in several countries on élites and intellectuals. As is to be expected from their varying social status in these different countries, the studies have been made from different points of view. But since the subject is a very complex one and the literature very vast, we shall confine ourselves here to mentioning only a few of the most suggestive items. There are, however, no systematic and comprehensive works on the subject.

The problem was probably first discussed in Czarist Russia, where the term "intelligentsia" was first used. We refer in this connection to Lavrov, *Historische Briefe* ; Mikhailowsky, *Collected Essays* (Russian) ; Ovesianko-Kulikovsky, *History of the Russian Intelligentsia* ; Masaryk, T. G., *The Spirit of Russia*, 2 vols., London, 1919 (German original, 1913). (I am indebted to Professor W. Postan, of Cambridge, for these references.) The writings of Wilfredo Pareto are of great significance for the understanding of the entire élite problem. I cite here Traité de Sociologie générale, Paris-Lausanne, 1917 (English Translation : *Mind and Society*, by Bongiorno and Livingstone, New York, 1935, 4 volumes) ; where in the "Table analytiques des matières", the references to "Classes sociales ou castes", "Élites et leur circulation" should first be consulted ; cf. further his *Les systemes socialistes* (Paris, 1926), especially the index references to "Aristocracies", "Persistance des mèmes phenomènes sociaux", and "Formation d'une aristocratie dans une société égalitaire". Apart from the works of Pareto, the discussion has been stimulated in France by Charles Maurras, *L'avenir de l'intelligence* and in a more comprehensive way by Julien Benda in his books, *The Great Betrayal* (New York, 1927), and *La fin de l'éternel* (Paris, 1929) ; cf. further Furlan, L., *La circulation des élites* (Paris, 1911) ; Maurois, *Les classes dirigeantes : Noblesse, Aristocratie, Élite* (Paris, 1910) ; Rousiers, P. de, *L'élite dans la société moderne, son rôle* (Paris, 1914) ; A. M. Carr Saunders and P. A. Wilson, *The Professions* (Oxford, 1933) ; W. Kotschnig, *Unemployment in the Learned Professions* (Oxford, 1937) ; Wm. MacDonald, *The Intellectual Worker and his Work* (New York, 1924). For the German discussion, cf. Mannheim, K., *Ideologie und Utopie*, 2nd ed. (1930), pp. 121–134 (transl. into English as *Ideology and Utopia*, by Louis Wirth and Edward Shils (New York, 1936), pp. 136—146 and the bibliography. Cf. further Speier, H., "Zur Soziologie der bürgerlichen Intelligenz," *Gesellschaft*, 1929, and the publication of the "Verein für Socialpolitik ", "Über die Lage der geistigen Arbeiter ", also Bruford, W. H., *Germany in the Eighteenth Century* (Cambridge, 1935), and Kohn-Bramstedt, Ernst, *Aristocracy and the Middle Classes in Germany* (London, 1937). Apart from the publication of the present study I have treated the whole problem of the intellectuals in detail in a study which is as yet unpublished.

[2] Here I will cite only the following of the literature of the organizing élites, whose significance is constantly increasing, Marsal, F., *Les élites industrielles et financières*, Revue de Paris (19), (5), 19, I, x–29. F. Delaisi, *La democratie et les financiers* (Paris, 1910) ; and especially Max Weber, *Wirtschaft und Gesellschaft*, part iii, chap. 6, "Bureaukratie " (Tübingen,

the moral, and the religious. Whereas the political and organizing élites aim at integrating a great number of individual wills, it is the function of the intellectual, aesthetic, and moral-religious élites to sublimate those psychic energies which society, in the daily struggle for existence, does not fully exhaust. In this way they stimulate objective knowledge as well as tendencies to introversion, introspection, contemplation, and reflection, which, although no society could exist without them, nevertheless would not play their full part at our present stage of development without more or less conscious control and guidance.

We cannot here concern ourselves in detail with the intricate psychological problems of sublimation, introversion, contemplation, and so on. We must, however, recognize that the different methods of cultural sublimation are determined by various circumstances among which the following play a part : first, the customary way in which the members of a society normally spend their free time ; and secondly, the way in which the intellectuals—who have more than the average amount of leisure time, and who have their own kind of life, are recruited. A society which uses up all its energies in organization leaves little opportunity for introversion, contemplation, and reflection. In such a society, the political and organizing élites would predominate, while reflective, scientific, artistic, moral, and religious élites would scarcely exist, and if they did, would be very ineffective. A society which did not allow a sublimating group to develop, could neither direct its culture nor further its creative powers. Only where, on the one hand, the average person has enough leisure to sublimate his

1925). Cf. also Taussig, F. W., and Joslyn, C. S., *American Business Leaders*, New York, 1932 ; K. Demeter, *Das Deutsche Offizierskorps in seinen historisch-soziologischen Grundlagen* (Berlin, 1930) ; Kurt Wiedenfeld, *Kapitalismus und Beamtentum* (Berlin and Leipzig, 1932) ; Beard, Miriam, *A History of the Business Man* (New York, 1938) ; J. P. Palewski, *Le Rôle du chef d'entreprise dans la grande industrie* (Paris, 1924) ; Tead, Ordway, *The Art of Leadership* (New York, 1935) ; Whitehead, J. N., *Leadership in a Free Society* (Cambridge, Mass., 1936).

It would take us too far afield to quote even the biographies of leading financiers and industrialists, but there still is an immense scope for research work in studying the autobiographies, letters, and documents of the past and present of men like Hansemann and Ballin, Fürstenberg and Bleichröder, as well as Hearst, Northcliffe, Ford, and others. This is equally true of the immense field of political biography and memoirs, which reveal the most striking and sociologically important ways in which the ruling classes are selected.

surplus energies, and where, on the other hand, there is a dominant cultural group, do there arise mutually adapted classes which create and assimilate culture. Sparta may be cited as an example of a civilization in which the political and military élites repressed all others, while in the United States the élite have been absorbed in problems of organization, and this has determined to a very large extent the intellectual outlook of the whole nation. Even in a mass-democracy, cultural sublimation, as for example, in art and in fashion, can take place only if small groups of connoisseurs, who create and mould taste, already exist, and slowly diffuse the content and the technique of sublimation over the rest of society. In all the spheres of cultural life, the function of such élites is to express cultural and psychological forces in a primary form and to guide collective extraversion and introversion ; they are responsible for cultural initiative and tradition.[1]   If these small groups are destroyed or

[1] We think for instance of circles like the aristocratic salons in Vienna at the time of Beethoven. Austrian and Hungarian noblemen in those days were devoted to music and Beethoven found great understanding and generous support. The portrait we have of him as the misunderstood lonely genius is more and more revealed to be a romantic legend (Walter Riezler, *Beethoven*, Berlin and Zürich, Atlantis-Verlag, 1936).

Equally important were aristocratic salons in Northern Germany where the Klopstocks, Matthias Claudius, and others met at Emkendorf, or where the Danish sculptor Thorwaldsen stayed with the Rantzaus at Breitenburg (Schleswig-Holstein) Cf. O. Brand, *Geistesleben und Politik in Schleswig-Holstein um die Wende des 18 Jahrhunderts*, (Kiel, 1927).

We need not go into the importance which the Court of Weimar had for Goethe, Schiller, and Wieland, and Munich had for Wagner. But it is essential to note how with the rise of modern capitalism the wealthy merchant and banking families play their part in cultural life. The brothers Boisserée who together with their friend Bertram did so much for the appreciation of medieval German art, belonged to a wealthy Cologne merchant family, which originally came from Belgium. Their collection and study of medieval paintings aroused the interest of the romantic school. Friedrich Schlegel became acquainted with them in Paris and went with them to Cologne. When Goethe in 1810 saw the collection at Heidelberg, he was deeply impressed. Schinkel, the great architect of Berlin, took a keen interest in Gothic architecture, and the kings of Prussia and of Bavaria were equally influenced by the romantic circle around the Boisserée brothers. If this interest in medieval German painting and art superseded the predilection of the German princes and their courts for French and Italian art, it contributed towards patriotism and the awakening national pride in " Germanic art " as opposed to " Latin art ". Similar circles of importance were to be found in patrician Hamburg, where Ph. O. Runge found much understanding among patrician merchant families. Towards the end of the last century the progressive spirit of this social group clashed with the official academic and sterile atmosphere fostered by the Kaiser. The " Tiergarten ", the new living centre of

thwarted in their selection, the social conditions for the emergence and persistence of culture disappear.

The crisis of culture in liberal-democratic society is due, in the first place, to the fact that the social processes, which previously favoured the development of the creative élites, now have the opposite effect, i.e. have become obstacles to the forming of élites because wider sections of the population still under unfavourable social conditions take an active part in cultural activities. A similar situation arises where the principle of competition obtains. There, too, it may be observed that under certain conditions it leads to the best possible achievements by those who are trying to excel in quality, whereas the same principle, in a different setting, lowers the social level because it leads to unfair competition. In exactly the same way there are situations in which the unregulated operation of social forces can lead to negative results in the cultural spheres. In what follows we will point out some of the symptoms of the destructive effects of liberalism and of cultural democracy in the period of mass society. These we will call cases of " negative liberalism " and " negative democratization ",[1] and will set them side by side with those processes in which, at an earlier date, liberalism and democratization through the

the new Berlin bourgeois society, became the public setting for " impressionism " and the " secessionists ", led by Liebermann, himself the son of a wealthy Berlin Jewish family. What the art dealer Cassierer meant in this field, the self-made publisher S. Fischer meant for modern German literature. (Cf. Paul Cohen-Portheim, *The Discovery of Europe*, London, 1932, part iii, 2. Berlin and the Tiergarten. See Ennen's contribution to *Allgemeine Deutsche Biographie*, Leipzig, 1876, vol. iii, p. 87, about the brothers Boisserée. Cf. also Dresdner, A., *Entstehung der Kunstkritik*, München, 1915, and Walter Benjamin, " Der Sammler Fuchs," *Zeitschrift für Sozialforschung*, vol. ii, 1937.)

[1] An example taken from the competitive situation in the book-market as it prevails to-day, will illustrate better than anything else, the way in which competition and the democratizing process may bring about negative effects. Recently there has been a growing tendency to publish books, which had previously appeared in more expensive editions, in a very cheap series like the Penguin library or the Reclam Baendchen, the Phaidon edition, the Ullstein novel, or the Rowohlt novel. Certainly these cheap editions reach a broader public which otherwise could not afford to buy these books, but since their publication involves a far smaller risk and less costs, the small publisher who is often the discoverer of new authors, does not publish them because he is afraid of losing the market. The risk of starting new things becomes too great and the same tendency which makes for democratization of cultural values makes for concentration of business and market control, leading towards monopoly and totalitarian bureaucratic influence.

operation of freely self-adjusting social mechanism, led to the highest degree of cultural creativeness. In discussing the problem of how élites are formed in a liberal society, there are four such processes which are of special significance to-day. They are :—

(1) The growing number of élite groups, and the consequent diminution of their power.

(2) The destruction of the exclusiveness of the élite groups.

(3) The change in the principle of selection of these élites.

(4) The change in the internal composition of the élites.

III

First Process : THE INCREASE IN THE NUMBER OF ÉLITES

The first effect of a liberal social order on the formation of élites is to increase the influx into these groups and so to increase the number of these groups. At first this increase led to a fruitful variety compared with the rigidity and exclusiveness of the rather limited number of these groups which had formerly controlled the smaller and more manageable societies. But beyond a certain point this variety gives way to diffuseness. Indeed, the more élites there are in a society the more each individual élite tends to lose its function and influence as a leader, for they cancel each other out. In a democratic mass society, especially one with great social mobility, no group can succeed in deeply influencing the whole of society.

IV

Second Process : THE BREAKDOWN OF THE EXCLUSIVENESS OF THE ÉLITES

A second change for the worse consists in the fact that the open character of democratic mass society, together with its growth in size and the tendency towards general public participation, not only produces far too many élites but also deprives these élites of the exclusiveness which they need for the sublimation of the impulse. If this minimum of exclusiveness is lost, then the deliberate formation of taste, of a guiding principle of style, becomes impossible. The new impulses, intuitions and fresh approaches to the world, if they have no time to mature in small groups, will be apprehended by the masses as mere stimuli. As a result of this they fade away with the many passing sensations which abound in the life of a modern metropolis. Instead of creative ability and achievement we find constantly increasing hunger after ever new sensations. In this lies the social cause for a symptom, which was pointed out by the eminent art historian Riegl at the end of the last century, namely that since the *Biedermeier* Germany has produced no individual art style of her own, but has drawn her inspiration from the revival, in rapid succession, of older styles which belong definitely to the past. A corresponding indecisiveness and lack of leadership may also be found, however, in other spheres of cultural life, in the field of philosophical interpretation, in politics, and so on. The student of such changes if he is not used to noticing the social mechanisms at work behind the immediate concrete events is inclined to believe that in such periods human nature has changed over-night, and that human beings are to-day less talented and less creative and have less initiative than in earlier periods. The lack of leadership in late liberal mass society can, however, be much better diagnosed as the result of the change for the worse in selecting the élite. We must recognize further that it is this general lack of direction in modern mass society that gives the opportunity to groups with dictatorial ambitions. If such groups succeed in achieving some sort of political integration, they can carry out their programme without any great resistance from the other groups in society. They meet with no real resistance because all the élites from whom values, tastes, and standards of judgment could emanate, have cancelled each other out.

The general lack of direction in modern mass society could be observed most clearly in post-War Germany, where primarily as a result of the inflation, the older middle classes were economically and psychologically wiped out.

The groups which have in this manner been jolted out
of their social niches are like an unorganized crowd, which
only very rarely becomes integrated.

In this situation these people became acutely sensitive
to new experience, but the chances of an enduring pattern
of response emerging are very slight.   In contrast with
Germany, England is among those countries in which the
recent tendencies in mass society have been stayed by the
persistence of the older organic ties and their accompanying
effects.   France, too, has the smaller cities and the provinces
as counter-forces to protect it against the mechanisms
of mass society.

V

Third Process : THE CHANGE IN THE PRINCIPLE GOVERNING
THE SELECTION OF ÉLITES

Recent changes in the ways in which élites are selected
have also stimulated negative democratization.   If, on the
one hand, the élites, in order to create culture, must be
fairly exclusive, it is equally important, on the other
hand, that they should be recruited from society in
certain definite ways.   One cannot deny that intellectual
groups of a caste-like exclusiveness can create cultural life,
indeed, even an over-refinement of culture—one need only
think of the esoteric priestly cultures of Babylon and Egypt
—but precisely because of this social in-breeding these
types of culture tend to lose their life and vigour.[1]   On
that account these groups should be reasonably accessible
as well as exclusive if culture is to flourish.   Every person
who comes into an élite from some other section of society
brings with him new interests and new points of view and
enriches the atmosphere in which this élite lives.   At the

---

[1] Concerning the rôle of the intellectuals in the older, non-European
cultures, cf. the works of Max Weber, *Gesammelte Aufsätze zur Religionssoziologie* (Tübingen, 1920), vol. i (China), pp. 276–536, particularly
chapter v, " Der Literatenstand," pp. 395 seqq.   Vol. ii, chapter ii,
" Die orthodoxen und heterodoxen Heilslehren der indischen Intellektuellen," pp. 134–250.   Vol. iii, " Das antike Judentum," seqq.

same time, he is a mediator between the élite and those other groups to which the élite must turn for its audience.

But even in this sphere of selection, mass democracy betrays negative symptoms. If one calls to mind the essential methods of selecting élites, which up to the present have appeared on the historical scene, three principles can be distinguished: selection on the basis of *blood*, *property*, and *achievement*. Aristocratic society, especially after it had entrenched itself, chose its élites primarily on the blood principle. Bourgeois society gradually introduced, as a supplement, the principle of wealth, a principle which also obtained for the intellectual élite, inasmuch as education was more or less available only to the offspring of the well-to-do. It is, of course, true that the principle of achievement was combined with the two other principles in earlier periods, but it is the important contribution of modern democracy (as long as it is vigorous), that the achievement principle increasingly tends to become the criterion of social success.[1] Seen as a whole, modern democracy is a selective

[1] In Germany during the seventeenth and eighteenth centuries it was easier for the poor but gifted boy to rise in the social scale through education than during the nineteenth century. The surviving medieval schools of the towns gave lessons in Latin and there was no special examination before entering the university. The divisions between elementary and secondary schools did not yet exist. When the wealthy classes and the nobility withdrew from all the schools and had private tutors to educate their children, the tutorship offered a good opportunity for the poor student to make a living not too far away from his work. Only with Humboldt's introduction of the Abitur and the prolongation of studies was that link between property and education, so characteristic of the nineteenth century, first forged (Bruford, W. H., *Germany in the Eighteenth Century*, London, 1935).

The tendency for a stricter selection among students and applicants for the civil service after 1800 brought about a division into two different types of intellectuals: the refined (and often highbrow) urbanized intellectual of the Berlin and Weimar Salons and the plebeian type found in the Teutonic movement under the leadership of men like Jahn and Arndt.

It is not without interest to note that there is a far-reaching resemblance between the mental attitudes, gestures, and symbols of this early plebeian intelligentsia and the intelligentsia of National Socialism. It is also to be noted that the ambivalent tendencies towards freedom and revolution on the one hand and nationalism and even antisemitism on the other is already present. It is mainly the general trend of evolution which makes them fit into one or the other mould.

The " organizing " élites, especially the economic and financial upper classes, form a new aristocracy which is almost closed. Friedrich Zahn, when he was president of the " Bavarian Statistical Landesamt " included in the economic upper classes :—

(1) The owners of estates of more than 100 hectares (about 250 acres) under plough.

(2) The independent persons in trade, commerce, and transport,

machinery combining all three principles. Its élites are a medley of successful men and women who have attained their positions by means of one or more of the

excepting all home industries and all those who, judging by their occupation, which was that of a skilled artisan, seemed to belong to the middle classes. (" Wirtschaftsaufbau Deutschlands " in *Handwörterbuch der Staatswissenschaften*, 4th edition, supplement (Jena, 1929), p. 986. With those assumptions Zahn estimated the upper class as being 1 per cent of the whole employed population according to the census of 1925. He tried to estimate the chances of social advancement into various positions by counting the biographies of eminent men which had appeared in *Unsere Zeitgenossen.　Wer Ist's* ? Leipzig, 1925. (Veröffentlichung des Bayerischen Statistischen Landesamts, *Sozialer Auf- und Abstieg im Deutschen Volk*, p. 61.)

Profession of Contemporary	Fathers belonging to		
	Upper Classes		Middle and Lower Classes
	Intellectual	Economic	
	%	%	%
Big Industrialist . 　 . 　 . 　 .	13·9	70·9	15·2
Wealthy Merchant, Publisher, Banker . 　 . 　 . 　 . 　 .	17·8	67·2	15·0
Landlord, Wealthy Tenant 　. 　 .	14·8	85·2	—
" Privatbeamter," Employee in 　. *Leading* Position of these with University Education 　 . 　 .	38·8 40·5	36·9 37·2	24·3 22·3
Engineers, Technical Staff, Architect, Builder and Contractor, Independent Expert . 　 . 　 .	31·7	34·1	34·2
Representative of Economic and Diplomatic Interests . 　 . 　 .	42·6	35·0	22·4
Altogether 　 . 　 . 　 .	28·9	51·4	19·7

These figures show that out of 100 leading industrialists 70 are the sons of leading industrialists, out of 100 wealthy merchants, publishers, and bankers 67·2 are the sons of wealthy merchants, publishers, and bankers, and out of 100 people holding landed property 85 are the sons of men in the same position. There are some newcomers. Fifteen per cent of those whose fathers belonged to the middle or lower classes, and 13·9 per cent, 17·8 per cent, and 14·8 per cent of those whose fathers belonged to the intellectual upper class have become leading industrials, publishers, merchants, or bankers, and landowners respectively. How often this social change was due to intermarriage with the upper classes is unknown, but it is a factor which must be taken into account in considering the importance of achievement as a means of entering this élite.

three principles. Whatever may be one's attitude towards this combination from the point of view of social justice, it does at any rate combine in a rather happy way the restraining conservative and the dynamic progressive principles of selection.[1] Selection by achievement is the dynamic element here. We have no clear idea how the selection of élites would work in an open mass society in which only the principle of achievement mattered. It is possible that in such a society, the succession of the élites would take place much too rapidly and social continuity, which is essentially due to the slow and gradual broadening of the influence of the dominant groups, would be lacking in it. The real threat of contemporary mass society does not, however, seem to consist in the sudden predominance of the achievement principle but rather in that it has recently shown a tendency to renounce the principle of achievement as a factor in the struggle of certain groups for power, and has suddenly established blood and other criteria as the major factors to the far-reaching exclusion of the achievement principle.

We need not elaborate the fact that the recently proclaimed racial principle is, interestingly enough, not a genuine blood principle at all. It is no longer a matter, as in an earlier age, of the purity of an aristocratic minority stock and its traditions ; here, on the contrary, it has become democratic and quite suddenly offers to the great masses of the population the privilege of social ascendency without any achievement. Hitherto it has been the often envied privilege of the nobility to lay claim to certain functions and positions primarily on the grounds of biological inheritance, and to base its success only secondarily on achievement. Now, however, in many countries even the least important members of a given group wish to be regarded as superior not out of recognition of any achievements but simply by virtue of their biological ˙descent. Here, again,

---

[1] On leading groups cf. Marshall, T. H., article in *Annales d'histoire écon. et sociale*, 1937, on " British Aristocracy " ; Ponsonby, Arthur, *The Decline of Aristocracy* (London–Leipzig, 1912) ; Wector, Dixon, *The Saga of American Society* (New York, 1937) ; Taussig, F. W., and Joselyn, C., *American Business Leaders* (New York, 1932) ; Lundberg, F., *America's Sixty Families* (New York, 1937) ; Myers, G., *The History of Great American Fortunes* (new edition, New York, 1937) ; Nickerson, Hoffman, *The American Rich* (New York, 1930).

we have a characteristic illustration of the process, which we have called negative democratization. Whereas the unrestricted principle of freedom and free competition in the first phase of modern democratic society served to proclaim general equality, and therefore the same duties and rights for everyone, in this instance the principle has the opposite effect. The populace as a whole now becomes a privileged group in this sense and the man in the street is entitled to the privilege of being a member of a pure race, relieving him at the same time of the responsibility for individual achievement. In the prevailing conflict between political principles which are rapidly changing their meaning, expediency rather than truth is the decisive factor. It is therefore irrelevant in this ideological struggle to put forward the objection that in the long run it is logically impossible to give everyone the same " privileges ". We will not go into the problematic nature of a mass society in which the achievement principle has been dispensed with, but will only point out that it was precisely this new principle of selection which justified the rise of democracy itself, It was only on the basis of this principle that it could find the courage to oppose the principle of tradition which had formerly prevailed. One can already see that unless the principle of equalizing opportunities is linked up with objective criteria of achievement and just principles of social selection, mass society is bound to degenerate into Fascism.

VI

Fourth Process : THE CHANGE IN THE COMPOSITION OF
THE ÉLITE

In recent years further disturbances in the creation of culture have arisen from the artificial changes in the composition of the élites, and the relations between the autochthonous and the mobile elements within the intelligentsia have undergone profound changes.[1] In order

[1] In German scholarship, a worthy attempt has been made to clarify the rôle of the autochthonous social elements in the history of literature. Cf. Nadler, J., *Literaturgeschichte der deutschen Stämme und Landschaften,*

to understand what these changes mean, it must be remembered that the cultural élite of Western civilization have from their very origin been a fusion of the representatives of local cultures, of fixed social position, coming from the country, and of intellectuals who were not bound to any definite locality. Inasmuch as modern cultural life had its origins in clerical education, it absorbed a considerable element of internationalism from the very beginning. Clerical culture was primarily the expression of an international order, and only secondarily was it the reflection of special local and national circumstances. Secular humanism succeeded the Christian humanism and it took the form of an international cultural movement based on worldly foundations. But with the democratization of culture there also began in the ranks of the humanists and patricians a tendency towards regionalism. It was a bourgeoisie which had already attained power, that first created in the late urban art style a genuine local colour, creating and thinking in terms of regions and provinces. Thus, contrary to a widespread opinion, the history of Western civilization cannot be described as evolving from regional and provincial to national and international culture. There was rather, following a magnificent surge of international cultural integration (even though it was limited to narrow circles of élites), a gradual growth of local, then regional, and later national, patterns of culture. Cultural life, in our sense, was first brought to Northern Europe by colonizing monks who imposed upon the barbarian peoples a super-local and super-tribal outlook and way of life. For a long time it was the migrants—those individuals not bound to any particular place—who furthered this

Regensburg, 1912–1928, 4 vols. Cf. also Klaine, H., *Der Verfall der Adelsgeschlechter*, Leipzig, 1882. Toennies, F., Über den Adel Deutschlands im XIX Jhrdt. *Neue Rundschau*, 1912. Fahlbeck, P., Der Adel Schwedens (und Finlands) Eine demographische Studie, Jena, 1903. Savorgnan, Das Aussterben der adligen Geschlechter. *Jahrbuch für Soziologie*, ed. by G. Salomon, vol. i, pp. 320 ff. Uspensky, G. J., Terpigoriew, A. N., *Verlumpung der Bauern und des Adels in Russland*, Leipzig, 1892. It would, in my opinion, be at least as important to reverse the question and to show the significance of the mobile elements in social and cultural life. Cf. also Stonequist, Everett, *The Marginal Man* (New York, 1937) ; Park, R. E. " The Mentality of Racial Hybrids," *American Journal of Sociology*, vol. 36, pp. 534–551, January, 1931 ; and " Migration and the Marginal Man ", ibid., vol. 33, pp. 881–893, May, 1928 ; and esp. Toynbee, Arnold J., *A Study of History*, 2nd edition, London, 1935.

tradition in our society. Only very slowly did the autochthonous elements come to have their own culture. From that time onward in every country, two cultural groups have been in conflict with one another. One of them, in fact as well as in outlook, has been bound to its local arena and has regarded as strange and foreign whatever has come even from the neighbouring provinces. Side by side with it there has been the influence of certain mobile individuals who have not become merged into the indigenous population, and who have preferred to live in places and among people where the cultural community of Europe was becoming more and more united in a single fellowship. The French Revolution on its intellectual side was the expression of the mobile, urban intelligentsia; the counter-revolution and the romantic movement which followed represented, on the contrary, the rise of those groups which were more deeply influenced by the unique, individual developments of their native regions and provinces. As long as organic evolution lasts, these two types of human beings and currents of thought mutually enrich one another. The influence of the mobile type saves from intellectual provincialism those indigenous types whom property, sentimental attachment to the native soil, and the consciousness of a secure future have rendered not only more stable, but also more comfortable and satisfied. At the same time, the latter type forces the more abstract and over-mobile elements to take account of the concrete facts, locality and slowly growing traditions of their immediate surroundings and to assimilate them psychologically.[1]

---

[1] The argument that many of the ruling group in German National Socialism do not represent a local but rather a mobile element does not hold good in this connection. It is well known that many of the leaders came from relatively outside positions in the German nation, that Hitler as an Austrian and a provincial one had an inferiority complex towards the " Reichsdeutsche ".   Rosenberg came from the Baltics, Hess came from Egypt, Klaus Heim, the prominent leader of a rebel peasantry in Schleswig Holstein, came from South America, Count Reventlow had been for several years in the States before the War, and von Ribbentrop worked in Canada.   (These facts are stated in John Günther's *Inside Europe*, and in Konrad Heiden's *History of National Socialism*.)   But when we are considering social mobility we have to take into account that it does not always mean the same thing.   There is a cultural lag between developments inside Germany and their effect on Germans outside the Reich, in the former colonies, or in old settlements of German peasants as in Rumania or Hungary, a fact which has been

Just as we may observe in the contemporary economic situation, that autarchic tendencies and movements arise in the midst of the highest development of technique and international commerce, so obstacles are now arising in the cultural sphere. The representatives of local culture are trying to exclude from their midst those who are linked with international culture, and thereby threaten to destroy everything that has gone to make up our civilization since the beginning of humanism. The process of counter-colonization which Professor Bonn has descried in economic life, is also taking place in a certain sense even *within* the boundaries of some of the great states of the modern world.[1] To be more precise, the indigenous groups are isolating themselves from the mobile elements and thereby alienating themselves from everything which our culture has derived from Christian and secular international tendencies.

Indeed, many of the psychological and intellectual phenomena that accompany this process of de-colonization can be explained only in terms of such a regression. Whereas, in the past, the normal mechanism of selection had tended to bring the bearers of cultural values to the top, or else educated the ascending groups as they rose, at present negative selection gives a position of pre-eminence to those who were unable to live up to the standards of modern culture and were deficient in the mastery of their impulses

well described in Wilhelm Schneider's book, *Die auslandsdeutsche Dichtung unserer Zeit* (Berlin, 1936), pp. 9 seqq.

For the most part these settlers formed minorities who had to defend their cultural heritage against the pressure of the people who received them. Because of this defensive position they very often became staunch conservatives, changing only with utmost dislike, and since the stimulus for national unification within a Reich was lacking their cultural development moved at a slower pace. It was this backwardness which made the National Socialist Auslandsdeutsche so popular as professional politicians in Germany after the War. Their personal backwardness corresponded to the general backwardness of the German lower middle class or what was left of it during the world crisis. So the extremely mobile groups of National Socialist professional politicians—Dr. Goebbels from Heidelberg University was the most sophisticated type they could produce—could advocate the very opposite of their personal experience, blood and soil and " Bodenständigkeit ". The backward classes of Auslandsdeutschtum reflected the needs and opinions of the backward lower middle class in Germany, which reads few books and the lowest type of newspapers and which, in its work behind the counters of small shops, and at office desks, does not acquire any other intellectual training instead.

[1] Bonn, M. J., *The Age of Counter-Colonization.* Public lecture delivered at the London School of Economics and Politics, 1933.

and in self-control.   As a result of their triumph, their values become the dominant ones, and an inner conflict of motives develops in the psychological life of the individual too.   Finally, in this sphere, too, negative selection occurs in the sense that the earlier bearers of culture begin to be ashamed of their slowly acquired cultural and moral values and come to regard them as the expression of weakness and as a form of cowardice.   The sublimation of impulses which required so many generations for its realization is gradually disintegrated and the chaotic and undisciplined elements of the psyche come more clearly into the open.   Thus the negative selection of the élites is ultimately transformed into a negative selection of the prevailing experiences and characteristics of the human mind.   In the sphere of culture, positive selection, the effective force of repression, which exists in every society, masters the anti-social, primitive impulses, but in the negative selection it only annihilates those sublimations which took so long to acquire.[1]

VII

THE FORMATION OF THE PUBLIC IN LIBERAL MASS SOCIETY

The task of a sociology of culture is not limited, however, to describing how élites arise.   It also concerns itself with the rôle of the élites in society as a whole.   The next question to be considered here is the relationship of the élites to the " public ".   In order to clear up this point it is first necessary to say a few words about the processes by which the public is formed.

The élites are not in direct contact with the masses. Between élites and the masses stand certain social structures, which, although they are purely temporary, have, neverthe-less, a certain inner articulation and constancy.   Their function is to mediate between the élites and the masses. Here, too, it can be shown that the transition from the

---

[1] The phenomenon of regression was noted as early as Herbert Spencer who called it " rebarbarization ".   He traced the symptoms primarily to the pressure of militarism.   Such symptoms appear, not merely when a nation has an army, but rather when the military outlook replaces the civil one.   Cf. the section in question in his *Facts and Comments*.

liberal democracy of the few to real mass-democracy destroys this intermediate structure and heightens the significance of the completely fluid mass. In the realm of literature and of the theatre, this could be demonstrated by the fact that in earlier periods, when once an author had a public for himself, he could count upon its interest for at least a generation. In the disintegrated mass society, a public becomes integrated only momentarily, it comes together only to see a given play, and then disperses. Before such a public it is not a permanent theatrical troupe which presents the play but one which comes together only to present this particular play. It is in a society in a stage of dissolution that such a public supplants the permanent public which was formerly selected out of well-established and stable groups. Such an inconstant, fluctuating public can be reassembled only through new sensations. For authors the consequence of this situation is that only their first publications tend to be successful, and when the authors have produced a second and a third book the same public which greeted their first work may no longer exist. Wherever the organic publics are disintegrated, authors and élites turn directly to the broad masses. Consequently they become more subject to the laws of mass psychology than when they act through the medium of the social unit called "the public". In response to this need an attempt has been made in the most recent stage of liberal mass society to reach a novel and somewhat forced solution in the form of the *organized* public. Thus the workers' theatre plays before trade unions or other similarly organized groups. At this point in extreme cases in liberal mass society there emerges the solution which has its future in a regulated and planned society. Thus we see a transition in the development of the public from the organic through the disintegrated to the artificially organized public of the future.

The phenomenon of the formation of the public, as we have shown with reference to the theatre, can be pointed out just as well in other spheres of social life, e.g. in the political sphere. Here, too, there was at the stage of the democracy of the few an intermediate body between the broad masses and the élites, as represented, for example, by the more or less constant electoral following and the different parties as defined by the press. In the stage where democracy broadens into mass democracy the rôle of those who have hitherto been non-voters, and of the younger generation which has not yet made up its mind, becomes much more decisive as a fulcrum in those more or less definite, political, intermediate groups described above.[1]   The parties which in liberal mass democracy strive to attain some importance, turn, for these very reasons, towards these as yet unorganized masses and seek by appealing to emotional, irrational symbols, as these are understood by social psychology, to influence them in the desired direction.   But here, too, as with the theatre public, as soon as it attains power the dictatorship transforms its once voluntary following, which was an intense and momentary form of group integration, into an organized party.

VIII

THE PLACE OF THE INTELLIGENTSIA IN SOCIETY

We are confronted with the further problem of the position of the élites in the social order and their relationship to the various other social classes.

The question whether the bearers of intellectual culture

[1] Cf. Tingsten, Herbert, *Political Behavior* (London, 1937), on degrees in which social classes become politically minded. Cf. also Dix, A., *Die deutschen Reichstagswahlen 1871–1930 und die Wandlungen der Volksgliederung* (Tuebingen, 1930).

The fact that the National Socialist Party attracted the younger generation much more than the pre-War type of party like the Social Democrats is not only shown in the election results but even more unmistakably in the various generations of party membership.

According to " Die Nationalsozialistische Parteikorrespondenz " in 1931 the composition of the National Socialist Party was as follows :—

Members 18–30 years old making 37·6 per cent of the total			
,,	31–40	,,	,, 27·6 ,, ,,
,,	41–50	,,	,, 19·6 ,, ,,
,,	above 50	,,	,, 14·9 ,, ,,

That is to say 65·2 per cent of the party members were not more than forty years of age and only about 15 per cent were over fifty. The significance of these figures will become clear if one looks at the same figures for the Social Democrat party.

Members 18–30 years old making 19·3 per cent of the total			
,,	31–40	,,	,, 27·4 ,, ,,
,,	41–50	,,	,, 26·5 ,, ,,
,,	above 50	,,	,, 26·8 ,, ,,

(*Berliner Tageblatt*, Nr. 27, 16.1.1927.)

are members of more or less aristocratic " society " or whether they depend on individual patronage, on a freely and automatically self-integrating public, or on organized groups, is by no means irrelevant to the destiny of these élites, and to the type of outlook which prevails in a society. The first negative consequence of the modern widening of opportunities for social advancement through education is the proletarianization of the intelligentsia.[1]

[1] The sinking of the intelligentsia in the social scale could best be studied in Central and Eastern Europe during the post-War period. First of all, savings and rents disappeared through inflation. The sections of the middle strata who were dependent on salary and other forms of money income lost their social security and only by an extreme effort could a middle class family afford to send one of its members to the university. In this connection it is interesting to note that the size of the family mattered a great deal. Parents who had many children to care for could not spend so much on the education of any one of them, and those who wanted their sons to go to the university restricted births. Nearly 50 per cent of the German students come from small families with one or two children, about 25 per cent have two or more brothers or sisters, and only the remaining 25 per cent have four or more brothers or sisters. (*Deutsche Hochschulstatistik*, vol. 12, 1933–4, Berlin, 1934, p. 21.)

If economic conditions affecting the professional chances of the middle classes make for overcrowded universities, post-War political changes, the rise of the new national states after the breakdown and splitting-up of the Austrian-Hungarian state have made life difficult for the professional classes. The University of Vienna before the War had trained lawyers, barristers, and civil servants for the whole of the Habsburg territory. After the War Rumania, Hungary, Yugoslavia, Czechoslovakia, and others built up new bureaucracies out of their own stock, and offered the indigenous middle classes, the peasantry, and urban bourgeoisie new chances of social advancement, and of assimilation with the educated class. They encouraged them to speak their native language, to foster a literature of their own, to build up a national press, and so on. This meant an enormous shrinkage of the market for German graduates from Vienna University. But the adjustment in the market of professions is particularly slow and probably only by the introduction of quotas, legal and other political measures is it possible to restore the equilibrium between supply and demand. (Kotschnig, Walter M., *Unemployment in the Learned Professions.* An International Study of Occupational and Educational Planning, Oxford University Press, 1937, p. 33 *passim.*) Kotschnig's study gives some striking figures revealing the lamentable state of the overcrowded professions in all countries of Eastern and Central Europe. To mention only a few works on the proletarianization of the intellectuals, Becker, W. M., " Aus dem Gelehrtenproletariat der nachreformatorischen Zeit," *Archiv für Kulturgeschichte*, vol. 8, 1911 ; Michels, R., " Zur Soziologie der Boheme und ihre Zusammenhänge mit dem geistigen Proletariat," *Jahrbücher für Nationalökonomie und Statistik*, 3rd series, 81, 6, June, 1932 ; Kassel, R., *Soziale Probleme der Intellektuellen*, Wien, 1920 ; Rauecker, B., *Die Proletarisierung der geistigen Arbeiter* (München, 1920) ; Eulenberg, H., *Die Frequenz der deutschen Universitäten von ihrer Gründnug bis zur Gegenwart* (Leipzig, 1907) ; Kotschnig, op. cit., chap. ii ; R. Schairer, *Die akademische Berufsnot* (Jena, 1933).

There are more persons on the intellectual labour market than society as it is to-day requires for carrying out its intellectual work.[1]

The real significance of this over-supply is not only that the intellectual professions lose their social value, but also that cultural and intellectual activity itself is belittled by public opinion. The layman believes that intellectual culture is always highly valued for its own sake. It seems, however, to be a sociological principle that the social value of intellectual culture is a function of the social status of those who produce it. It not only took a long time for intellectual culture as such to attain general recognition, but in the course of this development the rank in society of those who produced it was time and again decisive for the value which was placed upon it. The intellectual aristocracy only very gradually took its place beside the warrior class of noble blood. We can point to many curious cases, such as the determination of the status of a university professor by the number of aristocratic youths who sat at his feet. We know from Greek history that the plastic arts were looked down upon for a very long time because those engaging in these arts were originally slaves. On the other hand, it was very important for the social advancement of intellectual culture in modern times that the absolutist state suddenly required educated officials ; this decreased the market value of court theology and certain other forms of intellectual activity, while it caused a rise in the value of legal education.

To-day we are witnessing a movement in the opposite direction. The glut of intellectuals decreases the value of the intellectuals and of intellectual culture itself. The fact that this overcrowding did not appear in the preceding phase of democratic society is closely connected with the

---

[1] An example illustrating this situation in Republican Germany may help to show what we mean. The annual excess of supply over demand during the past few years was approximately : Physicians 100–200 per cent ; physicists 100–200 per cent ; chemists 100 per cent.

These figures refer only to the annual increases in persons who had just become qualified for these professions, and do not include the reserve army of those unemployed who were already in the profession. Cf. *Untersuchungen zur Lage der akademischen Berufe* (Berlin, 1932–3).

Kotschnig, op. cit., summarizes all the available data for a large number of different countries and provides a clear-cut factual corroboration of this statement.

faċt that it was an era of minority-democracy. Apart from the families of the aristocracy, the cultured class was recruited so predominantly from the property-owning class that wealth came to be an inseparable prerequisite for education. The intelligentsia therefore took its place in " high society ". Although it is true to state that in the eighteenth century many men of learning were recruited from the lower classes, the path they trod was an extremely difficult one,[1] and their adaptability to the desires of the ruling classes was guaranteed by the fact that in many ways they were dependent on these classes. The modern transition from a bourgeois democracy of well-to-do classes to a mass-democracy, in which culture was no longer the property of the few, had beneficial results at first. Their excessively close connection with " high society " led the intellectuals to form their cultural outlook according to class conventions. In consequence intellectual culture to a very considerable extent acquired a class character. The freedom of the intellectuals from " high society " and their development into a section more or less detached from other sections, and recruited from all social classes, brought about a wonderful flowering of a free intellectual and cultural life. The great plasticity of mind and the deep sense of moral responsibility as represented by the intelligentsia of Czarist Russia, or the really valuable and representative intellectuals of the last hundred years in Europe as a whole, was a human achievement in the very best sense, free to a very great extent from the class prejudices which previously had always entered into intellectual life. This selection, made on an increasingly broader basis, had an adverse effect, however, when with the increase in the supply of intellectuals, the classes from which they were selected became more and more barren for purposes of cultural creation.

---

[1] Cf. Winckelmann, for instance, who was the son of a poor cobbler. It is said that he spent his day in the following way : " He did not go to bed all the winter but sat in his reading chair in a corner, before a table, with a bookcase on each side. After finishing with his classes and his private pupils for the day he studied until midnight. Then he put out his lamp and slept in his chair until four o'clock. At four he relit his lamp and read until six, when he had again to busy himself with his pupils." Reicke, E., *Der Gelehrte*, Jena, 1910, p. 142. See also Bruford, W. H., *Germany in the Eighteenth Century* (London, 1936) ; one could equally well refer to Fichte, Heyne, and others.

It is not the economically poorest classes which are unquestionably the least fitted for intellectual activity but rather those which have the least promising future in the modern process of production. For this reason the fundamental impulses which develop in these sections of the population tend to produce types which are quite limited in their more human qualities. If a society in which the various classes have very unequal standards of life, very unequal opportunities for leisure, and vastly dissimilar opportunities for psychological and cultural development, offers the chances of cultural leadership to larger and larger sections of the population, the inevitable consequence is that the average outlook of those groups which have been doomed to a more unfortunate position in life, tends more and more to become the prevalent outlook of the whole society. Whereas in an aristocratic society in which a very small minority was culturally active, the low average level of culture of the less fortunate classes was confined to their own sphere of life ; now as a result of large-scale ascent, the limited intelligence and outlook of the average person gains general esteem and importance and even suddenly becomes a model to which people seek to conform. A gradual influx from the lower classes can be assimilated by the upper classes, as is still very largely the case in England to-day ; when, however, the influx assumes mass proportions, the older intellectual classes lose their assimilative power and are themselves submerged.

Recognizing this fact, we may now ask the question : " Why did culture not take on a mass character at the time when the proletariat came forth for the first time with its own cultural ambitions, and began to exert a cultural influence ? Why did the negative symptoms of cultural decay become visible for the first time only when the democratization of culture began to affect classes other than the proletariat ? " To explain this we must ask first of all which social classes have really been taking political as well as cultural leadership into their own hands of late. The answer is, the lower middle class. The minor employees, petty officials, artisans, small business men, small peasants, and impoverished *rentiers*.[1]

---

[1] In the above-mentioned (p. 90 n.) analysis of biographies of eminent men Zahn gives some data on the composition of the intellectual upper class.

Intrinsically, there is no reason why these classes should not supply cultural élites as well as any other, nor why a selection from these groups, should not have positive values.

Contemporaries Belong to	Their Fathers Belong to		
	Upper Class		Middle and Lower Classes
	Intellectual	Economic	
	%	%	%
Intellectuals and Civil Servants :			
Male	56·1	22·7	21·2
Female	69·1	30·8	9·5
Artistic Professions :			
Male	41·5	27·3	31·2
Female	53·7	34·0	12·3
Economic Upper Class :			
Male	28·9	51·4	19·7
Female	—	100·0	—
Otherwise (Politicians, Social Work, Sports, etc.) :			
Male	11·0	17·9	71·1
Female	32·9	13·7	53·4
Total :			
Male	46·2	26·9	26·9
Female	53·0	30·8	16·2

(*Sozialer Auf- und Abstieg im deutschen Volke*, Arbeiten des Bayerischen Statistischen Landesamtes, ed. by Zahn, Fr. No. 116, p. 56.)

Here, too, some characteristic figures relating to Germany may be instructive. In 1830 about half of the university students came from families of the higher officialdom, and the liberal professions, while only about a fifth belonged to the classes commonly called "intermediate officials", which then comprised primarily clergymen and teachers. In 1930, the percentage of these students whose parents belonged either to the higher officialdom or to the liberal professions fell to one-fifth, while the percentage of students from the intermediate officialdom increased from 20 to over 30 per cent. The unusually large influx into the universities of the children of the lower middle class can be demonstrated by the following approximate figures : in 1914, 30,000, and in 1930, 60,000 of the students came from the lower middle class.

Cf. on this subject the book of Robert Michels, *Umschichtungen der herrschenden Klassen nach dem Kriege* (Stuttgart and Berlin, 1934), esp. pp. 162 *passim* for the bibliography on the "Akademikerfrage". Kotschnig, op. cit., pp. 162 seqq. Cf. also Hartshorne, E. Y., *The German Universities and National Socialism*, London, 1937. By the same author, "The German Universities and the Government," *Annals. Am. Acad.*, November, 1938 ; and "Numerical Changes in the German Student Body", *Nature*, 23rd July, 1938. Löwe, A. "The Task of Education in Democracy" in *Social Research*, 1932. For the United States cf. O. E. Reynolds : The *Social*

In principle this is true. A more precise analysis shows, however, the reasons why, when these classes help to form the élites, the quality of culture changes. Since Marx Max Weber,[1] and others, we have been aware that the different social classes have quite different outlooks, and that the mental qualities of a class can to a very large extent be derived from its position in the economic process of production. Accordingly the interest which a group has in the progress of further industrialization and in technical rationalization is vital in the present situation. Certain classes and groups depend for their existence on the growth of industrialization and the creation of large-scale productive units. Their economic position nourishes in them a sympathy for technical rationality and for the further development of man's rational capacities and humanistic spirit. It is clear that the proletariat which owes its existence to industrialization, the technical invention of the large factory, and the rationalization of certain social relations, will be unconsciously inclined to push social development in this direction.[2] Thus,

and Economic Status of College Students, New York, 1927 ; and for Italy the excellent article of V. Castrilli in Archives de Sociologie, Series B. 5–6. (Institut internationale de sociologie), published by the Comitato Italiana per lo Studio dei Problemi della Popolazione (Rome, 1935.)

[1] The best summary of Max Weber's investigations in this field is to be found in the chapter entitled " Stände, Klassen, und Religion ", in his Wirtschaft und Gesellschaft, Grundriss der Sozialoekonomik, part iii. Much empirical investigation has been done on this subject. Representations are such articles as Kornhouse, Arthur W., " Attitudes of Economic Groups," Public Opinion Quarterly, vol. 2, 1938, p. 260. Cf. also Droba, D. D., " Topical Summaries of Current Literature : Social Attitudes," Amer. Journ. of Sociology, vol. 39, 1934, pp. 513–534.

[2] However, an important qualifying factor must be recognized. The worker who has become unemployed, has, sociologically speaking, a different outlook from one who is regularly employed. The destructive effects on culture of lasting unemployment can scarcely be overestimated, since the change in the attitude of the unemployed naturally exercises an influence beyond the limits of the particular class. The most important negative effect of unemployment consists in the destruction of what may be called the " life plan " of the individual. The " life plan " is a very vital form of personal rationalization, inasmuch as it restrains the individual from responding immediately to every passing stimulus. Its disruption heightens the individual's susceptibility to suggestions to an extraordinary degree and strengthens the belief in miraculous " cure-alls ". The prospect of continuous work and rational self-support has the same effect in the sphere of mental life that saving has in the economic sphere. This attitude leads gradually to the creation of a " life plan " and the repression, to a certain degree, of immediate satisfaction of impulses and wishes, for the sake of the later social use of one's spiritual energies (cf. concerning what has been said about " career ", pp. 56 seqq.).

in Russia, for instance, where it possesses exclusive political power, the proletariat carries this principle so far, that even if for no other reason it continues to accumulate and to invest in order to expand itself as a social class, as against the peasantry.

The petty entrepreneurs, who direct their own tiny individual economic units, the small shopkeeper and the artisan, whose enemies are technical invention and large-scale production, have a quite different attitude towards further industrialization and rationalization.[1] To maintain their independence they must destroy the big concerns, the great factories, and the department stores. If they were to have things their own way, technical rationalization would be brought to a standstill. Anyone who is at all capable of thinking in sociological terms knows that rationality cannot be suppressed in one sphere without causing a corresponding regression in the whole of man's cultural and spiritual life. Anyone who wants to return to the social and economic life of the pre-capitalist era must also remould our whole outlook along pre-capitalist lines. In order to save himself he must artificially arrest the whole process of social development which, impelled by technical rationality, is moving more and more rapidly towards further industrialization and large-scale organization. Just as the industrial proletariat strives to alter the form of the class system by turning everybody into a proletarian, so the " new middle class " attempts to rescue itself by using all the political techniques at its command in order to reverse the process of industrial development, to restrict the extension of rationalized industry, and to prevent the development of the modern rational type of man with all his humane ideals. From what we have said hitherto, it is clear that a change in social order according to the wishes of these groups or classes will not take place of itself, but must be brought about by force. Though one may be in favour only of the proletariat, only of industrialization, only of reason and enlightenment, such a social order has at the present stage no more chance of developing spontaneously than has the

[1] Cf. Pesl, L. D., " Mittelstandsfragen (Der gewerbliche und kauf-männische Mittelstand)," *Grundriss der Sozialökonomik*, ix, 1, " Die Gesellschaftliche Schichtung im Kapitalismus," Tübingen, 1926, p. 70 ; and Brauer, Theodor, " Mittelstandspolitik," in vol. ix, 2.

pre-capitalistic person we described. It seems to require the use of force or, at any rate, planned intervention. It must be systematically cultivated by various social and intellectual techniques of control. Thus here, too, the unorganized growth of democratic society culminates in dictatorship. And that brings with it in the cultural sphere all those dangers which come from replacing the process of spontaneous development by enforced institutions.

IX

THE PROBLEM OF INTELLECTUAL LIFE IN MASS SOCIETY

So far we have criticized some of the distorted developments in the functioning of liberal and democratic society—with no fear of being misunderstood as its opponent. We could do so because the great strength of the liberal system and of democracy consists in the fact that they can bear criticism, and as long as they are vigorous, they are elastic enough to find ways and means of bringing about reform. The source of our criticism consists neither in the snobbish condemnation of the masses which is so widespread nowadays, nor in cheap grumbling about the principles of liberalism and democracy. The ultimate drive is rather the wish to make an appeal to those to whom freedom and justice are still ultimate values, to think about the proper means to secure them under the changed technical and social conditions of the present world ; and this in the first instance means keeping a watchful eye on the deteriorative tendencies in liberalism and democracy which are emerging in this era of mass societies and the growth of monopolies. We are firmly convinced that modern society will sooner or later be able to form its various elements into stable and creative cultural patterns, like those more or less attained by the various societies in earlier stages of social development. The chief difficulty of modern society lies not so much in its vastness as in the fact that the liberal method of organization has not yet reached the stage where it can produce the *organic articulation* (*Gliederung*) which a vast and complex society needs.[1] Modern psychology and sociology

---

[1] Cf. concerning this the discussion on pp. 61 ff.

have shown—as we have already pointed out—that the same persons react differently when they form an uncoordinated mass.[1] The contemptible behaviour about which we hear so much is actually due to an uncoordinated mass, and the flaws in the working of liberal society are probably the symptoms of transition. The process of selection and its corresponding institutions, which were appropriate to a society with only a limited choice of intellectuals are cracking under the impact of the mass influx with which they were not designed to deal.

But even if the flaws we have mentioned in the working of liberal society are merely the effects of transition, that does not mean that they cannot wreck civilization. We must, however, insist at this point that a dictatorship is by no means a form of social organization necessarily opposed to the excrescences and negative trends of liberalism, i.e. it is not the alternative to the liberal-democratic social order and hence is not in and for itself a panacea for everything that has gone awry in that society. Dictatorship itself grows out of the negative working of the forces of mass democracy and is nothing more than a violent attempt to stabilize a stage in the development of liberal society, which was by nature transitory, to reinforce and to extend that stage with all its defects, in favour of the one-sided interests of a certain group.

[1] Of the literature on crowds and masses which began with the well known works of Sighele and Le Bon, and which since then has been raised to a much broader level of discussion in various countries, I will cite only a few general works in which the reader can find further bibliographical references. In the German literature on the subject, cf. Vleugels, " Die Masse," *Kölner Vierteljahrshefte für Soziologie*, 1930, Ergänzungsheft No. 3 ; Colm's article " Masse " in *Handwörterbuch der Soziologie* (ed. by A. Vierkandt), Stuttgart, 1931 ; Freud, S., *Group Psychology and the Analysis of the Ego*, New York and London, 1922 ; Wiese, L., *System der Allgemeinen Soziologie*, 2nd ed., 1933, the chapter on " Masse ". In English above all cf. the articles on " Crowd " and " Mass " in the *Encyclopædia of the Social Sciences* (London, 1930–5) ; Wallas, C., *The Great Society*, 1914 ; Christensen, *Politics and Crowd Morality* (New York, 1915) ; Thomas, *Industry, Emotion, and Unrest* (New York, 1920) ; Taylor, J. L., *Social Life and the Crowd* (London, 1923). Cf. also the aforementioned book by Ortega y Gasset, *The Revolt of the Masses* (1933) ; Theodor Geiger's *Die Masse und ihre Aktion* (Stuttgart, 1928) ; and R. Fueloep-Miller's *Leaders, Dreamers, and Rebels* (New York, 1935) ; Drabovich, W., *Fragilité de la liberté et séduction des dictatures* ; Essai de psychologie sociale ; Préface de Pierre Janet, Paris (ed. Mercure de France), 1934. Cf. also the bibliography on p. 60 n. of the present book.

X

SOME PROBLEMS ARISING OUT OF REGULATION OF CULTURAL
LIFE, PARTICULARLY IN A DICTATORSHIP

We cannot describe in detail here the whole mechanism
of a dictatorially governed society as it affects culture.
In order to do this we should have to trace the individual
effects of dictatorship on culture at least as carefully as we
have done in our analysis of the effects of a *laisser-faire*
society. We must refrain from this analysis, since on the one
hand the effects of dictatorship are quite obvious, while on
the other there are at present too few carefully observed
instances of creative planning in the cultural sphere. All
comments along these lines must be based on a few quite
simple facts.

First : Dictatorship as such is not planning. It is possible
that full dictatorial power is necessary for a certain measure
of planning—and this *certain measure* should be made more
explicit in future research and in the laboratory of actual
life.[1] But to wish to cure a society in a state of crisis merely

[1] We must try to point out here at least the decisive causes which have
given modern dictatorships a totalitarian form. None of the older forms
of dictatorship and cultural planning were marked by the totalitarian
control which distinguish those existing to-day. It is known of the older
forms of despotism that those people who were not at the very centre of
political or intellectual opposition to the reigning group were never so completely dominated by a centralized power as to-day. Thus, Czarist Russia
was never as " totalitarian " as present day dictatorships are. Even the
cultural planning of the medieval church—in spite of its grip on the
conscience—was not as powerful or rigorous as the supervision of cultural
activity which prevails in the dictatorships of to-day. The cause seems
to lie in two essential factors. First, the nature of the modern means
of communication—the railroad, telephone, and radio—render centralized
control more possible to-day than at any earlier period. Second, and more
important, is the " fundamental democratization " of the masses. As
a result of the far-reaching mobilization of the members of modern society,
the resistance which dictatorships must overcome is so great that they
must penetrate into the smallest cells and associations (even into the
small groups which meet for discussion in restaurants and coffee-houses)
in order to attain and preserve their power. The intellectual class which
is capable of criticism and opposition is too varied in its origins to be
brought fully under control without the use of some element of compulsion.
The ecclesiastical cultural planning of the middie ages did not have to
be so radical since the masses were still culturally dependent and had been
made pliant and obedient by tradition and ritual, while the intellectuals
were in the direct service of the church. Absolutism, too, could depend
to a very large extent upon the cultural and political passivity of the

by establishing a dictatorship over it is like the physician who believes he is curing a sick child by forbidding it to cry.

A single example will make it clear that dictatorship is not the same as planning. A correct scheme for the planning of culture, which would plan everything in the sense of the totalitarian state, would also have to plan the place of criticism. It would have to provide forums where the results of fruitful self-criticism, namely the experiences of those who are affected by planning could be brought together and publicly expressed. Arbitrary criticism and irresponsible public chatter may indeed have a destructive influence, but a complete suppression of criticism can have only negative results. Even the most convinced liberal must recognize the destructive effects of irresponsible criticism of the activities of the groups in power made with the sole purpose of gaining attention for the critics, who do not feel themselves bound to offer a single positive suggestion for improving conditions. Here again we have a negatively developing liberalism—which in an age of the domination of the masses allows the liberties which it provides to be used against itself without hindrance and permits the social mechanism which it has itself created to be misused by its opponents.

The further we advance in the history of liberal, democratic society, the more frequently do its opponents promulgate ambiguous " carry-all " programmes, giving something to everyone, or refuse to utter even the slightest word about their own proposed solutions for the future. Both these courses, which are a remarkable illustration of the psychological laws of mass suggestion, make it extremely

general populace. In contrast with this, the widespread participation in political life in modern society explains why contemporary dictatorships, in spite of all the great physical power and organization which they have concentrated in their hands, still have to use a gigantic propaganda machine, and why it is advisable for industrial and military dictatorships to give certain sections of the population a measure of control over the rest. We have presented here only those factors which cause the fundamental tensions in modern society. We have not, however, described the inner antagonisms and the concrete sequence of events which would be the result of these tensions. We can see at the same time, however, the general outline of a possible solution to the present tension, namely a sort of authoritarian democracy making use of planning, and creating a stable system from the present conflict of principles. Regarding the administrative obstacles to centralized control in the Age of Absolutism, cf. Heckscher, Eli, *Mercantilism*, Transl. from the German edition by M. Shapiro, 2 vols. (London, 1935).

difficult to deal with the social crisis in that they throw us abruptly back from a rational solution to faith healing.

These " carry-all " programmes of opposition depend for their support upon the mental passivity of the average person and on the limited outlook of the intellectual specialist who lacks judgment in social affairs. In the advanced stages of a demagogic movement it is regarded as a higher sort of wisdom to say nothing specific, to despise the use of reason in attempting to mould the future, and to require no more than blind faith. One enjoys then the double advantage of having to use reason only in criticizing one's opponents and at the same time, of being able to mobilize without restraint and to one's own profit all the negative emotions of hatred and resentment which—according to Simmel's principle of the " negative character of collective behaviour "[1]—can unify a large number of people more easily than any positive programme. By not asserting anything positive about one's goals, the danger of erecting schisms in one's own following is avoided. While the older forms of social opposition at least constructed so-called utopias, which were really uncritical in the sense that they confused day dreams with practical possibilities, at a later stage not even the intellectual effort of creating a day dream is required ; one need only work up feelings of frustration and dissatisfaction in the citizen's mind and need not consider intellectual consistency in one's programme at all.

As regards the impossibility of the older form of criticism, i.e. the liberal, uncontrolled type which is not integrated according to plan into the social order, even the most radical democrat will admit to-day that in a world in which the work of government requires increasingly specialized technical knowledge and in which the most important matters are settled by commissions and not by the deliberations of general parliamentary assemblies, adequate control cannot depend on general approval and thorough-going publicity. Exactly the same holds for the various spheres of cultural life, which in the main require such a refined special knowledge that irresponsible chatter has neither controlling nor guiding value. It is very probable that a planned society will provide certain forms of closed social groups

---

[1] Cf. Simmel, G., " Exkurs über die Negativität kollektiver Verhaltungsweisen " in his *Soziologie* (Leipzig, 1908), pp. 473–8.

similar to our clubs, advisory councils or even sects, in which absolutely free discussion may take place without being exposed to premature and unsatisfactory criticism by the broader public. The discussion in these groups would be quite free because no one would need to fear a premature broadcasting of views expressed. On the other hand, it must be constitutionally provided that any advice or suggestions coming from these exclusive closed groups would really reach and have an appropriate influence on the government of the day. On the other hand, admission to these " secret societies " or " orders " would have to be on a democratic basis and they would have to remain in close and living contact with the masses and their situations and needs. Liberal democratic society which first worked out the principle of public opinion, immediately lost sight of the real meaning of secrecy in society. It gradually disturbed a device which in previous societies was often very cleverly worked out—the system of gradual initiation into different stages of secrecy through, for example, age or rise in the social scale. We need not deny that public opinion in the early stages of its development did much good in that it made corruption much more difficult. But the more we develop into a mass society, the more the principle of inarticulated publicity (that is to say the conglomeration of the many in masses without organic sub-divisions) becomes incongruous, in so far as it tends to disturb the ultimate prerequisites of social creativeness and its transformation into concrete action. One of these elementary prerequisites is that the masses should not be able to criticize a social idea before it has been elaborated into workable form. The detrimental consequences of publicity in an increasing number of spheres can be best observed in the fatal fact that since the World War, external politics in a certain sense have become increasingly public, and in these spheres waves of mass sentiment have had to be reckoned with where previously internal discussions in diplomatic circles would have sufficed. This is naturally no justification at all for the earlier secrecy and intrigue of international diplomacy. We must see, however, that we only fall from the frying pan of secret diplomacy into the fire of a foreign policy increasingly at the mercy of public whim and fancy. We can at least learn the elementary principles of a reasonable solution from the distortions of these two extremes. In a well articulated society public opinion is not an incalculable, occasional integration of moods, but the principle of public control creates for itself organs of criticism. These organs are so incorporated into the society that they can, if necessary, count on complete secrecy. At the same time, however, they possess complementary institutions and regulations through which misuse of this secrecy—nepotism, graft, etc.—can be checked through the exercise of moral sanctions. Naturally the exact details of this planning for criticism cannot be worked out here. Social institutions, like medicines, can be compounded of different ingredients in different proportions, and the future will furnish us with the concrete details, provided that we are willing to observe society in the same analytical way as that in which we are accustomed to observing natural phenomena.

In the existing dictatorships we have an important laboratory for the study of this phenomenon. As long as they continue to exist the persons in the central positions of control must, in view of the vastness of contemporary society have at their disposal certain channels of information and criticism. Under a dictatorship, too, there must be ways in which the reactions of those governed can be observed.[1] Whether a secret system of espionage or the

[1] Authoritarian dictatorships certainly have far less elasticity than democratic forms of government where a necessary change of politics can always be achieved by a change in the cabinet brought about by arousing public opinion. This was seen during the Abyssinian war at the time of the Hoare-Laval agreement and the abdication of Sir Samuel Hoare. (Since then the power of public opinion is definitely decreasing in England.) In fascist countries " public opinion " does not so much express the opinion of the public as impress on it the opinion of the ruling strata ; whether they take the form of some cultural bureaucracy like the chamber of music, writing, etc., or of the party officialdom or of the labour front administrative body. Yet unless the leaders want to lose touch with the masses there must be some sort of organization providing for a stream of inside information for the benefit of the ruling classes in which all the conflicts, the shortcomings, the occasional inadequacies of command are circulated. And, in fact, such means of communication do exist. The German propaganda ministry with its " Gaupropagandastellen "—some twenty bureaux all over the country—have the means of quick contact because they are linked up with one another through telewriters. The central bureau in Berlin can communicate at the same time with all the local branches and can receive messages from all of them. So actually distance does not exist and one can organize some sort of conference by correspondence. Through these channels the local party organization

uncontrolled power of local authorities is in the long run the best solution has not yet been decided. As long as a dictatorship does not substitute new forms of canalizing opinion for the older ones—among which are parliament, press, etc.—the final result can only be disintegration. Thus here, too, dictatorship without planning causes regressions, since it has set up a number of unco-ordinated small despotisms in those subordinate positions which were formerly organized within a hierarchy of competence.

If in the course of time planned criticism is not integrated into the structure of the dictatorship, it must for this very reason fail. Either dissatisfaction breaks out in such a form that it can no longer be reassimilated into the social organism, namely in insurrections and counter-revolutions, or the dominant groups lose contact with the vital tissue of social life and become so bureaucratic that the insight born of day-to-day activity becomes impossible. An unrealistic sort of regimentation disrupts and in the end by means of " planning " prevents the orderly functioning of economic and cultural life.

After all this discussion the question may well be raised whether everything is not hopeless in this stage of mass society and whether we are not moving towards an inescapable social and cultural decline. This is by no means our own view. Our opinion is that liberal mass society has reached a point in its development where continued drifting leads to disaster. We shall not be able to get along without planning even in the cultural sphere

can hand on news which does not appear in the press, can criticize unworkable measures and so on. A similar means of control behind the screen of the regulated press—though in a different sphere—is shown in the publication of official book reviews, drawn up by a staff of several hundred reviewers under the direction of the *Reichsschrifttumskammer*. The newly published books are reviewed and the reviews appear in a periodical which is not on sale but is distributed to all newspapers and publications which review books. If a book is sharply criticized in this official organ no writer for a daily newspaper dare disagree and what is more, no journalist dare let such a book review go to press. Even if he succeeds in being quicker than the official organ he has every reason to fear that later on he will have to face an inquiry as to why he allowed such a criticism to appear. The " lack of instinct " is a reproach he learns to dread. So beside the privacy of political dinner-parties in private houses, casinos, hunting parties, select conferences, behind the organized façade of " public opinion " in the press stands the quasi-public of officialdom discussing and influencing current affairs by using all the modern techniques and equipment.

and we must finally recognize that a system of education which was suited for the individualized type of élite which prevails in a minority democracy cannot be successfully carried over to mass education without certain modifications.[1] We should, in a word, not wait until bad management brings to power these groups which understand by planning a one-sided reign of force, functioning in their own interest. Planning does not mean rule by arbitrary forces over the living body of society, nor the dictatorial attempt to supplant creative activity. Planning means a conscious attack on the sources of maladjustment in the social order on the basis of a thorough knowledge of the whole mechanism of society and the way in which it works. It is not the treatment of symptoms but an attack on the strategic points, fully realizing the results.

At this point we should not forget that in the cultural sphere (properly also in the economic) there has never been an absolute liberalism, that alongside of the undirected working of the social forces there has always existed, for instance, regulation in education. The liberal state, too, regulated whole institutions in which it decided not only the kind of knowledge to be supplied to the various classes but actually cultivated these model patterns of conduct which were needed for the continued existence of this society and helped the élites to acquire them. It is not, therefore, contrary to the nature of free democratic society if we maintain that the most satisfactory arrangement would be to fit a sphere of free creative initiative into a planned institutional framework. In the future this sphere of free creative activity must always be guided so as to guard against the possibility of distortion and breakdown. However, if in the future events are to be controlled we must have a knowledge of the laws of the social processes of cultural production and disintegration. And further, it must constantly be kept in mind that the transition from a minority democracy to an organized mass democracy does not take place spontaneously but must itself be planned.

[1] Concerning the pedagogical problem, cf. Part IV. *Thought at the Level of Planning*, pp. 219 ff; 225 ff; and 359.

PART III

CRISIS, DICTATORSHIP, WAR

Correlation between the Disorganization of Society and the Disorganization of Personality

In the first part we observed the factors which create crowd behaviour and irrationality in our society. In the second we watched the less eruptive, more slowly working social mechanisms which have a detrimental effect upon culture. The enumeration of these negative effects upon social life would not be complete were we not to study the causes of disorganization in their most disastrous forms as they make for crisis, dictatorship, and war. This rhythm of events is in everybody's mind; but in spite of it the interconnection and necessity of this sequence have not yet been sufficiently thought out. The tangle of economic, social, and psychological factors which brings about the general drift into war in our age has not yet been clearly enough analysed.

Recent experiences have shown us the starting point for our investigations by teaching us that there must definitely be a deeper correlation between the disorganization of society and the disorganization of individual behaviour, and even of certain levels of the human mind, and vice versa that the more strongly a society is organized, the more strongly forms of behaviour and the corresponding attitudes of the mind seem to be integrated. One has only to look at pictures like those of Bosch and Grünewald in order to see that the disorganization of the Medieval order expressed itself in a general fear and anxiety, the symbolic expression of which was the attention given to the underworld with its demons, and the widespread fear of the devil. In the Medieval order the luciferic element was present but had its place in the plan of the universe. When the social order goes wrong psychosis spreads, the diabolic forces are no longer integrated into the Cosmos. In an adequately functioning society the neurotic is only the borderline case.

In a state of general disorganization it is he who sets the pattern. But this correlation between social disorganization and mental disorganization seems to be much stricter than this general statement would lead one to believe. A careful observer, even on the basis of a preliminary contact with the relevant phenomena, would see that the predominant associations, for instance, of a man brought up in a well-integrated traditional society are more conventionalized than those of the average man in a society in the making, or in course of transformation. What we frequently call imagination is perhaps essentially characterized by unexpected mental associations and connections which do not form part of the usual chain of ideas. Also the increased awareness of the new and the sensational which is widespread in America seems to correspond to a society in the making where it was very difficult to stabilize social groups, develop folkways, and thus to determine the flow of mental associations. The lesser premium put on imagination in England, both in science and in life, in spite of its poets and social outsiders, perhaps also falls under that heading. As imagination and free association are mainly dissociated elements springing from the unconscious, their overflow or repression in the individual somewhere corresponds to the general pressure existing in society. The individual organism, according to its hereditary equipment and to its early life history, may put up with these pressures in different ways, but in the long run and in dealing with great numbers of people general causes will serve to create a single dominant pattern. But there are other indications, too. The study of disorganized behaviour as it prevails among delinquents, hobos, and primitives displaced from their community and brought into contact with industrial and urban civilization, shows that it is the disorganized part of a social structure in which disorganized behaviour and personality most frequently occurs.[1]

[1] Some bibliographical items : Park, E. R., " The Mentality of Racial Hybrids," *Amer. Journal of Sociol.*, vol. 36, pp. 334–551, Jan., 1931 ; Thomas, W. I., Znaniecki, F., *The Polish Peasant in Europe and America*, New York, 1927 ; Schrieke, B. J. O., *Alien Americans, A Study of Race Relations*. A Report on a Study of Negro Life and Education in the United States of America, undertaken for the Julius Rosenwald Fund, New York, 1936 ; Stonequist, Everett, *The Marginal Man*, New York, 1937 ; Park, R. E., " Migration and the Marginal

Another instance pointing in the same direction is that the individual by means of self-observation may realize that his psychological adjustment relaxes continuously according to the repressive power of the different social groups in which he lives. Thus the most conventional and most orderly people when they travel in foreign countries very easily drop out of their fixed mental associations and habits. All these are merely different forms of social and mental disintegration which naturally ought to be studied more carefully, but which reveal the meaning of general social tendencies only if they are watched from the point of view of a comprehensive theory. The corresponding phenomenon on a larger scale is presented to us if we watch the suddenly changing behaviour of people living in the socially disintegrated parts of the European continent. History is producing a sad experiment before our eyes, and shows what happens to the individual when the basic integrating factors are put out of action. This is the best place to study the continuous interrelatedness of sociological and psychological mechanisms. These transformations in the characters of individuals should be investigated in concrete field work by trained observers in connection with the transformation of social mechanisms. But such studies would not furnish us with the necessary answers unless two pre-conditions were fulfilled : first, we must have a wider hypothesis concerning the major trends of development in order to be able to allocate carefully the more detailed

Man," *American Journal of Sociology*, vol. 36, p. 534 ; Anderson, N., *The Hobo*, the Sociology of the Homeless Man, Chicago, 1923 ; Wilmanns, K., *Zur Psychopathologie des Landstreichers*, Leipzig, 1906 ; Elliott, M. A., and Merrill, F. E., *Social Disorganization*, New York, London, 1934 ; O'Malley, Mary, " Psychoses in the Colored Race," *American Journal of Insanity*, vol. 71, 1914 ; Dollard, J., *Caste and Class in a Southern Town*, published for the Institute of Human Relations by Yale University Press, New Haven, 1937 ; Alexander, F., " *Psycho-analysis and Social* Disorganization," *American Journal of Sociology*, vol. 42, no. 6, 1937, pp. 781–814 ; Adler, Alfr., " Psychiatric Aspects Regarding Individual and Social Disorganization," *American Journal of Sociology*, May, 1937, no. 6, vol. 42, pp. 878–887 ; Schilder, P., " The Relation between Social and Personal Disorganization," *American Journal of Sociology*, vol. 42, no. 6, May, 1937 ; Blumer, H., " Social Disorganization and Individual Disorganization," *American Journal of Sociology*, May, 1937, vol. 42, no. 6, pp. 871–8 ; Mayo, Elton, " Psychiatry and Sociology in Relation to Social Disorganization," *American Journal of Sociology*, vol. 42, no. 6, May, 1937 ; cf. in the same issue " Further selected References on Social Psychiatry ".

observations in the different parts of the social field, and secondly some widespread misrepresentations concerning human psychology and its relatedness to the social texture must be set right. As to the main trends in the events of the last decades, the facts are sufficiently well known to be able to reconstruct their inner sequence. It is possible to describe the great phases in the fundamental, social, and psychological transformation through which the Fascist states are passing. As to the latter, namely the false psychological presumptions with which we used to work, recent developments in psychology and sociology have done their best to revise some of our obsolete hypotheses so that we may be able to characterize these changes. The trouble is that in thinking about these great issues, we have never brought these two different pieces of knowledge together. This is the reason why in the present chapter I shall take at random some of the fundamental questions which invariably occur in discussions on these issues. Let us start with the more general question which is often put first in this context : " What is the contribution psychology can make to the solution of the problem of war or peaceful change ? Is there anything in human nature which necessarily makes for war ? If not, what is the process whereby a highly industrialized society becomes a martial state with a wholly different psychology ?

In this connection there is another question which presents itself : " Under what circumstances do people who were formerly striving for economic gains, for the raising of their standard of life, invert their scale of values in a relatively short time, and now seem to rank the honour, prestige, and glory of their country far higher than before ? In short, why do people sometimes prefer guns and sometimes butter ? And, finally, if such fundamental psychological changes do occur are they the ultimate causes of war or are they rather the effect of institutional maladjustments in society ? " [1]

---

[1] There exists a considerable amount of literature, very miscellaneous in nature, both on the psychological and sociological aspects of war and peace. A preliminary survey can be obtained through L. L. Bernard and I. B. Bernard, *Sociology and the Study of International Relations*, Washington University Studies, New Series, Social and Philosophical Sciences, no. 4, St. Louis, 1934. (In this I mostly refer to studies which have not been mentioned in the above survey.)

II

SOME OF THE AXIOMATIC BELIEFS CONCERNING HUMAN NATURE

Let me start with the ideas of the man in the street, which very often are also the ideas of the specialist in other fields untrained in sociology or psychology. If he is asked to what war is due his answer will be that human nature, with its instinctive inheritance and unchanging aggressiveness, is responsible for it.

There are few ideologies more dangerous in their consequences than this one, because it creates an acquiescence in the aggressiveness which leads to war. But if there is one view which has been revised during recent discussions in psychology it is this, namely the view that there are, in fact, any such definitely shaped instincts as aggressiveness or acquisitiveness. Rather, we can only say that there are instinctive tendencies, originally vague, which adapt themselves to varying circumstances, and can be shaped by society.

Discussions between instinctivists, endocrinologists, psycho-analysts and behaviourists (not to mention other schools) have led to the conclusion that, although inherited chromosomes, certain established nerve connections, and the gland system set limits to the changeability of the individual, there is nevertheless a great plasticity in man. Although both believe in the changeability of man, the behaviourists go further than the psycho-analysts. To the behaviourist, children start with only vague instinctive tendencies and as the child grows up these vague tendencies are gradually conditioned by behaviour-forming situations. In the course of time these moulded tendencies become habits which have the appearance of being as spontaneous as innate reflexes. Thus it is the situations peculiar to different societies which mould the actual form of these tendencies. The behaviourists therefore believe that if we could reorganize society so as to present man with different situations we could recreate his fundamental behaviour and attitudes.

The psycho-analysts are, as I said, altogether less

optimistic as to the range of plasticity of certain fundamental drives. According to their theory such impulses as sex and aggressiveness are the ultimate and unchangeable sources of human action. Plasticity for them can only be observed as far as there is a certain transmutability of these fundamental drives. Whereas most of them are perhaps too inclined to stress the fixation which occurs during early childhood, there are others, with whom I agree, who are willing to devote at least as much attention to the capacity of institutions for influencing the psychic life of adults. These institutions determine not only the impulses which it is necessary to repress, but also the kinds of channels which will be at the disposal of the repressed drives.

Let us take for example the so-called aggressive propensity.[1] Even if one agrees that it is a primary drive, breaking through under all circumstances, there is so much scope in it for metamorphosis that there is no need to build up a social order on the basis of aggression and combat.

Bovet, in his book [2] *The Fighting Instinct*, formulates some of the different ways in which one and the same instinct may be expressed. There are : canalization, complication, deflection, substitution, platonization, sublimation, etc. Deflection of the so-called fighting instinct occurs, e.g. when, as in the Greek legend, the angry Ajax massacres sheep instead of men, or when the lust for fighting is converted into competitive impulses. Examples of such sublimation are to be seen in such organizations as the militant order of the Jesuits, the Salvation Army, and the Boy Scouts, which subordinate this instinct to socially useful goals. Thus they sublimate it without renouncing

---

[1] On aggressiveness and anxiety cf. amongst others : Freud, S., *Hemmung, Symptom und Angst*, Vienna, 1926 ; Jones, E., " Fear, Guilt, and Hate," *Intern. Journ. of Psycho-Analysis*, vol. x, 1929 ; Isaacs, S., *Social Development in Young Children*, A Study of Beginnings, London, 1935 ; Glover, E., *War, Sadism, and Pacifism*, Three Essays, London, 1933 ; Ginsberg, M., and Glover, E., " A Symposium on the Psychology of Peace and War," *British Journal of Medical Psychology*, vol. xiv, 1934 ; Williams, F. E., *Soviet Russia Fights Neurosis*, London, 1934, chapter vi, " Hate." Cf. also on the Physiology of Emotions : Cannon, W. B., *Bodily Effects of Hunger, Fear, Rage*, 1915 ; Crile, G. W., *The Origin and Nature of Emotions*, 1915, and his *Man, an Adaptive Mechanism*, 1916 ; Kempt, E. J., *The Autonomic Functions and the Personality* : Nervous and Mental Disease Monograph Series, No. 28, New York and Washington, 1921.

[2] Bovet, P., *The Fighting Instinct*. Tr. into English by Greig, L. Y. I., London, 1923, 82 ff.

thereby the satisfactions to be found in strife and the sociological stimuli prevailing in the methods of military systems.[1]

Indeed there is nothing in the so-called fighting instinct which makes inevitably for war. Its existence only explains why, when the social structure presents us with certain situations, our psychic equipment enables us to fight, or in some circumstances even forces us to indulge in aggression. Once the very structure of a social order is so built as to avoid war it can, by the control of education, prevent the forming of warlike attitudes, or if these are already established, it can break them up into their constituent elements and reintegrate them or give them new functions.

One must bear in mind that anger, hatred and sadistic urges as they manifest themselves in the life of the individual, are by no means identical with warlike attitudes. This is a fact which the individual psychologist is apt to overlook. There is a big gap between simple and spontaneous hatred and what has been called trained hatred,[2] and there is a big gap between occasional outbursts of anger and the formation of a bellicose character. I would venture to say that it costs a social organization at least as much energy deliberately to build up warlike attitudes as peaceful ones. Moreover, peaceful attitudes being more in accordance with the ways of an industrialized society, it is more unnatural for us to behave like soldiers than like citizens.

It is obvious that here we reach the point where individual psychology calls for the help of sociology. Since the innate psychological equipment of men leaves equally open the possibility of their becoming either warlike or peaceful, it depends on the nature of social institutions and of social régimes, whether man in the mass has a character of one kind or the other.

[1] Bovet, op. cit., pp. 111 ff. Cf. also Joly, H. S., *Ignace de Loyola*, Paris, 1899 ; Bovet, P., *Le Genie de Baden-Powell*, Neuchâtel, 1921 ; Baden-Powell, General, *Scouting for Boys*, London, 1908 ; *Girl Guiding*, London, 1921 ; Classen, P. A., *Der Salutismus*, Jena, 1913 ; Begbie, Harold, *The Life of William Booth, the Founder of the Salvation Army*, 2 vols., London, 1920 ; Booth-Tucker, F. de L., *The Life of Catharine Booth*, 2 vols., London, 1892.

[2] Royce, J., *Race Questions, Provincialism and other American Problems*, New York, 1908, p. 48.

A sociology of war and peace aiming at completeness should therefore answer the following two questions : (a) Have there been any societies in history which, on the whole, have made for peaceful attitudes ?   (b) For what reasons and by what mechanism do peaceful modern societies turn into bellicose ones ?

The first question I shall not discuss in detail.   It is sufficient to state that nations once bellicose have lived for hundreds of years without war, and this in itself is answer enough to those who assert that war is the necessary consequence of the instinctive equipment of man.   First of all we find among the so-called primitive tribes some who do without war, or at least show only mildly bellicose attitudes.[1]   These attitudes, however, are less a moral achievement than the outcome of narrow conditions of life.   Mostly, as with the Eskimos, it is the hardness of the immediate struggle with nature and the absence of crowding that account for their freedom from aggressiveness.   Generally it is the food-gatherers and the agriculturists who are known to be peaceful.   Furthermore, trade and commerce very often make for peace ; it is dangerous to generalize, however, for under certain conditions the same factors might foster war.

Of the fact that, in our modern civilization, peoples can live for many hundreds of years without war, the Dutch are an example.   Although the bellicose peoples by far outnumber the peaceful ones, the mere existence of the latter, as I mentioned, is a sufficient indication that human nature can very well do without war.   The main problem, therefore, is to identify those mechanisms, those social processes, which tend to turn peaceful attitudes into pugnacity.

Once peaceful attitudes have been established in a given society the spontaneous growth of warlike attitudes *en masse* will represent a case of collective regression.   Our next problem, therefore, is :   What brings about such a social regression, such a dissolution of all those smoothly

---

[1] Davie, M. R., *The Evolution of War*, A Study of its Rôle in Early Societies, Newhaven, 1929, cf. chap. iv, " Where War Exists and Where it does not," chap. xv, " The Stress toward Peace," Appendix C ; Hobhouse, L. T., Wheeler, G. C., Ginsberg, M., *The Material Culture and Social Institutions of the Simpler Peoples*, London, 1930, pp. 228 ff ; Perry, W. J., *The Growth of Civilization*, chap. x, " The Origin and Development of War ", London, 1937.

working tendencies which are needed by a society based upon work as opposed to conflict ?

I think that one of the main causes of a sudden disintegration of socially established attitudes is any kind of *collective insecurity* such as leads to a partial or total dissolution of society. The present crisis especially has been making us realize that collective insecurity has been throughout history the great factor in the rapid dissolution of old attitudes and the creation of new ones.

III

DIFFERENT FORMS OF INSECURITY AND THEIR IMPACT UPON BEHAVIOUR. DISINTEGRATION IN ANIMAL AND HUMAN SOCIETIES

But it is not enough to make the general statement that collective insecurity may suddenly change human nature : one must define the historically specific forms of insecurity, and the ways in which they react upon the psychology of the individual.

The insecurity of nomadic peoples forced by drought, or animal epidemics, to migrate or to plunder their neighbours, differs in many ways from the insecurity from which nations suffer in the modern world. But even in modern societies we have to distinguish between several different causes to which a general feeling of insecurity may be due. In the first stage of capitalism, the maladjustment between absolutism and a growing industrialism led to dissatisfaction and to acute tension between the rising bourgeoisie, on the one hand, and the landed aristocracy and the army on the other. It was this tension which sought an outlet in war. In the monopolistic stage of capitalism, the underlying tension between capital and labour grows acute when structural unemployment of large masses transforms their latent hostility into despair. This leads to disturbances and even to that state of partial social dissolution in which war appears to be the simplest means of diverting attention from internal difficulties. Thus we must begin by clearly understanding the meaning of this partial dissolution of society and its reaction upon the attitudes and mentality of its members.

Although I am constantly stressing historical distinctions in the phenomena in question, I would not wish, at the very beginning of my analysis, to neglect the general biological foundations of human society as they are represented in animal communities.

No doubt much harm has been done by indiscriminately transferring analogies from animal life to the interpretation of human society.[1] Yet I am convinced that, if one is careful to make a clear distinction between the still-persisting framework of common features and those differences which are due to the special nature of man, it may be possible to throw new light on events which have hitherto been inadequately described. In this connection it may be helpful to observe for a moment how social animals react to a disturbance of their social organization.

Among the bees sudden changes of behaviour can be observed when the queen suddenly dies and the social order of the hive is disturbed. These changes in behaviour are so radical that they have been legitimately called regression, or even atavism. Such a regression can be observed most clearly among the workers, which are females whose sexual energies have been turned into working energies. Once the social fabric is disturbed these working bees fall back into an earlier biological stage of their instinctive behaviour ; all of a sudden they begin behaving like females and lay parthenogenetic eggs (i.e. eggs that have not been fertilized). They revive that former stage in their phylogenetic development in which their ancestors, although living in hives, were not yet compelled by a caste-like division of labour to turn their sexual energies into

---

[1] The suspicion against biological analogies rightly arises when one compares society as such with an organism. Such an analogy is usually misleading, because although there are similarities between the organism and society the differences are so great that the analogy as a whole becomes futile. For example, in human society one man can abandon his place and fulfil the functions of another man, whereas the cells which fulfil the functions of the heart cannot fulfil those of the lung. But it is not this kind of search for external similarities which stands behind the statements mentioned in the text. What is aimed at there is to elicit the still relevant biological foundations of human nature, and also the biological framework of human societies against which the differences characteristic of human nature and society can then more easily be sketched.

working activities. Moreover, many of these workers regress still further, to a stage when bees did not yet live in hives and, instead of collecting honey and caring for the larvæ, they become individual plunderers and robbers.[1]

Thus it would seem that already among the social animals there is a strict correlation between instincts and the social organization. Once this social organization is disturbed and partly or wholly disappears, the socially achieved reactions disappear along with it and there is, or may be, an atavistic reaction to the instinct patterns of an earlier stage.[2] To the individual bee, ignorant of the total social process, this catastrophe probably appears as one in which his instinctive drives are suddenly deprived of their normal objects and substitute activities, like the laying of eggs, consequently occur.

The analogy between the societies of bees and of men holds good in so far as in human society also a dissolution or partial dissolution of the social order brings about a regression to an earlier stage of behaviour; but this regression is not a biological but a social one. Man, unlike the bees, does not revert at once to earlier biological stages

---

[1] The above case is mentioned by Brun, R., *Biologische Parallelen zu Freuds Trieblehre*, Experimentelle Beiträge zur Dynamik und Ökonomie des Triebkonfliktes, Internationaler Psychoanalytischer Verlag, Leipzig, Vienna, Zürich, 1926, p. 24. Brun's main concern is to collect instances in animal life which could be considered as forms preliminary to the main psychic mechanisms, as e.g. repression, regression, substitution, transference, as described by Freud. The premises of the theory are to be found in Freud, and Hattingberg, H. von; Übertragung und Objektwahl, ihre Bedeutung für die Trieblehre, *Internationale Zeitschrift für Psychoanalyse*, vol. vii, 1921, pp. 401–421. A brief report in English on the latter is to be found in the *International Journal of Psychoanalysis*, vol. i, 1920, p. 346 f.

[2] Although the case described by Brun leaves open the question whether the regression of the working bees is due to individual causes or is strictly correlated with the dissolution of the social order in the hive, experiments carried out by von Buttel-Reepen, H., seem to favour my hypothesis, namely that the changes in the social order are mainly responsible for these regressions. Von Buttel-Reepen removes the queen from the hive, and as soon as the bees become aware of this they manifest great excitement and peculiar sounds of despair may be heard, p. 19, cf. von Buttel-Reepen, H., *Sind die Bienen Reflexmaschinen ?* Leipzig, 1920. For further references to the peculiar behaviour of bees in abnormal situations cf. Rath, O. v., " Über abnorme Zustände im Bienenstock," *Berichte der Naturforschenden Gesellschaft zu Freiburg i. Br.*, vol. xviii, Freiburg i. Br. und Leipsic, 1894 ; *Bienenzeitung*, vol. xiii, n. 20, pp. 229 ff., article by Dr. Dönhoff ; Cowan, Th., *British Bee-Keeper's Guide Book*. 25th edition, London, 1924, chap. xxiii, " Loss of Queens."

in the history of his instincts. Owing to the plasticity of his nature, he reverts from one historical-social elaboration of his attitudes to an earlier one, still based on the same instinct. A peaceful society, becoming insecure as a result of a partial dissolution, breaks up the peaceful attitudes so painfully established and tends to replace them by the social remnants of such militaristic patterns as still exist within it.

Even in the details of the transformation of attitudes connected with this dissolution of society, there is an analogy with animal life. In the case of the bee, for example, anxiety and regression begin with a dissolution of the social order which deprives the instinct of the objects towards which it has normally been directed. When the normal co-ordination of tasks characteristic of life in the hive is disturbed, the working drives of the bees are left with no means of gratification.[1]

Is not such a partial dissolution of the social order the outstanding feature of that social insecurity of which unemployment has become a general symptom ? For man, however, the catastrophe lies not merely in the disappearance of external opportunities for work but also in the fact that his elaborate emotional system, intricately connected as it is with the smooth working of social institutions, now loses its object-fixation. The petty aims towards which almost all his strivings are directed suddenly disappear, and, not merely does he now lack a place of work, a daily task, and an opportunity for using the integrated labour attitudes formed through long training, but his habitual desires and impulses remain ungratified. Even if the immediate needs of life are satisfied, by means of unemployment relief, the whole life-organization and the family hopes and expectations are annihilated. One has only to remember how much libidinous energy is normally invested, in a capitalistic society, in social ambitions to realize what this means.

---

[1] Probably in these cases we are presented with frustrated feeding instincts. The nursing bees whose task it is to feed the queen seem to be the first to realize her absence. As they cannot get rid of their amply-prepared food another instinct becomes discharged, namely that of building cells and laying eggs. Von Buttel-Reepen, who gives this explanation, adds : "One can well believe this procedure to be based exclusively upon reflexes. No thinking of any kind is needed." Von Buttel-Reepen, op. cit., p. 24.

The frustration of the desire to rise in the social scale means not only that hopes of raising the standard of life must be abandoned, but also that social esteem is shattered and with it self-respect. The symptoms of such general insecurity may differ in different strata : the petty rentier, the black-coated worker, the skilled artisan and the unskilled labourer, the intelligentsia and the student. But, despite their social differences, shattered self-respect is at work in all of them. Lasswell has shown that, when the former ideal of the " successful self " is once disturbed and former attitudes are left objectless, the old impulses turn inward and take the form of self-punishment, which degenerates into masochistic or psychologically self-mutilating orgies. In this situation the scapegoat, such as the Jew, affords a real relief by providing an opportunity for once more externalizing the aggressive tendencies, an opportunity that is equally welcome to the frustrated in every class.[1]

IV

From Unorganized Insecurity to Organized Insecurity

This is the stage of unorganized insecurity, which is fraught with incalculable possibilities. It is the stage of general psychological and emotional experimentation ; and of the decay of our belief in institutions, mores, traditions, and historically established prestige. These are the sociological conditions in which ideologies are unmasked and the validity of established principles and values comes to be doubted. This is the moment of scepticism, hard for the individual yet productive for science, as it destroys the petrified habits of thought of the past. In this general

[1] Cf. Lasswell, H. D., *World Politics and Personal Insecurity*, 1935, London, New York. Cf. also King, J., " Influence of the Form of Social Change upon the Emotional Life of People," *American Journal of Sociology*, vol. ix, p. 124. The idea of a catastrophic theory history has been expounded by Teggart, F. J., *Theory of History*, New Haven, 1925, cf. esp. p. 196. Th. Waitz, *Introduction to Anthropology*, ed. by J. F. Collingwood, London, 1863. Gothein, E., " Soziologie der Panik," *Verhandlungen des ersten deutschen Soziologentages*, Tuebingen, 1911. Waelder, R., " Aetiologie und Verlauf der Massenpsychose," *Imago*, 1935, vol. 21.

experimentation, the individual who cannot reorganize himself may perish, but for the social body it means the possibility of a selection of new models of behaviour and of new representative dominant types. That is why Fascism and Communism, and any other new social fixation, seem at certain moments to have equal chances as far as psychology is concerned. And, indeed, Michels [1] does observe that, in the rise of Italian Fascism, men who had once been Socialists often joined the Fascists.

Finally long-term calculation also ceases, at least among those social groups most strongly affected by the partial dissolution of society. The panic reaches its height when the individual comes to realize that his insecurity is not simply a personal one, but is common to masses of his fellows, and when it becomes clear to him that there is no longer any social authority to set unquestioned standards and determine his behaviour. Herein lies the difference between individual unemployment and general insecurity. If in normal times an individual loses his job, he may indeed despair, but his reactions are more or less prescribed and he follows a general pattern in his distress. Even if he rebels against society by stealing, his activities will fall into some mould not created by him.

The distress of man in a situation of insecurity is worse than that of social animals, such as Hodgson's " old unhappy bull "

> Sick in mind and body both,
> Outcast from the herd he led,
> Bulls and cows a hundred head . . .

because the bull may still rely on the prompting of instincts that are uncorrupted by membership of a society based on an all-pervading division of labour. Such a society destroys the spontaneity of responses ; and man, if the usual objects of his strivings are withdrawn, is lost and without orientation. His socially moulded instincts are useless when conditions alter, his old emotional strivings are homeless in a situation of unorganized insecurity, and his common sense is too narrow in outlook to understand what is happening around him in this invisible society with its unintelligible structure.

[1] Michels, R., *Sozialismus und Faszismus*, München, 1925, p. 266.

Here lies another difference between animals and men, for, whereas after the loss of the object the bee falls back on an earlier biological stage of instinctive reaction, man, deprived of his original goal, finds relief in the creation of symbolic goals and symbolic activities. For man is a being living in a community whose reaction is not based simply on instinct but on symbols of his own creation, such as words, images, and ideas, which serve as a fundamental means of communication.[1]

Some of these symbols, words for instance, stand for things that really exist, others are symbols or symbolic activities that serve as substitutes for real activities. When desired objects are withdrawn from our reach, when we find it impossible to get full and immediate gratification in real things, then we use these symbols as substitutes. Experimental psychology provides us with information showing how substitute activities function in simpler situations. I refer to experiments and investigations carried out by Lewin,[2] Ovsiankina, Mahler, Lissner, Hoppe, and others. An instructive case is quoted by Lewin.[3] A young feeble-minded child wants to throw a ball a long way, and although he fails, is happy because he finds a substitute in the vigorous movement he has made. Lazar[3] calls this type of child a "gesture-child", because he is satisfied with gestures when others are striving for concrete goals.

---

[1] As to the nature of language in animal life I would like to refer to the short but illuminating summary which Hempelmann gives. According to him the language of animals is but the immediate expression of a given physiological state. It is never founded on the conscious intention to communicate a definite meaning. Expression only works as a stimulus or signal for specific reaction. As animals mostly lack insight into the connection of events their correct reaction to these signals is merely the outcome of an appropriate adjustment. Hempelmann, F., *Tierpsychologie vom Standpunkte des Biologen*, Leipzig, 1926, p. 530.

[2] Lewin, K., *A Dynamic Theory of Personality*, Selected Papers, New York, London, 1935, chap. vi, " Substitute Activity and Substitute Value." Lewin refers to the following contributions : Mahler, W., " Ersatzhandlungen verschiedenen Realitätsgrades," *Psychol. Forsch.*, 1933, 18, 27–89 ; Lissner, K., " Die Entspannung von Bedürfnissen durch Ersatzhandlungen," *Psychol. Forsch.*, 1933, Bd. 18, 218–250 ; Ovsiankina, M., " Wiederaufnahme unterbrochner Handlungen," *Psychol. Forsch.*, 1928, Bd. 11 ; Hoppe, F., " Erfolg und Misserfolg," *Psychol. Forsch.*, 1931, Bd. 14, p. 1–62. Cf. also Koffka, K., *Principles of Gestalt Psychology*, London, 1935, pp. 670 ff.

[3] Quoted by Lewin, op. cit., chap. vii, " A Dynamic Theory of the Feeble Minded," p. 205.

During a period of unorganized insecurity, the normal person, owing to the lack of an immediate and real gratification for his strivings in the field of work and social acknowledgment, tends to become a " gesture-adult ", existing on substitute goals and being satisfied with gestures and symbols.

As Lewin realized, the term substitute goal, or substitute activity, has no meaning in itself, but only when measured against the original intention, or original tension-system, of the individual.   Since in capitalist society the normal working incentive is acquisition, a desire to raise the income-level, any goal will be regarded as substitute which compensates for some failure in this field.   The symbolic substitute is felt as being unreal only as long as the original tension-system, the striving for money, persists.

As soon as it is possible to change the original level of aspiration and to induce people to strive for symbolic goals as if they were primary goals, so that instead of butter they desire national prestige, they will cease to feel the latter as symbols and consider them rather as real gratifications.

According to the observations of individual psychology, once the individual tension-system is built up it is not very easy to alter, except in the case of children.   But in my view the characteristic feature of any revolutionary period is that failure of original expectations occurs to hundreds of thousands at the same time, the search for substitutes follows the same rhythm, and the meaning of what is real or unreal is established in common.   If there are many who think it is better to have guns than butter it will be easier for the single individual to change over from one tension-system to the other than it would be if he had to reorganize the system for himself.

The collective transformation of the system of symbols into new realities occurs in three stages.   The symbol may remain unchanged externally while the real dynamic transformation which changes its function and meaning takes place behind this façade.   The three stages of this transformation are :—

   (a) The symbol is a pure substitute goal ;
   (b) The symbol becomes the new driving force for new
       forms of spontaneous group-integration (this we
       may call the utopian stage of the symbol) ;

(c) The symbol becomes the rigid emblem of an organized group.

In the first stage men flee to symbols and cling to them mainly because they want to avoid that anxiety which, according to Freud, overwhelms us whenever the libidinous energy remains for long without an object. Hammer and sickle, swastika, brown and black shirts, red and black flags, outstretched arms, clenched fists, phrases like "freedom and glory of the nation "—are fictions providing an outlet and goal for displaced energy.

But as soon as people by these very gestures and substitute goals become integrated into spontaneously growing groups, they reach the utopian stage in the development of the symbol. The utopian symbol makes people act ; it makes them act against the system of established relationships, and in acting against it they not only try to wreck this network of relationships, but seek to call in question the former definition of the situation, devaluating the meaning and significance of the original level of aspirations.

Thus not only does the new symbol gain in significance but its reality-prestige is raised ; striving for the honour and glory of the nation seems to be every bit as real a business as striving for economic gain. Another reason why the new symbol seems to become more than a substitute, and indeed becomes a new social reality, is that it in its turn likewise generates its own network of inter-related activities. Although these activities may for some time remain sterile and may consist mainly of endless discussions without rhyme or reason, or of loitering in groups and marching about, later they will lead to quasi-military exercises and to the forming of " pressure-groups " which will from time to time press upon that social system which is still the acknowledged order.

During the utopian phase,[1] important changes take place in the individuals themselves. Whereas in the first stage the symbol was merely an occasional substitute in their lives, it now becomes both a factor in the reorganization of their whole personality and the ferment

---

[1] On the social function of utopias cf. Mannheim, K., *Ideology and Utopia*, an Introduction to the Sociology of Knowledge, London, New York, 1936. Especially part vi, " The Utopian Mentality."

which brings them to a new kind of group-cohesion. In such a situation it is obvious that radical changes in the individual only take place where some sudden shock has destroyed the network of his established habits and expectations, and that the stabilization of his new hopes and values is intimately linked up with the integration of new groups. Old traditions fall to bits, new forms of social adjustment occur, and we speak of a re-birth of men and society. It was perhaps this same psychological mechanism which in the ancient world produced the new spirit of Christianity, or which in the sects of the later Middle Ages gave rise to the modern forms of utopian spirit.

In the utopian stage of symbolic integration a certain social differentiation becomes perceptible. Not all the symbols appeal to everyone equally. Their growth is intimately connected with that of the particular groups to which they belong. Even if different groups have the same symbols, they stress different aspects of them, because memories of the pre-insecurity phase of society are, unconsciously, still active in their mind. Thus to one man perhaps the symbol of security and order has an appeal, because the group to which he belongs is a petty bourgeois one now threatened in its slumber ; or else, since the man is a member of a group such as the army or the bureaucracy whose prestige is bound up with the growth of the State, what he values is glory. There are still others, for whom local independence or folkways constitute the lost paradise, and those to whom it is equality that represents the supreme value, because even in the former, stable society they had been outcasts. The several symbols correspond immediately to the characteristic wishes of the several social strata.

But this stage of spontaneity in the recreation of man and of groups does not last very long, as in mass society it has to be succeeded by a stage of strict organization ; for, of the achievements of modern mass society, only those can endure which are sponsored by definite organizations or are continuously reproduced through the very working of the social structure. Thus spontaneous activity on the basis of enthusiasm gives place to rigid organization, for which the symbol has become nothing more than a lifeless emblem. Just as, in an earlier example, hatred, in order to become socially effective, had to be turned into trained hatred, so the new emotional attitudes and working incentives now tend to be inculcated and enforced by the group.[1]

Through this petrifying of human relations, which in modern nations tend to crystallize into the militarist pattern,[2] society passes from the stage of unorganized insecurity into that of organized insecurity. Society as a whole is still insecure, for the causes of the disorder in its functioning are not removed and the economic disequilibrium which brought about structural unemployment is still present, and is perhaps even increased by tendencies towards self-sufficiency. But, though the nation be insecure, new social formations are being built up which, while providing psychological substitutes to some extent for the lost honeycomb of work (e.g. unnecessary roads, labour-camps, and rearmament), at the same time help to run the national economy at less expense. It is now possible gradually to lower the standard of living, without resistance, by balancing every dose of deprivation with some psychological substitute, by finding scapegoats and creating occasions for collectively guided enthusiasm. The less bread, the more circuses !

The essential feature of this new type of society is that it affords channels not only for economic and administrative activities, but also for new psychological adjustments. Not only government and industry are planned, but the psychic disturbances and the general breakdown are deliberately guided for the benefit of those who still maintain their rational calculation and, because they stand more or less outside the focal points of the general collapse, are

---

[1] This passing from the purely emotional, through the utopian, to the organized stage, may have been the typical process of genesis of institutions in the past. Only to-day, when we are witnessing the sudden growth of new institutions in our midst, do we realize the importance of the symbolic element in primitive institutions. Most of our institutions have long since solidified into relations and functions with no symbolic aura (take, for instance, our business relations or, say, a post-office). In primitive communities the symbolic glorification of the institution still prevails and there is an appeal, through magic or mere customary rites, to the original emotions.

[2] There are special reasons for the choice in this case of the militarist model. We have seen how in the first stage of unorganized insecurity, when the old order of society is vanishing, a regression to earlier social patterns is to be expected. In inland states the old army pattern naturally had great strength. The officials dismissed from the old army were busy after the war in reorganizing the dissolved cadres of bourgeois society into quasi-military formations. The military mind had no other conception of organized security but that characteristic of a state at war.

able to remain sober. They may consciously desire even war or autarchy, for what is economically irrational for a whole nation may still be profitable to particular groups— of industrialists, army leaders, and officials. Their psychology is mainly to be explained in terms of a gamble in which, though the nation lose, they should still get rich. Just as the military caste re-establishes itself by using in its own country the same methods as during the war it used in occupied territory, the industrial and commercial bosses consider their country, once the stage of organized insecurity is reached, as a field for exploitation almost equivalent to a colony. And they use the new situation for the preparing of an imperialist expansion, because for their enormous monopolies the closed territory of their own country is too small.

Within the network of new pseudo-activities a psychological readjustment seems to take place. Through the instituting of inexpensive new systems of honours and distinctions, social ambitions are once more given satisfaction and the man who, following the loss of his job, had lost his self-respect finds it again through a position in some organization which puts others under his control. In the party there is no one at the bottom, for below the lowest is the outcast, the Jew. Foresight and calculation are restored, too, as tasks have some sort of pattern again, and festivities and manœuvres have to be prepared a long way ahead. There is no longer reason to resort to the diverse forms of self-mutilation ; the continuous exhibition of the organized power of the state does away with that.

The organization of insecurity has above all the advantage that there is no longer a feeling of object-loss and as long as the system functions and an emotional and symbolic atmosphere overlies its rigid military order people will willingly obey and subordinate their individual preferences to the dictates of the central machinery. Those who formerly lacked direction enjoy the inescapable automatism of the machine. To them it does not matter that in certain fields freedom has gone ; only social types who, like the intelligentsia and some of the entrepreneurs, have previously learned to use and value freedom of thought, lament its loss. Most men have their roots in the older types of traditional society and lack the habit of personal initiative and the capacity to enjoy responsibility. They crave rather for subjection to a rule and are glad when they can glide on from one well-defined situation to another.

In such a society those who are leaders enjoy the possibility of raising hatred on one day and appeasing it on the next. Society becomes a structure where one presses a button and the expected reaction occurs. One day the detestation of a neighbouring country may be preached, on the next you decide to live in friendship with it for ten years. In the phase of unorganized, as compared with that of organized insecurity, quite a different psychology characterizes the individual. In the former phase the psychological reaction of the people was important, the psychology of the masses governed everything. In the latter it seems as if the masses have abandoned their individual psychic life, at least as far as public affairs are concerned, and are ready to turn into robots. It is as if the sociologist had only to deal with the peculiar psychology of the leaders.

In the first stage of unorganized insecurity these leaders play no very important rôle. So long as everything is fluid numerous petty leaders arise—in place of the notabilities of the vanishing order—but theirs is only a transitory influence. After the first fermentation, however, a new differentiation into guiding, and guided, groups occurs. Spontaneous symbol-integration can take place only in a small community ; in mass societies after the first spontaneous reactions a more or less conscious control of these symbols and of the emotions connected with them is needed. This manipulation is performed by people whose personal psychological constitution and aptitudes especially enable them to take the lead.[1]

Max Weber observed that even in primitive communities the psycho-pathological types usually become the prophets, saviours, and reformers, changing the old ways of life and breaking down the old magical attitudes. In his view this is because in societies whose customs are sanctioned mainly by magic it is the psychopath who is unadjusted and who therefore dares to break these old habits, which are no longer fitted to the changed

[1] Lasswell gives in his books a valuable analysis of this management of symbols.

situations, and is able to discover new and better adjusted attitudes. Thus it was the Jewish ecstatic prophets who destroyed those established traditional attitudes personified in the official priesthood.

It is not to be expected that the old bureaucracy of the country or the former commercial and industrial leaders trained in the ways of rational calculation will find the secret of symbol-manipulation. They need an alliance with a new kind of leader, and this leader, and the petty leaders, must come chiefly from those holes and corners of society where even in normal times irrational attitudes prevailed and where the catastrophe of unorganized insecurity was most severe and prolonged. Thus the leader must himself have experienced that emotional rhythm which is common to those who have been most exposed to the shocks of a partial dissolution of society. But, by itself, mere emotional irrationality is not enough, and the leader and most of the petty leaders must also have a sense of calculation which will grow more acute as unorganized gives way to organized insecurity.

The calculation connected with symbol-manipulation is not the same as, for example, commercial calculation, and, as a woman may be of little use in business yet skilful in judging the moods of her husband, so an individual, hopeless as a bureaucrat, may be expert in calculating and expressing the changing shifts or emotions in others. In modern mass society these leaders purposefully transform the spontaneous symbolic attitudes into manipulated patterns of thought, sentiment, and action.

It is not very easy to distinguish, in the first stage, between rational interest and wish-fulfilling dreams and gestures. The interconnectedness between interest and irrational symbolic striving is far deeper than some abstract thinkers would imagine. Marxism, as the product of a highly rational and intellectualized age and group, not only over estimates the driving power of explicit economic interests, but puts alternatives in too sharp a contrast, as also did the commercial and liberal mentality of the eighteenth and nineteenth-century philosophers and economists.

Even in rational strivings irrational tendencies are latent, and Glover is not wrong when he says that, very often,

" conscious preoccupation with reality and mainly self-preservative situations " covers unconscious motivations.[1] It frequently occurs that through unconscious urges, such as transformed or displaced sadistic attitudes, or for the sake of glory, we indulge in rational calculation, in money making, and in ruthless pursuit of personal advantage. On the other hand the American sociologist Wirth hit the nail on the head when he wrote that " interests slumber below the surface of any kind of activity and it is only in certain spheres of life, in economics, and to a lesser degree in politics, that they have been made explicit and articulate ".[2] Therefore, in my view, the crucial problem is not whether irrational motives disguise themselves under rational attitudes, or whether behind rational behaviour some unconscious interest is at work. Taking it for granted that the rational and irrational are interwoven, we must discover in what circumstances the various forms of rational interests, slumbering under the surface, become explicit.

It remains, therefore, for us to ask what those social factors are which help to bring to consciousness the so-called rational interest and thus may possibly lead to the breakdown of the sort of society we have been considering.

The system has, as we have seen, a relatively great elasticity for not only does it manage production and consumption, the defence services and administration, but by means of regulation it assists in the adjustment of men's wishes to changing situations. It is capable of postponing the breakdown in that it controls the subjective side of the process, and is able to compensate if not for the economic dis-equilibrium at least for the psychological maladjustment.

There is, nevertheless, a fundamental contradiction which makes for its possible collapse. And this contradiction is to be found in the mutually antagonistic working of mechanisms within it which foster the growth of conflicting impulses. Everything depends on whether the new organizations which have been superimposed upon society during the period of organized insecurity are strong enough

---

[1] Glover, E., *War, Sadism, and Pacifism*, London, 1933, p. 133.
[2] Wirth, L., in his Preface to Mannheim, K., *Ideology and Utopia*, op. cit., p. xxiv.

to establish the new set of values and symbolic strivings as having more reality than the older motivations, the desire for economic gain and for a higher standard of life. This does not mean that I am assuming that man's wishes in themselves are only real when conforming to the concept of the *homo economicus*. We all know how very difficult it was for the absolutist mercantilist system in Prussia for instance to train people to strive for profits instead of keeping to their former humble standards. But I am convinced that any new system which departs from capitalism has to reckon with the possibility that the masses may rapidly identify themselves once more with the older tension-system, the original aim of which is economic gain. If this happens, the new standards of honour and prestige will be felt once more as mere substitutes. Thus the problem of the new élites who control the symbols is to suppress the older mechanism of capitalist society by means of the superimposed institutions of the new social technique. If there are factors in the industrial system and in the remnants of the property system which keep alive the old set of acquisitive wishes, then they may easily fail.

The underlying crisis produced by unemployment, even in the stage of organized insecurity, will make itself felt as soon as the new form of psychological adjustment, with its motivations of honour and prestige, ceases to function. The whole propaganda machinery becomes vain and meaningless as soon as the capitalistic aspirations break through and the new symbols are felt as being mere symbols and people cease to have faith in the corresponding activities. Once this happens on a large enough scale and penetrates even to the ranks of the armed forces, the crisis becomes apparent and panic breaks through once more. But at this stage the psychological breakdown, the panic, is much more dangerous than it was in the phase of unorganized insecurity.

It is not so much an object-withdrawal which brings about the general tension, but what I would call a " motive-withdrawal ". The institutions, the reified relations, are still present, but dissociated from those motivations which originally worked through them. Such an estrangement from the goods of the world, and its powers, occurred among the early Christians. Such an alienation or motive-withdrawal may occur as soon as the more fundamental mechanisms of industrial society assert themselves against the totalitarian superstructure. As is well known, the greatest danger of war lies in the situation just described. In capitalist surroundings, in a society which is still based on private property, it is very likely that sooner or later the symbols of prestige and honour will lose their character of reality in the estimation of the masses and loyalty to the social machine will thus become problematic.

In the stage of unorganized insecurity, the object-withdrawal had not led to war because the psychological breakdown was not canalized. The confusion was intense enough to destroy a part of the former élite, but could not be drawn upon for purposes of outward aggression. It may be simpler for the élites, now that the emotional channels have been established and the war machine is ready, to divert the mind of the masses from the growing social tension by taking refuge in war and so obviating the alienation of the population.

To sum up, this brief study has not attempted to give a complete analysis of the causes of war. My examples are not even meant as an exhaustive study of the evolution of unemployment, insecurity, and Fascism as factors making for war in our age, but merely to show more concretely the kind of help psychology can give if it is integrated into the economic analysis of capitalistic development in its present stage. The meaning of these considerations is not that psychological processes are independent and therefore ultimately responsible for what has happened and what is going to happen, but that the economic maladjustment cannot be fully understood unless its psychological implications and consequences are put into their proper place. It is the concrete sequence, the real concatenation of structural changes, which must be reconstructed in its main phases if a real control is to be achieved.

War itself is the outcome not of some invariable instinct like aggressiveness, but partly of the faulty elaboration of psychological tendencies through institutions, and partly of the desperate flight of people into collective aggression when unco-ordinated institutions clash and bring about the feeling of general insecurity.

Hardly anyone wants war. The new ways of drifting into a world catastrophe which neither the leaders nor their peoples really desire is the most tragic example of what one can call objective dynamics in history. Through the accumulation of effects, economic, social, and psychological, which are not intended by those who initiate them, things happen which are definitely repulsive to the people who are acting. It is a veritable nightmare that we should arm and drill men for ends which very few, if any of them, in their hearts really want. We are liars caught in our lies. Public utterances were never less believed. Most of our great ideals are being more discredited than ever by their wholesale use in the marketplace, and still we march whenever the command comes. In our solitary hours our most horrible vision is the collapse of civilization by the explosion of the bombs we store, but we blackmail each other with the fear of war until the blackmail catches up with the blackmailers. We anticipate that there will be war. People predict dates for its beginning. Only who fights whom and why is still unknown. Nationalist slogans call little people who love their homes and gardens to become heroes by killing other little people who love their homes and gardens. There has seldom been a generation which was less willing for petty sacrifice and more likely to pay the supreme one without even understanding why.

Hardly anyone wants war. It is in the main a calamity which occurs because men in their activities have not learned to take a long range view, to adjust one institution to another, and to think in terms of a real psychology. But how can they learn to act on the basis of a broader insight if not even the social scientists aim at correlating the results of partial observations in order to detect the reason for the maladjustment in the structure of society as a whole, if they, too, do not aim at real knowledge, but divide their investigations into watertight compartments in order to escape responsibility, and work with a fictitious *ad hoc* instinct-philosophy of some kind or other which itself is part of a mentality that is unconsciously making for war ?

The disentanglement of this network that is strangling us can only come about through action. But it is untrue, despite the scepticism so frequently put forward to the contrary, that we can know little or nothing about the working of our society and about the forms that action can take. We could know enough to understand the main direction of events if we only had the will to control the situation which will otherwise enslave us, and the courage for the kind of thought necessary in our age.

PART IV

THOUGHT AT THE LEVEL OF PLANNING

I

The Redirection of Man's Thought and Will

The main problem in the remaking of man is to transform his thought and action. Just as obstacles always arise in changing from one economic system to another, from one political opinion to another, so we meet with the same resistances when we have to think or act in a new way. We are experiencing a similar problem on a large scale to-day. The best solution for our present difficulties is to become fully conscious of these resistances, and to consider how far they can be counteracted.

It was one of the greatest achievements in the evolution of man when, with slow but unbroken progress, he learned to record his own history. He has taken a new step forward, when he can live his own history in the spirit of experiment and create out of the emergent forces of the social process the knowledge and the will to shape history itself. The older epic form of historiography placed the individual man and individual events in the foreground. The novel contribution of the sociological view of the past and present is that it sees history as a field for experiment and reform. Corresponding to this transition from the epic to the sociological view of history, there is now emerging a new type of self-analysis on a similar sociological level. The analysis of external events soon spurs man on to analyse himself in the same way. Anyone who would know how the world can be changed by changing man must first carefully observe how the present world has made us into the men we are at present. The history of autobiography is in this connection one of the most valuable sources of information, because two things can be observed at the same time : firstly, and indirectly, we can observe the nature of the introspective attitudes of men in the past—in which way and for what purpose they observed themselves ; further, we can see how different social and historical situations

147

fostered different forms of personality, and how these different forms of introspective attitudes unconsciously fulfil certain social functions. Seen from this angle the modern form of self-analysis is the expression of a new attitude to social events and is not to be confounded with older forms of self-observation.

There have been at least two forms of self-observation in history, which must not be confused. The older form was derived for the most part from a kind of egotism. The saints, for example, observed themselves mainly for the purpose of self-redemption and self-perfection. Even though altruistic in their philosophy, in the act of self-observation they were concerned with themselves and themselves alone. The modern observer (for instance Rousseau) is concerned, on the other hand, with himself mainly in so far as he can use his knowledge of the origins of his psychological defects as a universal remedy for society as a whole. In the same tradition, the modern sociologically inclined psychologist or psycho-analyst, having once traced certain of his own psychological troubles such as feelings of guilt and inferiority to environmental maladjustments in early childhood, does not rest content until he has produced a theory which enables him to combat similar psychological difficulties in other men. This form of self-analysis has a levelling tendency and disregards individual differences because it is concerned with the general aspects of the human personality and its capacity for transformation. Probably no one formulated this sociological view better than Lorenz von Stein who, following Louis Reybaud, described the life of Saint Simon as an " experimental " one.[1]

In this type of experimental self-observation planned thinking is already unconsciously at work. Man does not accept human nature as represented in himself or his fellow-men as the unalterable gift of God, nor does he, as on the pantheistic level, regard the soul with sympathetic resignation as a part of nature which cannot be intellectually understood and which can only be grasped through awe. Instead he approaches himself experimentally, just as he approaches the objective facts of this world.

[1] Cf. Stein, Lorenz von, *Geschichte der sozialen Bewegungen in Frankreich von 1789 bis auf unsere Tage*, new edition, edited by Gottfried Salomon, München, 1921, vol. ii, p. 141.

In order to understand this sort of attitude we must be clear that thought is not an independent self-contained and abstractly intelligible fact but is intimately bound up with action. The form and content of thought vary with the situation we are thinking about. Thought does not create the world, but rather in a given world with a given structure a given form of thought is an instrument which may, at a certain moment either be adequate or inadequate or else be in the process of becoming increasingly adequate. There is no thought " as such " ; a specific type of living creature thinks in a world with a specific type of structure in order to fulfil certain specific life-functions.

In the following paragraphs we want to show in detail how changes in the nature of thought are intimately and directly bound up with changes in the nature of the conduct and action of which it is really a part. As soon as a new type of conduct emerges in history a corresponding type of thought necessarily follows to accompany it. What even pragmatists do not, however, realize as a rule is that there are very different types of action, and that as long as they are not carefully distinguished, the basic transformations in thought cannot adequately be described.

We shall distinguish here between radius of action and radius of foresight. By *radius of action* we understand the extent of the causal sequences directly brought about by our initial activity and remaining more or less under our control. By *radius of foresight* we understand the length of the causal chain which can be more or less accurately forecast in a given situation as regards this initial activity. Normally, every action sets up unlimited causal sequences and man is usually only able to foresee and control the more immediate consequences of his action. Thus, the greater the degree of technical and institutional control in a given society, the greater the radius of both action and foresight.

If, for instance, I sow seeds in spring, at a certain level of technical and social development I can predict with reasonable accuracy that a considerable proportion will later come up as corn. There are, however, a large number of incalculable elements, both social and natural. I cannot know, for instance, whether or not my crops will be spoiled by drought or flood. I cannot know, either, that the warriors of some neighbouring tribe will not march across my unripe fields. But as soon as I introduce new institutions —for instance, irrigation, to counteract drought, or a body of armed guards to watch over my fields—then the radius of my action grows in so far as more and more links in the causal chain come directly under my control, and correspondingly my range of foresight becomes both larger and more reliable.

Before we can attempt to examine how the needs of a changed social order create a corresponding new type of thought, we must be clear as to the nature of the following three fundamental stages in the history of thought, which may provide a frame of reference for such an investigation.

The first traces of thinking, which still betray the relationship between animal behaviour and primitive forms of human thought are, as far as we can see to-day, characterized by the fact of chance discovery preceded by trial and error. Both the animal's adjustment to nature and the behaviour of the primitive group which is ruled by custom and tradition are based on chance discovery (Finden). In a world in which man carries on his struggle with nature directly, and in which natural selection regulates every process, some individual or group discovers accidentally, among a very large number of possibilities, the kinds of reaction which fit a given situation. The achievement of thought then lies in remembering the correct solution which has been discovered. Natural selection henceforth works through this achievement in the sense that those groups which cannot retain and transmit the right way of doing things, inevitably die out. In order to preserve this find, there is no need for a precise, reflecting knowledge of the environment which brought about the successful adaptation. All that is necessary is that the positive prescriptions and taboos which the tribal ancestors had worked out on the basis of such a discovery, should be faithfully kept. If the surroundings or the social order change considerably, so that a new kind of collective behaviour is required, the older form of group organization must either be broken or limited in scope, so that better adjustments may again be discovered by the more or less conscious " trial and error " experiments of the individual. These in their turn become traditional by the same method of imitation and taboo and are preserved so long as one can adapt oneself socially to these conventions and the social order can be made to work. The primitive stage of food gatherers and hunters is an example of this type of social life, which is now commonly recognized as the original form of social and economic organization. Even to-day we react to many situations with a type of thought and conduct which is still at the level of " chance discovery ".

Great progress was made beyond this " chance discovery " type of reasoning when single tools and institutions were consciously modified and then directed towards particular goals. This phase in the history of thought may be called the stage of *inventing* (Erfinden). At this level man had to imagine a definite goal and then think out in advance how to distribute his activities in a given way over a certain period of time with this goal in view. He did not in such cases have to think beyond the task immediately at hand. But he had at least to be able to imagine how the object of his thought fitted into the immediate environment. He had also to be able to foresee the most probable consequences of an event. The entire development of technology from the simplest tools and instruments through the use of the plough and the taming of domestic animals up to the use of steam and electricity and all inventions which, to achieve a given goal, deliberately combine ways of thought and action which we shall describe more exactly later, work within the framework of this type of thinking. In the same sense one can " invent " or establish an association or organize an administrative staff, with a definite goal in view, and give it a place in an existing society.

Once these objects, methods, and institutions have been invented within the framework of an only partially regulated society, a process of selection working behind the backs of the individuals concerned decides whether they will survive or die out. Historical events at this " inventing " stage of development are a peculiar mixture of the results of natural selection and of institutions which have been consciously formed and thought out. This means above all that this type of thinking, with its limited goals, is itself the product of natural events. What a man succeeds in perceiving in society and what he fails to see, what immediate tasks he sets as his goal, and the ends for which he organizes himself and society, depend on natural selection. He rationalizes and suppresses not in terms of his own whims, but rather according to adaptations and necessities, individual and collective, which in their turn are not created by the people involved. Social processes, controlled by the understanding on the one hand and intellectual achievements, regulated by social processes on the other, exist side by side. At one moment man has the upper hand, and at another human understanding bows to the actual social situation.

To-day we are in the main still lingering at this stage. But the tensions which underlie our conscious goals within the larger field of the forces of natural selection, are gradually compelling us to pass on to another stage. We will speak of *planning* [1] and *planned thinking* (*Planen*) when man and society advance from the deliberate invention of single objects or institutions to the deliberate regulation and intelligent mastery of the relationships between these objects. Formerly these relationships were simply governed by the random working of cause and effect, and regulated by conflict, competition, and the selection they bring in their train. The most

---

[1] For planning from the bibliographical point of view, planned economy, etc., cf. Emil Lederer's article, "National Planning," in the *Encyclopedia of the Social Sciences*; and K. Mandelbaum and G. Meyer, "Zur Theorie der Planwirtschaft," in *Zeitschrift für Sozialforschung*, Jahrg. 3 (1934), pp. 228 seqq.; also Mackenzie Findlay (ed.), *Planned Society* (New York, 1937); Hall, R. L., *The Economic System in a Socialist State*, London, 1937; Hayek, F. A. von, et al. *Collectivist Economic Planning*, London, 1935; Lange, O., and Taylor, F., *On the Economic Theory of Socialism*, Minneapolis, 1938, ed. by Benj. Lippincott; Wootton, B., *Plan or No Plan*, A Comparison of existing socialist and capitalist economic systems, London, 1934; Lewis, L. Lorwin, "Planning in a Democracy," in E. W. Burgess, H. Blumer, *Publications of the American Sociological Society*, August, 1935, vol. 29, no. 3; Heimann, E., "Types and Potentialities of Economic Planning," *Social Research*, vol. 2, 1935. Cf. also in the Bibliography, i, 2, and v, 1–3. As yet but little thought has been given to the problems of cultural and educational planning with reference to the aspects of the social structure. One of the most interesting attempts is to be found in Kotschnig, op. cit., chapters x and xi. An approximation to educational planning is contained in the *Conclusions and Recommendations of the Commission on the Social Studies of the American Historical Association* (New York, 1934). The numerous psychological problems of a planned society have been left untouched by social scientists, who have concentrated their attention primarily on the economic aspects. Cf. K. Mannheim, "Present Trends in the Building of Society," in *Human Affairs*, ed. by R. B. Cattell, J. Cohen, etc. (London, 1937), and Hans Speier, "Freedom and Social Planning," in *American Journal of Sociology*, vol. xlii (Jan., 1937).

decisive change occurs when man awakes to the necessity of regulating these gaps between existing relationships and when, in response to this, new patterns of thought arise. First, the pattern of thought is a linear one ; possible chains of causal sequences are foreseen of which only the first phases are initiated by the acting and thinking subject, the rest being left to take their own course according to their own laws. The linear pattern of thought takes the form of a circular flow where the first elements in the causal chain are in our new model of thought supplemented by further elements, the movement of which tends towards an equilibrium, and in which all the factors act upon each other simultaneously instead of in an endless succession.[1]

The circular flow works automatically and it is quite unnecessary to interfere with it. This closed circle of mutual relationships is still on the level of inventive thinking, for it is one-dimensional, as can be seen most clearly in the case of classical economics. This one-dimensional pattern is turned into a multi-dimensional one when at the highest stage of development the separate spheres such as politics, economics, etc., which were formerly thought to be closed circles, are seen to interact upon each other and lead to a multi-dimensional structure. This structure is not considered as a static one, as it is continuously subject to change ; and from now on the changes in its parts will only be felt to have been adequately interpreted if understood in terms of the changing whole.

This new way of thinking is balanced by a new way of acting. For planning not only changes individual links in the causal chain and adds new ones but also tries to grasp the whole complex of events from the *key position* which exists in every situation. The mechanism of the cycle of events can be mastered and guided only if the appropriate key positions are found and dealt with by a new method. Conduct directed from the centre of the cycle of events is

---

[1] Here we refer to the following scheme which underlies Adam Smith's conceptions : Technical progress raises profits—increased profits mean increases in capital and additional demand for labour, whence there follows an increase in wages—increase in wages raises the birth-rate and so, in the long run the supply of labour—increase in the supply of labour improves the opportunities for division of labour, leading thereby to new technical advances—whereupon the cycle begins again. (Cf. Löwe, A., *Economics and Sociology*, London, 1935, ch. iv.)

far more effective, for by using a key position, a number of links in the causal chain can be either initiated, or controlled, or even circumvented. Instead of a too limited power over immediate goals, there now emerges at various points the possibility of direct control of the whole, and of the more indirect type of control in individual cases. As soon as it is possible to plan the whole and the key positions become clear, the single links in the causal chain are no longer regarded as immutable and complete in themselves.

The most essential element in the planned approach is, then, that it not only thinks out individual aims and limited goals, but also realizes what effects these individual aims will in the long run have on wider goals. The planned approach does not confine itself only to making a machine or organizing an army but seeks at the same time to imagine the most important changes which both can bring about in the whole social process.

It is of course clear that the line which divides inventive thinking, which is rationally striving to realize immediate goals, from planned thinking, is not a hard and fast one. No one can say for certain at what degree of foresight and at what point in the widening radius of conscious regulation the transition from inventive to planned thinking takes place. This transition is just as vague as the previous one between chance discovery and invention. The most primitive form of discovery is probably that in which two almost blindly interacting natural factors collide with one another : when the infinite variety of situations confronts the finite number of possible responses. Out of these the right sort of behaviour is crystallized and stabilized through unconscious adaptation and selection. We may ask, therefore, whether a discovery which is based on the conscious search for a more favourable situation is already an invention or whether invention emerges only when factors are spontaneously combined in a new way. It would be idle to pursue the problem of determining the transition point any further, for the fact that there are in reality indeterminate transitions does not abolish the fundamental differences between these two types of thinking. " Planning " as a new stage of the development of thought and action is realized in so far as the previously vast arena of competition and the consequent process of selection are increasingly narrowed by regulatory intervention and the forces at work are consciously controlled.[1]

II

UNPLANNED AND PLANNED ACTIVITIES

There is, however, a decisive law which rules us at the present moment. Unplanned spheres regulated by natural selection on the one hand and deliberately organized provinces on the other can exist side by side without friction only *as long as the unplanned spheres predominate*. The greater the area and time-span of the social processes working according to plan, the harder it is to fit them into an unregulated society. Wherever plans to create and maintain particular objects and particular institutions (a factory, a school, a political party) involve regulation of the contacts between these institutions and others, these plans cannot be arbitrarily stopped at random at any point along the line. This is true for two reasons ; first because all planning makes the individual elements rigid and unadaptable, and secondly because even in the unplanned areas, there is less and less opportunity for change and individual adaptation.

[1] With the gradual integration of unplanned events into a planned society, an important stage in the technical control of nature is reached. The newly controlled provinces of nature lose their original character and become functional parts of the social process. That part of nature which is not mastered by technology and has not been drawn under the influence of social conduct will for the time being remain extra-social. This is not, however, true of those aspects of nature which have come under the domination of technology. They are suddenly brought into the field of social interactions and become, for practical men, problems just like any other genuinely social problems. Two illustrations will serve to clear up this point concerning the transformation of natural processes into problems of social life :

(a) Reproduction regulated by birth control can no longer be explained primarily in terms of biology, but only in connection with the other phases of the social process. The biological forces are not thereby suspended but are rather coupled with social ones.

(b) A whole series of inventions in division of labour and of technology, which have increased the productivity of labour and thereby saved great masses from death by starvation, can through their repercussions, so complicate the social processes of production and distribution that as a result of their incomprehensibility and their failure to function properly even more persons suffer than when natural forces were still uncontrolled.

Every element which has been created and prepared for a given purpose loses its adaptability when it enters into the free area of competition and selection. This is true of institutions as well as of living organisms. It is a general experience that small economic units, lesser industrial enterprises and small shops can maintain themselves better in an economic crisis than huge, inflexible concerns which cannot readapt themselves. The same principle holds true of a man with specialized training who is fitted to work in a highly rationalized and differentiated enterprise and who shows himself much less adaptable than the sort of person who has become versatile in the course of his natural growth. When families lose their social position, the father who has been trained as an engineer or as a higher official adapts himself with much more difficulty to a new occupation and in a new situation than the mother, who has no special training and whose life pattern, for this very reason, is elastic enough to be adaptable. The husband who has been trained for a particular occupation loses his adaptability as a result of the one-sided rationalization of his energies which his training and occupation have imposed. The wife, on the other hand, very often because she has had no profession of a specialized kind, retains those original forms of impulses and thought which are most essential in an unorganized social sphere. This form of thought,[1] which is best adapted to the unregulated sphere of social struggle, is, however, marked by the fact that it only sees one step at a time as the occasion demands and does not systematize its conduct too far.

In the free unplanned sphere where an unregulated selection based on conflict and competition prevails, thinking which is too far in advance of the immediate situation may be dangerous. He who thinks too far in advance and counts too much on certain events ties his own hands, in so far as he will find it harder to adjust himself to an unprecedented change in his situation. In the regulated sphere it is different. Here the regulation must be carried out in

---

[1] The English, who have realized this mode of thought and conduct most completely, have coined certain expressions in which this attitude is represented, such as "Wait and see" and "muddle through". Napoleon, the man of action, meant the same thing when in a social situation in a state of dissolution he based his thought and conduct on the maxim "*On s'engage, puis on verra.*"

thought to its logical conclusion and the chance of success depends to a large extent on the capacity to think things out in advance.

Individual chances of escape and the elastic texture of the unplanned sphere, on the one hand, and the growing necessity for planning can be illustrated by an example from everyday life. When, at a traffic crossing, every minute or so from both sides one or two vehicles appear each going its own way, there is no need for a traffic policeman. These individual cars are elastic enough in their movements to be able to adapt themselves to one another spontaneously on a fairly wide street ; that is, they can move out of each other's way. On the other hand, planned regulation by a policeman becomes indispensable as soon as five or ten cars appear every second from various directions. As a result of the increase in their number, they take up the entire width of the street and there is no more room for them to move out of each other's way. With such a crowd there can be no thought of individual adaptation. Each monad must give up its own purpose, and fall in with the policeman's plan, which covers them all and lets one group go at one time and another at another time. This simple illustration enables us to see precisely how the increasing *density of events* (*Dichtigkeit des Geschehens*) makes the possibility of a natural balance through competition or through mutual adaptation more and more hopeless.

The change in the sequence of objective events can perhaps be made more vivid by an example which a liberal thinker used a short time ago to support his opposition to state intervention during the crisis. He said : " If, when I was on a climbing expedition a cloud suddenly darkened my path, as an experienced mountaineer I should not go on trusting either in my stick or in some apparently sound calculations, because I might end up worse off than before. I should wait until the cloud had passed and then continue on my way with a clear road before me." Here we can see how the commonsense maxim falls short when it attempts to analyse late-capitalistic conditions with concepts relevant only to liberal society. The economic and social order in the liberal epoch did indeed resemble the unregulated processes of nature, since the rise and fall of the economic cycle, like the changes in atmospheric conditions, seemed to have a definite pattern with a rhythmical recurrence which could be confidently foreseen. Since the rationalization, however, of ever wider areas of the economic and social order, this type of waiting can have very disastrous results. It is no longer a question of waiting, as it once was, for the recurrent favourable phase of the cycle : under the changed conditions of the present situation it simply does not emerge " by itself ". Another illustration would fit the present state of affairs. It is as if while we were making a machine according to plan, difficulties arose and, having lost all faith in thought, we left the half-finished work to go on by itself.[1] To-day there is no longer a free movement of the natural economic elements which works automatically and tends towards equilibrium in the old sense. On the contrary, the elements which would tend to re-establish this equilibrium, deviate further and further from their course.

These " disturbing " deviations are partly due to wise or unwise attempts at regulation and partly to the interference of political, technical, and psychological factors. At this stage of development, economic events can be understood only when we grasp their connections with those series of factors which are fairly independent of them, but which are nevertheless in some way related to them. This implies, however, that we should try to create, instead of the unidimensional conception of economic events a polydimensional, structural view of the whole social process.

In the past, in the liberal social order extra-economic factors certainly influenced the economic sphere. But then the interaction of the various spheres was rather occasional and fluctuating. Not merely in theory, but in actual fact, at that time, there was something which was very like a separate functioning of the various spheres of social life. Theory tried to set up individual cross-sections of events as independent spheres—it formulated a pure economics, a pure system of ethics, a pure political science, a pure psychology, according to certain axioms and clearly definable points of view. When it did this, besides

---

[1] In communicating vessels, through the free movement of the tiniest particles, liquids tend to equilibrium at their own levels. In our present economic system the process is no longer like this ; increasingly large fixed crystals are suspended in the fluid, which in the end put a stop to circulation altogether.

the arguments which can always be used to defend the integrity of theory, it found a sanction for its undertaking in the actual situation of its own time. For owing to the nature of society as it was at that time, man did indeed live and carry on his work in apparently separate spheres, acting sometimes purely economically, at others purely religiously and at others purely politically and so on.

All the practical maxims of that period and the ideals of the ruling groups betray a change in the conventions which had formerly prevailed. Individuals reorganized themselves, and so indirectly reorganized society. The idea of the " policeman state " which was not to concern itself with the private affairs of individuals, the demand that economic life, too, should be free from state intervention, that religion should not influence education, that empirical observation should go its way independent of religion and metaphysics, that the external legality of law should not be confused with the sphere of inner life and of conscience, all these maxims reveal in the same way a complete separation of different spheres. If we want not merely to reveal this striking parallel between the characteristic thought of the time and the prevailing life pattern, but also to explain it, we should as sociologists raise the question : which hidden social mechanisms caused the life of that period to function as a number of separate spheres, any more than it does to-day, and which mechanisms brought the thinkers of the period to conceive of the world accordingly ?

To answer this question we must first remind ourselves that medieval society did not display a tangible separation of spheres any more than the stage of social development which lies ahead of us. The medieval guild combined in itself political power, economic activity, religion, art, and so on, and bound them all into an inseparable unity. It regulated almost everything in life from technology to prices, from religion to the use of leisure. It could do this because within the narrow limits of town economy, nothing was able to escape it, neither the individual as a whole nor any single phase of his existence. The central body which organized economic life was a totalitarian one, and it subjected to itself all spheres of social life and fused them into one. In this way it was able to dominate the individual completely, on every side, and so to plan the entire society.

Totalitarian planning was possible at that time because the relationship between the effective radius of action (of a purely political, economic, and psychological kind) and the extent of the territory to be governed was favourable to central regulation. That this was the decisive factor is clear from the fact that the free economy which followed the guild order arose among individual and productive units which could either from the very beginning escape the narrow boundaries of town rule (rural industry) or in spite of all regulations within the guild, became so powerful that they were able to disregard its regulations.

From this point of view, liberalism appears as a transitional phase between two forms of planned order—that of the local authorities, on the one hand, and of the territorial state organization which was emerging ever more clearly on the other. Liberalism appeared and only really existed in that free social area in which the economic subjects who could escape from the domination of the local authority could adjust themselves to the market directly without being subjected to other controls.[1]

They were able to maintain themselves in this position only so long and in so far as the state which was extending itself over this free area had not as yet discovered any sufficiently effective means of influence. Ultimately the radius of means of influence became so great that at a new level of integration they were able to control the entire structure.[2]

When we turn our attention to society in the liberal

[1] From the sociological point of view, the most abstract definition of freedom would be that it is nothing but a disproportion between the growth of the radius of effective central control, on the one hand, and the size of the group unit to be influenced on the other. As long as organized control lags behind spontaneous social integration, there are possibilities of choosing and ways of escape. Since freedom is essentially the chance for spontaneous initiative, everything is reduced to the question of how great are the possibilities of individual choice in a given situation, and what are the available ways of escaping the apparatus of coercion. The concrete elements in these possibilities of choice and escape, work like a matrix which more or less mould the character of the individuals and groups which emerge from them. The concrete historical forms of these characters can be explained to a large extent in terms of this matrix. (But cf. for further differentiation of the problem also the last part of the book.)

[2] Absolutism was only apparently totalitarian. In most cases it did not have the means for dominating all the spheres of life of the inhabitants of the territory over which it was sovereign.

epoch, we have to explain how the individual members of that society gradually came in their activities to break the total social process up into separate spheres and to distinguish step by step the *homo economicus* from the *homo religiosus* and this in turn from the *homo politicus*, and so on. These distinctions first developed in the daily lives of individuals. Only subsequently were they followed by the rediscovery of the fact which, it was said, could be perceived in objective reality, that whole spheres are rigidly separated from each other, pure economics, pure politics, and so on. It is a widespread illusion that spheres of social reality are separated. Properly speaking there are no spheres in social reality—only in human activity. When the individual in his daily life behaves in such a way that he separates his religious from his economic motives and conduct, then a new type of individual conduct emerges. On a social scale, when these new types of separated activities integrate so that the economic or religious chain of action of one individual finds its counterpart in the economic chain of action of another, then the various spheres tend to take on an objective form.

This change can be traced back to two series of factors. First the individuals who escaped the local authorities of the town economy and who gradually became free and mobile, entered into a variety of unplanned social groups and classes. There they behaved in a way which was neither regulated in advance nor prescribed. Instead, as the occasion demanded, they adapted themselves to the needs of the environment in which they were living at the moment.

When the mobile person appeared in the market place he behaved more and more as *homo economicus*. When he came in contact with neighbours in his private life he accepted the ethics of neighbourliness. When he met people with whom he had other social and economic relationships, he changed his tactics with every human contact. Occasionally a not too powerful state forcibly interfered by means of its taxation, police regulations, and so on. In private life religion might play a rôle, and then the contrast between everyday life and holidays became a growing indication of the gulf between these worlds, just as the separation of the office and the factory from the home played an active part in forming a new type of character. Thus the different spheres of social life affected the individual in the liberal era, too, but though these spheres existed side by side they rarely affected him simultaneously, or came into direct and lasting contact with one another.

Once this separation of spheres had emerged in the liberal epoch, it was stabilized by a second series of factors. There was as yet no central power which could organize individual activities over a wide range, or bind together the relatively small economic units. The integration of economic and social units makes it more and more difficult to separate the standards of conduct required in business and social life.[1] As, for instance, the competing economic and social units increase in size they seek to wrest for themselves powers of the most diverse sort (political, juristic, administrative, propagandist) and to co-ordinate them for their own advantage, to fit in with their own plans and institutions. Thus it might be said that at the latest stage of social development a new fusion of the spheres has been brought about by means of institutions which affect them all.

One can see signs of this tendency towards integrated social and economic units, and their struggle to unite the various social factors from within, in the trade-unions' attempt to gain a " political wage " and the " state-guaranteed " price of the cartels. This tendency is equally evident in the great economic enterprises which are ousting the consumer's freedom of choice by regulating his needs through advertisement. In this way, the interference of non-economic activities in the sphere of economics, which in the liberal era was only occasional, now directs the course of economic events themselves, and the old boundary between economics and sociology is thereby swept away.

All these details should make it clear that, as we pointed out before, there is a fundamental distinction between the type of thinking at the most recent stage of social development and the thinking adapted to the preceding stage. It must also have become clear that in the present situation of thought the same tensions occur that we have observed in the actual development of present-day society. The conflicts in which that partial thinking became involved through its insistence on half-hearted rationalization and the

---

[1] Integration and interdependence are two different principles. They are, however, closely related to one another.

separation of spheres are the same as those to be found in concrete political and economic processes.[1]

Both a political policy which rationalizes and integrates all the machinery of power and control but which allows the principle of conflict to continue at the very centre of its policy, and a type of economic activity which calculates every detail in its own province but which ceases to inquire into the psychological nature and origins of the forces which drive it, commit in practice the same error of partial rationalization and the separation of the spheres. These shortcomings cannot be overcome methodologically by means of the partial thinking of the theorists in those fields.

There are certain attitudes of mind which correspond to the stages of chance discovery, invention, and planning and at first these exist side by side. But as long as they are not in harmony with one another, and the relationships between them are not clear, they bring about the same confusion of thought as is caused in the outside world when actions are based, now on discovery, now on invention, now on planning.

Discovery and invention by no means lose their function on the emergence of planning. But problems in thinking which can be solved only by planning, cannot be left to discovery just as, on the other hand, planning always must build upon the stages of discovery and invention. In the same way, thinking in terms of interdependence (which is one aspect of planning) does not supersede abstraction with its separation of spheres. But one must know precisely how each stage of thought is related to the others and how they supplement one another. All this, however, can only be answered when we know more about the nature of planned thinking and have distinguished it more clearly from other forms of thought.

[1] It would not be entirely correct, however, to insist that this is the only reason for the specialization of sociology among the social sciences. It is quite likely that one reason why sociology became a special science, the subject matter of which did not or was not supposed to overlap with that of any other social science, was the purely interacademic dispute concerning the legitimacy of sociology. From the first sociologists have felt that if they were to prove their right to existence, they had to demonstrate that they had a subject matter on which no one else worked. Thus it happened in America that sociologists became preoccupied with the family, city growth, immigration and assimilation, criminality, delinquency and other subjects which were not treated by history, economics, anthropology and political science—the sciences which had preceded sociology.

III

THE TENSION BETWEEN THEORY AND PRACTICE

The educated layman, startled by the terrific tension between scientific theory and practical thinking, realizes for the first time that two kinds of thinking, and two fundamentally different ways of dealing with social affairs, exist side by side.[1]

The layman has the general impression that what the social scientists know they know more clearly and precisely than the practical man, but after a certain point they make no attempt whatever to answer those questions which actually disturb practical people living in society. Here lies the issue. First, however, we must work out in detail the discrepancy between theory and practice which underlies this feeling. In a certain sense the practical man is undoubtedly right, for the problems arise just at that level from which the social tensions really spring. To go to the root of the matter in terms of the distinctions which we made above : the dissatisfaction of the practical man is a sign of the tension which arises from the fact that the social sciences are still at the stage of partial thinking, whereas in the practical adjustments which are bound up with the real conflicts of social life people are forced more and more to attack their problems in terms of interdependent thinking. The sciences dealing with social relations both in their approach and in their frame of reference are still at the historical stage where man wants to understand individual objects and relationships in order to be able to reproduce them. The contemporary thinking of the practical economist or politician, arising out of the needs of society as a whole, is actuated more and more by the conflicts which spring from the interactions of the spheres and the clash between projects

[1] The remarks made above on the problems of thinking in the social sciences are summaries of a longer methodological study which is as yet unpublished. Here we have entered into the question only so far as the limited space of this book permits. There is an attempt to state similar problems from the point of view of economics in Löwe, A., *Economics and Sociology*, London, 1935, and his " Economic Analysis and Social Structure," in *Manchester School*, vol. vii, no. 1. Frank H. Knight's " Nationalism and Economic Theory," in *Ethics of Competition* (New York, 1936), contains many penetrating remarks on this subject. Cf. also in the " Bibliography ", III, 1g, " Psychological and Sociological Elements in Economics."

which have been independently worked out. The distinction
between theory and practice is by no means only that which
scientists have naïvely been accustomed to conceive it to be
—namely the distinction between superficial and more
exact knowledge, between obscure and clear concepts,
although of course this distinction, too, has a very large
element of truth in it. It is primarily a matter of attitude to
quite different levels of reality and of distinctive ways of
dealing with reality. In pure theory and in empirical precision the scientific investigation of social phenomena has
attained a high level. But as regards the technique of
synthetic observation an intelligent journalist or a leading
man of affairs often states the problem in a much more
sophisticated way.

We can now consider a few examples which show how
partial thinking at the level of discovery underlies the
whole approach and framework of the main achievements
of modern sociological research. We shall show further how
this frame of reference excludes everything which would
facilitate the transition of scientific work into planned
thinking with its interdependent approach to social problems,
and so into the real world of practical life as it exists in
present day society.

What are the greatest accomplishments of the social
sciences and on what are they based ? Inasmuch as we are
not concerned here with a detailed methodology and logic,
we will summarize briefly the most striking processes of
thought in those achievements which lie within the framework of our problem.[1] In an ascending series from the concrete to the most abstract, we have the following types of
theoretical approach :—

(a) Exact description [2] of concrete, individual social facts

[1] As regards the following study, cf. my statements in *Die Gegenwarts-
aufgaben der Soziologie* (Tübingen, 1932), where I tried to make use of
a framework not unlike the methodological outline given above to determine the fields of sociology and their doctrinal form.

[2] Obviously this pure description of unique phenomena already contains
within itself a tendency towards generality and repetition. It can be
either " scientific " or " artistic ". Scientific description is on the level
of inventive thinking, because it unconsciously picks out those features
which are fairly general and are needed for the reproduction of the object.
That scientific description is not indiscriminate description can be seen
by this fact—that *everything* is not described but only those characteristic
features which are " necessary for the understanding of the object ",
which simply means that we describe only what we would have to

(e.g. an exact description of the condition of a given family, of a given constitution, etc.).

(*b*) Comparative description of a number of individual social facts which belong in the same category. We try to find out how the same phenomena may vary. By comparing a large number of families or constitutions in various periods and in various countries we may succeed in accurately defining the scope and the characteristics of the corresponding general concepts. Or we may find it more useful to introduce " types " which, just because they are less abstract than general concepts, will reflect more adequately the variability, and do more justice to the concrete individuality, of the single facts compared. All this is almost entirely in terms of observation and description, but is not properly analytical knowledge. We ascend from this to :—

(*c*) The explanation proper of social objects in terms of causal connections. In order to arrive at these we conceive of the existing objects as the result of past developments. At the same time we break them up into elements, the present combination of the latter as being the result of the interplay of forces and factors operating upon them. Thereupon we come to :—

(*d*) The point of view which searches for regularities in the operation of the general factors. This, however, works itself out at two levels—

(i) in which the factors (forces) are understood *on the level of descriptive concepts* in their concrete tangibility and immediacy, as common-sense observation usually copes with them.

(ii) in which they are reduced to even more general, more *abstract*, more *formalized* principles (which are emptied to an increasing extent of their historical content).

At the level of concrete description one could, for instance, define a constitution as the institutional stabilization (based on contract) of the fundamental duties and rights of citizens and officials of the state. Only a precise analysis shows that the concepts which are applied here are ad hoc concepts, that is to say common-sense observation produced them rather vaguely. They can be further

know if we wanted to change or to produce the object. An artistic description of the unique has a quite different guiding principle, namely the stimulation of moods and sentiments, cultural values, and so on.

investigated and reduced to those simpler processes of which they are made up. " State," " contract," " institutionalization," " duties," " rights," " freedom," " obligation," " power," etc., are complexes which must be carefully observed in their actual working and reinterpreted as potentials of forces or as the interplay among them. A second definition which would conceive of the constitution as a formal crystallization of the existing balance of power between the various groups in the community struggling for supremacy can indeed transcend the concrete facts to the extent that it finds that the essence of the constitution in something which is not directly perceptible, but which is a principle from which most of the specific contents of concrete individual constitutions could be explained.

Now one can be even more precise in the explanation of these principles which represent fundamental forces and can ask further : What is really meant by power ? The answer, " It is every action which compels certain actions in others " —will, because of its still greater abstractness and generality, bring out the common elements in a wide range of phenomena which, at the level of concreteness, are still radically different from one another. By means of this abstraction, it becomes evident that in addition to the quite obvious and tangible forms of power in which physical coercion appears, there are also elements of power in economic life, in administrative machinery, in the agencies which form opinion. Hence, in considering the struggle for state power by various groups and in the definition of the balance of power, all these factors must be brought under a common rubric and taken fully into account. In other words : by deepening the process of abstraction in the right way, the increasingly formal definitions embrace more and more concrete processes and phenomena which could formerly be regarded as ultimately irreducible facts. (In the same way, " freedom " can be further formalized and reduced to the most abstract principles. Cf. our own attempt at a definition, p. 160, footnote).

The tendency in all these processes of thought, to reduce concrete ideas to more abstract ones (a stage through which all sciences which strive for precision must pass), is to be found also in the attempt to reduce the multiplicity of social phenomena to a number of fundamental processes and axiomatic concepts. This method aims at explaining every social event in terms of these axiomatic processes and relationships. Where questions of control and social guidance are at stake, it is hoped that ultimately certain desirable ends can be brought about by working in terms of these basic concepts. At the same time this reductive process implies a tendency to measure those elementary factors in terms of quantity.

If one examines this programme more closely, it is obvious that two things have been omitted, apparently intentionally. One is the absolutely exact perception of the individual event as we meet it in unique situations (the " accidental ", the " historical "), and the other is the investigation of those regularities and inter-connections, those *principia media*, which do not operate in every society but which define the particular character of a certain social pattern. We will have something more to say about these *principia media* later on. In what follows we will point out that implied in the scientific frame of reference described above, is a mode of thought which begins with the setting of immediate goals, i.e. it is on the level of inventive thinking. Only the man who is interested in producing isolated individual objects according to a general principle will try to discover the general laws governing their origin and transformation of a whole class of object. Such a person has advanced beyond chance discovery to the extent that he does not take the objects as he finds them ; he ignores their unique and individual qualities and goes back to general factors, in order to recombine them so that he may " invent " a new object. The tacit intention which is at work even in the most remote processes of sociological thought in its search for laws and generalizations, is the question : How can I satisfy this or that social need with the aid of a measure or institution which is to be based on general principles of social interaction ? But this question is asked without entering more deeply into the way in which this institution is embedded in the concrete environment. A direct leap is made from immediate con-creteness into the sphere of the most general laws and principles. In this—as in every attempt to transcend the particular historical framework—the fact remains that in these processes of thought a type of mind is at work which sees individual objects and individual relationships within the framework of a " world in general " but which does not at the same time, try to rebuild the actual framework in which these individual objects are expected to function. The seemingly great abstraction which prevails in this treatment does not arise from the broad and creative conception of the world peculiar to the abstract type of approach, but rather from a *remoteness* from the world, if by " world " one understands the interdependence of a particular event with the manifold factors which really cause it. This highly abstract method of thought is the highest refinement of an approach which seeks to realize both practically and theoretically only isolated individual objects, isolated individual causal sequences, isolated individual complexes of wishes, but which does not yet dare to concern itself with the concrete structure into which this individual object is to be integrated in either theory or practice.[1]

The social scientist in the next stage of social development will be actuated neither by bravado nor by idle

---

[1] It is one of the peculiarities of the history of thought that the development of a particular style of thought tends to suppress or totally to obscure the significance of the remaining styles of experience and thought. We shall show later (cf. Part V, I, esp. p. 241 ff., of the book) how our modern scientific development which is based on " inventive " thinking and ultimately on the needs of technique, tends to obscure the fact that the direct physical and psychic contact and perception of an object affords an equally valid source of knowledge. It is by no means true that these offer no *knowledge*—the knowledge we obtain thereby is merely an entirely different type from that abstract inventive knowledge which tries to " produce ", and " use " the object and therefore conceives of it in functional terms.

Inventive thinking does not confine itself to the object as it presents itself immediately. The above classification of theoretical approaches, ranging from the most concrete to the most abstract, shows this clearly. Knowledge based on intuition, on the other hand, keeps very close to the object at hand and tries to extract its information from the object as it finds it. The intuitive approach does not aim at understanding the object with a view to constructing it out of its elements. Inventive thinking, however, even when it is more abstract, is concerned with reproduction of the object. Intuitive knowledge is for this reason condemned to remain mute and unconstructive. Just as the unconscious forces which are at work at the level of chance discovery may in time become explicit in the nature of their achievements, so there are ways of becoming aware of that knowledge which is implied in intuition. We may describe as romantic all attempts to maintain the intrinsic value of the intuitive approach, and of all types of human understanding which are being suppressed or at least obscured by increasing technological rationalization. They have a historical function because they save older forms of knowledge, which otherwise would be threatened with extinction. To these

ambition when he searches for methods which will do justice to the actual context in which the individual object exists. He will be forced to seek such methods, since a mere mass of single objects abstractly construed and an accumulation of partially regulated practices and institutions will no longer function smoothly. The practical man of affairs who notices for the first time how various actions conflict with one another will be led more rapidly than the scientist from the experience of these real conflicts to a qualitatively different type of thinking about them. The social scientist, on the other hand, at first scarcely does more than intensify those strivings for accuracy which he has inherited from a previous stage of social activity.

This discrepancy between science and practice (the scientific approach lagging behind the practical one) seems to be vitally important in the social sciences. It is due to a social division of functions, so that in our field the practical person is much closer to the subject-matter than the theorist. Nevertheless, as in every case of division of labour, here, too, those who are working at a common task must guard against getting too far away from one another. The necessary correction, however, at the advanced stage of differentiation at which we now find ourselves, can

---

belong Goethe's " theory of colours ", and, in a certain sense, modern " Gestalt " theory, phenomenology, and the German " philosophy of existence ", and so on.

Everything we have said above concerning interdependent thinking and *principia media*, is contrary to the trend of intuitive thought. But our aim is not that of the Romantics—to escape the general rationalizing process of modern times. We want so to refine and extend the methods of rational analysis that they enable us to grasp scientifically the concrete object in its concrete context. This is true even when the type of investigator who still works on the level of abstract invention and the separation of the spheres looks upon interdependent thinking as an incursion into the realm of the irrational. For him facts which lie outside his plane of abstraction are incomprehensible, irrational facts, which he will gladly leave to the intuitive-immediate perception and irrationality of the romantics. He forgets, however, two things, namely that these *principia media* are irrationalities only when measured by his abstract system of co-ordinates, and that the method which has been described here does not try to grasp the individual by intuition or by apprehension (*Schau*), but rather through a further differentiation of the rationalizing frame of reference. When once this is seen, it is interesting to observe further that the highest stage of rationalization—planned thought—has in the end the same tasks as intuitive thought—viz. to grasp the concrete object in its concrete context. But whereas intuition does this in avoiding rational analysis, planned thinking does it with the use of refined and elaborate instruments of thought.

succeed only if we come back again and again to the original frame of reference, compare it with the new situation, and so discover the next steps to be taken.

To look at the problem from another angle, let us now ask of what the prevailing methods of thought and the most important accomplishments of our scientific research consist, apart from the methods already mentioned. The answer is primarily in *specialization*. Specialization will always exist as long as there is anything like a division of labour in scientific research. Only the following remain then as decisive questions :—

(*a*) In which direction and on what principle is the specialization conducted ?

(*b*) To what degree and at what later stage of the investigation is the reality which has been divided up for purposes of specialization, recombined and reintegrated ?

Modern specialization in scientific work follows two lines. First that of subject-matter, and secondly that of method. Specialization of subject is a self-evident necessity. A single investigator cannot occupy himself with every possible phase of social life. In this sense we must give our assent when one investigator concerns himself with the family, or, specializing still further, with the family at given period or of a given social class ; another with constitutions, and so on. This specialization will not do any harm as long as one remembers that one is dealing with fragments of a larger context.

If we look at specialization from the point of view of method, we shall see that it follows the method of abstraction we have already described. We do not examine every fragmentary aspect of the situation which confronts us ; we consider the situation according to abstract principles, which when logically carried out, lead to the creation of the so-called " pure spheres ". One studies, for instance, the family in its different manifestations from a political, an economic, an educational, a biological, or a psychological point of view and on the basis of this abstraction, homogeneous fields are set up in which only political, economic, educational, biological, or psychological aspects emerge. This type of specialization does not so much deal with fragments as cross-sections of the whole and it is clear cut and consistent when it carries through its abstractions with unambiguously defined concepts. This way of cutting out a cross-section of the total context which arises from the necessities of the division of labour, is admissible and highly fruitful as long as it is not forgotten that we are dealing only with fragments, cross-sections, and spheres of reality.

Thus the organic unity of events is severed by analysis in two directions, and this division becomes even more marked when specialization in subject is combined with a rigid separation of spheres, so that the family, the constitution, and so on, are investigated only from some abstract point of view. Thereby a double removal from concrete reality is realized : the degree of abstraction which has been brought about through specialization of subject-matter is intensified by a division into separate spheres.

But this, too, is admissible and indeed even necessary, for without preliminary specialization in subject-matter precise observation is not possible ; without abstraction from some point of view, no concepts are possible which will be sufficiently clear-cut for analytical purposes. For us the question reappears in a different form : How far does our science attempt to reintegrate, after the two-fold act of specialization has taken place ?

Here we can make the following remarks. Either we remain at the level of specialization of subject-matter and no one undertakes to bring the fragments together according to their real structure, or, if integration does take place, abstraction and the separation of the spheres still persist and integration occurs only in the specialized individual disciplines, so that we have pure economics, pure psychology, pure sociology, etc. But no one reconstructs theoretically the whole from the pieces, or shows the real interdependence of the spheres in an everyday concrete setting.[1]

[1] American sociology became famous in the fifteen years after the World War for its intensive thematic specialization which bore very fruitful results, in the form of new techniques for empirical research and in the exact knowledge of specific subjects. Since the great depression, however, a growing discontent with this type of specialization has been evident and has borne fruit in a number of works. Most recently the Social Science Research Council, through its Committee on Studies on the Social Effects of the Depression, has published a series of thirteen monographs which outline possible research projects on a wide variety of subjects, and which represent a great advance in the overcoming of this earlier unplanned specialization. Cf. *Studies on the Social Effects of the Depression*, Social Science Research Council, Bulletins 27–39 (New York, 1937).

Here, too, it could be said that as long as this method of splitting up reality continued to work smoothly in the sense that it corresponded to the kind of practice prevailing in that age no objection could be made to it. The most important criticism of this approach as the only possible scientific way of thinking arises, however, from the fact that at the stage of reconstruction and planning reality can no longer be mastered by the exclusive use of these older methods.

It has become clear that we cannot do without the kind of thinking which distinguished the stage of invention. Neither the demand for theoretical accuracy which this mode of thought expresses—nor the detailed precision which is the result of specialized observation—should be pushed into the background. It must, however, be made equally clear the tasks that which confront the social sciences to-day reach far beyond the framework of investigation presented above.

IV

THE INDIVIDUAL AND THE UNIQUE

The use of general principles as instruments for perceiving and controlling individual objects and relationships and compassing immediate ends, meets with obstacles when society consciously begins to direct its own course, not in isolated details, but as a whole. At this stage it is evident for the first time that every object exists not in a " world in general " but rather in a particular world with a structure which becomes more and more cramped and rigid, because it is built on unchangeable foundations. Of course it was previously known that the individual object as it is found in concrete reality is something more than the result of the interplay of a number of general laws. It was assumed, however, that one was dealing only with a " world in general " and that the deviations in the individual case were due to some as yet unknown factors which in their turn also sprang from general principles. The uniqueness of the individual fact was regarded as inscrutable, not because it existed in a particular world with its own peculiar forces, governed by *principia media* which were not necessarily contained in general laws ; but either because a still unrecognized general factor was thought to be combined with known principles in its occurrence, or because its individuality seemed to spring from a source of its own.

Every society based on specialization and division of labour, produces in practice separate and more or less isolated institutions and relationships, but does not create the whole social fabric. This was the reason why such a society could afford to minimize all those deviations which arose from the peculiar individual character of certain situations and patterns of culture. At this stage of development most institutions grew up by themselves and were modified by conscious action only in a very gradual way. Any independent invention, such as a new constitution, a new military organization, a new type of school, was only apparently an entirely new creation. The essential part of it arose from a slow, traditional, selective process of discovery. It was only at a later date that constitutions were codified, systematized, and institutionalized—originally they were the direct product of infinitely complex conflicts, the expression of varying conditions of equilibrium in the social structure. Exactly the same is true of a new military organization or a new educational programme : each of them makes use of what already exists, consciously modifying it according to principles with a view to some more or less explicit goal, so that in the end it takes on the guise of a new creation. But it was largely assumed that the excessively abstract principles used in constructing this new social creation would lose their rigidity and adapt themselves to the *particular principia media* of the *particular* concrete situation, and the entire structure would in this way adapt itself to the larger world in which it would have to exist. The product of abstract principles would be " run in " through usage and practical experience, and would become individualized—at least, so it was hoped. But the more thoroughly organized the division of labour and differentiation of functions in our society become, the less they can rely on uncontrolled " chances " to bring about adjustment and to give a vital elasticity to " artificially " constructed social institutions. As time goes on, even the individual case must be thought out in advance if it is not to have an arbitrary effect on its surroundings. The handicraft system of production could still transmit the technique of making things to its apprentices knowing that individual combinations and adaptations would produce the best results. The large taylorized plant must exclude every individual personal operation. The older forms of administration could work with a staff of voluntary and unpaid administrators whose traditional class-outlook, combined with a general education and worldly wisdom, made for the best decisions in each particular case. The thoroughly organized administrative machinery of a modern industrial society requires a technically trained specialist to occupy the positions formerly filled by voluntary officials from among people of rank. Every decision both in its formal aspect as well as in its inner intention must be made according to rules and the individual cases must be foreseen as completely as possible.[1] In this way men are forced even against their will to give their attention not merely to general laws, which must be known here, too, but also to the task of thinking out those special laws which hold good only in special spheres of society at a given place and time. The increase in the complexity and interdependence of events, the necessity of predetermining the exact individual form of a process or institution and its individual adaptation, which formerly took care of itself, compels us to search for *principia media*.

The accurate description of a social situation confronts us with a problem which we meet with in nature, but in a far less urgent form.[2] In nature, too, we deal with special spheres. So a marsh provides a closed system of special conditions which are produced by ecology, by the interdependent metabolism of the creatures living together in this particular environment, and by the history of the marsh in question. But we have never had to set up and direct the entire system of nature as completely as we are forced to do to-day with our society, and therefore we have

---

[1] In this connection cf. Max Weber, *Wirtschaft und Gesellschaft*, vol. ii, part iii, chap. vi, " Bürokratie," pp. 650 seqq.

[2] When, in the sphere of technology and natural science, we say a machine must be " run in ", we mean precisely this close adaptation of the parts to each other and to the external situation which is so difficult to grasp by means of abstract principles.

never had to penetrate into the history and structure of the individual worlds of nature. Mankind is tending more and more to regulate the whole of its social life although it has never attempted to undertake the creation of a second nature from the primary forces which are given in nature. When we have gone so far as to regulate the movements of clouds and, to make use of individual forces regularly and for particular purposes according to certain rules of experience, when we have controlled climate in the same way as it is becoming necessary for us to control social factors, and when we try to draw into the framework of our regulation all the laws of biology in their concrete interactions, then we will be faced with the same problem in the world of nature as now confronts us in the world of society : namely the treatment of a particular historical and local stage in the total system of nature as a relatively self-contained whole, working according to certain principles which are peculiar to it. But since we have not yet gone so far and since it is also doubtful whether we will ever arrive at such a point in nature, we must, rather, content ourselves with the observation of general forces in order to combine them for the attainment of unique and partial goals.[1] There does not seem to be any immediate need here for absolute interdependent thinking, and we can rest content with the vague statement that uniqueness in nature is made up of countless contingent situations and forces.

This last formulation, however, obscures the fact that in certain spheres of life not all situations are accidental and that certain facts, forces, and principles are characteristic. In general the expression " accidental " applied to facts, forces, and principles makes sense only if one explains at the same time how one defines for purposes of contrast the terms " constant " and " necessary ".

If the question is put in this way it becomes clear that at the stage of abstract thinking most concrete events were thought to be accidental, because people's attention was focused only on the creation of an abstract object and

[1] Here our previous remark that we exclude nature from our construction of social relationships becomes significant. Nature enters into our social regulations only in fragments torn from their context as for example, where it becomes a part of technical manipulation. (Cf. p. 155 n.) Nothing that is excluded from these relationships becomes a problem from a social point of view.

on the factors which formally could be said to determine it. Had we sought also to remould the concrete environment, everything we had hitherto called " accidental " would have become divided into those facts, forces, and principles which were really accidental and those which in their concrete form were really essential to this particular sphere. In other words we would then be working on the level of *principia media* of the sphere involved.

V

THE UNIQUE AND THE GENERAL IN HISTORY AND THE PROBLEMS THEY PRESENT TO LOGIC

It is now time to speak about these *principia media* in greater detail.[1] We have so far observed that they are in a certain sense a kind of regularly recurring special laws, special relationships of a certain historical phase in a particular social setting. Superficial insight into their character has led many thinkers to speak of a special historical logic and has misled them into believing that the individual destiny of each historical epoch is entirely independent of the general laws of events. Historians have tried to grasp the uniqueness of each epoch as something which can be understood only by immediate intuition (Romanticism) or to deduce it as a type of unique historical dialectic (historicism, Hegelianism, and Marxism). The first solution renounced scientific methods in the study of history completely. The second constructed two independent and co-existent logics ; a generalizing logic which deals with what is general, and another which traces the relationships

[1] John Stuart Mill in *System of Logic : Ratiocinative and Inductive*, vol. ii, book 6, chap. 5, sec. 5, employs the expression *principia media*. He himself derives it from Bacon. To a certain point our use of the expression *principia media* and Mill's are alike ; the differences arise where our general principles differ from his. Since the German edition of this book in which I presented the theory of *principia media* against the background of planned thinking, Adolf Löwe in his *Economics and Sociology*, London, 1935, has fruitfully further developed some of the main aspects of it. A very stimulating criticism of his presentation is to be found in T. Parson's article in *American Journal of Sociology*, 1937, vol. 43, no. 3, pp. 477 ff. Cf. also M. Ginsberg's presentation of the *principia media* in his *Sociology*, London, 1934, which discusses the corresponding problems in the traditional setting as they appear in Mill's writings.

between events in a unique historical issue. As the latter, theoretical approach creates a dialetic which is entirely independent of a generalizing theory of factors, it is also inclined to use unscientific methods. In its concrete form it is mainly inspired by a philosophy of history, which draws its vision of the course of history from the particular aims of certain groups. We think that in spite of this the exponents of the dialectical approach rightly understood that the individual development of certain historical and social units had to be studied scientifically and could not simply be left to the causal epic style of the historian. The mistake they made was to reconstruct the individual framework of a society, or its individual development without taking universal factors into account.

The *principia media* which we wish to introduce into the discussion are in the last analysis universal forces in a concrete setting as they become integrated out of the various factors at work in a given place at a given time— a particular combination of circumstances which may never be repeated. They are, then, on the one hand, reducible to the general principles which are contained in them (that is why the method of abstraction, described above, has achieved so much). But on the other hand, they are to be dealt with in their concrete setting as they confront us at a certain stage of development and must be observed within their individual patterns, with certain characteristic sub-principles which are peculiar to them alone.

The layman who observes the social world intelligently understands events primarily by the unconscious use of such *principia media*. His thinking is characterized, however, by the fact that he constantly tends to confuse general principles of the social structure *as such* with their concrete forms as they come to exist at a definite time or in a specific social order. In static periods he is unable, in any case, to distinguish between a general abstract social law and particular principles which obtain only in a certain epoch, since in periods of only slight variability, the divergences between these two types do not become clear to the observer. The real constants and the principles peculiar to a single age have the same degree of fixity at such a time.

Let us now try more accurately to trace the emergence of *principia media* in everyday experience. Everyone lives in expectation of possible events. In this sense all human life is bounded by an horizon of expectations. Our horizon of expectations reckons with events which rest on the constancy of social experience, as for example, the constancy of the social guarantees that certain social customs and usages will be followed, that certain social hierarchies will be respected, and so on. It also takes into account, however, a great number of unforeseeable facts. When we eagerly take up a newspaper we are already prepared for the occurrence of certain kinds of events which interest us for the very reason that we cannot foresee in detail what they will be. Although we always leave a gap in our horizon for unforeseen facts, that certainly does not mean that we are prepared for anything—that we have an equally intense and concentrated attitude towards all categories of events. We think it probable that the newspaper will report a case of robbery or that the cabinet has fallen, or that certain commodity prices fluctuate in a certain area. In other words : we are prepared to perceive facts and complexes of facts of a certain type, of a certain order of significance, which we expect as " normal " and relevant. The single facts may vary ; the framework and the system of co-ordinates into which they must be dovetailed remains more or less constant as long as the whole social situation is stable, and its development is continuous.

The range of expectations of the man who lives in an age where the social structure is changing through and through is quite different. He not only takes into account innumerable individual facts which he has never experienced before—for in this respect he is like the person living in a static society ; he is also prepared for a possible change in the principles governing the new kinds of facts which emerge and combine in unexpected forms. One then takes into account, for instance, not only fluctuations in the buying power of money but also the possibility of a complete collapse of the monetary system ; one reckons not only with the possibilities of a cabinet change but also with the possibility that a non-parliamentary government will seize power or even that no state power at all will be able to establish itself, or that a state power will change its principles with regard to the use of force and propaganda. One has to allow for the fact, not merely that individuals may suddenly become untrustworthy and untruthful, but that in whole spheres of relationships, in the economic realm or in private life, the former trustworthiness and honesty on which one could normally rely, has suddenly disappeared because war, revolution, and disintegration almost amounting to civil war have destroyed the framework of social events on which, in the last analysis, the older behaviour was actually based. In such times we may speak of discarding an earlier, more limited, " horizon " for a broader range of expectations. In such periods the history of mankind reveals itself in a much more essential form ; it gives the observer the chance to understand the now shifting levels of those *principia media* which were the basis and framework of a single age in social history. In cases like these social scientists are given the opportunity of dividing those structural laws, which they thought were eternal, from those on which a single epoch, or stage of development was founded. There is the further possibility of diagnosing correctly those facts which first emerged individually and in apparent isolation, which did not fit into the older structure and which suggested the new principle of organization, and of formulating the new structural law which is emerging in the grouping of these facts.

In order to give a more accurate picture of what we call *principia media* we will cite, in contrast with the more complicated laws mentioned above, further types of *principia media*, which are bound up with a definite historical structure. Recent studies in the sociology of law [1] once more confirm that the fundamental principle of formal law by which every case must be judged according to general rational precepts, which have as few exceptions as possible and are based on logical subsumption, obtains only for the liberal-competitive phase of capitalism and not, as Max Weber believed, for capitalism in general.[2]

The aim of this basic principle was to allow the capitalistic parties to a contract to calculate the results of a lawsuit in advance. At an earlier period of capitalist development the contracting parties appear before the law with approxi-

---

[1] Cf. concerning the facts cited Neumann, F., *Koalitionsfreiheit und Reichsverfassung*, Berlin, 1932, p. 53 ; Hedemann, J. W., *Die Flucht in die Generalklauseln* (Tübingen, 1933) ; Geiler, K., *Beiträge zum Wirtschaftsrecht*, Mannheim, 1932.

[2] Cf. his " Rechtssoziologie " in *Wirtschaft und Gesellschaft*, vol. ii.

mately equal strength at their disposal; but in the later stage of monopoly capitalism, the partners are of unequal political and economic power, and we find an increasing element of juridical irrationality in the shape of legal formulæ which leave the decision of the case to the discretion of the judge, dispensing with the old principles of formal law. Such clauses as the consideration of " public policy ", " good faith " or the interests of the " concern in itself " give the judge the chance to disregard the formal and equalitarian application of the law and to open the door to the influence of the real holders of power in society. That corporation law is being increasingly applied to the prejudice of the small investor is likewise a symptom of this development which favours the few who already have power against the many who have not.

In this way, under apparently democratic rule, at the stage of monopoly capitalism, a situation is developing which in Fascism is openly proclaimed: i.e. inequality before the law.

The correlations between liberal competitive capitalism and formal law, and between monopoly capitalism and increasing legal irrationalism are (as far as they can be proved correct) historically limited *principia media*.

There is another psychological generalization which can be shown to be in fact only a principium medium. It used to be generally accepted that enforced unemployment would always create rebellious attitudes. But this is not true of the unemployment characteristic of the late capitalist age in which we live. Chronic or structural unemployment as we know it, for the most part creates apathy rather than rebellion in the minds of its victims. The primary reason for this is that modern unemployment destroys the " life plan " of the individual. Under these circumstances rebellion and aggression lose their purpose and social direction.[1]

Let us take another principium medium which does not apply to all human behaviour but is bound up with a particular state of society. At the stage of late capitalism the classes which are most typical of earlier economic forms (small shopkeepers, artisans, small peasants), are

---

[1] I intentionally cite examples which we have dealt with in the course of our discussion in order to relate the methodological problem to the sequence of ideas that we have been dealing with here. Cf. p. 104 n.

anti-proletarian as long as their hopes of social advancement are not completely destroyed and their proletarianization has not yet been carried through to the bitter end. To them must be added that new class of black-coated workers which is the product of modern large-scale business administration, and which in spite of its recent origin, tends to act in a similar way to the older type of the lower middle class. But it would be wrong to infer that the lower middle classes whether the old or the new are always anti-proletarian. How they will behave and with whom they will co-operate depends entirely on their historical circumstances. But however much we must take the *principia media* and the corresponding concepts (" late capitalism ", " structural unemployment ", " lower middle class ideology ", etc.), as concrete expressions of a special historical setting, it should nevertheless be borne in mind that what we are doing is differentiating and individualizing abstract and general determinants (general factors). The *principia media* are in a certain sense nothing but temporary groups of general factors so closely intertwined that they operate as a single causal factor. That we are essentially dealing here with general factors in an historical and individual setting is evident from our example. Our first observation implies the general principle of the functioning of a social order with freely contracting legal personalities ; the second, the psychological effect of unemployment in general, and the last, the general law that hopes of social advancement tend to affect individuals in a way which obscures their real social position. It is no less a mistake to believe that the particular psychology of white-collar workers in its historical setting can be completely explained in terms of a general psychology of social advance, than it is to believe that the particular psychology of this social type in the late capitalist epoch can be worked out in full detail without taking into account the general principles of the human mind.

These examples show that the *principia media* are constantly at work in everyday thinking and that they fill the horizon of the man in the street. The insecurity of modern man does not arise—as we have seen—from the occurrence of too much that is unexpected and novel. He has evidently accustomed himself to the variations in individual facts. His disturbance is due rather to the fact that he has

to transform the " principles " of his " horizon of expectations " at a very rapid rate. If he fails in this, he despairs
and like a character from Hebbel can only say, " The world
is beyond me." Anyone who does not revise his *principia
media* in time and cannot acquire an insight into contemporary problems, will not only find the world " beyond
him " but will indeed be overcome by it.

Since the beginning of modern times, it has been the
special task of sociological thinkers to understand the
principia media of each new period. The existence of
thinkers like Machiavelli and Thomas More was first made
possible by the collapse of the feudal world and the emergence
of the new capitalist structure of society. The achievements
of Adam Smith, St. Simon, Lorenz von Stein, and Karl
Marx also represent intellectual responses to important
changes in the course of social development. Our day, too,
must strive with ever more determination to acquire such
knowledge. But in our present situation it is no longer a
matter just of discovering such new *principia media* without
reference to their context : we must constantly study them
in their mutual relationships and strive to exert some
influence on them in our practical activity.

The more we emphasize the total situation in our study
of society, the more the concept of *structure* imposes itself
upon our analysis. An epoch is dominated not merely by
a single *principium medium* but by a whole series of them.
A number of mutually related *principia media*, however,
produce a structure, in which concrete patterns of factors
are bound up with one another in a multidimensional way.
In our frequent references to this multidimensionality, we
have meant that while the economic, political, and
ideological spheres (according to the cross-sections taken by
different observers) each represent a single dimension of
events as a whole, existing reality in fact consists in the
mutual relationships between many such spheres and the
concrete *principia media* at work in them.

Every concrete complex of events, e.g. a change in
cabinets or the rise and fall of an economic cycle—is in
itself a section of the whole structure, which every com-
petent analysis must be able to trace back more or less
exactly to the individual events in question. Every important
complex of events, on the other hand, is not only a section

of the existing structure but at the same time carries the multidimensional pattern a bit beyond the preceding stage. This structural change which is caused by the force of the cumulation of individual events must also be taken into account in every adequate description of the events themselves.

A large number of mutually related *principia media* form a structure. An interdependent change in a number of *principia media* constitutes a structural change. But there is nothing more mistaken than the assumption that the organization and trend of the structural changes taking place in our society can be discovered by a scientist or a statesman at a glance. The so-called intuitive perception of a configuration (*Gestaltschau*) may claim to be able to grasp fundamental phenomena in a single psychological act—in a single act which is not simply the sum of elements which have previously been analytically understood. One is reminded in this connection of the well-known example of a melody which is immediately perceived as a whole and not as the mere sum of the single tones and intervals contained in it. But only in the sphere of sight and hearing are wholes in this sense immediately present and perceptible in a single psychological act. The structure of all the social and historical events of an epoch is by contrast too intricate to be understood at a glance. Nor is it directly perceptible. It can only gradually be grasped after long thought, in which all its elements are noted, compared, and combined.

The most we can really see to-day is the interdependent modification of various *principia media* in the political, economic, technological, and psychological spheres. These modifications must be viewed as interdependent, i.e. the points must be discovered where changes in the political sphere, for instance, touch upon those in the economic, and where the changes in both these objective spheres bring about a subjective change in the form of a new psychological attitude. It is the proud claim of periods of sluggish development that they observe individual facts and the general abstract laws which govern them ; but we have the chance to reveal more comprehensive relationships and the fundamental changes taking place in them as they emerge.

Every method of investigation has its own particular

standards of accuracy, as I pointed out elsewhere, and nothing could be more mistaken than the indiscriminate transfer of these standards from one problem to another. When one is trying to analyse isolated individual objects and the way in which they emerge and function it is probably best to reduce the concrete phenomenon to its most abstract elements, and to express these elements in a measurable form as far as possible. Where it is a question of the determination of a concrete " trend " or some other *principium medium*, this type of quantitative precision can be attained only very gradually and perhaps never completely. As a first approximation the problem is to make a qualitative analysis of these *principia media*, to distinguish various factors and tendencies and to translate the chaos of facts into a correct description of the complicated interplay of forces. It would be quite wrong to renounce this qualitative analysis only for the reason that it does not or at least does not yet, come up to the ideal of measurability.

The forced imposition of mathematical and mensurative methods has gradually led to a situation in which certain sciences no longer ask what is worth knowing but regard as worth knowing only what is measurable.[1] As against this point of view we should insist that in the social sciences we are absolutely bound to concern ourselves with the immediate task presented by the total social situation, and this can only be adequately grasped through qualitative analysis. Only when this has been cleared up should one consider how the complex problem can be analysed into simpler elements. When this, too, has been achieved, we should inquire how the results can be verified by means of simplified elements and how the broader original thesis necessarily follows from the individual points we have verified. Quantitative analysis cannot take place until a qualitative analysis has been made. The mere reduction of a complex of social facts to measurable elements, gives proof of little scientific insight. But it is a strictly scientific undertaking to verify our knowledge at points where qualitative analysis admits of a quantitative control.

---

[1] Thus, many empirical investigations in the social sciences are made merely because the data are at hand, and not because the investigators are faced with problems which they are seeking to solve.

In this way we can make the following assertion : (*a*) Individual facts and the factors which produce them should only be subject to measurement if their qualitative analysis has been sufficiently developed to make it clear that figures do not register facts in the abstract, but verify the answers to clearly formulated hypotheses. (*b*) The abstract determinations of quantities themselves are largely inexact, inasmuch as they do not take into account the divergence from the general laws which are due to different simultaneously existing *principia media*.

For the research method which attacks its problem by counting and measuring, which only seeks abstract laws and aims at the description of units, regardless of their particular historical context, the studied neglect of these *principia media* is a source of error. Even the greatest precision in this sphere does not succeed in being precise as far as historical concreteness is concerned. If social research wishes to be loyal to its claims to accuracy, it must welcome every step which even through divergent methods, leads to the discovery of *principia media*. These principles are, it is not to be denied, very vague at first. The determination of their relative importance rests first on estimates which can to a considerable extent be demonstrated or refuted by the further course of development. When, for instance, it is stated that the present-day concentration of military instruments in a relatively small army, made up of professional soldiers, weakens the chances of general democratization and of the autonomy of the civil population while it strengthens the groups already in power, the thesis can be demonstrated or refuted by the development of military technique and course of political events. At any rate, history can either confirm or refute such observations concerning the actual existence of certain *principia media* only when the social process has previously been analysed into a larger number of such *principia media*. When only one or two such *principia media* are used to understand the total process, the investigator easily falls a prey to the danger of including changes which are due to another principle. This, for example, is the danger of an exaggerated economic interpretation, which from the standpoint of its universal principle, as I wish to emphasize again and again, is easily led either to obscure entirely all the other psychological, and political factors, or else to attempt to derive them from economic elements alone. But if, on the other hand, the investigator has at his disposal a rich network of such *principia media*, he has the chance of discovering further ones as time goes on and of noting, more and more accurately, how they interact in creating social changes.

If there is, on the one hand, the danger of dogmatizing about various *principia media* and their significance in the social process (for instance, regarding as absolute the rôle of economic or political factors in a given period), there is, on the other hand, the opposite danger that the *principia* will be simply placed side by side as equally significant forces, without any attempt to relate them with one another. It is very probable that the forces at work in a given society are of unequal weight and that there is such a thing as a hierarchy of *principia media*, particularly when the multi-dimensional structure is being described as a whole. As against a method which assigns equal weight to all factors and principles and which is at the very best, merely cumulative, there can be no doubt that those methods which give an axis to the structure in the sense that they seek to establish either " independent variables " or a " hierarchy of causal factors ", are on the right track. But such a " hierarchy " can be constructed only empirically, whereas most theorists are guided in deciding what is significant by certain expectations and prejudices which are characteristic of a prevailing scientific fashion or the interest of a given social class. The technician defends a technological inter-pretation of history, the economist an economic inter-pretation, the politician a violence theory, and the unworldly scholar an idealistic one. Their conflict can be settled not " philosophically " but rather empirically by uniting the standpoints of various observers.

VI

Obstacles to the Discovery of the *principia media*

The main difficulty in the discovery of new *principia media* is that we have to search for them among objects which are still in the process of formation and which are closely bound up with all our practical concerns, and further, because the standpoint from which we try to observe them is in itself not entirely stable. We ourselves stand in the midst of the development and interplay of these active forces. Whoever believes that he knows in advance what path the individual *principium medium* will take, and exactly what structure society will tend to adopt, weakens from the very beginning his capacity for empirical observation of newly emergent changes, and treats a structure in the process of becoming as though it had already taken its final shape. A scientific technique for describing the developing historical process must be worked out. This technique should serve those who are trying to discover existing trends and who are determined to deal with future events in terms of open alternatives, i.e. to approach ambiguous facts with an open mind. This type of thinking conflicts with the need for security felt by the historian who likes to present a clear-cut picture of what is essentially an ambiguous past, and with the desire for certainty of the warring political groups.

In order to make clear our own point of view, we wish to call to mind the distinguishing characteristics of two opposing views of history. The first is the post-mortem point of view of the specialized historian.

It is based on the idea that the present cannot be scientifically studied because it is still in the process of emergence and that it is impossible to know which series of facts is really important. This emphasis on the post-mortem point of view compared with an approach *in statu nascendi* does not appear to arise from the objective difficulties of the problem, but rather from the subjective anxieties of the scholar. The danger that in the study of past events one will fail to grasp that detailed network of human relationships which lends itself to immediate observation in the present, seems to be much greater than the danger of going astray in evaluating and weighing present factors. As a matter of fact, no one has as yet really understood the present from the past who did not approach the past with the will to understand the present. The normal process is as follows: we comprehend past situations by means of analogous or contradictory forms which occur in our own contemporary world. This sense of actuality (in the best meaning of the word) which views life *in actu* and thereby gives actuality to the past, remains the *nervus rerum* of all historical and social knowledge.

The post-mortem point of view is entirely in the wrong when it attempts to determine after a series of events has taken place which factors and *principia media* were important. The most fundamental error of which the post-mortem view of history is guilty is that it regards everything that has happened as the only thing that could possibly have happened. Thus it obscures what is always clear to the rational observer who studies the subject *in statu nascendi*, namely that in every historical event numerous factors are acting upon one another and very often the ostensible triumph of one by no means annihilates the rest, but merely makes them less apparent, on the surface, than those factors the significance of which is more immediately perceptible. The sudden emergence of surprising new situations is very often nothing but such previously suppressed and obscured factors coming to the fore. In times of turmoil the " horizon " of expectations, as we have seen, discloses all the contemporary *principia media in statu nascendi* and through the uncertainty of the entire future, emphasizes the wealth of the various possibilities. The task of really scientific observation is to describe these *principia media* as multiple possibilities.[1]

Also opposed to the scientific attitude are the political groups, which, in their view of the present, treat the developing *principia media* as if they knew for certain what their outcome would be. Thus they renounce the experimental attitude in favour of a prophetic one. This, too, is a post-mortem approach, and is basically related to that of the historian. What it really does when it claims to grasp the significance of events which are taking place and to render unproblematic what is really problematic is no more than to describe dogmatically what will happen in terms of its own wishes. Then, on the basis of this as yet unrealized future condition, it undertakes to give meaning to what is

---

[1] For instance, as we tried to do with the conflicting principles of the concentration of the means of power making for minority rule, and fundamental democratization counteracting it : or with the description of the typical situations making for the growth of rationality counteracted by the forces making for the growth of irrationality. Cf. Part I of this book.

still in process of development. Events are accordingly interpreted in terms of this anticipated future. This point of view may have its advantages for political behaviour. The fact that one can pretend to state with certainty which road to follow sometimes enables one to influence broad groups as well as individuals, whose attitude is decisive in crucial situations. In doing this one not only prophesies history but also, in part,- makes it. The political advantage of this unswerving loyalty to the one desirable possibility has, however, the disadvantage that, when in times of crisis, mistakes are brought to light, the over dogmatic politician cannot easily readapt himself. Under these conditions self-correction, which is indispensable for group activity, can be carried out only after severe setbacks and with heavy sacrifices.

Besides the post-mortem approach to history and the prophetic attitude of determined politicians, we must plead for a third method of observation which is *in statu nascendi* and proceeds in terms of an experimental attitude. A method of approach must be developed which treats the horizon of expectations as an open horizon, and not as a map which charts already established facts. The map serves only a traveller who treads a road already prepared for his coming. We, however, who are on the point of traversing a new section of our history, must find the way for ourselves. But we cannot build our roads just as we please. History presents us with a world full of obstacles. Faced with such obstacles, men in the age of magic would have tried to compel the hidden forces to act as they wished. In a later age religious fatalism, though active in carrying out individual undertakings, sought to leave events as a whole in the hands of God. The essential attitude of the planning age seems to be a synthesis of these two types of approach. Once more it displays the courage to intervene in the interplay of fundamental forces ; on the other hand it inherits something of the humility of the religious mind in that it does not pretend to act as a creator of these forces, but rather as a strategist, who only watches over the factors at work in society in order to detect the new possibilities which are coming to the surface at the proper moment, and to reinforce them at those points where vital decisions must be made.

VII

The Concepts of Establishing, Planning, and Administrating must be Distinguished from one Another

The last sentence compels us to make a clear distinction between *establishing* or founding (*Gründung*) and *planning*. *Establishing* is one of the most advanced stages of invention. But within the meaning of our definition it is not, in fact, planning. We have already touched on the problem which arises here when we spoke of *reconstructing* society instead of building it anew. If the social world could be formed in the way in which one deals with single problems or immediate aims, rationalizes a factory or founds a city, or, in other words, creates individual things according to abstract laws and rules of thumb, then planning would not in itself be a new type of thinking. But since planning means an ever deeper penetration from central points into intervening areas which hitherto had been only very indirectly related to one another; and ultimately involves the control of the whole of this still unplanned territory, behaviour which derives from the stage of inventive thinking could only have a disastrous effect in this sphere. It is not planning in our sense when colonizing peoples found an entire city. Such an enterprise is very like planning but it differs from it in two essential respects.

The colonizing, *founding* or *establishment* of a city is distinguished from planning first by the fact that it builds the city in an abstract milieu. It considers the surrounding areas in its calculations from time to time as occasion demands but does not plan them as such. In spite of all precautions with regard to the inner course of events, the total structure, as far as the outer world is concerned, is set up without a plan and can, under certain circumstances, go down like any historically " evolved " city in the face of the competition of other cities and other external difficulties. The second way in which *establishment* is to be distinguished from planning is that in establishment the materials of construction are first brought together and then placed in a predetermined relationship with one another. The house which is to be built exists first on paper. If the finished building differs from the blueprint there is an error either in the blueprint or in its execution. This certainly does not mean that *establishment* is an act of creation. It would be creation only if the inner nature of the materials and the physical, chemical, and other regularities were created by the builder himself, it is sufficient for *establishment* or *founding* that the person who draws up the plan makes use of forces given by nature, but does it in such a way that he produces something new in the sense that from the very beginning he brings together all the elements he needs for his building and organizes them according to his immediate aim. According to this definition a large scale organization, a rationally outlined system of railways and postal service, for instance, may have the character of an *establishment*.[1]

In this sense society as a whole can never be *established* or *founded*, for the elements of which it is constructed are always found in a certain historical relationship. The factors are never found as pure forces but are linked up with *principia media*, in certain groups, and interacting on different levels in a constantly changing society.

All this does not mean that planning is impossible but rather that it should not be thought of as being the same as *establishment* or absolute innovation. *Establishment* proceeds from a fixed and finished scheme which exists in the minds of the founders before it is carried out, and like the Fichtean ideas it is translated from this supersensory condition into actual fact. The problem of execution is no more than the problem of adequate means. Planning, on the other hand, begins with the use of what is immediately available. The ends, means, and foundations of planning exist on the same plane of historical reality : the crowding together of men and things in society is the foundation of planning. This provides the means, and only on this basis can we attain our next goal, and undertake the moulding of society in the right way.

In dealing with *principia media* we have no free, unlimited power of disposition. Instead of this, what we need is the right *strategy* by which to work with or against

---

[1] *Establishment* in its pure form is perhaps possible only in colonization. But even this is enough to indicate its theoretical possibility. The fact, for example, that our transport facilities have really grown up traditionally in the sense that they have passed through every stage from discovery to the rationally regulated invention of a railway system proves nothing against this theoretical possibility.

the current in which these principia are moving, according to the most favourable points of control, which the planning will can find.

In order to understand rightly the chief characteristics of planning, it must be distinguished from *administration*,[1] which is no longer political. This latter emerges as soon as the social structure passes from the stage of planning into a completely organized state, and as soon as all or most of the historical forces, which have arisen in the struggle, have been brought under control through strategy. We could, of course, decide to describe this stage as planning, too. We should like, however, to reserve this word for the predictive strategy which strives to bring under its control the as yet unco-ordinated *principia media* of the social process. Planning is the reconstruction of an historically developed society into a unity which is regulated more and more perfectly by mankind from certain central positions. It is possible, of course, that the age of planning will be followed by one of mere administration. It is also possible that at a later stage all that we now call history, namely the unforeseeable, fateful dominance of uncontrolled social forces, will come to an end. As contrasted with administration, planning is thus a form of conduct still operating within the framework of history. As we understand it, planning is foresight deliberately applied to human affairs, so that the social process is no longer merely the product of conflict and competition. Whether we will ever fully succeed is not at issue here. It is also not a question of whether we prefer a planned society. What we must realize is that we cannot escape this task ; that all the tenseness in the atmosphere of our times arises from this redirection of human willing and thinking which is now in progress, and that without recognizing this trend, we cannot understand the age in which we live.

VIII

THE VOLITIONAL AND EMOTIONAL ASPECTS OF PLANNING

With this we imply that social planning is no empty theory unconnected with practical life. This is why we

---

[1] Cf. further on the nature of administration, pp. 294 ff.

spoke, previously, of a strategy of planning. If planning involves the discovery of those key-positions from which the ultimate *principia media* of the social process can be bent to do one's will, then planning implies the existence of that will and the power to intervene at the very points where intervention is required.[1]

Now this enterprising " will to plan " cannot be confined to the individual alone.   It need not, on the other hand, be the majority which supplies the original impulse. Minorities can now take the lead in decisions of the collective will and in carrying out a social reconstruction.   Owing to the fact that modern economic, political, administrative, and cultural institutions have a tendency towards centralization, the minorities which obtain power can make use of this machinery. We have already shown, however, that it is the paradox of the period of reconstruction that those groups which are seeking to realize the new society still retain the old outlook and try to plan one-sidedly for themselves or for the groups which they represent.   Because of this they create a twofold contradiction in their scheme.   First they want a totalitarian system for the benefit of a particular interest, namely to make the planning which is possible only for all useful to the special interests of particular groups.   Secondly to bring it about they intensify the competition and conflict for power to an extreme degree, furthering thereby the typically unplanned and irrational process of natural selection. These contradictions are not imaginary, but are directly demonstrated from events, especially since this struggle for key-positions in planning is waged more vigorously

[1] Freyer is right when he says in his *Wirtschaft und Planung* (Hamburg, 1933) that planning is not a purely theoretical act and is not conceivable without power. This assertion agrees with our contention based on the sociology of knowledge that all thinking is determined by the actual situation and by the will. The fascist element in Freyer's formulation, however, is shown in the fact that an over-emphasis on power leads one to think that power and violence are the really decisive phases of planning. One confines oneself to the maxim that once one has power, the plan will emerge of itself. This is an attitude which has a certain justification at the level of discovery and invention but which, at the present level, leads only to violent crises, since, by dictatorship alone, the conflicts which exist are by no means abolished. Instead, it freezes the life-giving mobility of those elements which had formerly the best chances of discovering new adaptations.

Cf. Paul Tillich's book, *Die sozialistische Entscheidung*, Potsdam, 1933, which in many respects has found the right approach to these problems.

under dictatorships than anywhere else. As long as this stage of one-sided control prevails one cannot speak of successful planning, since the rigorous struggle which was once carried out between different social groups, is now concentrated at the head. Tensions arise which are focused on the positions of authority as they exist within the national political and social units as well as in the world arena. The question is now whether this conflict can be ended and planning can be achieved in such a way that this violent struggle for hegemony will cease. Can this more and more integrated network of relationships be used to secure, not opposition but co-operation? Or, in other words : is there any chance that this social system can so direct our impulses, that either spontaneously, or by planning and guidance, the prevailing antagonism can be changed into co-operation ?

It is possible that a new social situation will never produce new human beings who will think and integrate their impulses in a new way. It is possible that a new social situation will never produce the types of persons required in the proper numbers. But it is also possible that there are tendencies in the social system, which rightly guided by minorities will make it possible to bring about a change of thought and will.

Theoretically, there can be no objections to the possibility of a change in the expression of the elementary human impulses, for we have experienced far greater changes than these in history. Even without planned control the bourgeois type was gradually produced from the appropriate enclaves in the feudal surroundings. And modern industrial bureaucracy, superseding competition, arose in response to the growth of large scale industrial technique.

Such a process of the redirection of impulses and ideas may be seen at work within our own generation and surroundings, whenever an opposition group comes to power. In the new position the old problems appear in a new guise, and unconsciously the attitude of the group to the problems changes completely.

The rate of transformation can indeed—as we shall see later—be accelerated, if deliberate changes in education are planned, corresponding to the parallel social tendencies in the same direction. Whereas education becomes empty preaching when there is no real situation to which it refers, it accelerates the process of transformation when it is bound up with social forces which are moving in the same direction. Here, too, the decisive question is whether the *principia media* in the transformation of man are successfully co-ordinated with the *principia media* of the social system.

On this occasion we wish to explain only the formal [1] mechanisms which are at work in the integrating tendencies of the present stage of social development and to think of this problem, too, in terms of open alternatives. It is conceivable that conflict can lead to ever greater integrations, so that there remain in the end only a few, and in extreme cases only two conflicting power-groups within the individual state and the international system. For the sake of clarity we will consider this process separately as it occurs within political groups and between them. If large units become integrated according to the old principle of the still unplanned society, i.e. by conflict, something like this will happen : Conflict has hitherto been a means of integration as well as of disintegration. Thus it is not impossible that up to a point the use of violence will bring about a more and more intensive centralization. In an extreme case only two powerful antagonists might remain. The integration which follows takes the form of a victory for one party which subdues the other completely. In such a case there is still the chance that the conquered group will indirectly absorb some of the power of the victorious one and from below influence the planning to its own advantage It is, however, also possible that the struggle will end in a deadlock or in mutual annihilation. In the conflict which takes place within the boundaries of the

---

[1] We are perhaps not wholly justified in construing the problem of power integration in such a formal and abstract way as we are doing here—by disregarding the actual opponents who are taking part in it. But our excuse is that, on the one hand, in the general flux into which things have fallen at present, the concrete power groupings cannot be determined in advance, and on the other hand, it is not our task to make political prophecies. For the examination of our problem—which kind of social forces and circumstances could either in the past or future convert hostility into rational insight and co-operation—a rough outline of the possible trends of events is enough and may sometimes throw more light on the basic forces than an analysis which holds very closely to historical and concrete forms.

national states there is still the possibility that pressure from the outside will force the parties to a peaceful compromise—such as the arbitration of their difficulties. It is a much more difficult matter in conflicts on an international scale, where large integrated power units, nations or continents or other types of associated groups, confront one another. Since only the principle of conflict is at work here, there is a considerable possibility that one of the great warring groups will triumph over the entire field and through this victory carry out a unified plan. Much more likely, however, is another possibility, namely that such a final contest will lead to mutual destruction.

Yet another way remains open—it is that unified planning will come about through understanding, agreement, and compromise, i.e. that the state of mind will triumph in the key-positions of international society which hitherto has been possible only within a given national group, within whose enclaves peace was established by such methods. Such a change of outlook would, it is true, be a real revolution in world history, since it would represent a solution to a major crisis, which for the first time would be based not on fear or coercion but on understanding. It has hitherto been part of the nature of conflict that two warring groups would only make peace of their own free will if they feared a common enemy. If we had to rest our hopes only on the conflict principle, it would be necessary at the penultimate stage of world-wide integration to invent some external enemy, e.g. the inhabitants of Mars, who because of their potential threat would compel the still antagonistic groups to come to terms. But since such an enemy from another world cannot be considered, we must try to find out whether it is possible to come to an understanding which would exclude violence and oppression in the field of conflict in another way. The following method is theoretically possible, but cannot be guaranteed to work.

In all previous wars one of the combatants could always hope to annihilate the other. In contrast with this, it becomes more and more obvious that modern war destroys them both. Fear of the horrible destructive power of a future war might become so intense that it would act just like fear in the face of a real enemy. In this case compromises might be reached from fear of a coming general slaughter and the national states would subordinate themselves to a central organization which would undertake to plan for everyone.

Nothing is further from our intentions than to construct what are sometimes called utopias. But it would be a matter of utopias only if we were to assume that the conflicting parties " suddenly " underwent a conversion, out of a spontaneous change of heart without being brought to it by some social device. We have, however, assumed that fear was the motor impulse behind insight and have merely expressed the hope that situations would emerge in which fear would work in the way we have suggested. The question remains, then, whether war in general or the certain destruction which it represents can engender the same type of fear as a common enemy. Fear of an enemy led to a change of mind in certain situations and called forth, so to speak, dialectical understanding through discussion and solution, by compromise. In the instance we have mentioned the frightful power universally possessed by modern military weapons might possibly act like a *second nature*. Just as men in earlier times banded together against the enmity of Nature and in this way arrived at an organized division of labour, this mass of munitions of terrific explosive power might play the part once played by Nature.

To be sure, there is not much in favour of this hypothesis at the present time, especially now when we are witnessing the most overwhelming regressions in the irrational search for power and in its exercise. Nevertheless, it is not entirely beyond the limits of possibility that at the stage of late industrial development, the rising effects of mass irrationalities and the overwrought suspense might recoil and that there might arise a sort of " catharsis ". Of course, this dissolution of tensions can also lead to lethargy. It is, however, quite possible that as, for instance, after the Wars of Religion, when the religious fanaticism and irrationality in general, were in a certain sense transcended, there should now emerge, following this great tide of irrationalism, a new readiness to listen to reason. In this comparison we must keep in mind that the reverence for reason and the tolerance of enlightenment were confined to limited groups of élites ; nevertheless, disenchantment itself was rather widespread. To this should be added the fact that the changes, which at that time took place only in small élite groups, can in principle be realized in modern times in the masses, too, especially since in this case we are dealing with classes which have already undergone what we have called " fundamental democratization ".

The new vigour of the masses and the surge of irrationality which it brings in its train can be appraised from the point of view of a possible development other than the one we mentioned in the first part of this book. One can regard the events which are now taking place as the first stage in a general process of enlightenment in which, for the first time, broad human groups are drawn into the field of political experiment and so gradually learn to understand the structure of political life. When looked at in this context, it is not entirely inconceivable that contemporary mass enthusiasm is the first symptom of the penetration into political life of classes which hitherto have been politically indifferent, and that in spite of the extremely tense atmosphere and against the will of those who seek to control the process, the practical education of the masses in political thinking is taking place before our eyes. It should not be forgotten that the labour movement, which is typically rational in its attitude towards the social process, began as a machine-wrecking movement. These are obviously only possibilities which are contained in the conflicting tendencies of our epoch and nothing is further from our intentions here than to present these prospects as prophecies. It would, however, be an unpardonable error if, for fear of appearing utopian, one failed to mention certain existing factors and suppressed certain tendencies of development only because they imply the possibility of a transformation of man.

IX

THE PROBLEM OF TRANSFORMING MAN

The immediate task of our time seems to be to think out our economic organization in dynamic terms and according to a strategy which will so co-ordinate the now prevailing tendencies that they will no longer conflict. The political problem, therefore, is to organize human impulses in such a way that they will direct their energy to the right strategic points, and steer the total process of development in the desired direction. If these are the problems, then a static psychology which conceives of " man in general " on the basis of what man is to-day is on the wrong track. It may be noted that often those thinkers who are economically and politically progressive, in their political analyses take an eternal human nature for granted. In doing this they unwittingly confuse *Man* with the man as he is found in the present social order. In our approach to psychological problems we must find a way of mediating between this unconscious conservativism and a misdirected utopianism.[1] For it is just as erroneous to believe that human nature remains eternally the same as it is to assume that it can be moulded at will and is infinitely plastic.

Our approach to problems of social psychology should also be quite different from that of the epoch which is now passing. We should neither start our analysis with " man in general " nor should we confine ourselves to purely individual cases, deducing them from the most abstract principles. Rather should we always attempt to view

---

[1] Hertzler, Joyce O., in *History of Utopian Thought* (London, 1923), thinks that the chief characteristic of the so-called " utopians " is that they assumed a type of human nature which did not exist but which once it was constructed, was favourable to their ideals. In truth, such a construction which is based on non-existent and impossible human beings deserves to be called " utopian " and has nothing in common with scientific sociology.

Another question is whether we are also bound to believe that human existence is conceivable only in the form in which we know it under capitalism, and whether we are not justified in analysing more precisely the scope of human transformability. Even if one is convinced that man can be modified, the planned approach is obliged to start with those forms of psychological responses which we find in our present society. This realism as to the point of departure need not, however, lead to the rejection of that other form of utopia which has the courage to regard that which does not exist or which hardly exists in our society as possible in a society which has a different type of organization. Every attempt at planning is utopian in this latter positive sense : it seeks to direct given facts—including psychological ones—in such a way that new facts will come into being in place of those now existing.

Concerning this positive sense of the concept of utopia cf. my *Ideology and Utopia* (English translation by Wirth, L., and Shils, E.), New York and London, 1936, pp. 176 seqq., as well as my article " Utopia " in the *Encyclopædia of the Social Sciences* where further literature on the problem is referred to, also Hans Freyer, *Die politische Insel. Eine Geschichte der Utopien von Plato bis zur Gegenwart* (Leipzig, 1936).

individual facts and individual human beings in their particular social context as it reflects itself in their character. Just as inventive thinking assembled an individual machine or formed an individual organization according to general principles of mechanics and organization, without at the same time considering the *principia media* of the particular sphere involved, so the older psychology occupied itself only with the human mind in general and *in abstracto*. In therapeutics it concentrated on the individual to be cured, whose characteristic symptoms were diagnosed and treated according to general principles. The approach of the planning era is heralded by new developments in psychology. We no longer leave those modifications, which are individually necessary in a given situation to unconscious adaptation or, as we used to say, to " chance ", but rather attempt to provide for the best possible adjustment in advance. Similar developments are to be found in all those scientific tendencies which use a sociological in place of an abstract psychology (i.e. those which instead of speaking of man in general, speak of the mind of the child, of the adolescent and even more concretely of the mind of the proletarian adolescent, of the young girl worker, of the unemployed, of the various occupations, etc.) and which divide up the problem further along historical and sociological lines. Thus, one tries to investigate the origin of the monastic, the feudal, and the bourgeois types. These represent the first steps toward an *interdependent* approach. There is no variation of the human mind in itself, but reasonably enough only a variability determined by the situation (in which, obviously, certain situations as, for example, the family situation, are of special importance) nor is there any change in the economic or social structure which takes place in isolation. No economic order can be brought into existence as long as the corresponding human type does not also emerge.[1]

---

[1] In this connection, the case which stimulated Max Weber to make his investigations of Calvinism, remains highly instructive. An attempt was made to introduce piece-rates in areas where a traditional outlook prevailed. The result was that the Catholic women workers in certain sections where the new principle of increasing one's earnings had not yet been realized, stopped their work as soon as they had earned the amount needed for their customary level of maintenance. Even capitalism can function only when it simultaneously created the corresponding human type which in the earning of money is dominated by the principle of " more and more ". Cf. Max Weber, " Die protestantische Ethik und

When psychology turns its attention to social phenomena it perceives first of all the immediate environment—the immediate situation. But it will push forward inevitably into that sphere of social history from which not only the changes in the environment, but also those social forces which mould the age first spring—i.e. its *principia media*. When it concentrates its attention on this level of social events it will no longer explain the changing individual solely in terms of his immediate environment. It will rather integrate the outstanding characteristics of an historical human type according to the corresponding characteristics of the society in which we live. In order to distinguish between these two types of approach, we might use the expressions : " environmental social psychology[1] " and " structural social psychology ".

Psychology will in our opinion take over the methods of planned thinking to the degree in which it discovers key positions in the sphere of structural sociology, when certain kinds of behaviour can be predicted or produced with a high degree of accuracy, even in otherwise differing individual types. It will seek for laws which turn aside the aggressive impulses and guide them towards sublimation. It will note the correlation between rational and irrational impulses in the human mind and the thoroughgoing rationalization of a society. It will investigate how thought and experience are formed by the social positions arising out of the social structure. With these observations as a beginning, it will be possible to mould personal intercourse in a more realistic way. The planning approach is already at work here, and with it men will have outgrown the notion that psychological attitudes and types of personality can only take the form

der Geist des Kapitalismus," in vol. i, pp. 94 seqq., of his *Gesammelte Aufsätze zur Religionssoziologie*, Tübingen, 1920 (English translation by Talcott Parsons, *The Protestant Ethic and the Spirit of Capitalism*, New York and London, 1930).

[1] As an example of environmental social psychology, I will refer to Busemann, A., *Pädagogische Milieukunde* (Halle, a. d. S., 1927), and the *Handbuch der pädagogischen Milieukunde*, ed. by Busemann (Halle, a. d. S., 1932). Both have good bibliographies. The first and the third study of our book in contrast with these works must be viewed as a study in structural social psychology. A large amount of the literature of environmental social psychology is summarized in Murphy, Gardner and Lois Barclay, *Experimental Social Psychology*, 1st edition (New York, 1931) and 2nd edition with Theodore M. Newcomb (New York, 1937). Both editions contain extensive bibliographies.

in which they occur to us in our age and in our society. Thus our main concern is to discover or to reconstruct the range of variability on a broad historical scale, and then to relate these attitudes and types to the historical and social setting in which they occurred and to which they belonged.

This striving is clearest in recent tendencies in education which no longer aim at forming an ideal person in general, but a person which will probably be needed in the next stage of social development. When, for example, grades and marks are done away with in the school,[1] in order to check the nurture of over-ambitious and competitive persons, one brings to an end a human type which is too well represented in the highest ranks of our society and which finds its own reward by success in contest with others. At the same time modern education should and could cultivate those existing types which have the capacity to sublimate, to strive for intrinsic values—i.e. for goods which can be had without depriving others. In as far as group education is redirected along these lines, man can be transformed so that he is fit for a society whose mainsprings are not competition and natural conflict. Previously it was only in special technical training that we gave a man an education which supplied him with the necessary technical knowledge to do his job. In contrast with this, contemporary education is slowly but consciously beginning to plan not only the communication of skill, knowledge, and technique, but also those *principia media* of character formation [2] which have hitherto been left to themselves and through which even the principles on which the social structure rests are to be transformed. In other words, through these efforts, the entire person is to be remoulded so that by using these new types of personality, it will be possible to transform the social structure in its psychological dimensions.

It could be objected—and not without justification—that this attempt is not entirely new and that, for example, the church, too, has claimed that it was educating the whole man. It constructed a human type according to a pattern

---

[1] Cf. Curry, W. B., *The School and a Changing Civilization* (London, 1934), especially the chapter "Competition and Marks". Cf. in the Bibliography: iii, 7, "Education as a Means of Social Technique."

[2] Cf. in the Bibliography: iii, 1, "The Science of Influencing Human Behaviour".

which it thought desirable, just as later, following its example, the state brought up the citizen and before this, court society set up the "courtier" as its educational ideal. The main distinction between present-day attempts and those which took place earlier seems to us, however, to be a two-fold one.

First, whereas former societies confined themselves to the production of types which were adjusted only to partial situations and could only function successfully there, we are to-day attempting to produce a type which is not only adapted to certain social milieu, but also to the *principia media* of our social structure. Thus, it is from the very beginning more flexible and better able to adapt itself to all the various situations presented by contemporary life.

Further, it is much more important to assume that hitherto educational ideals have taken shape through unplanned chance discovery and selection, whereas reflection has now increased to such a degree that we can consciously make our selection of ideals or reshape them, according to the social function they have to perform.

In this connection we can recall with what sociological consciousness the long enduring ideal of asceticism in the various countries was revised and reinterpreted ; how, in England, the Puritan and Victorian roots of self-denial, frugality, and repression gradually became apparent (for example, in the spiritual revolt manifested in Butler's *The Way of All Flesh*) ; how in Germany the same anti-ascetic tendency was expressed in the works of Nietzsche, Max Weber, and Freud. In all these cases, moral arguments were used less and less, and were gradually replaced by utilitarian analyses of a sociological and psychological kind. Take, for instance, the sociologists' attempt to relate the asceticism of early Protestantism with the primary accumulation of capital.

It is by no means true that we have to deal with a given human type and hence must order our society according to the dictates of an immutable human nature. What we do is rather to accept the older human type as it stands in the first place, and then try, by a wise strategy, to guide it while it is still in action. It is promising and thoroughly realistic to try to transform a person when we meet him in a dynamic environment, so that we can stimulate a change in his psychological reactions, conduct and ideas, with a continuous reference to the changing stimulii of the social background. Whenever a school is conceived of as an experimental community, this kind of planned transformation seems to be at work.

Once we have reached this stage of thought, the progressive significance of certain psychological and philosophical currents suddenly becomes clear. This is particularly true of pragmatism, behaviourism, and psycho-analysis among others.

In what follows we want to investigate how these fundamental tendencies in psychology and in certain schools of philosophy arose from the main social trends of our time, and how they fulfil certain functions in the social process. It is for the most part not recognized that the different philosophical, psychological, and educational theories which exist in a period are not the accidental discoveries of individuals but are the result of a collective experiment ; and that even in these spheres the human intellect is confronted with tasks the real, but often hidden, interdependence of which is only apparent to the sociologist. The individual psychologists, educationalists, and philosophers are so completely adjusted to their particular tasks and so taken up with the difficulties and details of their special spheres that they cannot see why just these particular tasks presented themselves in the course of history. They do not see the connections which produce these difficulties and problems ; they take them for granted without realizing that every maladjustment and every conflict is typical of the society in which it arises, and that consequently the sociological diagnosis is best once it knows how to analyse the social situation. At the same time, however, from these philosophical, psychological, and educational theories, and indeed from the social sciences in general we can see how the scientific man approaches the object of his studies. In his approach to the psychology of other men, and to the conflicts of society in general, he is unconsciously guided by certain dominant habits of thought which have spontaneously grown up in society and which the scientist unwittingly takes over. The unconscious implications of the scientific treatment of society (for instance, how this treatment relates theory and practice to one another) are thus symptoms of the changing nature of society itself, and no sociology is complete which fails to treat these changes in science as symptoms of changes in society.

The positive significance of *pragmatism*,[1] i.e. its meaning for the approach to a new mode of thought in preparation for a new era of planning, as I see it, is that it no longer sets an abstract barrier between thought and action. In a certain sense this is an important step towards inter-dependent thinking. Pragmatism was aware of that organic process by which every act of thought is essentially a part of conduct and rejected the older artificial distinction between action and pure theory which certain philosophers, isolated from the world, had invented. Only to those who live a cloistered life can the nature of thought appear as purely contemplative, i.e. as self-contained and not as an instrument of life and action. In life as it was originally lived there was no thought which was not directly linked with action. To overlook or to deny this integration of thought in conduct is to deny that thought in its very nature is determined by the situation. From the scientific point of view it is very wholesome to make clear once more the creative significance of action and to realize that only a new type of action can give birth to a new type of thought. This spirit has borne fruit in education as can be seen in the attempt to replace the older abstract sermonizing by a new technique of transformation. This consists in creating situations in which the children can practise the principles which they have been taught. Mere admonition and exhortation have been abandoned.

Although there is the healthy element in pragmatism which rejects the idealistic abstraction which breaks the unity of thought and action, its limitations in its present form are that it has too narrow a conception of the context of action in which thinking arises. If by action one understands only the practical everyday handling of things, and focuses one's attention only on the individual with his immediate

---

[1] Of the literature on pragmatism I cite only James, William, *Pragmatism*; and Dewey, John, *Studies in Logical Theory* (Chicago, 1903 and 1909), his important *Human Nature and Conduct* (New York, 1930), and his *Logic* (New York, 1938). Cf. also Mead, G. H., *Mind, Self, and Society* (Chicago, 1935); *The Philosophy of the Act* (Chicago, 1938).

tasks and limited interests, it should be made clear that one is dealing only with thought at the level of chance discovery —a state of affairs in which the practical, immediate, and often unconscious acts of adaptation are primary. At this stage thinking plays only a secondary rôle, as it is lacking in constructive power. It only fills the gap between isolated "hunches" and its only task is to exemplify the significance of things as they emerge in the course of the trial and error process. Thinking first becomes distinct from immediate chance discovery when invention projects in advance an idea of the object to be constructed and analyses this concrete object into abstract elements in order to recombine them into a new object to promote its own purposes. In any case, this stage proves that the capacity for abstraction springs from a higher level of activity than that of chance discovery— i.e. from the stage of inventive thinking.

As soon as thought passed from the stage of chance discovery to that of invention, it became impossible immediately to grasp the connection between thought and action, and this was the origin of the distortion of idealist philosophy which conceived of thought as independent of practical necessity. This stage of thought made it plausible to speak of "ideas" which anticipate conduct and which guide it. As the classical illustration has it, the idea of the house exists in the mind of the architect before it exists in the external world.

Once thought was conceived of in these terms, one very soon was led to conceive of all mental activities as *a priori* to any experience. It would, however, be just as incorrect to deny that on this level of practice, i.e. on the level of inventive thinking, a certain degree of abstraction, anticipating the object to be invented, is necessary, just as it is dangerous to over-emphasize the independence of this abstraction from its background of concrete activity. Thought at the stage of invention is independent of the demands of immediate activity. It is not, however, absolute or autonomous.

The solution of the difficulty seems to us to lie in the fact that inventive thinking cannot be understood within the radius of action of the single individual. For that reason it appears to be absolute if by absolute one understands that it is severed from the context of individual activity. But inventive thinking is, still obviously bound to the context of action in a broader sense. This is clear when one focuses attention on the web of thought and action of the whole historical group within which it arises. Thus the pragmatic nature of thought is not revealed at this stage by considering individual action alone, but only if one focuses attention on group action of which the former is a part. Even the transition from discovery to invention is not to be attributed merely to an individual achievement, but rather to the fact that the group in its collective adaptation passed from a more primitive form of production with a very slight division of labour (as, for instance, primitive hunting and gathering) to a more complicated division of labour. Owing to the progress of division of labour and of social functions, the objects and institutions which formerly were handled as wholes seem to be merely fragmentary to the individual who approaches them thinking only of his own share in the collective work. Abstraction is by no means determined by the object but rather by the form of activity of the knowing subject and especially by the group organization of which the subject is a member. Thinking signifies then " thinking for a group ". The wider the scope of activity, the greater the division of labour, the larger the number of members for whom the same thing must be made clear from the point of view of different tasks, the more are the socialized individuals compelled to divert their attention from individual institutions and processes, as they would appear from a purely personal standpoint and to develop a technique of abstraction which can be used by the group as a whole. Hence, there are just as many possible forms of abstraction as there are collective, active approaches to the handling of things in an historical community. Thus, division of labour and social functions produces more points of view in any given community than any single individual actually needs, so that it is possible for him to learn more than he will need in real life. The community in its language and concepts builds up a store of experiences and abstractions, corresponding to approaches which were current in its history. This is the reason why the individual, when he contemplates the vast body of abstractions which is available to him, has the feeling that the categories and processes of thought were given to man when he first entered this world ; mythologically expressed, this takes the form of the belief that his concepts and his perceptions are drawn from a world beyond. In actual fact the existing body of ideas (and the same applies to vocabulary) never exceeds the horizon and the radius of activity of the society in question. Thus the illusion that thought at the level of invention is completely independent of the context of conduct arises from the fact that in a highly stratified society with a complex division of labour, the collective framework of action has already been lost to the eye. The individual can retain the illusion of his intellectual independence since he no longer has the chance to see how his own actions and experiences grow out of the collective ones. At the level of inventive thinking, the pragmatist explanation is valid for the group but not for the individual—not directly at any rate.

That the radius of activity of the individual is not the same as that of the group can be confirmed by much simpler facts. It has often been observed that the individual inventions which are made in society, do not arise from chance inspirations but come about through a slow accumulation of discoveries and inventive actions. The framework of the individual invention, which develops in apparent isolation, grows up along the lines of collective interests, which for their part are closely bound up with the common radius of activity of group life although there are many intermediate links. This is the only true explanation of the fact of simultaneous invention by independent individuals within the same society.[1] What is true of discovery and invention is true also of the forms and technique of knowing. The error of pragmatism, as a product of the age of liberalism, is that it has in mind only the activity of the individual and does not see that the individual really represents only a section of the activity and experience of the whole social group. The determination of thought by situations can never be demonstrated if one tries to understand it exclusively in terms of the practical activity of the single individual. The point where action passes over into thought

[1] Cf. for numerous illustrations concerning this point, Vierkandt, A., *Die Stetigkeit im Kulturwandel*, Leipzig, 1908. Also Ogburn, W. F., *Social Change* (New York, 1929), pp. 90 seqq. And more recently, Gilfillan, S. C., *The Sociology of Invention* (Chicago, 1935), pp. 71 seqq. (The Un-importance of the Individual), cf. also National Resources Committee, *Technological Trends and National Policy*, Washington, D.C., 1937.

will be found more easily if the whole background of the historical community is considered. The concrete tangible actions of the individual become intelligible only when, in order to place them correctly, the historical conditions and the tasks and functions of the group from which they spring have been reconstructed in imagination. It is only within these larger contexts that the special functions of individual classes and persons and the inhibitions which they impose can be understood. The sociological history of intellectual life is fundamentally nothing more than the *post factum* reconstruction of the functional units and the trend of action in a given society, through which, even with the help of many intermediate links, we can explain why this or that person was interested in this or that subject and why from his standpoint he saw, or distorted, things in such and such a way.

At the stage of *planned thinking* the gap between knowing and acting is in a certain sense greater than it is at the level of invention, where it is directed towards immediate aims. For the total plan is even farther in advance of direct action than at previous levels. As we have seen, thought, as the synthesis of all the acts of thinking taking place in an historical community actually covers more than is required by the immediate tasks which single individuals have to solve in their own narrow range of experience. In a complex society in which the various activities are interdependently organized, the individual in the course of his own experience, finds himself more and more involved through his own actions in the collective activity and organization.

In liberal society the connections between different goals as they supplement each other in society can only be followed with difficulty by the individual as he sets about his daily business. The individual, caged in by his own private motives—the search for profit, and so on, sees nothing more in society than many other individuals similar to himself acting individually one against the other. How these individual acts are socially integrated is quite outside his range of vision. In the liberal social order, the integration of the social-economic structure takes place, so to speak, behind the backs of the participants. The individual remains blind to the larger society which is coming into being, and to the consequences of his own actions, since he can see merely his own field of enterprise and thinks only of his own activities. One can, it is true, think out an elaborate scheme of " pre-established harmony " by which these conflicting actions, contrary to appearances, form a self-equilibrating cycle of events.[1]

It is given only to the philosopher, or later to the social scientist, to complete these missing links in the chain binding the individual to society ; and then only hypothetically ; he cannot actually trace out all their effects in everyday life. It is a different matter in a society which is becoming more and more closely organized. If I act in this more organized society, the consequences of my actions are more clearly visible since they do not immediately run off into an overwhelmingly vast network of competition as in liberalism, but run along the well-worn tracks of a fully co-ordinated division of functions. It is true that the final step is not immediately visible from the first one, but our actions lead us with much less ambiguity into the network of integrated activities in society. In such a society the individual merchants and producers and all the other socially dependent human beings are forced, as a result of the increasing interdependence, to take political and psychological probabilities into account in deciding how they will act. The individuals in leading positions who, to some extent, act independently—and in a crisis even those dependent individuals whose security is threatened—are given a sharper impetus towards a point of view which takes into account not merely their own immediate interests but also the ultimate effects of their activities on society itself. In this way actions which seem to be effective in the short run can be seen to defeat their own ends when viewed with a longer perspective. The individual who achieves this point of view is thus enabled to see his place within the larger historical situation, and this in turn in its place in the field of forces at work in the total social process. In this way he can at least perceive the connection between his own actions and the collective actions, between his own horizon and the collective horizon (understanding by the latter, the integration of all of the social relationships which have

---

[1] Such an approach is found in English intellectual history from Mandeville to Adam Smith.

become visible at a given stage of historical development).[1]
The individual discovers, or at least has the chance of
discovering in his own conduct, those aspects of dependence
on the larger context which in the liberal order were so
hidden [2] that it was difficult to see even the contradictions
prevailing in the contemporary social system.

Thus the planning approach outruns the immediate
actions of the individual even more than in liberal society
where separate individual ends were pursued. The tension
between individual actions and thinking becomes greater
than ever before. But at the same time, the difference
between the individual and the collective radius of action
diminishes in as much as it now becomes possible for the
single individual, realizing the implications of his actions,
to integrate them into the collective activities. But this
only becomes possible if a new type of self-observation
corresponding to the level of planning is developed. This
new attitude consists in the fact that in the process described
above, the individual is able to perceive not only all the

[1] It would lead us too far here to follow up the really important problem
of how this collective horizon is in fact integrated in various societies.
In certain periods, the integration really consists only in an exchange of
social experiences. The craftsman and the industrial worker, the peasant
and the town dweller exchange their impressions of the different ways
in which the world presents itself to them. In the same way, scientists
at this stage confine themselves to the exchanges of achievements between
different specialists. This kind of synthesis, however, is for the most part
only mechanical and it is really the task of the intellectual with the help
of constructive imagination to evolve a sort of picture or idea of the world
from these partial segments. Whether such a form of systematic integration is desired by society as a whole, which place is given either to philosophy
or to synthetic knowledge in general, depends ultimately on society's concrete
needs (cf. next note).

[2] It is not unimportant to ask here whether this possibility of tracing
the relevant links in the interdependence of events and the position of
the individual relative to this process is actually exploited and if not,
why not. We touched on this problem of social psychology when we
were dealing with the deadening effects of functional rationalization
(pp. 58 ff.). That is to say we are only concerned to ask whether the
objective nature of the social structure is such as to make it readily
apparent to the thinker within that society. We speak of subjective
chances when we seek to estimate the inhibitions which might prevent
the individual becoming aware of the objective factors which are, so to
speak, potential aids to his comprehension of the social system. Thus, if
one utilizes this distinction and compares the last results of our analysis
with that of page 61, there emerges the paradox that while the most
recent stage of social development offers a better chance of objective insight
into the social situation than the liberal social order, it also creates
mechanisms the functioning of which makes it extremely difficult psychologically for the individuals to realize these objective possibilities.

relevant facts and all the relevant ways of looking at things (ultimately he must perceive them if he is to avoid destruction), but he also becomes capable of seeing his special position in the social process, and of understanding that his thought is shaped by his position. New possibilities of planning now arise which hitherto were difficult to conceive, even theoretically. The individual not only attains a knowledge of himself but he can learn to understand the factors that determine his conduct, and can thus even attempt to regulate them. In a certain sense, his thought has become more spontaneous and absolute than it ever was before, since he now perceives the possibility of determining himself. On the other hand, he can never reach this stage by himself, but only through sharing a social tendency in that direction.

His understanding still remains a product of the historical process which arose independently of him. But through his understanding of this determination the individual for the first time raises himself above the historical process—which now, more than ever before, becomes subject to his own power. At this stage the determination of thought by situation is raised to the level of consciousness so that in so far as it is a source of error it may be corrected. Men seek to transcend the relative narrowness of their own horizon because life itself has become broader. They try to anticipate coming events in order to overcome their limitations by their own efforts. And they also correct their limited horizon because they desire to get rid of the discrepancy between deed and opinion or between theory and practice in the individual as well as in the group.

Behaviourism is a typical product of thought at that stage of mass society in which it is more important, from the practical point of view, to be able to calculate the average behaviour of the mass than to understand the private motives of individuals or to transform the whole personality. In this sense behaviourism belongs essentially to the first stage of planning, where in the sphere of individual conduct, one seeks to induce reactions which will be " correct " and appropriate to a thoroughly organized society, without, however, transforming the personality as a whole or even trying to adapt the entire personality to an entirely changed society in all respects.

Just as inventive thinking confines itself to placing individual objects and activities in the world as it is given, so behaviourism to a certain extent is related to it, in that it only seeks to co-ordinate certain spheres of reality and for this purpose assumes a resigned and agnostic attitude to all other spheres.[1]

The sphere of life which behaviourism seeks to calculate and control is that of pure action—external individual behaviour. Moreover, it is interested in this only to the extent that it must be accurately understood in order to deal with it in corresponding practical situations. For this purpose one must exclude in advance all those meanings which conduct derives from inner motives and which make it really difficult to understand. In the murder trial which is the centre of the Brothers Karamazof, Dostojewski tried to show how the same action can assume completely different meanings according to the different motives which underlie it. It is this multiplicity of meanings which can be grasped only by the " understanding " interpretation which behaviourism attempts to exclude. Its existence is denied so that it need not be dealt with. Behaviourism is interested in human beings only as part of the social machine, not as individuals but only as dependable links in a chain of action. The behaviour of a human being is simplified to such an extent that it becomes measurable in an elementary way. Natural behaviour, as it is formed by living adaptations, is observed so carefully and analysed into such abstract components and factors that it can be reconstructed by psycho-technics with an excellent chance of success.

Behaviouristic thought still moves within the framework

---

[1] Thus in so far as it is thorough-going and consistent, it denies the existence or at least the relevance of that dimension of the mind which an " understanding psychology " seeks to comprehend. Cf. Watson, J. B., *Psychology from the Standpoint of a Behaviorist* (Philadelphia, 1919) ; also *Behaviour : an Introduction to Comparative Psychology* (London and New York, 1925) ; Watson, J. B., *The Battle of Behaviorism*. An Exposition by J. B. Watson and an Exposure by W. MacDougall, 1928. For an interesting and by no means too dogmatic attempt to construct a sociology on behaviouristic foundations ; cf. Davis, Jerome, and Barnes, H. E., *An Introduction to Sociology* (Boston and New York, 1927), which also contains a detailed bibliography. Cf. also the articles of Read Bain and George Lundberg in *Trends in American Sociology* (New York, 1929), also in *Zeitschrift für Völkerpsychologie und Soziologie* (*Soziologus*) and *American Sociological Review*, and in *American Journal of Sociology*.

of inventive thinking in so far as it is abstract, i.e. as it deals only with partial, that is to say abstract spheres of social life, in harmonizing external behaviour. It still works piecemeal and is not really synthetic in its approach as it refuses to understand the environment and the individual as a whole. Nevertheless, it is already on the way to planning in so far as it tries to make it possible to calculate and manipulate an abstract cross-section of the course of events, i.e. the organized external conduct of all the units of a society. The intention is to co-ordinate only a few spheres of social life with one another and these only in so far as they represent the outward aspect of behaviour and the outward aspect of the organized environments. But there can be no doubt that planning is involved here since the attempt is made to grasp the *principia media* of a period from some strategic vantage point. As far as planning is concerned, behaviourism has limited itself from the start by renouncing the need for the real transformation of the individual and of society.

Once this essential feature of behaviourism has been perceived, its resemblance to Fascism is unmistakable.[1]

[1] A bibliographical guide to Fascism is to be found in Santangelo, G., and Brocale, C., *Guida Bibliographica del Fascismo*, Rome, " Liberia del Lettorio," 1928. It should be supplemented by the *Bibliographica Fascista*, issued by the same publisher. There is considerable information in L. Rosenstock-Franck, *L'économie corporative fasciste en théorie et en fait* (Paris, 1934) ; H. Finer, *Mussolini's Italy* (London, 1935), and G. Salvemini, *Under the Axe of Fascism* (New York, 1936).
On the bibliography of National-Socialistic publications, cf. Unger, E., *Das Schrifttum des Nationalsozialismus*, 1919–1934, " Forschungsberichte zur Wissenschaft des Nationalsozialismus," Heft 1, Berlin, 1934. Pollock, J. K., Henemann, H. J., *The Hitler Decrees*, Ann Arbor, 1934. There is also an Institute for the Study of Fascism in Paris. Also Schuman, F. L., *The Nazi Dictatorship* (New York, 2nd edition, 1936) ; and Robert A. Brady, *The Spirit and Structure of German Fascism* (New York and London, 1937) ; Rauschning, H., *Die Revolution des Nihilismus*, Zürich, 1938. Engl. transl. as *Germany's Revolution of Destruction*, London, 1939.
Concerning the literature about the Soviet dictatorship, cf. Mehnert, Klaus, *Die Sowjet-Union*, 1917–1932 (Berlin, 1933). Also, more recently, the extensive work of Sidney and Beatrice Webb, *Soviet Communism* (New York and London, 1936), 2 vols. *Dictatorships : A Sociological Study*, by Hermann Kantorovicz, with an excellent bibliography by Alexander Elkin (*Politica*, i, 4, August, 1935), and Cambridge, 1935, should also be consulted.
Concerning the methods used by the various political systems to educate their citizens to civic loyalty, cf. the series edited by Merriam, C. E., *Studies in the Making of Citizens*, University of Chicago Press. The introductory volume is written by Merriam himself and is called *The Making of Citizens : A Comparative Study of Methods of Civic Training*

It is not as though behaviourism itself is fascist, but rather that fascism in the political sphere is to a large extent behaviouristic. Fascism plans and changes the political world at the level of behaviourism. This is demonstrated by the type of propaganda in the various countries and the way in which it is used neither to change nor to enlighten the populace, but rather to subordinate it and make it loyal. Fascism creates an apparatus of social coercion which integrates every possible kind of behaviour or at least brings it into an external harmony by force. Fascism in its ideology eulogizes the instinctive forces in man, but in fact it does not penetrate to the depth of human personality or do justice to its genuine complexity. It has, however, an abstract ordering principle which changes man through the maximum combination of external coercion and suggestion with no wider aim than the regulation of outward behaviour and the integration of the sentiments. In its external co-ordination it reaches the highest stage of functional rationalization without even beginning to approximate to any sort of substantial rationalization. Just as the typical fascist leader combines sharp calculation with an irrational unsublimated energy, so in this particular type of society a formal optimum of order and an amorphous irrational residue, with a constant tendency to anarchy, exist side by side.

What we have tried to describe in our analysis is expressed very vividly in the following programmatic speech of an outstanding fascist leader, in outlining his programme : " The temperaments, characters, and capacities of individuals are so varied, that it is impossible to fuse a large mass completely into a unity. Nor is it, moreover, the task of the political leader to try to cultivate this unity by education. Every such attempt is doomed to failure. Human nature is a given fact which cannot be changed in individual details, but can only be transformed by centuries of evolution. In general, however, changes in fundamental racial characteristics are prerequisites for these other

(Chicago, 1931. The most important single volumes in the series are Schneider, H. W., and Clough, S. B., *Making Fascists* (Chicago, 1929), and Kosok, Paul, *Modern Germany : A Study of Conflicting Loyalties* (Chicago, 1933). (The latter work does not deal with the period of the National Socialist dominance.) All the volumes contain bibliographies.

changes. If a political leader sought to attain his ends in this way, he would have to think and decide in terms of eternity instead of years and even decades. He can count on bringing to his movement, not ideal 'universal human beings', but men of widely different talents who can form a harmonious pattern only by adapting themselves to one another in a group. If a political leader recoils from such a realization, and searches only for persons who are the very mirror of his ideal, not only will his plans be wrecked, but organization will soon be merged in chaos."

If we want to change the human personality as a whole and not just its external behaviour, we must penetrate beyond the external behaviour to that realm of consciousness in which the different meanings of external acts can only be comprehended by sympathetic understanding. Thus we must try to pass from the accessible surface-indices to the more deep-lying background of psychological phenomena. It is not without symptomatic significance that psycho-analysis of the Freudian, Adlerian, and other types emerged and became popular at a time in which another group of psychologists (the behaviourists) was obstinately opposing the " understanding " method.

Psycho-analysis [1] in its general approach at least, is one of these types of psychological investigation which do not regard man as he is found at any given time as immutable. The discovery of the unconscious makes it possible to penetrate into those hidden mechanisms through which psychological adjustment on the deeper levels of the self can be brought about. Whereas behaviourism is concerned primarily with external behaviour and shuns the type of " understanding " observation which is necessary for dealing with the deeper levels of mental life, the Freudian theory

---

[1] As a bibliographical introduction to the literature of psycho-analysis, cf. Rickman, John, *Index Psychoanalyticus*, 1893–1926. International Psycho-analytical Library, volume 14, London, 1928. Cf. in addition to Freud's *Gesammelte Schriften* the psycho-analytical periodicals, *Internationale Zeitschrift für Psychoanalyse*, *Imago*, *Zeitschrift für psycho-analytische Pädagogik*, *Psycho-analytische Bewegung*, and the other publications of the Internationaler. Verlag für Psychoanalyse.

Concerning individual psychology, cf. above all the writings of Alfred Adler and Erwin Wexberg, and the *Internationale Zeitschrift für Individual-psychologie*.

For a bibliography orientation in the problem of personality, cf. Roback, A. A., *A Bibliography of Character and Personality*, Cambridge, Mass., 1927

and similar points of view turn their attention to injuries, the after-effects of which influence the whole psychological organization of the individual. Traumas, which have arisen from external causes, are included here as well as the inferiority feelings which develop in the course of the competition which has been so important in our own society. In the last analysis—without deciding whether it can succeed or not—psycho-analysis seeks to transform the whole man.[1] It is a question here of formulating these ultimate abstract principles which govern psychological life in general, as well as those psychological *principia media* which comply only to a typical human being of a particular historical period and in a particular society. Abstract principles are attained when the most complicated psychological changes are reduced to a few fundamental laws of the theory of drives, such as, for example, the pleasure principle, the reality principle, the death instinct, and so on, and moreover, when the attempt is made to interpret the whole mechanism in terms of fundamental processes, such as repression, sublimation, projection, etc. The existence of *principia media* which are valid only for certain epochs, has recently been demonstrated in investigations which show that in a patriarchial society emotions appear in quite a different form from those in a matriarchal society.[2] In this connection,

---

[1] This tendency is best expressed in V. von Weizsäcker's *Soziale Krankheit und soziale Gesundung* (Berlin, 1930). " The medical attitude which alone is suited to cure a neurosis and not just to isolate it (and thereby maintain it) we will call the comprehensive one. It consists in the fact that the physician by collaborating with the patient from the very beginning, goes with him, so to speak, into the field in which the neurosis is at work, as if he himself were in the same position, and, as regards knowledge and the formation of judgment, places himself on the same level. . . ." " It will no longer be permissible to confuse the health of a person with the anatomical and physiological normality of individual organs and functions. This truly hypochondriac approach binds the minor specialist on the one hand to a once great idea, and on the other to the patient who wishes at any price to have his symptoms treated in order not to have to undergo the deeper change in his human existence, which is indicated by the symptom."

[2] Cf. Malinowski, B., *Sex and Repression in Savage Society* (London, 1937), p. 178. Malinowski employs in addition to the Freudian theories (which he applies only with qualifications) the fundamental psychological principles laid down by Shand, A. F., in his *The Foundations of Character* (London, 1930). Cf. among anthropological and ethnological studies on the same theme, Mead, M., *Coming of Age in Samoa* (New York, 1928). The authoress of the latter work shows from strikingly vivid observations of the life of young girls in a so-called " primitive " tribe

our endeavour to describe the historical variations of mental life is presented with an entirely new task. Namely to investigate every society to see what sort of repressions and taboos it brings about in the individual in its efforts to maintain its authority and order. Every social order and the various special social situations which make it up breed various neuroses, which they in part repress and in part foster.

The will to transform and to plan is manifested in the daring which is involved in the attempt to regulate even those phases of psychological life which hitherto were most obscure and which worked like natural forces, i.e. the adaptation and the malformations of the unconscious. In short even the inhibitory and liberating mechanisms of the individual are to be recognized, analysed, and turned in the best possible direction. Dreams are to be studied and those men and women whose spiritual growth has been warped in a social situation are to be completely transformed. Originally the psycho-analytical approach was purely individualistic, it was able to perceive only the individual with his abstract injuries in some abstract society. The sociological approach was followed to the extent that only early childhood experience was dealt with in terms of a few standard situations, without taking into account the social distinctions between the various families (e.g. the proletarian family, bourgeois family, and so on). The individual was to be transformed within his own framework through a process of inner enlightenment and through the cathartic effects of a wisely guided analysis. What was lacking, however, for thoroughgoing planning, was the pragmatic insight which in its possibilities at least has been too little exploited by psycho-analysis, namely that psychological make-up and activity go together, and that a human being can be changed only when together with the revelation of his customary maladaptations and injuries, a new environment is created in which the adjusted and enlightened individual will be able to stay on the right track. Moreover, it lacks the

---

that the psychological crises which are typical of the stage of puberty in more advanced cultures do not exist there. The psychological conflicts of the stage of puberty seem then to be due not to the biological structure of the individual, but to the conflict laden atmosphere of present-day society.

insight to see that certain maladjustments cannot be put right without a change in society as a whole.

The place in which psycho-analysis originated, i.e. the consulting room of the physician, entered into the scheme of things in both a positive and negative way. Its concrete relationship with psychiatry gave it the chance to observe a large number of cases very carefully, but it allowed it to become only very vaguely aware of the social environment. It lacked the sociological insight into the social mechanism which is indispensable for complete planning. The person was to be reorganized as an individual although this reorganization penetrated to depths which had never been touched before. But the level of inventive thinking still persisted in as far as psycho-analysis sought to adjust or establish the individual object, the individual person, without really fitting it into its actual situation in life. The planned approach, however, is already manifesting itself in so far that the abstract processes of action, the correct and incorrect adaptations are analysed from the point of view of the whole spiritual economy of the individual. In this context the concept of economy of the libido is of greatest significance. Thus, the aspects that behaviourism completely neglected are here raised to the level of a central problem. But all that still appears to us in the first phases of psycho-analysis is a product of the approach characteristic of the liberal-individualistic epoch : the typical isolation of the individual when diagnosed, the obscuring of social interdependence, and the over simplification of the individual's relationship to his environment—all these are being overcome step by step and revised in a new process of sociological readjustment which is already visible. Owing to this more concrete and sociological point of view various important differences are discovered. Thus the family in general gives way to the family in a given social class at a given period in time. The observation of psychological crises, which are brought about by unemployment in various types of personality in various stages in their development, becomes a major interest of psychological research.[1] The special

---

[1] Serious works in this field are Lazarsfeld-Yahoda, T. M., and Zeisl, H., *Die Arbeitslosen von Marienthal : Ein soziographischer Versuch über die Wirkungen langdauernder Arbeitslosigkeit mit einem Anhang : Zur Geschichte der Soziographie* (Leipzig, 1933). *Men Without Work*, a report made to the Pilgrim Trust, Cambridge, 1938. For a bibliography, cf. the very

problem of the proletarian or bourgeois child arises out of the abstract problems of childhood as such.[1]

The process of the formation of symbols is studied not only in the life of the single individual but in the various classes. The classes are themselves not treated without distinctions, but rather as historically and socially stratified, and one traces the way in which the general mechanism produces particular mechanisms in various historical social situations in varying degrees of detail.[2]

With this we enter upon the level of planning. The understanding of those key-points which connect the psychological with the social mechanisms, the comprehension of the *principia media* which govern psychological and social

valuable bibliographical survey of Eisenberg, Philip, and Lazarsfeld, Paul F., " The Psychological Effects of Unemployment," *Psychological Bulletin*, vol. 35, No. 6, June, 1938, pp. 358–390, also Williams, James Michel, *Human Aspects of Unemployment Relief* (Chapel Hill, North Carolina, 193) ; Bakke, J., *The Unemployed Man* (London, 1933) ; Sutherland, E. H., and Locke, H. J., *The Homeless Man* (Philadelphia, 1936) ; Kardiner, Abram, " The Rôle of Economic Security in the Adaptation of the Individual," *The Family*, October, 1936, pp. 187–197 ; and " Security and Cultural Restraints ", ibid., October, 1937, pp. 183–196. Cf. also Lasswell, H. D., " What Psychiatrists and Political Scientists Can Learn from One Another," *Psychiatry : Journal of the Biology and Pathology of Interpersonal Relations*, vol. i, No. 1, pp. 33–9, 1938 ; and " Psychoanalyse und Sozialanalyse ", *Imago*, vol. 19, pp. 377–383, 1933 ; also Lewin, Kurt, *Dynamic Theory of Personality* (New York–London, 1935) ; Brown, J. F., *Psychology and the Social Order* (New York, 1936) ; and Moreno, J. L., *Who Shall Survive* (Washington, D.C., 1934). Cf. also *Sociometry : A Journal of Interpersonal Relations*, 1937.

[1] Cf. for illustrative literature Aichhorn, A., *Verwahrloste Jugend* (Wien, 1931) (English translation as *Wayward Youth*, New York, 1936) ; Homburger, A., *Psychopathologie des Kindesalters* (Berlin, 1928) (with an extensive bibliography) ; Franzen-Hellersberg, L., *Die jugendliche Arbeiterin* (Tübingen, 1932) ; Thomas, W. I., *The Unadjusted Girl* (Criminal Science Monograph No. 4) (Boston, 1931) ; Reuter, E. B., Mead, Margaret, and Foster, R. G., et al., " Sociological Research in Adolescence," *American Journal of Sociology*, xlii, 1 (July, 1936), pp. 81–94.

[2] We will mention here only a few examples of this approach : Fromm, Erich, *Die Entwicklung des Christusdogmas* (Wien, 1931), and his essays in the *Zeitschrift für Sozialforschung*. Reich, W., *Massenpsychologie des Faschismus* (Copenhagen, 1933) ; Dollard, John, *Criteria for the Life History* (New Haven, 1935) ; Horney, Karen, *The Neurotic Personality in Our Time* (New York, 1937), and " Culture and Neurosis ", by the same author in *American Sociological Review*, i, 2 April, 1936) ; Dollard, John, *Caste and Class in a Southern Town* (New Haven, 1937) ; Erich Fromm's contribution to the collective work *Autorität und Familie*, edited by Max Horkheimer (Paris, 1936), is also a step in this direction. An important work in this field has been done by Harold D. Lasswell, cf. *World Politics and Personal Insecurity* (New York, 1936), also the bibliography of his publications in *Psychiatry*, vol. i, No. 1, 1938. Cf. also in the Bibliography (III, 1, d and f) at the end of this book.

types in a given time and place, move more and more into the foreground. We have now reached a stage where we can imagine how to plan the best possible human types by deliberately reorganizing the various groups of social factors. We can go on to alter those inhibitions which are a legacy of past societies and are no longer necessary. This was already the meaning of the Enlightenment which in its attempt to eliminate superstition and those forms of asceticism which became meaningless fore-shadowed, at least, a new social economy in the control of impulses and a new self-conscious guidance of the restraints which are still necessary. Even though much still remains obscure and very many assertions problematic, nevertheless this approach has reached such a point that we can, logically at least, foresee our goal, which is the planned guidance of people's lives on a sociological basis, and with the aid of psychology. In this way we are keeping in the foreground both the highest good of society and the peace of mind of the individual. The promising beginnings of psycho-analysis, together with the subtler forms of pragmatism like that of Dewey [1] give a good start and may well lead to promising consequences, the nature of which we are not yet able to foresee.

It is not our task here to decide just whether in the attempts of our time to bring about a transformation of mankind we are striving for the impossible, but it cannot be doubted that the sociological problem of social change will never be solved without an exact analysis of the problems with which we have been dealing here. There is, no doubt, a line beyond which innate hereditary traits and certain principles of social organization hold sway. This line cannot be known in advance, but will reveal itself only through experiments. The apparent limits to the transformability of men are not themes for abstract philosophical discussions but for realistic approach, education, and social research.   Philosophical

---

[1] Dewey, John, *Democracy and Education* (New York, 1916). Cf. also Russell, Bertrand, *Education and the Social Order*, London, 1932, and his address *Education for Democracy*, London, 1937.

For a stimulating collection of essays on recent problems in education, together with further bibliographical references, cf. Calverton, V. F., and Schmalhausen, S. D. (editors), *The New Generation* (London, 1930). Cf. also Cohen, J., Travers, R. M. W. (ed.), *Educating for Democracy*, London, 1939 ; Laborde, E. D., *Problems in Modern Education*, Cambridge, 1939.

discussions are most likely to result in ontological and anthropological dogmas about the nature of man which spring from the analysis of situations which are already passing away, and which no longer give valid grounds for philosophical generalizations. Such discussions serve only to spare us the trouble of transcending a form of human life which is moulded by our particular society In fact, philosophy often runs the risk, as a late-comer in the scientific field, of basing its generalizations on empirical data and principles of discovery which empiricism itself is in process of repudiating. Apart from the cloistered systems of philosophy which merely sum up the results of past ages, there has always been another type, that of the pioneer who produced principles which at the next stage of social development were to become important tools of research, and set up the frame of reference into which specialists were later to insert the details. Seeking to follow this example, it seems to be our task to pick out the factors unconsciously at work in the empirical researches now under way, i.e. to demonstrate that in the scattered and apparently isolated philosophical, psychological, and educational tendencies of recent years, the will to plan is everywhere at work, though in most cases, it has not yet become conscious. To-day it is not enough that individual scattered researches which are fundamentally related, should go on without knowing of each other's existence. Planning means fitting the isolated fact into place, so that the individual research workers realize the often latent connections between their discoveries.

Is mass transformation of external behaviour the right way to begin, or must we start with the complete transformation of the individual ? In answering this question, it must be remembered that planning is not *establishment*, where the major materials of construction are found in a relatively finished state and have only to be assembled. Planning is strategy, and strategy is a process in which an action requires only the means to carry it out during the action itself. In such a context, actions are to be directed primarily not to attaining the best possible qualities or to following the more favourable path, but towards means which are most likely to lead from the *status quo* to the desired goal and which will gradually transform the person who uses them. A psychological and sociological method of influencing and forming human beings which is in itself the best, may be quite unsuitable from the point of view of strategy. Here, too, it would be best to think in terms of open alternatives, and constantly weigh the pros and cons of each way of doing things.

If, in planning, we keep the strategic point of view in the foreground, it is possible that in order to transcend the given social situation, we may have to begin by using the behaviouristic technique. One begins with the technique which will transform human beings from their external behaviour inwards and which will compress the processes which can be organized from the outside into a properly working interdependent whole. Only when a certain order has been brought about in this manner will we be able to assuage the uneasiness of those who feel that this method neglects the " whole person " and in the last analysis deforms it. This kind of approach is favoured by the fact that man has hitherto been changed from the outside through uncontrolled processes of growth and selection, and real assimilation and inner adaptation to a situation have followed a long way behind. The normal way has been for man to find himself a new situation first, to adapt himself to it through a series of more or less unconscious acts and then, later, to make those inner psychological changes which bring the individual into harmony with the situation. To take a simple example : when a man, who has been a slave to his work, retires towards the end of his life, and suddenly finds a tremendous amount of unused energy available, he will at first from sheer imitation, spend his spare time in the conventional ways. Only quite gradually after severe crises will the inner workings of his mind be transformed. He will then, according to his character, and the situation, cultivate his capacities for play, for sublimation, for contemplation, and so on. Classes [1] which have recently risen in the social scale remould themselves in the same ways, and turn their energies from work and competition to culture and sublimation only after their outward circumstances have been changed.

The natural processes of education work from the outside inwardly, and if it often seems in history as if an intellectual revolution preceded the " real movement " as for instance, in the Enlightenment with its new kinds of sentiments and

---

[1] We shall have to say more on this topic later.   Cf. pp. 316 ff.

ideas, one overlooks the fact that even before these " ideas " emerged the transformation had already begun to take place in a great many real situations, which to-day are hidden from us. The Enlightenment as an all-embracing intellectual trend with its obvious social consequences could be integrated into a movement only after social changes penetrating from the outside inward had already prepared the minds of individuals in society to accept certain things. A further fact, which testifies to the way in which the technique of transformation begins with the outside and moves inward, is our experience with delinquent adolescents. In the light of results in this sphere, it can be said that it is, for example, almost impossible to change an individual member of a well organized criminal gang by taking him out of the group and trying to improve him by himself. The whole group must be given a new direction, starting with its leader. The individual will then move with the general current.[1]

The second strategic method of social transformation would be to begin with the inward transformation of the individual. By far the greatest difficulty is that this method can obviously only be applied to a very few, to minorities, inasmuch as neither the political, nor the institutional, nor the economic possibility for a large-scale change in educational methods exists at the present moment. This remains the special problem of our experimental schools, which carry out their experiments on a small minority. Such experiments—even were they to fail—would still be a heroic undertaking, which is reason enough for briefly explaining the sociological meaning of their method.

The transformation of society through the transformation of the personality of each individual, can at first create only pioneer types. Even if these methods succeed completely, they produce only a few more perfect human types, and there is always the danger that when these are placed in the middle of practical life, which is quite differently organized from their own, they may break down. These apprentices will always suffer from the fact that their inner transformation has been brought about by an education which is out of step with the transformation of society. Here the law that human nature must be transformed

[1] Thrasher, F. M., *The Gang. A Study of 1,313 Gangs in Chicago*, new edition (Chicago, 1937).

through the group, as we saw in our example of the gangs of delinquent children, does not hold to the same extent. Only the man who is still not far removed from primordial horde solidarity can be transformed through the group alone. Those individuals who come from social groups which are already individualized can be remoulded individually, even if not entirely, at any rate, to a much greater degree than delinquent children with a poor background. This is especially true when they are placed in artificially isolated surroundings and educated under such special conditions such as boarding schools, and so on.

Everyone who does not underrate the significance of pioneers in history must admit that this inward transformation of the individual, which sets him in advance of his time, is more or less justified.[1] And it should not be overlooked that in the older, more stable and hierarchic societies, the special education of the élite was much less dangerous for the individual than it is to-day, when it is unlikely that these few who have been trained for a special pioneer work will be able to live and maintain themselves in their own class with its own individual atmosphere.

An unequal, more or less caste-like, static society can approve the cultivation and sublimation of the personalities of its ruling classes as advance guards. In these circumstances it is probable that these leading groups will have to prove their worth only within the special atmosphere of the ruling classes. On the other hand, the new method of training the élite merely by education and from the inside outward is faced with the paradoxical task, even where it is entirely successful, of developing pioneers who will remain completely balanced in spite of the external structure and the average conditions of the existing society. Something is then expected of these élites which a static society did not require, namely that they maintain their personality and stability of character even in an uncertain environment and in completely unpredictable situations. The only solution here is to find a way to make these pioneers so supple, adaptable and decisive that in spite of the broad outlook their education has given them, and a personality which is in advance of their time, they will continue to exist in the

[1] Cf. pp. 75, 86–106, where the inevitability of advance guards was made evident. Cf. also in the Bibliography, IV, 4, and III, 1, d.

ups and downs of a revolutionary world. It will be necessary, therefore, to combine steadiness of purpose and a farsighted policy with an unusual capacity for adaptation and action.

A continuity between the older and newer élites seems to be desirable here. This continuity is not only important for the older élites but also for the newly developing society. Never has mankind been able to maintain a level of culture which it had once attained without establishing some sort of continuity with the bearers of the older cultural heritage and their techniques of rationalization and sublimation. Just as a revolution, however radical, should not destroy the machinery of production, if there is not to be a relapse into backward standards of living, so the bearers of the accumulated cultural heritage cannot be cast aside if one wants to avoid a cultural catastrophe. Here, too, there must be methods of planning, which by amalgamating older and newer groups of leaders, can combine the valuable heritage of the older élites and the new outlook of the younger ones in the best possible way. The function and the rôle of the élites, their continuity and the manner in which they are integrated into society, constantly reappear from whatever angle we regard the problem. The historical and sociological investigation of the functions of élites is vitally important if the older as well as the younger groups of élite are to understand their work in society.

To summarize : The danger of the external method of transformation consists in the fact that it only outwardly changes society without really transforming man.

As a result formal order and functional rationality exist side by side with an inner disorganization and lack of direction which constantly threaten to undermine important social institutions. The danger of the internal method consists of the fact that the few who, because of this kind of education, have a certain spiritual richness and personal culture, break without resistance as soon as the special surroundings in which they move are destroyed by a sudden social upheaval. Here we can be helped only by interdependent action and thought which make use of both the internal and the external approaches in the sense that they combine at every step the transformation of society with the transformation of individual personality. Moreover, as with most theoretical paradoxes, the problem is insoluble on the level of abstract thinking. The exaggerated consistency of one-sided logical systems of thought tears out of their context things which if reconciled in action, can be gradually united into a more and more appropriate pattern of conduct. The solution of these theoretical paradoxes is always possible in practice if the carefully thought out alternatives are used not as final formulæ but as signposts to indicate the possible trends of events.

We have now seen from many angles that planned thinking rests primarily on the new capacity for perceiving interdependent connections in a social structure. By *interdependence*, we mean that the effects of a particular element are first traced out in one of the abstract spheres (such as economics, psychology, and so on), and that later the interaction of the spheres itself becomes a problem. This kind of thinking has its difficulties like every other. One of the greatest difficulties is the question of the division of labour and equally difficult is the method of control.

Abstract thinking, which tries to deal with single isolated objects, has created a division of labour for itself which works very well. We must abide by this division of labour as we shall constantly have to solve individual problems which must be treated up to a point as if the question of interdependence were irrelevant. There are technical questions concerning the structure of an association, the organization of a school, the constitution of a state, and so on, which can be handled largely according to abstract rules which are universally valid, and not limited to a given social milieu.

On the other hand, we must always return to the point at which the general rules must be modified to fit the concrete situation. *Principia media* limited to the situation will have to be sought out again and again. The uniqueness of a given form of government cannot be explained only by an abstract functional principle. The way in which authority is organized, the kind of economic system in force and the outstanding characteristics of the citizen—all these will affect the concrete working of the constitution.

The old division of labour in the sciences is adequate as long as individual objects, processes and institutions are to be accurately studied. It is, however, completely inadequate if one takes as one's central problem the concrete relations of the individual object with its particular environment. When the problem appears in this form, the integration of once separate spheres becomes an issue. The obstacle to the realization of the necessity for such a new type of integration is mainly to be found in a philosophy and methodology which belongs to an earlier stage of history. As often happens in history, an earlier outlook or an earlier type of investigation builds up a philosophy which is intended to justify its own inability to solve the new problems which are emerging. In this case, for instance, it is maintained that it is not the task of science to unite the fragments which have been taken from their context. Or else it is contended that the nature of reality itself is such that it does not allow the separate cross sections to be recombined in thought, or the individual form of society to be reconstructed.

It is already sufficiently obvious to us that as far as the concrete, historical, individual societies and their *principia media* are concerned, scientific agnosticism necessarily belongs to the stage of knowledge which has not yet reached the level of planning, and where thought in every sphere still works within the framework of the invention of isolated single objects. The most essential aim of this book is to show that the claims to absoluteness of this type of thinking have been invalidated by the tasks set by the social process and that the transition to *interdependent thinking* has become a necessity.

It is now clear that if the vast field of knowledge could not be mastered by a single investigator under the previous division of scientific labour, this new type of thinking which strikes out in all directions has even less chance of being achieved by an individual thinker without the help of a far-reaching division of labour. The result is that division of labour and specialization become even more necessary than before. But the lines along which the division of labour takes place must be completely different from what they have been in the past. The fields and subjects which the old as well as the new division of labour has to take into account must be arranged.according to a new principle. This new principle, however, can only consist in bringing together everything which is required to explain a concrete situation, whether the themes selected fall within one or several fields of the already existing special sciences. The division of labour will be determined by *problem-units* which will be concrete analyses of situation and structure.

Abstract inventive thinking, having failed to reproduce the total structure, tried to provide a substitute to gratify man's craving for a total picture, by an exaggerated systematization of its principles and facts. Instead of taking as its problem the whole network of interdependent social events, it has tried to construct a formal *system of sociology* which undoubtedly has a certain educational value.

Now it is not to be denied that all abstract thinking reaches its highest level in a system of thought which orders all its contents from a few axiomatic principles, until the concrete historical types are reached, according to a single criterion. A system is, of course, a praiseworthy accomplishment within certain limits. But this tendency towards formal systematization can be harmful if it diverts research workers and theorists from *interdependent thinking*. Interdependent thinking is most useful when it works out as fully as possible all the relevant factors—their relevance being determined by the problem to be solved. It is less useful when it limits itself to applying a few formal principles which are imposed on the subject matter from the outside. The bias towards classification in the type of textbooks used in American education and the overwhelming tendency to systematize according to the pattern of philosophical systems, so marked in German thought, can sometimes be an obstacle to seeing the object itself. This, for instance, happens when one believes that the formally ordered facts in themselves comprehend the whole of reality. System and structure are two entirely different things. A system is an intellectual, self-contained ordering principle ; structure is the organizing principle of social reality itself. It can never be directly observed because it is always more inclusive than any partial social situation. It is to be approached only when different empirical trends and results are combined. Thus theoretical considerations are here inevitable, although they must be so undogmatic and flexible that they are capable of adjusting themselves to all the deviations and ramifications of events, in order that the real structure of society as a whole may be extracted from them.

The analysis of concrete situations will therefore have to begin at first by stressing those facts and interconnections of facts which are structurally relevant. This choice of relevant facts can be achieved only by means of the sociological translation mentioned at the beginning of the book.[1] It presupposes a special training in observation and an intellectual tradition accustomed to theoretical analysis. Certain types of events have a special significance because they reflect the transformation of the older *principia media* into new ones. These are the facts which must be sought out in any empirical investigation. It is, therefore, quite wrong in the name of a falsely conceived empiricism to collect all facts indiscriminately as though one were as good as the next. Facts are only of equal value for someone who is more or less indifferent to the real course of events and who does not have to take action, so that the major trends in events seem unimportant. Human knowledge, however, even in its most isolated spheres, is somehow linked up with the social process, and it is fatal to this sort of knowledge if an unordered empiricism with its senseless collection of facts is allowed to produce a cultivated blindness to the real nature of the society in which we live. As contrasted with this method, the right way of studying society is first to grasp those significant facts, which so to speak, represent the key positions in the social process. Once these are grasped, they will almost spontaneously force the investigator to use synthetic methods. Important as it is to stress the uselessness of an indiscriminate empiricism from the point of view of social conduct, it is also dangerous to exaggerate the importance of activism in human thought to the point of a dogmatic denial of the value of a searching questioning method. The greatest danger is a certain lack of openness of mind which is apt to treat statements about the *principia media* as axioms, instead of flexible hypotheses, always ready to be checked by the smallest contradictory fact.

The findings in the field of the *principia media* cannot be judged by the same standards as the inductive confirmation of general laws. The sociologist devoted to their study must use the results of the special sciences in analysing the situation as a whole, but it is no part of his work to obtain the specialized results themselves. It is true that the synthetic method is largely based on the facts that the

[1] Cf. page 26.

special sciences have collected by induction, but it frees them from their abstraction, and shows how they work in a concrete setting. Comparing, relating, synthesizing and referring theories to concrete facts are the basic methods which have to be used here.

Sociology in coping with these tasks must take the risk that a certain amount of intuition will be involved. But it is an unfortunate habit to call everything which cannot be measured " intuitive " in a pejorative sense, just as though genuine perception were only possible through quantitative measurements. There are so many different forms of intuition that they really cannot all be included under one heading. The intuition of a poet who conceives of an object in his fancy so that it eventually becomes only an exaggerated or idealized picture is on quite a different level from the intuition of an empiricist in the deeper sense of the word. Although admittedly not measurable, the imagination of the genuine empiricist is nevertheless so well directed towards the object as it really is, that in a certain sense it achieves a new form of exactness, *sui generis*, so that to use the same word " intuition " here that one uses for the fancy of a poet, only serves to obscure the real nature of this type of perception. In this sense, there is only imagination in the thought processes of the genuine empiricist in so far as he has to use his faculty of calling up things which are not immediately present, or reconstructing aspects of the object and its interrelations with others which are not directly perceptible. If conceived of in these terms the intuition of our empiricist is something which can be analysed and broken down into its elements and at all its stages converted into a method of control and demonstration. Constant comparison and corrective analysis, flexible, undogmatic hypotheses, which bear all the possibilities in mind, and the readiness to learn from fresh events guarantee that anything learned from intuition will be carefully tested by the facts. What is more, the intuitive approach is inevitable in inventive thinking, too, as long as we are dealing with a subject which has not yet been explored.

The characteristic unit of *planned thinking* is the " situation " and even more complex configurations.[1] At the level of planning it is more and more necessary to think in terms

[1] Cf. in the fifth part of the book, pp. 299 ff.

of situations as wholes. It is essential, not only in practical life but in science itself, to know how to fit together in one's mind the different series of events, and to see how the individual events, institutions, and attitudes of mind are determined by each other.

We need, of course, specialized knowledge, which is accurate in the sense that it can demonstrate regularities with inductive certainty in a purposely limited field. But this latter type of thought, which is extremely exact by its own standards, is extremely inexact when measured by other standards, because it has no horizon and tears the individual object out of the context in which it works. It is estranged from reality, because it destroys the unit of action of which the individual object is a part. For this very reason the analysis of a situation is the right approach to reality.

It is essential to thought on the level of discovery that it should be entirely " instinctive " and that it should produce its very best results without being aware of itself. It is of the nature of inventive thinking as it expresses itself in abstract and specialized terms that it loses sight of the fact that it is not an end in itself. In contrast with these *planned, interdependent thinking* is more rational and more reflective, and at the same time less abstract than inventive thinking in that it is constantly aware of its function and is constantly scrutinizing its methods to obtain better control over them. Planned thinking conceives of itself in terms of thought which is part and parcel of the total life process.

The danger zone of each of the modes of thought which we have dealt with so far is that it either runs ahead of or lags behind the kind of thought best fitted to a given stage of history. The possibility and the necessity of certain modes of thought at a certain period of history are defined primarily by the nature of the problems to be solved and by the level of reality to which it is necessary to penetrate. We noted the disastrous effects of this lag (pp. 10 ff., 162 f., and *passim*), where we showed how man tried to solve problems which arose from the interdependence of events by thinking only in watertight compartments and considering only individual, isolated goals. Here we could see very distinctly how greatly thought can lag behind the tasks set us in certain fields of social life. Our predicament consists in that we are approaching an age when it is necessary to regulate not only single institutions but also the manner in which they are interrelated.

Besides the danger of the lag, there is an equally great danger of " running ahead " which consists in the premature use of complicated ways of thinking and acting in situations where the simple ones still work quite well. In this way the original " interplay of forces " in which actions and habits of thoughts are unconsciously adapted to one another is broken up. This spontaneous behaviour, with its unconscious adaptations, cannot easily be surpassed by reason in certain spheres. On the contrary : every act of reflective thinking in these spheres blunts spontaneous capacities and is rarely more than a poor substitute for them. This does not mean that thought in itself is an evil, but rather that it only applies to certain fields of action. Invention only spoils things as long as discovery still goes on its way successfully, and it is probable that we first passed from discovery to invention only in situations where certain problems could no longer be mastered through the simpler modes of behaviour. On the other hand, where inventions are called for, every single act of inventive thinking takes the place of many generations of unconscious experiment.

Thus through historical changes, different fields of action gradually emerge, which in their turn evoke different forms of conduct and thought. Although these types of conduct and thought are related to each other as stages, this does not mean that the newer modes of conduct and thought must always replace the older ones, since it is possible for the most diverse historical levels to exist side by side. Even to-day there are many difficulties in our lives to which we adjust ourselves quite simply without knowing precisely how we do it. Even to-day every technological innovation is brought about on the level of inventive thinking and the social process of production would come to a standstill if, at those points where abstract thinking focused on immediate goals is required, we tried to suppress it in favour of the *planned approach*. The real danger in planned thinking is that instead of constantly experimenting, it tends to turn into a rigid system. " Dogmatism " on the planning level is nothing but a mistaken view of planning as being a purely theoretical scheming. In planning the highest level of experimental thought and conduct is reached. Dogmatic, systematic consistency is possible only where the rigidity of purely administrative methods has been attained—or where, as we have seen, on the level of inventive thinking, one tries to systematize the general principles collected from concrete facts. Doctrinaire, rigid consistency is useless when we enter into what is still unknown. Here even planned thinking, to become the appropriate instrument, has to take up the questioning, searching attitude.

If planned thinking is to remain a strategy, then it must have the courage and the leap into the dark required by the interdependent method of investigation. But it can never afford to be so authoritative as to exclude the element of inquiry which is an essential part of planning.

An illustration will make this clear. Anyone who to-day concerns himself with the transformation of man, will have to make use of the insight offered by psychology, and the ends and means which he has learned to appreciate through a study of society. He would, however, be a poor educator if he simply included the person he was to educate in a preconceived category. By contrast he would have the proper approach if he first submerged himself in the real difficulties and conflicts of his pupil, and then remembered to apply his theoretical knowledge. This means, as far as thinking is concerned, that we should think things out as far as possible, but that in action, we should continually be aware that planned thinking, for a long time to come, will have to work in as yet uncharted territory.

Principia media cannot be deduced and their transformations cannot be prophesied in advance. But in spite of this it is possible to press forward *intellectually*, in a spirit of inquiry. This reckoning with facts which are not yet fully understood from the intellectual point of view is by no means to be confused with the thoughtlessness which to-day calls itself irrationalism. In our present historical situation planned thinking counterbalances this growing and ever more destructive irrationality.

Contemporary man must learn to rise to the historical and social occasion, so that he will not be driven arbitrarily by the blind forces of his time. He must have the courage to face his present position intellectually with all the acuteness of scientific analysis. But at the same time he must set about it in such a way that he will transform not only himself but also his habits of thought.

The distinction between the accumulation of factual knowledge and the capacity for independent judgment, between the mere arrangement of details and their interpretation in terms of a situation, has long been clear in everyday life. This distinction is now becoming the concern of the theorists. A new type of scientific accuracy has taken the problem in hand. At the level of planned thinking, it is for the first time really scientifically possible to " grasp a situation ", to be " master of a situation ", as the common-sense expressions put it. In contrast to the abstractness of thought at the level of inventive thinking, planned thinking is at last concrete, because it starts with the context of things, and it is into concrete *situations* that one integrates the otherwise disconnected elements of knowledge.

Part V

PLANNING FOR FREEDOM

I

The Concept of Social Technique

1. *Our Ambivalent Attitude Toward Planning*

In the last section we saw that thought adapts itself to the needs of the social process and to the new and difficult problems which planning involves. It is hard for the spectator not to watch this transformation in our thinking with very mixed feelings. On the one hand he is filled with legitimate pride that human intelligence is ready to accept the new challenge and look farther and farther ahead. On the other he is haunted by a sense of oppression, wondering whether the whole undertaking is not a mere intellectual adventure, a reckless project of the modern spirit, which is determined to direct practically the entire course of social history by its own unaided skill. We all have this ambivalent attitude to planning to a greater or less degree, however good a face we may put on it, for we are all children of an age of transition, in which two kinds of motives are combined : the liberal distaste for meddling in human affairs, and the passion for experiment marking a social age, which wants to explore the new possibilities of human nature.

In many ways we are like Goethe's apprentice in the magic arts, who when his master left the house, conjured up the spirits of the underworld with his secret formula, and when they appeared cried out in terror : " The phantoms I have summoned will not go ! " We should all really prefer to leave the great decisions of our time to fate. At bottom we are afraid to take the responsibility. But in periods when the change goes very deep we have no power to decide whether we wish to accept responsibility or not, to plan or not to plan. In the light of sociological analysis the decision how to act or think does not rest entirely with the individual, neither does his attitude to destiny. How far he is conscious of himself and of his relation to history seems largely to depend on the problems which confront his age. In a society in which there are few technical means of controlling the forces of nature or averting catastrophe, the prevailing philosophy of life will regard almost every event as the work of a blind fate. It is possible that the lack of objective security may be compensated at this stage by two conflicting attitudes. Either society can teach the individual to face risk and danger by heroic principles and training, or it can foster his passive inclination to submit to a higher and inscrutable will. These reactions to objective insecurity will be replaced by others as soon as an improved social technique makes it possible to regulate certain spheres of life. In a relatively short time the sense of personal responsibility will increase, especially in departments that are now under control. Thus it is quite probable that the citizens of some well-planned future age will regard our anxiety over the problem of the intellectual mastery of our social destiny and our reluctance to create new forms of social organization as the last vestiges of an obsolete frame of mind.

Once we have realized that the popularity of determinism is bound to decrease in view of the number of social controls which will fall into our hands, it soon becomes obvious that nowadays we cannot take a fatalistic view of our social destiny or reject the thought of planning. After drafting a whole series of regulations and deliberately interfering with the moulding of human character, we cannot retreat when a crisis occurs and all our institutions are in conflict.

This increased interference results in a new approach to society and human affairs. Instead of the passive and contemplative outlook which takes people and things at their face value, we are developing an active and managing attitude. This new approach is reflected in a corresponding frame of mind : the functionalist type of thought which gradually supersedes the traditional methods of thinking. Functionalism made its first appearance in the field of the natural sciences, and could be described as the technical point of view.[1] It has only recently been transferred to the social sphere.

[1] For a history of the functionalist type of thought and its impact on philosophy, cf. Schuhl, Pierre-Maxime, *Machinisme et Philosophie* (Paris, Alcan, 1938), and my study on " The sociological history of the concept of organism " to be published in the *Economic History Review*.

In looking at an object the unspoken question which the functionalist has in mind is never : " What is that thing ? " or " What is the essence of it ? " but always : " How is it to be produced ? " He never regards anything as an end in itself ; it only reveals its true nature in its relationships with other entities.

The antagonism between these two types of thought tends to become really bitter, but instead of taking sides we ought to try to understand the specific contribution which each of them has to make to the development of the human mind.

The Romantic thinkers were the first to realize that a fundamental change was taking place in our outlook, and they were deeply alarmed by the new rise of the technical spirit. In their struggle against the abstract, mechanical kind of thought which was prevalent among the revolutionaries, they tried to preserve the dignity of the older, " organic " ways of thinking. They felt, however dimly, that once this technical approach was transferred from natural science to human affairs, it was bound to bring about profound changes in man himself. They had a presentiment that it makes all the difference whether we apply the functional pattern of thought to dead things or to our fellow creatures. In the first case, we are handling things which are alien to us, but in the second, the new and managing attitude tends to become inhuman, because it forces personal relationships into mechanical categories. In this sense the traditional mind has every right to rebel against this expansion of the technical spirit. The Romantics and their contemporary disciples were defending the unsophisticated immediateness of human experience, the desire to accept things simply as they presented themselves. People and things exist in their own right and not simply as functions of other entities. Their very existence is a fulfilment of their inner nature. The only proper way to treat them is to approach them directly and not by roundabout routes, as a function of something else. In the same way, spiritual experiences, whether moral or religious, once reverenced as transcendent realities, are in the modern approach deprived of their true nature when they are conceived as artefacts. The functional approach no longer regards ideas and moral standards as absolute values, but as products of the social process, which can if necessary be changed by scientific guidance combined with political practice.

This Romanticist criticism is undoubtedly a profound one, and will still preserve its value in the future. Its task is to remind us continually of the limitations of the functional approach and of the danger of it becoming universal. The functional approach is only one of the many the human mind has created, and the world would be the poorer if it were to replace our more genuine ways of approaching reality.

But the Romantic attack does injustice to the new ways of thinking if it fails to realize their necessity, or to see how deeply they are rooted in the social process. It is short-sighted if it does not understand that the stronger the impulse to change society, the more people are compelled to think of things which once they passively accepted, in terms of function. We must repeat that the application of scientific methods to human relationships is not purely arbitrary ; our society has been forced into planning by the heritage of regulations accumulated from the past. Once the preliminary steps have been taken, we cannot escape the task of acquiring sufficient technical skill to steer the social machine instead of letting ourselves be crushed beneath its wheels.

But the technical management of human affairs did not merely produce a new style of thought, it was also combined with a philosophy which declared technical inventions to be the dynamic factor in the making of history.

The significance of technics first became obvious in the field of economic production. According to Marx, it was these technical inventions which set the ball rolling. First they reacted on economic relationships proper, and later their influence translated itself into changes affecting the remaining social spheres as well. The human mind was not excluded from this transformation. The changing ideas of men are ultimately functions of the social process, which, as we have seen, has for its independent variable the changing economic technique.

Technical inventions, however, in the sphere of economic production provided merely the first tangible evidence of the new technical spirit. Since then the scope of technical inventions has enormously increased, and one cannot fail to see that improvements in the field of military technique, of social organization, education, and persuasion—to mention only a few instances—are equally significant, and that each of these changes tends to affect the whole texture of society.

The extension of the doctrine of technical supremacy which I have advocated in this book is in my opinion inevitable, even if it means abandoning the much simpler scheme which was current in the economic interpretation of history. Our impression of the dynamics of history naturally becomes far more complex than that of Marx when the wave of change no longer originates solely in a single sphere of the social process. There is no reason why technology should be significant only in the economic sphere and should be the sole factor decisively influencing the framework of events. We are all of us bound to acknowledge that the invention of bombs and aeroplanes, the use of tanks and gas, and the mechanization of the army have had the most far-reaching effects, and have been more than capable of upsetting the whole economic order and diverting its course into entirely different channels. The change in the technique of warfare altered the forms not merely of international war but of civil war as well. It made it possible to recast the class system and to produce a type of mind which was characteristic neither of the bourgeoisie nor of the proletariat. The changes in technique outside the economic sphere made way for the modern dictatorial system. These systems, by their influence on economic development, produced something entirely different from what one would have expected, had one been guided by a purely economic diagnosis. Thus as independent forces these different techniques deserve a separate investigation which will do justice to their inner nature, and classify them according to their impact on society.

2. Preliminary Classification of Social Technique

In analysing these techniques, we shall begin with an elementary distinction, which will later lead us on to a rather more essential classification. Originally, the words "technique", "technical invention", were only applied to tangible objects like machines. Inventions in this sense of the word were television, telephony, telegraphy, wireless, (means of mental communication); railways, motor cars, aeroplanes (means of locomotion); guns, bombs, tanks (means of defence and attack), the spade, the plough, the tractor (means of production), sanitary improvements for preserving health and so on. These things make it possible to build up a social order on a large scale and to maintain it efficiently. But beyond that there is another level of technical progress which at first we hesitate to describe as technical, because it is concerned, not with visible machinery, but with social relationships and with man himself.

And yet progress in the technique of organization is nothing but the application of technical conceptions to the forms of human co-operation. A human being, regarded as part of the social machine, is to a certain extent stabilized in his reactions by training and education, and all his newly acquired activities are co-ordinated according to a definite principle of efficiency within an organized framework. The technique of organization is at least as important as any of the techniques we have described. It is even more important, as none of these machines could be used in the public service without giving rise to a corresponding social organization.

But what we have to consider in discussing these social techniques is not social organization in the narrow sense such as taylorization and business administration. The rationalized forms of organization with their completely standardized behaviour are only the most blatant example of the changes which are taking place. Any deliberate re-building of human groups in terms of more elastic organizations represents another chapter in the development of social techniques. It demands a division of labour and a distribution of responsibilities (involving foresight, initiative, and a calculation of risks) among the varied individuals who compose the groups, in accordance with a definite plan. The innumerable problems created by the rapid growth of mass society have found a variety of solutions. But we have not yet succeeded in making adequate comparative studies on a large scale, so that these more elastic forms of organization current in politics, in public life, in the family, in social work, in art, and in the intellectual sphere can be contrasted and their under-lying principles worked out. The varying degrees of freedom and coercion to be found in them, their external relations with other units, the connections between competition and co-operation have never been developed. We must not forget that the family, for instance, has a foreign policy in dealing with other groups, just as much as the state in dealing with other states, and even clubs and sects are based on similar rules.

The more we come to realize that the swift dynamics of modern society produce not only community disorganization, but also a disintegration of the other social groups and institutions, the more important it is to study the technique of elastic organization on a large scale. Skilful reconstruction is essential, but it cannot be effected without a sounder knowledge of the principles of a healthy community life. In the past a disorganized community could readjust itself by trial and error or by the acceptance of traditional patterns. In an age in which unemployment and unplanned migration upset the balance of community life and whole suburbs and cities have to be built at a moment's notice, it is impossible to create a new order without understanding how to co-ordinate the forces of society.

But if we adopt some definite pattern of communal organization, we shall be able to discover criteria for determining the best ways of employing our leisure or of creating enthusiasm for our common ends. Only if we have a clear conception of the moral aims which a community can reasonably be expected to pursue and of the social conditions under which community spirit can develop, shall we be able to take the lead in planning these vital experiments. The time will come when the considerations involved in organizing a new community centre will be as obvious as those which enable a chairman to decide which topics can best be dealt with in a general assembly and which in special committees. In both cases we have to deal with the more elastic types of social technique.

Thinkers and scholars have been interested in the principles governing an elastic social organization from the time when they first began to discuss the merits of the different political and administrative systems which have flourished since the age of Aristotle, or to analyse the miracle of the English constitution and its practical possibilities. But the problem of discovering the best working system is not really confined to politics at all, it is a matter of general organization. Even in considering the autocratic and democratic alternatives with all their intermediate shades, we find that we are concerned not with the merely legal relations between the legislature and the executive, but with a problem of group organization in general which arises just as frequently in the family, the workshop, the school-room or the club. This becomes even more apparent when we examine the problems of economic democracy and discover that the principle of democratic organization is not confined to politics ; it very often occurs in economics as well, just because it is a general principle of group regulation and its essence can only be revealed by a general theory of organization or scientific guidance. The researches which deal with the transformation and moulding of human behaviour [1] represent another province of social technique. Although these investigations and experiments have so far mostly been confined to the laboratory, their real significance will only become apparent when they are studied in the social context in which they actually occur. The advantage of artificial experiment is that it is easier to isolate the different factors under such conditions and to work out the correlations between specific stimuli and their effects. The more we know about them the clearer and more skilful both our field-work studies and our historical investigations will be.

But for the sociologist these experiments are merely preliminary, for his principal aim is to discover how far social situations can be conceived of as composite collections of stimuli which condition behaviour in certain specific directions. The fact that every new form of organization, every change in human intercourse inevitably involves a partial or total transformation in human behaviour shows how inseparable these sciences must be. Only when they act in unison will it be possible to discover the full impact of social conditioning upon mankind.

The sociologist trained in psychology regards group integration and social organization as techniques for producing specific behaviour. With this hypothesis in mind he is able to show how certain individual reactions are produced by an authoritarian regime and others by a democratic one. One has only to remember how differently the average Englishman and the average Prussian behave.

[1] Cf. III, 1 and 4 in the Bibliography.

The former is more inclined to respond to a tentative statement, the latter to an absolute statement. In the same way professional activities, or at any rate the methods by which they are organized, have a marked effect upon the individual. To take a typical contrast, the professional attitude of the man who works in an industrial groove will differ from that of the writer or free-lance journalist. While the former standardizes his work and tries to divide his time up evenly, the latter works almost regardless of time, guided by more or less creative moods. The whole spiritual economy of the latter will differ from that of the former, for he will try to base his work to a far larger degree on the ebb and flow of inspiration. Although in all these matters constitution, habit, individual· differences, vestiges of childhood experiences play a considerable part, one must not under-estimate the psychological issues created by the systems of organization which prevail in a society. A man tends to become the counterpart of the specific group organizations in which he finds himself : they influence different sections of his life at different times and call out different patterns of response. Each pattern of response can best be understood from the standpoint of the particular form of group activity in which he was engaging at the time of the reaction.

We begin to realize ever more clearly that these techniques, which set their seal upon mankind, are not merely accidental, but form part of an entire social and cultural system. They can only be understood if we bear this fact in mind, and instead of being satisfied with a purely descriptive approach we must try to investigate their interaction and their functions.

These practices and agencies which have as their ultimate aim the moulding of human behaviour and of social relationships I shall describe in their entirety as social techniques. Without them and the mechanical inventions which accompany them the sweeping changes of our age would never have been possible.

Although it is to Marx's credit that he realized the dynamic significance of technique in the sphere of production, owing to the peculiar character of the age in which he lived he can be charged with a twofold oversight. First, as I have already pointed out, he failed to realize the

significance of technology in non-economic fields, and
secondly he did not see that just as economic technique
may become the centre of certain social changes which
permeate the whole social structure, so the remaining
techniques in their turn also tend to radiate influences which
have an equally far-reaching effect. Any new invention in
military technique, group organization, government, or
propaganda helps to change society.

But we can give reasons why he was bound to underrate
the significance of the political and military systems—as
opposed to the economic system—and to regard them
merely as the by-products of changes in economic technique,
and not as the direct consequence of changes in the technique
of war and force. The reason was that in the industrial
revolution economic technique was advancing so rapidly
that it dwarfed the significance of everything else. The new
economic society with its technical inventions and increased
division of labour overwhelmed first the feudal order and
then the organization of the absolute state. It looked for a
time as if economic technique would determine the tempo of
events and form the foundation of the new society. This was
because the new achievements in military and administrative
technique and the psychological methods of propaganda and
persuasion had not yet been perfected.   This distorted
perspective is also responsible for the error current in most
of the thought systems of the time ; that of confusing the
motives of *homo economicus* with those of real human beings.
The human counterpart of economic society has been
accepted as a true picture of mankind, thus promoting a
very one-sided concept of man.

The narrowness of this view and its restriction to a
particular period became apparent at the time of the Great
War and was even still more marked shortly afterwards,
when the economic organization of the nations became
completely subordinate to politics, and even trade had to
give way to military ends.   The significance of military
influence is not affected by the fact that in imperialistic
wars the two motives and the two forms of organization go
hand in hand, and nations often rearm for the sake of
economic expansion while, on the other hand, their whole
economic life is subordinated to military rearmament.
Thus in certain circumstances there will be war, although

there is obviously little to gain by it from the economic point of view ; in other cases the naked economic interest prevails. As both motives and actions very often originate not from within but from the situation in which individuals find themselves, it is obvious that in the late phase of monopolistic capitalism where the military sector of society overlaps the commercial, we shall find individuals in whom the militaristic motive and the commercial one will be blended. Thus in the dominant types of leading groups the soldier and the industrialist will join forces in obedience to a principle which remains obscure to themselves. But to those who look behind the scene it is evident that the progress of the different social techniques, and the social relationships, institutions, and typical tensions they create is reflected in the motives which actuate them. Whatever the importance of the principle that the centre of gravity shifts from sphere to sphere with the progress in the different fields of technique, the economic sphere does not appear to be entirely supreme, although of course it has a vital social function to perform. One thing is clear. We are not far from a multidimensional conception of society, in which a dynamic survey of social history must be prepared to reckon with several focal points of influence, such as the technical progress in economic production, in political power, in administration, and in psychological influence. Every real theoretical advance consists in discovering that a phenomenon which was once believed to be an independent variable, only seemed to be such because we had failed to take into account the special historical circumstances which gave it such extraordinary importance.

Thus insistence on the doctrine of the absolute supremacy of the economic principle is already out of date to a large extent, and only hinders our investigation of the significance of the remaining spheres and their relation to the progress of technique. To-day it is wiser to be pluralistic at first, to keep each of the various principia media of technical progress in mind, and to study their intervention empirically as it occurs.

But although we must be cautious in our attempts to establish the existence of an independent variable, this does not mean that the problem of the interaction of the different spheres ceases to be a problem. The greatest achievement in economics has been to conceive of the economic sphere in terms of a dynamic equilibrium. Even if the ultimate impulses which make for change in society as a whole may come from other spheres than that of economics, and may vary with the epoch in which they occur, they still tend to create an equilibrium. The great theme of social dynamics is the continuous mutual adjustment between the basic institutions of society. Even if the centre of gravity temporarily shifts from one sphere to another, it involves the rearrangement of all the different spheres. And although the ultimate source of the change may vary, there is still an unconscious unity of purpose behind these innovations : the solution of the few vital problems which form the basis of our social life.

There is always the problem of the security of the group as a whole, to which must be added, first, material provision for its needs, then the task of administration, and last but not least the various methods of moulding human behaviour in the combinations in which they occur in that particular society. It is possible that we shall be able to find a common denominator for these rearrangements, this shifting of the centre of gravity within the different spheres of social technique, but already to-day it seems to be more likely that the security of the group as a whole will prove to be more decisive than anything else and in the long run will form the basis of all the other functions.

On the other hand, it is also possible that we have not yet studied a large enough section of history to be able to decide by experience whether any master principle exists. At this stage of empirical study we must be content to emphasize some basic principles which are to be found in all these spheres and which can be established without undue risk.

In this book I have ventured to suggest three hypotheses for diagnosing the course of events and have applied them to several different spheres.

1. That most of the symptoms of our time are due to the transition from *laissez-faire* to a planned society.

2. That the transition from a democracy of the few to a mass society explains another set of changes.

3. That the changes in social technique account for yet a third group of changes, which has profoundly modified our social life.

I have deliberately concentrated all my attention on these three basic trends of development, because they are so fundamental that their effects are likely to continue, whatever further changes may occur. As compared with these trends the struggle for power (especially the class war) proves to be purely secondary in its results. This does not mean that I wish to underrate its significance, but the various factors which arise out of the class struggle serve only to modify the concrete shape these tendencies may take.

To put it in another way : the suggestion that the great theme of our time would be the struggle between the proletariat and the bourgeoisie was understandable in terms of the situation which provoked it, but overrated the significance of a single alternative. This distorted perspective was also responsible for another statement : that the basic possibilities were dictated by the development of economic society, so that class antagonisms would be the principal characters in the drama. Since this statement was made we have seen new classes grow up which could not be placed in the same category as the bourgeoisie, the proletariat, or the military caste ; party organizations have been created which ignore the economic divisions between workers and industrialists. These issues dwarf the significance of the continuing class tensions.

Thus the problem of the struggle for power remains, class conflicts are still important, but the concrete patterns they produce are much too changeable to be accepted as the eternal framework of future events. In contrast with them the themes created by the transformation of *laissez-faire* into planning, the advent of a mass society, and the growing significance of social technique are bound to endure. One cannot think of the future without assuming their existence, whereas no one can predict which class pattern, which form of planning, will prevail. From the theoretical point of view, therefore, the abstractness of these principles is not a defect but a virtue. It has always been the task of scientific thinking to discover the fundamental principles which determine the framework of events. Only later can it turn to those rules which merely modify the structure of society.

To the politician these modifications may be more important than fundamental hypotheses, but we should not allow our political interests to define the hierarchy of principles. Theoretically speaking, the disadvantage of treating one group of factors as though it were the only possible combination is that this hypothesis becomes worthless when other configurations come into prominence. The test of my hypothesis, that the three principles I have proposed are more abstract and therefore more fundamental than those we have examined, is that they sufficiently explain a large number of changes which will endure after the special class patterns have been modified. Once this has been agreed, I am the last to underrate the significance of the struggle for power between the nations, and the class implications of that struggle. Whenever my analysis has become historical enough to examine any particular phase in the course of events, I have never failed to mention the contributions made by the different classes to the changing social structure.

Our three principles, therefore, do not claim to solve all the concrete problems of our society, but they try to draw attention to various factors which have so far been neglected although they go very deep. They will, therefore, explain symptoms and problems which are likely to be permanent, whatever may be the cumulative effect of isolated events.

So far we have devoted most of our attention to the first two principles; in this last part of the book I wish to deal at length with the analysis of the third.

II

SOME PHASES IN THE DEVELOPMENT OF SOCIAL TECHNIQUES

1. *Their Change from the Craftsmanship Level to Mass Organization*

Now our task is to interpret, however briefly, the most important changes in social history in terms of changes in social techniques. If it be true that the ultimate cause of the transformation of democratic countries into totalitarian states is to be found in a changing social technique, it is worth inquiring into the part played by the more primitive techniques of the past and their influence on the nature of society.

The older forms of institution which developed in tribal times and continued to make themselves felt in medieval society were also based on the necessity for influencing human behaviour. They worked within such a narrow compass and changed so slowly that people were scarcely aware of the pressure they exerted—a pressure as natural as that of the atmosphere itself. Customs, habits, education, at first in the home and later in the church and the school, the conventions of community life, all these acted on the individual, in the effort to create a type of human being who would conform to the ideals of society.

In former societies this influence remained at a stage which would correspond to handicraft in the sphere of economic technique. Its methods were founded on the unconscious use of everyday experience. They were almost always taken over from the past and readapted, and were hardly ever calculated to obtain the best possible results or even deliberately thought out. Nevertheless they were effective, owing to the very gradual development of traditional societies and to their lack of social mobility. Economic progress was so slow that these societies scarcely changed at all within one generation. The customary family upbringing, the ideals of the Church, and the current public morality had time to mature and to slough off the unsuccessful methods. Thus a traditional human type was created whose standards of thought and action were sufficiently uniform to guarantee the smooth working of society. At the same time, owing to the lack of specialization, these habits of thought and action were elastic enough to leave the individual free to make his own adjustment in situations which could not be foreseen.

The characteristic features of hand-made goods are also to be found in social institutions. These features are a profound traditionalism in the choice of pattern, combined with ample scope for individual variation and a contempt for mechanical exactitude. Owing to their sluggish development, the societies of the past managed to survive in spite of a technique of character building which was still of the home-spun order. Most people spent their lives in the groups in which they were brought up. Migration from place to place or from class to class rarely attained any large proportions. There were no rapid changes to conflict with the narrowness of the traditional outlook.

Although as we have seen in another context, the coming of the liberal age meant a tremendous influx of energy which penetrated to the very heart of economic life, the rest of the social order was in many respects unaffected. The psychological upheaval which occurred in the age of enlightenment was slight compared with that of our own time ; for the class of people who brought about this revolution was comparatively small : only the entrepreneurs, the intelligentsia, and a fraction of the bureaucracy took any active part in the change. Nevertheless, a sensitive ear will hear the same pulse beating in the changes of our time as was audible among the tumult of the pioneers of enlightenment. In their aims one can trace the beginning of a process in which the traditional forms of life gradually become the subject of rational discussion. But there was no radical attack on the traditional patterns, for economic and spiritual equilibrium was still restored by small, adaptable social units. It is not as yet the organized masses who took part in the struggle for a new economic and social order, but small industrial units and barely organized groups. These are far readier to adapt themselves to meet the new demands than our modern mass organizations, which, once a rigid organization has been established, are dragged along by the sheer weight of inertia. At that time it was easier to incorporate new types of malcontent into a society which was based on free competition between small units : displaced craftsmen, isolated intellectuals, unsuccessful business men, reformers crying in the wilderness, all after a brief or prolonged struggle found a niche in society. As a result of their struggle social reforms were often introduced in the shape of new institutions. The traditional and slowly gliding stream of social life can resist small gusts of wind ; the waves ruffle the surface, but the river does not overflow its banks.

To-day hundreds of thousands of people are shifted from one place to another in obedience to the law of the labour market ; more structural changes have taken place in a decade than in the whole century preceding it, more psychological incentives are produced each week than in years of former life, and the man in the street experiences a greater tension between adjoining worlds than was felt perhaps by the Christian knights who first went East on the crusades.

How can one work in such a world with a technique which corresponds to the stage of craftsmanship ? Just as craftmanship can only satisfy a small circle of customers, so the traditional methods of forming character are very often inadequate for a mass age.

The groups who were the first to learn by personal experience how difficult it is to steer a mass society, were also the first to realize the necessity for doing justice to the problem. One may think of the medieval church as a possible forerunner, but in spite of its desire for the planned control of thought and feeling, the church is not a good example, for owing to its agricultural environment and the immaturity of social technique, it was forced to leave too much to traditional authority. Then it did not make sufficient use of rationalized methods to be regarded as the real pioneer in the history of modern social techniques. The army of the absolute states was the first great institution which not only devised rational methods for creating uniform mass behaviour artificially by means of military discipline and other devices for overcoming fear, but also used these methods for educating large masses of men (who were taken for the most part from the lowest classes) to act, and if possible to think, in the way prescribed.

This army had worked out certain social and psychological patterns of obedience, which constantly reappear as soon as it is impossible to conceal the compulsory nature of a social body. Thus, for instance, the type of organization which prevails in the Prussian army always has more success, as far as quick results are concerned, than any other method of integrating mass society. This is particularly noticeable in times of crisis, when democratic methods fail. Yet in the long run, the stern, despotic, military system is not the most effective. Too blatant a parade of violence leads to a waste of energy and requires a large bureaucratic organization for control and espionage. A growing society needs pioneers ; an over-centralized, rigidly disciplined mass technique leaves too little scope for individual adjustment, thus it fails to keep pace with the problems created by social expansion. For this reason the forms of organization and psychological technique which were used to establish a mass society in America were far more permanent in their results than any insistence on military discipline. The exponents of American mass propaganda found that the most successful psychological technique is largely based on the spontaneous action of the individuals to be guided, or at least gives them the illusion that they are making their own decisions—in spite of the fact that they have previously been exposed to a torrent of suggestion and persuasion. America had no feudal system, and this prevented the rise of many territorial traditions and customs. She did not have to reckon with these, and could easily break with local traditions when need arose. Owing to the gigantic wave of immigrants of every nationality which poured into the new settlements, " Americanization " became a problem of mass psychology. It had to be solved by democratic methods, not merely in the absence of any real central authority, but also because at least some sections of these immigrants were men of a highly independent and original type. As this technique originated in a democratic country, it never occurred to the inventors to impose any particular psychological outlook upon the people by dictatorial means. They were content to foster existing attitudes or to change them gradually as the occasion demanded.

Russian propaganda made use of these new discoveries concerning the practical guidance of mass impulses in an unstable society, and incorporated them into the enlightened dictatorship of the masses. In America the two most difficult problems which confronted the new social technique were social welfare and the modification of human behaviour by the skilful manipulation of mass psychology. The psychological influences of home and community had often been destroyed by the extraordinary restlessness of American society ; the authorities had to see to it that by means of these techniques the necessary social conformity was established up to a point, even if its growth had to be artificially stimulated. On the other hand the problem of enlightened dictatorship in Russia was to change masses of peasants into industrial workers in an incredibly short space of time, so that they could be relied on in their new jobs, and further to persuade them to accept the rational conception of the world which was believed to be essential for the maintenance of a planned state in the machine age. In America, propaganda had to solve the problem of creating uniform emotions and actions at election times and on other occasions in masses which were completely dissimilar in character and which had no common tradition. Russian social technique was confronted with much harder problems ; it had gradually to transform a fleeting emotional unity into an educational campaign which should embrace the whole man and gradually transform him into a citizen of a new society.

This could not be done by emotional propaganda alone. In addition to that, it had to develop original techniques to meet the new situation. Quite apart from its deliberate appeal to the emotions, a totalitarian state has all the other means of psychological persuasion at its command. It is not simply a question of propaganda ; there is the whole system of education, and behind the standardization of thought which is based mainly on imitation, there is the standardizing power of fear, instilled by the organized coercion of the state. The aim is to transform passing moods into a permanent frame of mind. Crèche, kindergarten, school, university serve to deepen the effect of occasional propaganda. But even the remaining spheres of social life, such as professional societies, newspapers, and hobbies are subordinated to the same purpose : to develop social technique to the very limit of its powers. These methods are more rational than those of the old traditional schools, churches, and national associations which set to work with a vague popular psychology and indefinite aims. The totalitarian states are more efficient because they co-ordinate their resources instead of letting their institutions work in opposite directions.

In the traditional societies of the past the Church with its religious influence was usually in the hands of men who held a particular set of philosophical and political opinions, while the state schools were directed by men of quite a different type. Naturally they cancelled each other out. Any moral teachings which Church, school, and home in spite of all their differences tried to instil into the individual, were effectively counteracted by what was known as " life ". This was simply the anarchic struggle for existence, which aroused an uncontrollable impulse for self-assertion. Regarded purely from the standpoint of efficiency, the liberal technique wasted an immense amount of energy, for owing to its lack of planning it weakened or even destroyed with one hand effects which it had achieved with the other. Co-ordination of purpose unquestionably saves time and energy. So much can be admitted even when one has no sympathy with the aims in view or believes that the gain is more than balanced by the loss.

In any case, the Russian state translated this realization into action, for with its co-ordinated social techniques it has carried the rationalization of psychological influences as far as it will go. This almost mechanical co-ordination of social forces which were once kept severely apart is, together with the conscious manipulation of psychological influences, the most important discovery modern society has made ; but there is nothing new in a mere attempt by society to influence people in one way or another.

The German and Italian Fascists have copied this whole-sale co-ordination from Russia but with a difference. Certainly Fascism has forced its way into the schools and has not confined itself to propaganda, but it cannot convert its discipline of thought and behaviour into a real work of enlightenment for a very simple reason. Russian socialism and industrialization can tolerate more rational thinking in their campaign, although many lines of thought have been tabooed. But Fascism has to make use of irrational and emotional methods in every major phase of life, in every vital social relationship ; for the Fascist system does not solve the fundamental difficulties of the new economic and social structure, but merely conceals them. In one respect, however, the Fascist countries are superior to the liberal states. The crisis through which they are passing has compelled them to make some attempt to solve the psycho-logical problems of modern mass society, particularly unemployment. It is true that Fascism has not yet succeeded in circumventing the economic crisis by the artificial expedient of the armament industry, to say nothing of achieving lasting prosperity or a higher standard of living. On the contrary, its economic position is deteriorating. But it does at least try, however brutal its methods, to remove the psychological effects of permanent unemploy-ment. Its social technique deliberately repudiates the en-lightenment of the masses and appeals to the most primitive impulses, but even in this distorted form it is at least con-cerned with questions which every future mass society will have to solve. This is where the prosperous mass states in democratic and liberal countries are in danger of lagging behind. They, too, are suffering from unemployment, and have little prospect of recovery as long as world depression lasts. But they have not yet managed even to face the psychological problems of the new age. In other respects, society is working fairly smoothly and those who determine the policy of these comparatively thriving countries have therefore failed to realize the precariousness of their position. The Fascist labour camp is of course an extremely uncongenial solution to the psychological crisis involved in unemployment, but from the point of view of social technique it represents a later stage than the liberal method, which thinks it can solve the social and psychological problem of unemployment by the dole.

Thus the English middle class observer hardly realizes that he is living in a mass society. He still does not perceive the symptoms of mass existence in his own country because the traditional methods of character building by custom and religion at home, in the state and public schools, and at the university are still working fairly smoothly. The accumulated wealth of the Empire, which is always creating new loopholes of escape from economic and social difficulties, has prevented many ugly symptoms of the problems of mass society from becoming immediately apparent. This does not mean that England and the other relatively prosperous countries will always be spared these problems, but they may perhaps be fortunate enough to be able to study the experience of other lands and plan their transition from the household and craftsmanship stage of social technique to large-scale methods. This respite should be used for a careful study of ways and means. Countries like England which have not destroyed their democratic and liberal institutions and are anxious to retain them, will have to face new problems should the question of new social techniques for dealing with the masses become acute.

2. *Lessons Democracy could Learn from the use of Social Techniques in Totalitarian States*

We must constantly bear in mind that once the basic traditions of social life have altered beneath the surface, we are living in a building which is already undermined, and the change from traditional order to temporary chaos may be accomplished without warning. Thus in a sudden crisis the uncontrolled influx of new social techniques might lead to the very same symptoms as those which are spreading in the dictatorial states. Thus there is every reason to study the nature of these techniques before they overwhelm us, and it is useless to treat them with contempt. We have first to arrive at a genuine understanding of their significance and to distinguish the permanent elements from the temporary distortions caused by dictatorial abuses.

So one should not ignorantly oppose these new techniques by regarding them merely as propaganda. We must.not judge them purely from the aristocratic standpoint of a minority culture, which produced a few élites on the one hand and tolerated the fact that the masses should remain uneducated on the other. Modern social technique is a vital necessity for every large industrial society : it is equally important for its psychological, economic, and industrial preservation. Like other kinds of technique it can be both magnificent and in-human. It is magnificent because it solves gigantic difficulties. One has only to ask oneself how a mass society, with all its conflicting tendencies and its danger of disintegration, could possibly continue if it were not in a position to reconstruct its whole social technique. The invention of a planned technique for influencing human behaviour offers some hope of deliver-ance from a chaos in which home, church, and school are losing all power of impression, though it must be admitted that in its present form this technique is still only a makeshift. We have called it inhuman because it is a machine working in a vacuum and is in itself neither good nor evil. Its effect depends to a large extent on the purpose for which it is used. The German authorities provided an excellent instance of its positive value when they succeeded in abolishing the hatred of Poland for as long as they wished in a very short space of time. This hatred is one of the most deeply rooted of all collective sentiments, and even if all Germans did not suddenly grow to like the Poles, it is significant enough from the sociological point of view that feelings of hatred can be handled in a way which prevents them from becoming socially integrated, and thus politically effective.

How it would simplify our common life, if this power of

planned persuasion were used, not for stirring up strife, but for encouraging behaviour on which all our hopes of peace, co-operation, and understanding depend. We would gladly consent to considerable interference at strategic points provided it confined itself to fostering those elements in the education of human nature which make for peace, understanding, and decency. An international agreement to co-ordinate education and propaganda so as to secure at least a minimum sense of decency and moral obligation would be a kind of conformity against which no objection could be raised.

If we are to realize the full possibilities of the new social technique, we must remember that in its present form it still has to work with a very primitive psychology. It is based on a collection of rules compiled from the experiences of agitators, officers, and wholesale merchants, and is coloured by their point of view. It is still far from attaining a degree of sincerity and subtlety which would enable us to estimate its real value. The propagandist works with a very superficial analysis of human possibilities. But side by side with this psychology, a subtler, more sociological psychology is developing in our society, and has not yet been fully assessed. We are thinking of the tremendous progress in modern social work, in children's courts, in education both for individuals and for groups. We are thinking of attempts at what behaviourism calls reconditioning, which makes it possible to shake off bad habits which have developed in early childhood and to create new and useful habits in their place. We are thinking of the results obtained by re-educating adults, which have proved that most of the characteristics generally ascribed to faults of character or lack of talent are produced by an unsatisfactory environment in early life. An almost pathologically arrested development of our impulses and the mental life can be corrected in such cases by further education.[1]

The experiments in adult education throw some light on the senseless way in which people behave in politics. Instead of finding a facile explanation in Le Bon's popular psychology of crowd behaviour, it is wiser to suggest that people who have had no chance of political responsibility are bound to

---

[1] Cf. III 1, III 6, III 7 d in the Bibliography.

behave foolishly until they have gradually obtained some experience of politics and have learnt to act like responsible adults. Why should a man be expected to develop into a fully fledged politician overnight without any preliminary training and experience ? No one would expect him to run a steam engine without being taught, or to give an intelligent opinion on intricate business matters. Among the refinements of social technique we must not forget to mention psycho-analysis.[1] In its revelation of the unconscious mind it has made discoveries which, although only too hypothetical at present will in time give us power over a new dimension of the spirit.

When we consider the possibilities of social techniques, we naturally regard them with very mixed feelings. It is impossible to rid ourselves of the idea that the subtler the influence over the human mind becomes, the more skilful our handling of social relationships, the greater the danger that we may be caught in a trap. The greater the pride of achievement, the greater the alarm at the power which one man has over another. But just as there is no retreat from rationalization, so it is impossible to turn our backs on this increasing knowledge ; the problem is rather to draw the right conclusions from the new possibilities.

It cannot be denied that directly men realized the power that could be gained from this expanding social technique, they began to abuse it. The fundamental error at the root of this abuse is plainly revealed if one analyses the word with which this co-ordinated use of social technique is described. It is extremely characteristic that in the atmosphere of mass dictatorship co-ordination is expressed by " Gleichschaltung ", although the two words have entirely different meanings.

Rightly understood, co-ordination means the intelligent correlation of all the resources at one's disposal, the harmonizing of the various instruments of an orchestra. This mutual harmony can be used to produce either monotony or polyphony. It is very significant that co-ordination has been interpreted as a kind of goose-step standardization—the creation of a barren conformity. As opposed to this if the problem were properly thought out, it would be obvious that a centralized social technique

[1] Cf. III 1 e in the Bibliography.

need not entail conformity, that it need not necessarily be used to create human sheep. The present experiments are only a travesty of the possibilities contained in the idea of co-ordination. Social co-ordination is like orchestral harmony. Social co-ordination only means that we do not let the instruments under our control—in this case the social institutions and techniques, such as family, school, work, leisure, and so on, cancel each other out but harmonize their creative powers with one another. Whether they are used to produce uniformity or a many-sided individuality depends on the will of the planner.

Quite apart from the dictatorial levellers, this insight is denied to those who still think it possible to give free rein to the social forces, without any attempt at planning or co-ordination. These old-fashioned liberals must remember that we cannot return to this conception of freedom. The arbitrary tyranny of the social forces, unbridled liberalism, at the stage of mass society leads not to freedom, but at the first real shock, to chaos. In a mass society it is just this chaotic welter of groups all struggling for mastery which causes reaction, a desire for the totalitarian and monopolistic control of social technique and the belief that planning means standardization and the suppression of spontaneity. If in this early stage men realize the enormous power that the co-ordinated control of social technique can give, but do not realize in time that the best planning is not planning for conformity, then further progress inevitably leads to the enslavement of mankind, so that it is almost a matter of indifference under which flag it takes place. Even a social order which is built on firm foundations and is sound in aim and function will in time fall a victim to bureaucracy through the institutional surrender of its citizens to the technicians who run the social machine, unless it becomes aware in time of the dangers inherent in the situation.

I believe, therefore, now that the countries with liberal and democratic traditions have reached the stage of mass society, they must use those traditions to interpret the problem of mass education with greater wisdom than the dictatorships have shown. These countries can rely on customs which provide them with a powerful combination of attitudes, based on ideals of individual independence, mutual consideration, and fair play, together with enlightened and acceptable conventions. These ingrained attitudes are diametrically opposed to the authoritarian propensity for laying down the law and to the masochistic pleasure in submission. In democratic countries there is thus the possibility of a gradual re-definition of the meaning of planning, so that the word is not associated with conformity but with co-ordination in the sense of harmonizing the instruments of social technique, in short, of meaning by planning, planning for freedom. True liberalism in our collective age must act as a supplement, suggesting every type of planning and social technique which is likely to foster individuality, and must not obtain order at the cost of freedom.

Planning in this sense means planning for freedom ; mastering those spheres of social progress on which the smooth working of society depends, but at the same time making no attempt to regulate the fields which offer the greatest opportunities for creative evolution and individuality.

This freedom is not of course that of *laissez-faire, laissez-aller*, which can no longer exist to-day. It is the freedom of a society which, since it has the whole co-ordinated system of social techniques within its grasp, can safeguard itself of its own accord against dictatorial encroachment on certain spheres of life, and can incorporate the charters of these citadels within its structure and its constitution.

Anyone who plans for freedom, that is, provides for citadels of self-determination in a regulated social order, has of course to plan for necessary conformity as well. The liberal age could give its whole attention to the propagation of the idea of freedom, for it could build on the foundations of the traditional conformity it had inherited from the old community culture of the Middle Ages. We shall have to waste a great deal of energy in the next few years replacing the old pattern of traditional conformity which is now disintegrating by a new one. We shall discover new values which were lost to us in the age of unlimited competition ; identification with the other members of the society, collective responsibility, and the necessity for possessing a common background for our attitudes and behaviour. But once the new community has acquired the necessary unity of outlook—a conformity which is not to be discouraged—there is no reason why provision should not be made, both in the educational system and in the very structure of society itself for gradual modifications, culminating in individual personality.[1]   To-day we can afford to create opportunities for encouraging the growth of individuality, because modern social technique can offer much sounder guarantees for the smooth working of society in the basic spheres of life than societies of the older type.

But the mere fact of the existence of masses is not an obstacle. It is by no means impossible to split them up into small groups in which there is scope for initiative and individuality.   In these small groups in which everyone feels that a great deal depends upon his actions, and learns to act upon his own responsibility instead of losing himself in the anonymity of the mass, social patterns grow up in which individuality can almost certainly develop. Sociology has already reached a stage in which it is possible to say which social forces and constellations have fostered individuality in the course of history.   Planning for freedom does not mean prescribing a definite form which individuality must take, but having both the knowledge and experience to decide what kind of education, what kind of social groups and what kind of situations afford the best chance of kindling initiative, the desire to form one's own character and decide one's own destiny.

III

THE CONCEPT OF SOCIAL CONTROL

Planning as the Rational Mastery of the Irrational

Society is almost ready to pass into a new stage. Unless we realize this, we shall lose the boundless opportunities which a co-ordination of social techniques would put into our hands.

Planned freedom can only be achieved by a deliberate and skilful handling of these techniques, so that every kind of

---

[1] I have dealt with the opportunities which planned society could offer for the growth of personality in three public lectures " Planned Society and the Problem of Human Personality " given at the London School of Economics. These lectures are as yet unpublished.

influence which can be brought to bear on human beings must be theoretically understood. The planning authority should be able to decide on empirical grounds what sort of influence to use in a given situation, basing its judgments on the scientific study of society, coupled if possible with sociological experiments. Such a tendency is already apparent in certain fields. For example, to-day we are developing a new kind of scientific study, e.g. the sociology of taxation,[1] in order to discover which methods work best in different countries. In the same way it is to be hoped that we shall be able to decide by experience what tactics to adopt in other spheres of society in view of the customs prevailing at the time. For just as different citizens in different countries feel differently about moral obligations when it comes to paying taxes, so there are different habits of thought, beaten tracks in the psychology of nations, which lead them to do some things in obedience to military orders, others in a spirit of free co-operation.

Social science in pondering the right techniques will obviously have to work with varying conceptions of efficiency. Apart from the purely technical conception which could be defined as " achieving the maximum effect by the minimum of effort ", other more human considerations must be taken into account. A drastic form of taxation may be efficient for the moment from the purely technical point of view because it extorts the largest sum in the shortest possible time, but psychologically and in the long run it may be inefficient, because it may shake the confidence of the tax-payer on which every future collection of taxes depends. Thus every economic, administrative, and educational code must be ready to consider not only the short-lived technical efficiency but the deeper psychological effects. A society in which profit is not the only criterion of economic production will prefer to work by methods which, though less effective from the point of view of output, give the workers more psychological satisfaction. Has not even our own brand of capitalist society, although it is prepared to fight for purely economic ends, been forced to cut down its profits

---

[1] On the Sociology of taxation, cf. Sultan, H., *Die Staatseinnahmen, Versuch einer soziologischen Finanztheorie als Teil einer Theorie der politischen Ökonomie.* Tübingen, 1932 ; and Mann, F. K., *Finanzsoziologie,* Kölner Vierteljahreshefte für Soziologie, vol. 12, No. 1, 1933.

in favour of the social services? A planned society would be still more likely to invent new forms of calculation owing to its greater interest in the good of the whole. The changed conception of efficiency which we have just discussed would not confine itself to the economic sphere. The psychological, social, and technical means applied should be judged by their effect on character and individuality as well as by their purely technical efficiency. Why should not a planned society which could deal not only with economy proper, but with human economy as well, make allowance for this point of view? We can go even further. A finer mastery of the social keyboard, a more accurate knowledge of social technique, does not necessarily result in excessive interference. I believe that the wisdom of the planner would very often lead to a deliberate refusal to interfere in many fields. I can perhaps explain what I have in mind by giving an example on a smaller scale. An experimental boarding school for instance which aimed at planning the whole scope of its activities, might proceed to think out its syllabus and time-table in detail, but at the same time would see that recreation hours should be provided in which the children were invariably left to themselves without advice or interference so that they could develop their own initiative. Arrangements could at the same time be made for the boys to go off for a tramp on their own, or find themselves work in which their individual initiative would have free play. This is by no means contrary to the principle that educational influences should be carefully controlled. Even in our present society sheltered zones and open battlefields exist side by side. In a planned society they will still be there, but they will be brought into harmony by a deeper understanding of the contribution they make, both to the formation of character and to the efficiency of society.

This rational mastery of the irrational which does not rob it of its peculiar charm, this deliberate recognition of irrationality is only possible when there is a thorough grasp not only of the standardized techniques involved, but also of the spontaneous forms which develop in life when it is left to itself. The keyboard and the polyphonic harmony of musical instruments of which we spoke were no chance metaphors. The analogy is justified in so far that only the man who has fully mastered musical technique can really express the irrationality of musical experience. In the same way a truly planned society does not suppress the genuine dynamics of life or intellectualize them, but tries through a skilful handling of situations to make a fuller use of organic forces than was possible at a stage of more primitive, inflexible control.

Even the greatest expert in social technique does not imagine that he himself creates the elementary psychological and social processes. The greater his knowledge, the more clearly will he see that a genuine improvement in social technique means an ever fuller use, an ever increasing mastery of the original material. Real skill will not make us inhuman, but human in a deeper sense. Only those who feel that the present state of society is " natural " because they were born into it will oppose true planning, thereby completely overlooking the fact that this alleged naturalness is the chance product of spasmodic interference with the course of social events and the development of the individual—an interference which usually does more harm than good because it is not consciously applied. The clumsiness of our society in which different man-made institutions frequently clash and different moral codes continuously lead to conflicts, is reflected in the rising tide of neurosis in the individual and in disastrous panics and crises in international relations.

If society can be controlled, we must ask ourselves how we can improve our technique of intervention in human affairs, and where this intervention ought to begin. The problem of this " where ", the right point of attack, brings us to the conception of social control.[1] The societies of the past made use of this control in many forms, and we are

---

[1] C. F. Ross, E. A., *Social Control : A Survey of the Foundations of Order* (New York, 1901), a book which has the merit of having directed attention very early to that problem. But I think in that early stage it was not yet possible to see its ultimate implications, which only become visible as soon as one discusses them in the context of social techniques and planning. Cf. also Cooley, Ch. H., *Social Organization*, New York, 1909, and his *Social Process*, New York, 1918 ; MacIver, R. M., *Society*, a Textbook of Sociology, esp. Book II, part ii, New York, 1937 ; Case, C. M., " Some Sociological Aspects of Coercion," *Publications of the Amer. Sociological Society*, 1922, vol. 117, pp. 75–88 ; Lumley, F. E., *Means of Social Control*, New York, 1925 ; Bernard, L. L., *The Transition as an Objective Standard of Social Control Thesis*, Chicago, 1911 ; " Social Control," *Publications of the American Sociol. Society*, vol. 12, Chicago, 1918 ; Smith, W. R., " School Discipline as Training for the Larger Social Control," *Publ. of the Amer. Sociol. Soc.*, vol. 17, 1923 ; Mead, G. H., " The Genesis of the Self and Social Control," *Intern. Journ. of Ethics*, vol. 35, 1924–5. Cf. also I, 1 in the Bibliography.

justified in speaking of the " key positions of social control " in the sense that there have always been foci from which the most important influences emanated. A new approach to history will be achieved when we are able to translate the main structural changes in terms of a displacement of the former systems of control. Looking at society as a whole, the replacement of individual controls is never due solely to immediate causes but is a function of changes in the whole configuration.

The question emerges whether in the past the controls grew up side by side haphazard, or whether even then they were unconsciously co-ordinated, and whether in the future such a co-ordination could be deliberately encouraged. The key to an understanding of shifting social controls lies partly in the changing nature of social techniques and partly in the transformation of human beings themselves.

In a society where the technique of social control is still in its infancy the influence comes from near at hand, from the father, the neighbour, the chieftain. Standards of behaviour must be inculcated and everybody must conform to them if the society is to work. This kind of primitive group with its narrow range of social influence will tend to impose too many taboos and will anxiously insist on what Durkheim calls a " mechanical solidarity ".

But in a society in which a more detailed division of labour occurs human conduct can be influenced by subtler and less obvious means. As Durkheim points out, division of labour creates functions which are complementary to each other, so that everyone is much more dependent on his neighbours than in a society where no such division exists and each as it were produces for himself. Owing to the division of labour and the consequent dependence of the individual on society, new kinds of pressure come into being which continue to take effect when there is no one to give orders. Certain situations constantly recur and exert a pressure from which there is little chance of escape. This " pressure of circumstances " admittedly allows the individual to make his own adjustment, but the number of possible adjustments is limited. Even if society is not in a position to deal with these situations, they can nevertheless be foreseen and are easily recognizable in the most important spheres of life. This similarity appears in its most striking form when we study the biographies of men who belong to the same period and class : they are usually confronted with the same type of situation even when they believe their circumstances are unique. It is clear that the social control which consists in confronting certain social classes with certain definite situations is radically different from that of primitive society where the individual is directly affected. Only when the social structure has reached a fairly complex stage of development can the social controls become flexible enough to provoke a number of possible reactions to typical conditions instead of laying down hard and fast rules of behaviour. The types of social control which work through situations or through force of circumstances are only to be found at a certain level of society, and their significance increases as its complexity grows. In the same way the vital question whether social control is exercised by a central group of leaders or is democratically diffused throughout society depends for its answer both on the social order and on the social techniques.

In this connection it again becomes clear that discussion of the problem of social control is hopelessly abstract when it is not related to the workings of society as a whole but is artificially divided into water-tight compartments such as economics, political science, administration, and education. As long as we specialize only in one of these fields its nature is hidden from us. We do not realize that all these seemingly separate sciences are in fact interrelated, that they refer to social techniques whose ultimate aim is to secure the functioning of the social order by bringing an appropriate influence to bear on the behaviour and attitudes of men.

Once this unity of purpose is recognized the political and social character of all human institutions becomes clear. They are not as they seem at first sight designed simply to achieve a limited object, they are permanent elements in the political organization of society and have grown up side by side. Economics in their broader aspect are not merely a device for regulating production and consumption, they are also an efficient means of regulating human behaviour as well, and in some spheres of action they help to adjust it to the general trend of affairs. Administration is not merely a form of social organization created for the purpose of carrying out certain decisions; it is becoming more and more obvious to-day that administration is turning into an instrument of political interference and that the methods used in executing the prescribed regulations can serve as an indirect means of altering the balance of power in a society. The dogmatic distinction between making the law (legislation) and expounding it (jurisdiction) does not seem to be as clear cut as it used to be, and we see ever more plainly that in the process of jurisdiction the judges are creating the law. Sociologists do not regard education solely as a means of realizing abstract ideals of culture, such as humanism or technical specialization, but as part of the process of influencing men and women. Education can only be understood when we know for what society and for what social position the pupils are being educated.[1]

If, instead of studying every branch of activity separately, we consider all social activities as a whole we shall be able to classify them as social techniques, whose sole *raison d'être* is to influence human behaviour as society thinks fit.[2] This leads us on to the working hypothesis that the quantum of mental energy needed to produce the habits and outlook of a society remains constant and that only the concrete forms of expression change. In this sense we can speak of a transmutation (metamorphosis) of this energy.

Let us now proceed to examine this transformation of mental energy in greater detail and give an example to show how the same activity (manual labour) was enforced in different ways in two successive phases of history. It is well

---

[1] K. Mannheim, "Mass Education and Group Analysis," op. cit.; and cf. in the Bibliography III 3a, III 4, and III 7a.

[2] We will only indicate here what we have explained in another place— why it should be in the liberal age that a tendency arose to divorce the spheres from one another. The habit of thinking in terms of pure economics, the unquestioning distinction between legislature, executive, and judiciary, the autonomy of education, mark only a certain stage in the evolution of society, in which, for structural reasons, co-ordination takes place through checks and balances. But even in this sense the different spheres of action were not so simple and unpolitical as they appeared to be in an abstract analysis. The regulation of property for instance was always political, for it was not only a means of guaranteeing a certain standard of living but regulated human activities in different spheres. Even when there was no authority which consciously set the different parts of the social mechanism in motion, they constantly influenced each other and tended towards equilibrium. This equilibrium was not totalitarian, however, in the sense that it was planned beforehand on theoretical principles to function as a single machine.

known that in Roman society, especially on the great estates (*latifundia*), the work was done by slaves and the principal incentive was the whip. Towards the end of Roman rule, at the beginning of the Middle Ages, this system of slave economy was transformed into serfdom, and now instead of brute force a combination of methods was used to arouse the will to work. First the slaves, once condemned to celibacy, were allowed to marry, so that instead of living in barracks they could have a home and family. This was a more or less deliberate attempt to mobilize the instinct of self-preservation in the economic interests of their masters by strengthening it through family ties. Then this motive was reinforced from another side and a strip of land was given them with a share in the harvest, so that they would take an interest in the output. And finally they were bound to the soil by law, and thus the ambition which society itself had aroused was checked by social regulation, for they had no hope of moving to the best manors in the country. These restrictions on their freedom of movement were further reinforced by the lack of communications.

The transformation of slaves into serfs is an example of the different incentives employed in these two solutions to the labour problem. Instead of the primitive method of brute force applied in slavery, in serfdom there is a combination of stimuli. Blood ties, an emotional attachment to the land, the legal inability to leave it and a vested interest in its produce, all combined to create a skilfully balanced system for arousing the necessary will to work. The particular course which human initiative takes, the changing forms of incentives, are once more functions of the changing social techniques and can only be completely understood with reference to the whole social order. People turned in our example to the more complicated system, not merely because it gave the serf a keener interest in his work but because imperialistic wars, which were a kind of slave-hunting, ceased and with them the source of slave labour.[1]

In this example the transmutation of social energy (metamorphosis) is obvious when we notice how certain systems

---

[1] Cf. Max Weber, " Die sozialen Gründe des Unterganges der antiken Kultur," in his *Gesammelte Aufsätze zur Sozial- und Wirtschaftsgeschichte*, Tübingen, 1924.

used different methods of pressure and stimulation in order to achieve the same result. In spite of its relevance in this particular case the principle of the transmutation of social energy is only a metaphor ; it would be a mistake to carry it too far.[1] It would also be foolish to attempt to measure the quantum of energy [2]; we might be led into theoretical trifling. For the vital element in the physical principle of the conservation of energy is that quanta of energy can be measured as they actually occur in various forms. Here the analogy of the conservation of energy only serves to emphasize two important facts : First, there is only one single principle underlying all social techniques, that of influencing human behaviour, causing people to act in a desired way. Secondly, the same behaviour (manual labour, in the case we have just analysed) can be obtained sometimes by a single act of direct compulsion, sometimes by a combination of social controls, expanding throughout the whole social texture.

[1] C. J. Friedrich, *Constitutional Government and Politics*, New York, London, 1937, pp. 12 ff., speaks of interpreting human action by the power principle, but forgets to emphasize that the idea of the conservation of energy is only adequate if it can be measured. Moreover, he ignores the primary assumption of the unity of social techniques, which in spite of their external differences have in our opinion a single task to fulfil— the influencing of human behaviour. Only if one makes this the basis of one's study is it possible to speak of the transmutation of energy. Otherwise it is impossible to interpret the changing expression of the same tendency as variations of that tendency. Certainly Friedrich has taken an important step in this direction in so far as he regards not merely the compulsory activities but also the spontaneous ones as an expression of this energy. Indeed, obtaining obedience to a distasteful order is a method of influencing behaviour just as much as creating agreement or a spontaneous desire to do one's duty. It is just in this ability to create agreement where authoritarian methods only obtain obedience, that the greater efficiency of democratic methods lies.

[2] In order to measure the mental energy expended in the above mentioned two methods of making people work, the results obtained by slave labour would have to be compared with the energy consumed by the overseers, and then with the results produced by the serfs, in order to contrast the energy expended by the overseers with the energy needed to keep the whole system going. It is clear that these quanta are not measurable, so, as we explained in the text, it is not the equality of the energy expended on which we lay such stress but on the question by what means (pride in one's work, enterprise) and through what combinations of social techniques, identical functions are created in different societies. As to the psychological effects of spontaneous and authoritarian methods, cf. the following recent contributions : Lewin, K., and Lippitt, R., "An Experimental Approach to the Study of Autocracy and Democracy : A Preliminary Note," *Sociometry* I, Nos. 3–4, 1934. Lewin, K., and White, R. K., "Patterns of Aggressive Behaviour in Experimentally Created Social Climates," *Journal of Soc. Psychol.*, May, 1939.

IV

The Classification of Social Controls

Once we have explained the major premises on which our argument is based, our next task will be to make a detailed investigation of the general hypothesis of the transmutation of social energy. The outstanding problem which a sociology of government will have to face is to demonstrate that different countries have different social controls at their command and to explain the nature of their working. This shifting of controls, the transmutation of the methods of influencing human behaviour, can only be studied in detail after a preliminary scheme of classification has been worked out. We still have a long way to go before we can determine through which controls our society functions, and farther still before we can form a concrete plan for securing the best possible disposition of these controls. Nevertheless much would be gained if social science were able to make a sound theoretical survey of the key positions of social control. At any rate this would be the best approach in studying the structure of any society.

In the following section I will try to classify social controls in this way. I am fully aware that I am unable to do more than to work out the main principle underlying them and to give some examples of their effects. For the purpose of this survey I propose to classify the relevant techniques of influencing human behaviour as follows. First we have two main groups :

1. Direct Methods of Influencing Human Behaviour.
2. Indirect Methods of Influencing Human Behaviour.

1. *Direct Methods of Influencing Human Behaviour*

These are always based on personal influence and work from near at hand. Thus the effect of this influence is always identified with the man who exercises it, and the layman does not notice that he is merely the unconscious exponent of the claims of society. So if the parents tell the child not to do certain things, we believe that it is they who wish to establish these particular rules. The sociologist, on the other hand, knows that a definite society is speaking through them,[1]

---

[1] Cf. Jessie Taft, *The Dynamics of Therapy in a Controlled Relationship*, ch. ii, " Thirty-one Contacts with a Seven-year-old Boy," New York, 1933.

and that it is more or less dependent on these rules for its smooth working. School masters and priests fulfil the same function. The leader of an opposition uses means of influencing behaviour just as much as the Government; the only difference is, that owing to his dislike of certain institutions he proposes to put others in their place. From the sociological point of view he might fulfil as important a function in transforming human behaviour as those who only care for conformity, for he fosters the dynamic change which is needed in the course of history.

As opposed to these personal influences, we speak of influencing human behaviour indirectly, when it is a question of influencing the action, outlook, and habits of the individual by conscious or unconscious control of the natural, social, or cultural surroundings.

The chief characteristic of indirect influence is that it works from afar, and the control originally springs, not from close at hand, but from distant sources. Far away there is a social authority, which by managing natural, institutional, or cultural factors persuades or compels the individual to react as it pleases. Of course, there are human beings at work behind this cluster of influences; these institutions represent real people, yet it is not private individuals, but the invisible pressure in the situation itself which makes the average human being do what is expected of him, apparently of his own accord, without external bribery or pressure.

In these circumstances the individual might have an illusion of freedom, and indeed he does in fact make his own adjustment. But from the sociological point of view the possible solutions are more or less determined in advance by social control of the situation.

In spite of this diversity of methods we must not forget what we have already stated, that indirect influence in its final stages works through direct influence. If certain provinces of society are regulated by free competition, the individual does not keep his eye on the system, but on the actual competitor who is pitting his prices against his own, or on a customer who wants cheaper goods and thinks he can get them elsewhere. The abstract power and pressure of competition as far as the individual is concerned is embodied in the concrete actions of other individuals with whom he has personal dealings.

According to this account there appears at first sight to be no real distinction between the direct and indirect methods of influencing human behaviour. For in both cases the social order is speaking through the mouth of a concrete individual and in both it seems as though the individual in question were the ultimate source of the influence. Yet when we look into the matter more carefully we realize that a father who is punishing his son provokes a different response from that called out by the process of competition. If a father hands on some opinion or other he is the author of it and we can only state in quite general terms that society is speaking through him ; while if I obey the laws of competition it is possible to point to the particular pattern of social interaction which has conditioned my behaviour. This distinction is absolutely vital to the planner, for if he wants to alter the position, in the first case he appeals to the father and in the second he tries to change the process of competition. We shall have more to say about this distinction later on.

Whether a society relies more on direct or indirect influence depends on a great many factors, but especially on its size, range, organization, communications, and social mobility. The feudal society, for instance, retained its pattern of direct personal influence and dependence because, in spite of its vastness, it was an agrarian society in which social regulation was based on neighbourliness and personal relationships. It never approached the conception of abstract officialdom, which was confined to the absolutist state and the democratic bureaucracy. As it grew it still clung to the hierarchic scheme in which everyone had his own overlord to whom he was bound by ties of fidelity. The emphasis on direct control may have forced this society to assume the complicated structure of a pyramid. Systematic generalization and the application of universal principles to social affairs were alien to the medieval mind in feudal times. It thought in terms of personal or class privilege. To do justice did not mean to accord every one equal rights before the law, but to guarantee to every man his own right, the right to which his estate entitled him. There was no liberty, only liberties. The method of generalization and subsumption only became operative in legal thought when through the idea of citizenship all men became equal, at least in the political sphere. Until this had been achieved it was impossible to think of law or political organization in the abstract.

Accordingly the prevailing pattern of thought expressed itself in terms of symbols and analogies rather than in logical generalization. The symbolic representation of authority still belongs to a world where personal contacts prevail, and the highest degree of abstraction can only be reached by means of images and not of general concepts. The libidinous energies which flow into these symbols are still of the same nature as the allegiance to a personal over-lord. There is no leap into the abstract as there is in obeying systematic legal regulations for their own sake or for the sake of the state.

The patterns of personal influence develop in those social units which Cooley called the primary groups [1] : the local units of a society, the family, the neighbours, and the village community. This personal influence exists in modern society too, in the family, in the nursery, school, and kinder-garten, in neighbourly relationships and during leisure time. It does not disappear in mass society but tends to be confined to certain aspects of life. Its real working can best be seen in our midst when small new groups arise : friendships, fraternities, political sects, and cliques. It is mainly these small and active bodies which invent new customs, so that the first patterns are created by a process of trial and error. The habits, feelings, sympathies, and idiosyncrasies of these groups will be determined, far more than in larger and more permanent communities, by the personal peculiarities of individual leaders and prominent members. The more stable and institutional these fluctuating groups become, the sooner these personal peculiarities will be abolished or will auto-matically be transformed into an impersonal tradition.

The detailed study of the problem by what means and on what plane of consciousness the sense of personal influence becomes effective, would require a whole treatise on psychology. We will, therefore, merely indicate certain important aspects of direct influence. First of all there is the whole mechanism of habit which is conditioned by

[1] Cooley, C. H., *Social Organization*. A Study of the Larger Mind, New York, 1924. Park, R. E., and Burgess, E. W., *Introduction to the Science of Sociology*, 2nd ed., Chicago, 1924. Chapter V, II, C., *Primary and Secondary Contacts*.

training and which guarantees a certain conformity among the members of a society—a conformity which is largely independent of rational and emotional judgment.

One usually distinguishes two kinds of habits : those which are uniform throughout a given society and those which conform to special institutions and co-operative schemes. When, for instance, a man acquires habits connected with the times appointed for eating, working, and sleeping, he is learning to share in the general activities of society ; but if he acquires the habits of a certain profession, or the manners of a certain social class, this can only be regarded as a preparation for particular institutions.

The principal aim of education is usually to achieve a basic social conformity ; it transmits by direct tradition the patterns of behaviour for which society is always groping in the past. The customary methods of carrying out certain collective activities such as a fishing expedition among primitive tribes, and the techniques for promoting co-operation and suppressing selfish motives fall into this category. Even such trifles as the art of winning approval, the intuitive power to realize which petty stratagems are permissible in personal intercourse, what is best left unsaid, and what must be stifled at all costs are communicated by private example. Thus from the skilful handling of commonplace situations to the traditional routine of group organization, everything is subject to the same law. But not only overt behaviour but also emotional and volitional reactions are transmitted in the same way.

Who can tell how the English form of self-control is handed down, or how emotional rhythm differs in the Germans, the French, or the Americans ? The normal methods of self-expression are openly transmitted by personal contact just as other social habits are. This is equally true on the intellectual plane and applies to style both in writing and in speech. We are justified in using the term habits of thinking in order to show that there are planes of thought which are taken over almost mechanically without being subjected to responsible control. We think as we do, not because long consideration of the facts has led us to this or that conclusion, but because our opinions were directly instilled into us in childhood.

But even if we decided one day to reconsider all our

prejudices, to think out all our opinions for ourselves, we should find that owing to the intensity of these methods of direct transmission, unconscious inhibitions would make themselves felt at certain points and would prevent us going any further. These inhibited fields in the mind exist in many spheres, of which the sexual sphere is only the best known. A patriot is inhibited from shaking off the collective narcissism of his group, just as a Communist can only compel himself sorely against his will to make a critical analysis of the dogma concerning the chosen destiny of the proletariat. Both men have not only adopted certain habits of thought at critical phases in their life but have also established certain inhibited fields of consciousness which react like a *noli me tangere.*

But these conditioned reactions, these ruts in the pathways of the mind, are sometimes exposed to change. In some of the feelings we acquire there are mental explosives hidden, which under favourable circumstances may convulse our whole system of habits. Small hidden resentments, repressed longings, may become revitalized. In this sense every conversation, every method of teaching either encourages or discourages such mental rebellions. In case of discouragement, hidden elements of fear and anxiety are implanted and inhibit the individual who is striving to surpass the boundaries of his limited sphere of action. Reconsideration is, therefore, never a purely intellectual act. It is emotional and volitional for it has to be preceded by the courage to break the spell cast by former habits of mind.

One of the many methods of establishing a certain conception of the world and thus of creating conformity is what has been called the definition of a situation. Certain interpretations of the situation, certain accepted valuations, and certain prevailing ideologies are taken for granted. We adopt them in the family, the nursery, the school, try to live with them and only when the tension between them and our direct experience becomes too great, do we gradually revise them. We usually make no attempt to do this by ourselves, but join forces with those who find themselves in a similar position and collectively rebel against an established definition. At first people are merely inclined to grumble and be generally discontented, and later out of their trivial disparagements new values and a new definition of the situation arises.

Not merely our smallest mannerisms, but the integrated pattern of our personality may be formed by our immediate surroundings and by the direct influence which is brought to bear. Ideal characters, the hero, the gentleman, the honest broker, become popular in this way in a given social structure.

If one asks how these alien standards are imparted, and how the desired behaviour is produced, a complete scale of methods, ranging from brute force [1] to spontaneity could be given. At one end of the scale is violent coercion with every means of causing pain and fear. At the next stage we find non-violent coercion, withdrawal of love, sabotage,[2] cold-shouldering, and indifference. We must also examine in a class by themselves the gratifications which arouse spontaneous action by stimulating the desire for profit and advancement. Praise, flattery, and persuasion can be used to create spontaneous responses and it depends on the social context and on established conventions whether they are more certain in their results than tangible possessions. The advantage of adopting a technique based on reward is that it creates the illusion of free choice. Here I must emphasize the fact that a society not only creates the hope of reward, but it has to foster the desires which go with it. If it offers only new gratifications for which no one is prepared to strive it meets with no response. If it fosters expectations which it cannot on principle fulfil, it will create discontent and finally rebellion. From the subjective point of view free choice and disinterested motives are a reality, but from a sociological point of view they are largely nurtured by society and are not in this respect totally unlike the reactions produced by brute force. If the individual studies his own mind, he is right in thinking that his reactions are spontaneous, but that does not alter the fact that society has, as it were, conditioned him without his knowledge to struggle for the prizes it offers. Indeed, it often depends on the form of social organization employed whether the individual does something because he must or whether

---

[1] C. M. Case, *Some Sociological Aspects of Non-Violent Coercion*, New York, 1923. Cf. also III. 2a and c in the Bibliography.
[2] Lumley, F. E., *Means of Social Control*, New York, 1925.

society has adjusted its emotional values with such skill that he sets his heart on doing it or feels that his honour is at stake. Mark Twain's *Tom Sawyer* illustrates this point very well in a limited setting. Tom is ordered as a punishment to paint the garden fence and he manages to make the other boys give him all sorts of presents in exchange for the privilege of doing the painting ; so that we see once again that much depends on the way in which a fact is socially presented. Punishment in a different setting becomes reward.

Though reward and punishment are both social incentives, and the rewards for which we strive are socially determined, it is true, nevertheless, that a society which is based chiefly on command and punishment is more brutal than one based on reward. The methods which try to rouse men to act by kindling their desires are much subtler in conception and more sublimated in effect. Their efficiency cannot be rightly assessed by noting the speed of reaction in isolated cases alone. We must also remember that the strain of waiting for orders and the fear of punishment destroy both individual spontaneity and the general power of response, so that these become atrophied in spheres in which they are essential.

It seems that society itself instils the wishes and determines the range of possible gratifications, and the dynamic tension which springs from them is strictly correlated with the needs of the changing social order itself. The different levels of expectations as they exist in the different social classes are the direct expression of strivings which set various groups in motion and give them direction. They are, therefore, the most important psychological key-points from which society can influence the minds of its members.

A planned society will naturally strive to influence these levels of expectation among the different classes. Such a society avoids many of the difficulties in which a free society is involved because it is capable of adapting the level of expectations, to wishes which it is possible to fulfil. If it cannot produce enough wealth it can make a virtue of renunciation or create satisfaction in economy itself. In a free society on the other hand the level of expectation is produced by external conditions which usually cannot be controlled, and it is in no way adjusted to the needs of the different social classes or of society as a whole. Our theory is, then, that the creation of rewards as well as that of wishes and expectations, is a product of the social process, and that the origin of the dynamic impulse which impels us to work and to make sacrifices is to be sought in tension between expectation and reward. This creative tension in favourable cases was spontaneously produced in the past. In modern society, however, owing to rapid changes, and to the mechanism of competition which gives rise to new expectations, without at the same time creating the means of gratifying them, a general dissatisfaction will naturally arise, and if it is to be avoided in the future guidance and planning will be needed. This theory that rewards are correlated with certain socially conditioned expectations will of course only be appreciated by those who have already seen that material interest is by no means final, and that men are not primarily bent on material gratifications. Even our interest in food, as Knight has clearly seen, is largely a matter of social standards rather than of biological need.[1] Here we meet with another fact of the same order. Not only does society co-ordinate its rewards with the level of expectations, but even the threshold of sensitivity, as we have already mentioned, is different in different societies. It is remarkable that an English upbringing creates a delicacy which is sensitive to the slightest shades of criticism, while in many other countries the coarsest abuse and exaggeration would be necessary as a deterrent. In dealing both with children and adults, an English rebuke is often concealed in a casual remark, or must as it were be read between the lines. Thus personal intercourse in England teaches people to notice the smallest change of manner, to feel good-humoured

---

[1] Knight has realized this fact very clearly. He has rightly emphasized that economic interests are not, for the most part, final, but that other values are set on apparently material things, and that the human struggle really revolves around these inherent valuations. Once this is understood, the new problem arises under what conditions these valuations become attached to material goods. When, for instance, do food and housing carry social prestige, and when can the desire for prestige be satisfied by badges and titles ? Knight, F., " Economic Theory of Nationalism," in his *Ethics of Competition*, p. 315. On the problem of Prestige, cf. Nicholson, H., *The Meaning of Prestige*, Cambridge, 1937 ; Hans Speier, " Honor and Social Structure " in *Social Research*, vol. 2, 1935. Cf. also IV 4 in the Bibliography.

ridicule and chaff as though they were a sharp rebuff.   This leads to great economy in the technique of rewards and punishments, and the general English tendency to under-statement is merely a particular expression of society's subtle grading of psychological satisfactions and rebukes. But probably an improved technique of this type is only possible in a more or less static society, where sensitivity is impressed on the mind in early childhood, and is more or less implied in the whole social order.   Here again we have an instance how various subtle qualities which are indispensable in a particular society are instilled by our immediate surroundings through the medium of personal contacts.

After dealing with gratifications, which we may regard as lying half-way between violent coercion and absolute spontaneity, we must pass on to mere imitation, which is a kind of no man's land between spontaneity and submission to brute force.   Many things are done in society, not because of special gratifications or coercion, but because people discover certain simple solutions and adopt them as a con-ditioned reflex or from imitation.   " It is always done " and " it simply is not done " are slogans, which help to pave the way for such solutions.   The lack of social mobility again makes it possible to hand on most conventions by imitation without giving them a second thought.   If there is no variety of experience to show that in other countries or in other social classes the same things can be done in a different way, the same problems solved by other methods, much can be achieved by sheer routine and inertia.   So, too, in the economic sphere people will be satisfied with current con-ditions if there are no other possibilities with which to com-pare them.   Thus Gide rightly remarks in his *Return from the U.S.S.R.* that shoddy goods are accepted in Russia without a murmur.   As long as my neighbour is no better off than I am, my mind is at rest, he adds.   The necessity for adopting a system of coercion or reward instead of leaving the desired behaviour to tradition and imitation seems to depend on definite social conditions.   Reward and punishment are only necessary when tradition is unequal to the task.   Detailed observation and experiment are needed on this point ; but in any case it is becoming more and more obvious that the various methods in use which attempt to bring about a definite type of behaviour cannot be interpreted in the abstract without reference to the countries in which they are found. It seems to be that dynamic society is compelled continuously to introduce new incentives and qualifications in order to break up, and to replace many of the habitualized patterns of tradition. But this perpetual search for new interests makes life far more difficult, for people who only react to new pleasures are infinitely harder to control than those who are governed by routine.

But a dynamic society must not merely encourage its members to work for reward, it must also develop fresh initiative and spontaneity, especially in the ruling élite. Here we come to the next position in the scale of techniques for influencing human behaviour directly. From the socio-logical point of view it is remarkable that society can provide incentives to persuade people to use their initiative and to enjoy the experience. We all know the type of man who prefers to live quietly, has no spirit of adventure and does not like responsibility, and on the other hand the type who is only happy in a profession which gives scope for his initiative. But these differences in type are rooted not only in physiology and heredity but to a large extent in early conditioning. There is a whole series of methods for encouraging and discouraging initiative by education within the framework of immediate influence ; and the way in which the different societies handle the feelings of anxiety and security forms a significant background to their educational strategy. If a society sets out to govern mainly by coercion and military command, the general feeling of anxiety is heightened and intimidation becomes one of its principal techniques. It is impossible to deny that the traditional religions have made considerable use of this fear mongering and have done their best to create a feeling of guilt. On the other hand, if a society needs heroes and pioneers it will see that its citizens are educated so that neither death nor the unforeseen holds any terrors for them. One of the principal features of Islamic teachings is that death has no horror in it.

But we can go a step further. At one end of a scale ranging from complete passivity to initiative there is the possibility of training for creative imagination—an education which not only encourages the desire for initiative but also quickens the imagination or at least gives rise to the necessary frame of mind. Here we must realize what the creative faculty is. Among other qualities it certainly implies a gift for curious and unexpected psychological associations, but this gift can be tabooed or welcomed by society. If a society values unconventional trains of thought it will set an æsthetic, moral, or scientific premium on them. We know that some primitive peoples only encourage their children to play a few monotonous games and others encourage games which cultivate imagination.[1]

It is once more obvious from these examples that applied techniques of influencing human behaviour by personal contact cannot be wholly understood if they are studied apart from their context. In order to understand the behaviour both of those who influence and those who are influenced it is sometimes sufficient merely to consider the relationship between father and child, teacher and pupil, actor and spectator. But as a rule the process of conditioning and persuasion can only be fully understood if we glance at the wider social configurations. The ultimate source of this changing behaviour is, in such cases, social control with a focus outside the personal relationship. This type of control originates in the last rešort, not in the person who is actually exerting the influence but in a wider social context, and thus is acting from afar. For this reason we shall speak of indirect methods of influencing human behaviour.

2. *Indirect Methods of Influencing Human Behaviour*

We shall deal with this indirect influence in five sections.
(*a*) Influencing behaviour in unorganized masses.
(*b*) Influencing behaviour in concrete groups.
    (*a*) In communities by means of traditional institutions, customs, and so on.
    (β) In organized bodies by means of rationalized behaviour.
(*c*) Influencing behaviour by means of field-structures.
(*d*) Influencing behaviour by varying situations.
(*e*) Influencing behaviour by means of social mechanisms.

[1] Cf. Mead, M., *Growing Up in New Guinea: A Comparative Study of Primitive Education*, London, 1931, page 6, 93 ff.

The last section was based upon the theory that as far as indirect methods of influencing human behaviour are concerned it is the objective context of social activities which ultimately conditions individual reactions, and not the immediately perceptible influence of the tutor, father, husband, wife, or neighbour. In many cases direct and indirect influences work hand in hand, but they often come into conflict. A young man's competitive tendencies may be aroused by personal contacts, for instance, by living with a brother who constantly provokes them or with a family which sets the example. But if he becomes a tradesman, these tendencies are stabilized by the objective social pattern of the market-place and after some reconstruction they take their place in the objective context of society. Reconstruction consists in co-ordinating the psychological impulses—envy, self-assertion, the desire to excel—and turning them in a new direction so that they may be used for an objective purpose which is of value to society. Whereas in rivalry these impulses serve a purely subjective purpose, that of annihilating his fellow-man, in competition they lead to objective achievement.

But once this reconstruction is accomplished the individual can no longer be explained in terms of his immediate surroundings, but only in terms of the objective social task which the competitive mechanism is designed to fulfil. From this time onwards his reactions are determined by the social background of the market-place rather than by his own character. His competitive attitude tends to become automatic and to emerge from the fluctuating private motives in which it was steeped. It becomes incorporated in the business aspect of his life. From then on the boy's action must be interpreted in the light of his competitive environment rather than that of his subjective unconscious, or of the demands and stimulation of his immediate surroundings. These do not entirely disappear, but his life has many different facets and the professional side of it is apt to become relatively independent. To turn to an example perhaps different in nature but which conveys the same principle : The choir-boy sings a part which is meaningless in itself, but which can be understood if one hears the whole choir singing together. Most human activities which develop in the context of division of labour are of that nature.

Their meaning does not become clear if one focuses attention upon the subjective aspects of personal motives, but only if they are seen in the objective context of collective purpose. As an example, the objective meaning of barter is only apparent to the man who sees how it involuntarily regulates the whole division of labour. Subjectively everyone is merely working for his own advantage. The subjective desire for profit is aroused by the whole fabric of barter and competition but does not in itself contain the meaning of the entire process. From the point of view of society barter and competition are devices which work as objective controls and constantly compel people to behave as they think fit.

How many of these social contrivances are there?

There are a great many social controls, but we will not describe them in detail, only try to work out the fundamental principle by which they can be classified. The simplest and most easily recognizable social units which act as visible controls are the groups. These are very numerous and need not be specified, since they are well known in the form in which we meet them in every day life. They include every concrete group from the family to the state, from the club to the joint stock company. They have their own controls which vary with the purpose and function of the group. Apart from these well-defined groups there are, on the one hand, the unintegrated and unorganized casual masses and crowds, which are governed by special psychological rules. On the other hand, there are functional units, configurations of activity, which cut across the contours of concrete groups and crowds. In their context we shall discuss in full detail the situations, field-structures, and social mechanisms. From the point of view of planned society these controls gradually become far more important than the concrete social groups which have so often been described, and which can only remain the centre of activity as long as a slowly developing society attempts to invest them with all its powers of control. As soon as society has outgrown them they cease to become political. That means society no longer uses them as the most relevant foci of social influence. Just as the tribe once undermined the family as a political agency and the state in its turn undermined the tribe, so the concrete groups tend to be superseded by the functional social units, and the more abstract social configurations become the real agencies of control. We shall pay special attention to these functional units as instances of control, partly because they have never been adequately investigated from these angles before, and partly because mass society seems to show an increasing tendency to reorganize itself through them. But we must begin with those forms of social conglomerations such as casual masses and crowds, which have not yet been integrated into concrete groups.

(a) Influencing Behaviour in Unorganized Masses

From the standpoint of the social conditioning of human behaviour the crowd or mass is an extreme case. In a normal society it represents a transitional stage between two forms of group integration. In revolutionary times when the older types of group have been destroyed, the individual often finds that his behaviour is prescribed, not by the internal organization of the group, but by human beings in the mass. A crowd has as yet no social aim or function, so that the conduct of the individual cannot be determined by his function in it or regulated by the mutual control of its members, for these members have not yet entered into personal relationships. The effect of the crowd on the individual is purely contagious ; it does not subordinate his impulses to functional tasks. This particular type of crowd behaviour has been justly described as uncontrolled. The reason why we behave as we do in a crowd is that the inhibitions connected with our family, our neighbours, our work, are cast aside ; and in the anonymity of the mass, sober citizens throw stones and scared employees fire on the police.

Most of the erroneous descriptions of mass behaviour are due to the fact that to the sociologically untrained eye all masses are alike. We have seen in previous parts of the book that only an unorganized mass gives any evidence of crowd behaviour, and that every specific form of socially organized activity has its own peculiar effect on human conduct. It is not only the number of people involved—or at least not primarily—which reacts upon the individual in various ways, but the purpose which guides their activities and the internal organization which goes with it. Here it is sufficient to mention the crowd as an extreme case of a group : a horde of men whose activities are still unorganized and have not acquired any particular function.

I shall not analyse the significance of mass behaviour in any detail here, for it has been described more carefully in Part III. Nor shall I go into the suggestion that the function of the crowd as a transient social entity is to break down the older forms of behaviour in order to combine them in a different pattern. We must now turn to the social control exercised by the group as opposed to the crowd

(b) Influencing Behaviour through Concrete Groups

By concrete groups we mean those social units whose contours are clearly defined in space and time. There is usually no doubt as to their existence ; their names, functions, and members are known. The family, the clan, the club are concrete enough, compared with the vague and indefinite public which listens to a wireless programme or forms part of a movement in literature, religion, or art, united only in its interest in new ideas or in its slavery to fashion. Like situations, field structures and mechanisms, these fluctuating publics form social units, but they are still too shapeless and indistinct to be assigned to any fixed location in society or to have any definite contours.

Concrete groups are usually divided into two classes : communities and associations.[1] The first class, which includes the family, the tribe, the village community, is in many respects like a living organism. These groups have never been planned, and they embrace every aspect of their members' lives. Membership is a matter of birth and not of deliberate choice.

Associations on the other hand such as a bureaucracy or a joint stock company, are consciously organized with some definite, rational purpose in view. They do not embrace every aspect of their members' lives, and one can join them or leave them at will.

(a) Through Communities by means of Traditional Institutions

The community is usually dominated by some special form of control and is governed by unwritten laws such as customs, habits, and conventions. Rights and prohibitions exert considerable pressure although there are no elected

---

[1] MacIver, R. M., *Society : a Textbook of Sociology*, New York, 1933. Cf. also F. Tönnies, *Gemeinschaft und Gesellschaft* (Leipzig, 1877).

officials with the power of sanction. Standards are maintained by what one might call mutual control. It very often depends on the situation who is likely to act as the representative of the community and insist that the rules must be obeyed. To give an example : A young man wants to marry ; he has to support his old mother and cannot afford to support a wife as well. A sister, an aunt, or a neighbour will express the public opinion on the subject. In psychological terms, this means that anyone can represent the super-ego and become the exponent of the group.

This does not cease to be true in spite of the fact that there is a definite traditional hierarchy of prestige among the members of these groups. On the other hand in an association there are statutes, regulations, and an administrative staff to see that the rules are kept—rules which in no way affect the ordinary life of the members outside the group. The prescribed pattern of behaviour varies widely with the type of community and association involved.

Communities and associations produce different types of collective behaviour, and this variation roughly corresponds to the distinction between institutional and rational responses.

It is merely for the purpose of definition that I shall describe as " institutions ", or as " institutional ", those patterns of co-ordinated activity which are the product of unconscious tradition, and shall describe as " rational " those co-ordinated social activities which are consciously directed to some definite end and are more or less strictly adapted to that end. Institutions, apart from their function, embody certain symbolic and intuitive values. These values appeal to elements in the human mind which remain untouched by abstract reasoning and can only be brought into play by a direct appeal to the unconscious. Rituals and ceremonies, such as those practised at initiations, weddings, ordeals, or coronations, are subject to this pattern. They originally developed from casual activities, from findings in the process of trial and error, and became habitual in static societies where customs change slowly. It is rightly assumed by some thinkers that an institution is never a simple, direct answer to a social need. It is rooted in the past, and can never be fully understood without reference to its history.

In contrast to this traditional form of collective adjustment, rationalized collective behaviour begins by abolishing the traditional symbolic elements in favour of those which are essential to the function of the body concerned, judged exclusively by the needs of the present situation.

These traditional institutions, taken collectively, constitute the prevailing customs, folkways as W. G. Sumner [1] called them, of a society. It is an extremely difficult question whether a planned society should refrain from changing the customs which regulate the life of the community. It is unwise to make too vigorous an attack upon them, for they are deeply rooted in the habits and emotions of the people, who often react more fiercely when these habits are disturbed than when material goods are taken from them.[2] Another fact tells heavily against the destruction of traditional attitudes and institutions, as retained in customs and religion. Under normal conditions it is exceedingly hard to replace them overnight by other values, for it is they which keep human conduct within bounds. Their destruction creates a gap in the social structure and in the individual's system of behaviour, and modern mass propaganda pours into the breach.

On the other hand, we must remember that it is usually not the planner who destroys them ; industrial society itself has really dissolved the substance of these customs long ago in most spheres of life, and that is why it is so easy for propaganda to instil new values by mass methods. Even after taking every precaution that this living tissue demands, one cannot help saying that it is unwise to be wholly deterred from changing this system of habits, however ingrained it may be, because we often cannot reconstruct the social order without changing human beings and their conventions. We must not attempt to deny that these traditional practices in education, in the family, in the nursery, in the old-fashioned school, are frequently full of

[1] Sumner, W. G., *Folkways*, a Study of the Sociological Importance of Usages, Manners, Customs, Mores, and Morals, Boston, 1907.
[2] This need not surprise us after what we have already said, for we have seen that as far as material goods are concerned, the standard of living is largely a conventional conception. Once the most elementary needs have been met, the loss of material possessions only creates unexpected agitation because people can no longer live according to their traditional habits.

superstitions and create distorted minds. If we do not change these things organized reform is hopeless.

The solution will probably be the invention of a kind of strategy which more exactly defines the stages in which reform has to be carried out. First of all it must distinguish between the harmful elements, which should be abolished, and those which still help to bind people together and have power to influence the course of events. If we uproot them, we are only replacing living forms by the highly artificial values hammered in by dictatorship and mass decree. After the experiences of the last decade, the intellectuals of to-day should see more and more clearly that the war waged by enlightenment in reason's name against conventions and traditional institutions must in part be lost. It is right that it should go on where traditional methods prove to be clumsy and could well be replaced by a more rational form of control, supposing that the problem is simple and unambiguous. On the other hand, this war on tradition led to hopeless impoverishment, where the new social forces were not in a position to replace the old folkways by new ones. Apparently the new patterns of behaviour can only be created at an especially slow tempo and require a genuine imagination which is almost opposed to calculated thought.

The symbolic elements in folk-lore have their own peculiar appeal—an appeal to the unconscious elements of the mind. For reasons which psychology has not yet adequately explained, the modern consciousness has rarely succeeded in stirring the depths of the unconscious by means of new and authentic symbols. This may well be the reason why the Catholic Church usually took over the heathen cults and incorporated them in its system, giving them at most a new interpretation. It felt itself powerless to oppose the genuine primeval archetypes of tribal times. This far-sighted policy has shown us how to bring about a Renaissance in this field without entirely destroying the older system of archetypes, customs, and traditional institutions. The charm of the original pattern can often be preserved by giving a new meaning to former institutions and absorbing them in the new way of life. This is especially true of those traditions which are still of value to a society after it has reached a new stage. Applying this to our central problem, that of devising a planned society which will be democratic and constitutional, the Anglo-Saxon countries should not try to shatter their traditions which have kept the texture of social relationships almost unbroken from the ancient common law until the present time, only to replace them by an authoritarian pattern. They form a traditional heritage which is easier to destroy than to rebuild, should it once again be needed.

(b) *Through Organized Bodies by means of Rationalized Behaviour*

Associations are, as we saw, concrete groups with ascertainable contours, and are composed of members who have come together for certain rational ends. They are informed by a spirit which leads to the rational regulation of behaviour, for the necessary action is determined solely by their central aims. In extreme cases, this behaviour is completely organized and association develops into organization. Thus it is largely a matter of degree whether we speak of associations or organizations ; it depends on the amount of rationalization applied.

If an institution is governed by formal statutes and regulations and maintains an administrative staff to see that these rules are kept, and yet leaves room for a variety of decisions, a number of different views as to the wisdom of a given policy, we shall speak of rationalized but not of rationally organized behaviour. The procedure at a club or at a business meeting is of this kind.

But if regulation goes farther, if the behaviour of the individuals who take part in this co-ordinated action is carefully calculated and completely predetermined, and its effectiveness can be appraised in more or less quantitative terms, we shall speak of rationalized and organized behaviour. Our group has developed into an organization. In all probability, there is a high correlation between the growth of population and the growth of technology, the greater number of tasks to be dealt with by organization and the necessity of standardizing an increasing number of activities. Owing to the rapid development of these systems of strongly correlated activities, they should be considered in a separate category. Armies and factories are usually governed by this type of organization. Not only their basic procedure but their ultimate aims, and the means used to attain them, have been calculated in advance and are in this sense organized.

Administration is the most important example of the modern phenomenon of organization, and we shall confine ourselves to analysing it, for it clearly illustrates the scope of the new problems in this and allied fields. Administration cannot be created at random, it implies a pre-defined aim. In social affairs, this means that administration can only be set up where activities are no longer political. By political activities we usually mean the kind of group action that is fighting for ultimate opinions and values. Administration does not fight and does not determine aims but is merely a means for carrying them out.

If we consider the politics of action, of taxation, of trade, we mean by " action " the struggle between the rival groups and authorities which determines the trend of development. Those who control policy—the inner groups or the élite— find themselves directing organization. If both ends and means have for a time been determined in advance, the conflict over ultimate aims naturally ceases, and the measures which must be adopted to secure these aims can be regulated by hard and fast rules. An administrative staff can be created to carry out decisions, and we shall call their department the administrative province of group action. This has a very different nature from the political department at the head of the group which determines its external policy towards other groups. At bottom, every little group, family, and party has this political aspect for it has its own tactics, activities, values, and policy, requiring foresight, decision, and a calculation of risks.

In modern society as social techniques become more intricate, little units once in conflict are merged into larger groups both in the sphere of economics and of power. Thus they acquire a common leader and a common policy, and the non-political, administrative sphere of action which forms an enclave becomes more and more extensive. Owing to the dual nature (political and administrative) of social activities, we must train two types of men. One must be capable of directing policy and must have political initiative in the wider sense of the term : the other must be able to carry out this policy exactly with unquestionable efficiency. These qualities were often united in one man ;

they were to be found in government officials and in the managers of the smaller business units, but the growth of administration tends to separate them.

This example clearly shows once more that the creation of the social types which are to prevail in a given society largely depends on the nature of the groups and spheres of action in which they have to work. As the gulf between legislative and executive action widens, the older type of man who was able both to frame a policy and to carry it out will become scarcer, and will make room for the few who have initiative and the many who are capable only of executive action.

Organization and administration [1] are typically modern forms of social control. They have been investigated with such care that it is possible to direct their operations from key positions in the state. It is extremely important that the public at large should be familiar with the modern conception of bureaucracy. Here too a genuine sociological investigation into the new possibilities is the first step towards a sound policy.

(c) Influencing Behaviour by means of Field Structures.

There are social controls which are based on the interdependence of human action without being centred in concrete groups, communities, or associations. This means that our actions can be controlled by the actions of others, even though they may not be members of a definite group.

The sociological category through which this control operates can be called a field structure ; it lies somewhere between concrete organic groups and huge organizations. [2]

If a man's behaviour is conditioned by his local group and he assimilates its customs and convictions, we recognize the influence of this group immediately. We see how the individual and his habits are stamped with an institutional

---

[1] Cf. in the Bibliography, III 4a-c.

[2] K. Lewin introduced the conception of the field into psychology from physics. J. F. Brown has recently made use of it in sociology but our approach is rather different from his, in so far as we discuss the phenomena in relation to the system of social controls. It is only in this context, I think, that its meaning becomes apparent. Cf. Lewin, K., " Field Theory and Experiment in Social Psychology : Concept and Methods," Amer. Journ. of Sociol., vol. 44, 1938. Brown, J. F., Psychology and the Social Order, New York, 1936.

pattern, which corresponds to the impressions pouring in from his immediate surroundings. We can also see what happens when, instead of the traditional, flexible imprint of the institution, he is exposed to the mechanized patterns of organization. In other words, we see how a man can be conditioned in one way by the influx of local customs and mores, and in another by his activities in an administrative bureau, whether it be owned by the state or by a private firm. But obviously, there are certain human qualities which do not correspond to these influences as the following example will show.

When the trader and later the merchant developed within the towns of the late Middle Ages, with their purely regional interests, it was found that the outlook of these men differed in some ways from the traditional outlook of the local community. From the outset the merchant represented a peculiar social type. The more he depended on his international relationships, the clearer it became that he was not a citizen of his community like other people. While most of his fellow-citizens were stamped by the personal influences of the community, he was only partially affected by them, and the greater part of his reactions were responses to the field-structure which we call the world of commerce. This is a unique phenomenon, a peculiar network of interdependent activities, which even in the late Middle Ages embraced the commercial centres of the contemporary world. Competition and the interdependence of markets were important, but were still only isolated factors. (In so far as they were units in themselves we shall deal with them separately under the heading of Social Mechanisms.) Commerce being a field structure is greater than the sum of these mechanisms. New trade, economic exchange, transport, commercial travelling, correspondence, bookkeeping, and speculation formed a sector of coherent activities and of new forms of behaviour cutting clean across the world of concrete groups. In order to describe this world, which as we have seen does not express itself as a concrete group either in terms of a community or of an association, we must draw on the conception known to physics as the magnetic field.

We speak of the influence of a field structure on the character of an individual, if we cannot explain his behaviour by group institutions or by the mechanical patterns of organization, but only by a more or less free adjustment to the pressure of segmental influences.[1] The pressure prevailing in the field is conveyed by the interdependent activities of individuals which very often cut across a given society as a whole.

Whenever society instead of expanding in concentric circles, develops new spheres of action which traverse the boundaries of the concrete groups, we speak of a field structure. Where fresh markets must be won after economic or political conquest overseas, where new industries create fresh trade at home, or propaganda is needed to persuade people to take up unfamiliar work, the predetermined patterns adopted by the concrete groups are apt to break down. Whenever conflict and competition are in full swing, and individuals have to make their own adjustments, whenever it is impossible to foresee the trend of events, the laws which govern the magnetic waves of the field structure have more effect on human nature than established custom or rational organization.

Under the segmental influences of these field structures, new character traits of the economic man developed which differed from the ideals of his organic community.[2]

The question arises whether social control is possible in spheres where conflict and competition are the usual forms of adjustment. Even here regulation is possible, for conflict and competition on a large scale do not lead to chaos but unite in a process of dynamic equilibrium. If one wishes to interfere in these fields without doing violence to the spontaneity of events, a specific kind of regulation is necessary. Regulations which are adapted to the nature of the field structure intervene only at certain points in the course of events. They do not determine the line of action in advance as in custom or administration.

[1] We understand by segmental those influences which do not affect the whole personality, but only certain classes of responses in the individual which fall under the influence of the field structures. The latter, as the text will show, traverse society like a magnetic ray emanating from a distant focus.

[2] Cf. Brentano, W., *Der Wirtschaftende Mensch in der Geschichte*, Leipzig, 1923 ; Sombart, W., *Der Bourgeois*, Zur Geistesgeschichte des modernen Wirtschaftsmenschen, München, Leipzig, 1920. Mannheim, K., "Über das Wesen und die Bedeutung des wirtschaftlichen Erfolgsstrebens," *Archiv für Sozialwissenschaft*, vol. 63, 1930.

It is to Lippmann's [1] credit that he realized how law can sometimes take this form. It was he who showed that the difference between legal regulation and administrative regulation is that administration prescribes in advance what must be done and creates a standard pattern, while law lets the parties act freely and decide when to ask the judge to straighten out a difficult situation. But Lippmann failed to see that it does not rest with us whether we let certain actions take their course and submit them only afterwards to legal procedure or surrender them from the very beginning to administrative control ; because law can only be applied in terms of retrospective regulation as long as relatively independent small units are competing for the conquest of a new province of social life. As soon as these units grow in size, economic and social techniques, strengthened by the concentration of power in a few hands, transform the free field-structure into a monopolistic and organized one with a leader or a small band of leaders at its head. Policy is now fixed and in more and more fields only administrative regulations are in force.

Thus we shall only speak of a field-structure as long as the warring social atoms are regulated by social and natural laws, such as conflict and competition. Their activities are then co-ordinated by spontaneous adjustment and the flaws in the system take effect in a series of waves, like slumps in the trade cycle. This interplay of forces does not prevent the game being played according to certain rules, such as property laws or the laws of contract, but usually these define only the framework of the system and not the individual moves in the game. As soon as power and initiative are concentrated in a few hands, we should prefer to speak of a completely organized sphere rather than a field-structure.

Our mind, trained only to see the crude alternative between complete freedom (*laissez-faire*) and traditional and rational regulation, has seldom become aware of the controls governing the field-structure. These controls are a combination of spontaneous adjustment of the social atoms and the deliberate adaptation of the rules of the game by a central authority. A planned society might succeed in incorporating in its structure fields where competition and

[1] Lippman, W., *The Good Society*, London, 1938, p. 316 ff.

spontaneous adjustment could prevail, while the final controls could be exercised from strategic points within these fields. The central authority would only make its influence felt when it was forced to modify the rules of the game in order to prevent results which might be injurious to society or to the central plan democratically agreed upon. Such a solution would stimulate the creative impulses of acting individuals without leaving every social activity in a state of chaos.

(d) *Influencing Behaviour by means of Situations.*

Another social pattern which has a decisive influence upon men's lives and forms a hidden mainspring of their actions, is the situation. By a situation, I understand a unique configuration formed in the process of interaction between certain people. Although the participants in the situation need not necessarily have any common purpose explicitly in mind, their activities must be related to some common theme which defines the nature of their efforts. The term " the pressure of the situation " hints at the fact that unique configurations in the process of interaction may be such as to act as a control on our behaviour. We can be compelled to act in a given way through explicit taboos and commands ; but also without the latter, solely through the pressure of the situation. Situations do not emerge out of the vacuum, but are rather cross-currents in a stream of events, in a process which is governed by certain social forces. In the correlated activities of a group of enterprising friends, thousands of situations emerge out of the tensions, rivalries, emotional ties involved, and if only a few seem to be conspicuous, it is because these situations throw more light upon the dynamic trends which govern the common action, or because they change the course of events. Although situations are not independent but are, so to say, the by-products of this process, they have a controlling power of their own. If one is involved in a situation one is not entirely free ; the combination of forces represented both by the material and moral factors at stake and by the wills of the other persons concerned, acts as a brake upon the individual. · As I have already pointed out, situations can be classified according to the tendencies which make them conspicuous.

First there are the catastrophic situations, which are unusually vivid. They express the failure of a relationship which can no longer be continued owing to the impossibility of adjusting the factors involved. Thus a hopeless love affair may end in suicide or a business enterprise may go bankrupt. Both these situations affect the lives of a number of people and bring many different factors, material and moral, into play. Then there are rebellious situations in which one partner tries to alter the balance of power after the tension has become unbearable. If a child breaks away from his family in adolescence because his parents fail to realize that he must now be given more freedom we are dealing with a rebellious situation.

Although situations do not, as a rule, become conspicuous unless they reflect a conflict of forces, harmonious situations and those which bring about a readjustment by establishing a new equilibrium on a higher plane should not be overlooked. The celebration of a happy marriage or a close friendship by an exchange of presents or by joint festivities symbolizes the equilibrium attained in the relationship. In such cases, one situation is deliberately chosen out of many, for the sake of emphasis, to represent the happiness achieved through adjustment. Situations of readjustment are reached when after continual conflict both the spiritual and the material factors which have not yet been adapted become clearly visible, and can be rearranged so as to meet the needs of the case. Plant,[1] in his new book, is right in choosing catastrophic situations—" the casual break-down " as the best means of diagnosing the social forces in play. This is the first step from purely descriptive field-work under artificially static conditions to dynamic penetration into the life of the group. If the child in our example after breaking away from his family succeeds in establishing his status as an adolescent, or if the bankrupt merchant succeeds in making his creditors agree to a fresh financial arrangement, a situation of readjustment has arisen.

Situations are of special interest to us, because like field-structures and mechanisms (which will be discussed later), they represent controls which differ from those of the concrete groups, yet influence the individual. The field structure was

[1] Plant, J. S., *Personality and the Cultural Pattern*, New York, 1937,

important, because the magnetic waves of influence and the key points of control from which they are governed extend beyond the boundaries of the concrete groups and are, so to say, independent of them. These waves, radiating through the group, influence the individual while evading the normal controls at work in his surroundings. Situations also evade the control of the concrete groups, but for entirely different reasons. They achieve a certain autonomy, not because they are more comprehensive than the concrete groups but sometimes precisely because they are more microscopic. Thanks to their uniqueness and their infinite variety they can more easily escape the vigilance of centralized group control. They owe their relative independence to the difficulty of penetrating into the life of social atoms. Although their movements and changes are also guided by general forces, their unforeseen combinations progress in a creative evolution, constantly producing something entirely new. Thus genuine situations combine to produce independent controls which escape the standardized forms of guidance.

These new controls are more diffuse than those which emanate from the concrete groups, but it is to this diffuseness that they owe their independence. Although situations are in their very nature dynamic and unique, as soon as they become socialized—that is to say, built into the framework of society—they tend to become standardized to a certain extent. Thus we must distinguish between what is called patterned and unpatterned situations.

Unpatterned situations can best be studied where pioneers are breaking new ground, and unforeseen situations occur for which no established patterns exist. Under the guidance of a leader, new forms of adjustment must be found. This is what happens on a smaller scale after revolution or war, when the old institutions break down and unprecedented situations constantly arise. But once a new order has been established around the new situations there will be a tendency to harmonize them with the more familiar situations. Society cannot, in the long run, tolerate the unpredictable, and is rarely willing to do justice to the variability of life. It will smooth the irregularity of these situations by sorting them into patterns which impose some degree of conformity. Thus we get the phenomena of patterned situations. The social process is continually moving between two extremes : producing situations which are controls in themselves or controlling them from the outside.

When society tries to limit the variability of situations, it uses every means in its power. First it makes use of practical methods to ensure that its economic and political foundations are as firm as possible. By storing food, by building dykes, by accumulating capital it helps to remove economic insecurity. By recruiting armies and police forces it attempts to stabilize the political order. By drafting rules and securing uniform behaviour it limits the possible number of situations in advance. In addition, there is the intellectual method of concealing the variability of situations. By forcing the situation into a recognized category, society can refuse to admit its novelty at the cost of ignoring its uniqueness. In Ibsen's play, Nora's husband refuses for as long as possible to admit that his wife's problems cannot be interpreted as those of the old-fashioned marriage and the old-fashioned housewife. Here he has the traditional forces of society behind him.

Society is, up to a point, compelled to act in this way, for it is obvious that it is only these partly real and established resemblances, however artificially produced and intellectually over-emphasized, that give people a chance of dealing with their difficulties. If they were constantly faced with new problems, and a full realization of their novelty, they would simply be bewildered.

We have to pay careful attention to these elements in our social life, as our task is to detect as many dynamic controls as possible, that is to say, controls which can do justice to the change and individuality of society. The question which puzzles us is : " How has society dealt with these new situations up till now ? Has it left them entirely alone ? "

On closer examination we come to the astonishing conclusion that society has generally succeeded in establishing automatic devices, which, however unconsciously, have acted as social controls on situations. The vital and unadjusted forces at work in a social situation frequently assume the form of conflict. The management of conflicts therefore is a special method of controlling situations. There are professions whose principal task is to study the technique of adjusting conflicts. The judge and even more the arbitrator can be described as the typical peace-makers within the nation,[1] while the diplomat tries to smooth away friction between the nations.

The technique of managing conflicts very often consists in diverting tension from the channel in which it originally occurs. Many unadjusted emotional forces find satisfaction if they are given an outlet in another field. Duels and ordeals proved to be useful because they led to a solution in which the fervour aroused by resentment and the thirst for revenge found its catharsis. Even disputes in Parliament and in the courts of law provide a vocal outlet for the feelings of dissatisfaction which are bound to develop in a given situation. Very often a judge settles a border-line case, in which both parties claim to be in the right, simply by redefining the situation in terms of general principles of law. In such cases he may not satisfy material wants, but readjustment will consist solely in removing intellectual uncertainty. Social workers observe that many family conflicts occur because in modern society the age of adolescence is not as clearly determined as among primitive tribes, where the fact of growth is publicly acknowledged by initiation ceremonies.[2] If this dynamic change is left undefined, as in our society, both parents and children will try to define it in their own interests.

These methods of removing conflicts which we have described so far, have dealt only with the psychological side of readjustment. They seem rather unsatisfactory because they do not touch the deeper forces responsible for the growth of conflict. Although they are very often less significant than the controls which try to readjust the basic material factors they should not lightly be dismissed. Much of our maladjustment is psychological, and we ought to be able to cope with psychological problems as well as social ones. Any careful analysis of the legal adjustment of conflict will show that it frequently deals with its problems on the plane of psychological readjustment. Only too often the judge acts like a conjurer, using the power and authority of the state to squeeze all changes into the framework of

---

[1] Cf. Friedrich, C. G., *Constitutional Government and Politics*, New York and London, 1937, part i, chaps. 5 and 7.

[2] Foster, R. G., "Sociological Research in Adolescence," *American Journ. of Sociology*, 1936.

existing regulation and to define them in terms of established categories of offences, ignoring the novelty of the cases for as long as possible. But a promising new trend is now developing.

In many spheres where order was secured in the past at the cost of doing violence to reality, more realistic experiments are now being made. Conciliation Committees and Courts of Arbitration represent the new technique of dealing with dynamic situations. Pigou among others drew attention to their significance.[1] These bodies, with their greater knowledge of the social foundations of the evils they were established to remove, are trying to find solutions which do more than cure the symptoms. One of the most interesting experiments of this kind in the field of sociology proper was the Chicago Commission's report on negro riots.[2] After the outbreak of these riots, a Committee was set up in order that it might use its sociological knowledge to discover the causes, both small and great, which were responsible for the disturbances. Even if one realizes the limitations of the report, it provides some indication how collective maladjustment could one day be treated by arbitration based on scientific knowledge. As compared with scientific reconstruction and sociological readjustment of these conflicts, the prevailing legal procedures seem to be in many respects still on the plane of magic. Instead of curing the causes of the evil, they give an abusive name to behaviour which in itself is consistent. It has been rightly said that very often society is the patient, and what we usually call punishable or pathological reaction, when more closely observed, proves to be the healthy reaction of a healthy organism to an unhealthy social situation.

As to the special case we have been discussing, i.e. situations acting as controls, it is essential to realize that not only the concentration of power but also its diffusion is vital to society. The value of diffused power is that it helps to keep the authorities in touch with the life of social units and to do justice to the changing factors involved in concrete situations. A centralized power once its sovereignty is assured, should immediately delegate many of its functions to local and

[1] Pigou, A. C., *Economics in Practice*, London, 1935, p. 117.
[2] Chicago Commission on Race Relations, *The Negro in Chicago*, a Study of Race Relations and a Race Riot, Chicago, 1922.

professional bodies whose arbitration should consist, not only in the customary subsumption of new cases under old laws, but in the immediate expression of the actual needs of society as they are clearly reflected in individual conflicts. They should continuously report to the central lawgiving authority the way in which the statutes work in any concrete setting and what the creative tendencies in the living material are.

The significance of distant controls as opposed to those vested in concrete situations and groups is equally striking in the educational field. The essential changes in the methods of modern education spring from the discovery that the vital clue to the moulding of character and the integration of personality lies in the mastery of the situation by the pupil. Only authoritarian teaching tries to develop isolated qualities, attitudes, and habits, and to instil ready-made knowledge so that the citizen may become ever more ready to respond to centralized command. Any education which aims at producing citizens who will be capable of independent judgment and spontaneous co-operation will train its pupils to respond to situations. The situation is the simplest context in which the child can be taught to use his own judgment and thus to face the elementary conflicts of everyday life.

There are professions which train the mind to think in terms of situations. Any good judge or social worker will naturally be inclined to think of society as composed of a variety of characteristic situations. The disadvantage of such an outlook—should it become general—is that it will never arrive at the more comprehensive principles underlying the working of society, or learn to think in terms of *principia media* or of the social structure as a whole. The revolutionary who is anxious to change society overnight will be only too apt to focus his attention solely on the broader principles and to lay too great a stress on the total social structure, the field structures, and the centralized controls in concrete groups. In my opinion, neither of these approaches is satisfactory if it becomes exclusive, and only a judicious combination of the two is likely to do justice to society.

The danger of an over-organized society with too great a weakness for centralized regulation is that it will lead to the abolition of the battle zones and to the absence of any situations in which the process of life could develop. But just as modern education makes deliberate use of planned situations in its training (for what is an experimental school but a bundle of planned situations ?) so a planned society must be careful to retain dynamic situations wherever it can afford to do so.

(e) Influencing Behaviour by means of Social Mechanisms.

The best illustrations of this type of control are competition, division of labour, distribution of power, the methods of creating social hierarchy and distance, and the mechanisms which determine whether we shall rise or sink in the social scale.

It is extremely difficult to distinguish social mechanisms from situations and field-structures, chiefly because they are not mutually exclusive and their boundaries tend to overlap. Situations and field-structures can both be partly or wholly produced by social mechanisms. Competition in itself for instance is a mechanism, but if it produces trade and the trade of one country becomes dependent on the markets of another, a homogeneous sphere is formed which conditions the reactions of the individuals concerned, so that we should speak, as we have seen, of a field-structure. On the other hand, competition may give rise to situations. Out of the process of competition, competitive situations emerge. It is purely a question of emphasis whether we turn our attention to a single cross-section of the process and some particular combination of factors involved, that is to say, to situations, or whether we study the whole process of competition as a mechanism with all its cumulative effects. Competition may be legitimately regarded as a basic process in society. This is evident from the fact that it always tends to create the same effects as long as it can function undisturbed. If the social mechanism of competition for instance be introduced into an existing sphere of social life its consequences will be seen immediately. If commercial activity be stimulated by introducing a railway into a remote part of the country, one can watch the effects of competition, and how it always arouses new ambitions, breaks up ancient customs, and shatters group solidarity. Competition has often been mistaken for a purely economic process. In fact it has never been confined to the economic sphere. There may be competition within the framework of administration, in the army, in science, in love, or in any other field of social activities. The head of a bureaucracy, of an army, or of a scientific body may decide that a certain result could best be achieved by competition. This is bound to change the attitude of his subordinates towards their work, towards their colleagues, towards the administration of the available resources, and so on. The mechanism of competition in these cases acts as a new kind of control, with a focus and an influence of its own.

The more closely one examines the psychological effects of mechanisms like competition, the more obvious it becomes that our previous distinction between direct and indirect influence needs amplification. Although it still remains legitimate to consider the education of the child by its parents and neighbours in technical skills, in inventiveness, in trustworthiness, as a personal influence, it is always possible to find this education stimulated and even controlled by situations and thus by the mechanisms of a given society. It is ultimately the nature of these mechanisms : competition, division of labour, the division of social functions, the division of power, the necessary hierarchy, which creates both the need and the opportunity for definite types of activities. It is these mechanisms which either foster initiative, ability to take risks and responsibility, or create obedience and submission. To take this latter view, i.e. that mechanisms are the ultimate controls, becomes especially important if, by trying to correct some of these educationally harmful influences, one comes to realize that they cannot be altered by simply recasting the form of personal influence but only by altering the nature of the situation in which it occurs. This is in my view the significance of the recent sociological trend in psycho-analysis and psychiatry. Thus Karen Horney, for instance, is right in stating that neurotic competitiveness is strictly connected with our competitive system.[1] Here the individual therapeutic approach reaches its limits, for in order to achieve results the whole social mechanism of competition ought to be altered. At the present level of our discussion we realize that it is gradually becoming evident that mechanisms are working behind personal influences, and

[1] Karen Horney. *The Neurotic Personality of our Time* (London, 1937).

although for certain educational purposes it is not without value to act as if direct influences were to a large extent autonomous.

Let us take another example : the mechanism which determines whether people shall rise or fall in the social scale. Sometimes this mechanism is not a completely independent one, as it very often depends on another mechanism, competition. But there are other cases where the mechanism of advancement is independent, when, for instance, a rise in the social scale is dependent on the principle of seniority. Here the mechanism of advancement will act as a direct control, not merely as a by-product of competition. Thus, in these cases, the deliberate regulation of the principle of rising and falling in the social scale is a control *sui generis*.

Although it is very important, from time to time, to decide whether two mechanisms are independent or dependent on each other, and thus to elaborate a whole list of existing mechanisms, it would be a mistake to think that all are of equal weight. Therefore one can always rightly ask whether any one of these mechanisms is supreme. Both the Liberal and the Marxist theories were right in emphasizing the supremacy of the division of labour and in pointing out the way in which it regulates the institution of property, the whole legal system, and class stratification. I wish once more to stress that the question of primacy, though an important one, in no way alters the fact that in some periods emphasis may be shifted from one mechanism to another, and that this in itself may depend on the changing nature of social techniques. If military techniques gain in importance, the division of labour will be regulated according to military needs. Social advancement may also be controlled not by competition but according to the needs of the military pattern. People will simply rise in the social scale just as they do in the army.

One has to guard against two extremes, that of focusing attention exclusively on the minor and dependent mechanisms, and that looking only at the major principles regulating the whole social structure. A study of the social structure without a knowledge of the minor mechanisms is worthless. A study of the minor mechanisms without a sense of the major dynamic processes is equally shortsighted.

Fascism is very apt to juggle with separate mechanisms, without the slightest inkling of their reaction on society as a whole. For instance, the Fascists control the mechanism of social advancement by treating the Party as an organized means of promotion, and racial discrimination as a means of social disinheritance. Thus they have shown how immensely powerful these mechanisms can be, and how much harm can be done by applying them irrespective of their long run effects and of the injustice they cause.

The most promising possibility in the regulation of social advancement would be the hope of securing a better co-ordination of supply and demand in the various professions and a fairer selection of candidates. Employment ought not to be so dependent on luck, unfair competition, patronage, wire-pulling, and nepotism. The real difficulty lies in the present artificiality of the objective methods of selection. Tests and examinations frequently reveal only simple, static qualities and do not do justice to complex and integrated characteristics, which only become apparent in dealing with concrete situations. There is some prospect of improvement in this sphere as well. Just as a skilful child psychologist does not confine his knowledge to test results, but also watches the children at play and studies their individual characters in ordinary intercourse, so examination methods can be supplemented by a careful investigation of the candidate's ability to deal with situations. The Wawokye Camp Experiment provides an interesting example of these joint methods in a combination of mechanical tests with natural observation of the children's behaviour in spontaneous situations.[1]

These instances show that academic methods are improving by becoming more realistic and adaptable. The gap between mechanical methods and the changing conditions of real life is being steadily reduced. Mechanisms lose their artificiality, and when adequately applied can be used to develop the deepest forces of living material.

The various controls we have already described are not exhaustive, and are not based on any single principle of classification. There is a deeper reason for the lack of any unified

[1] Newstetter, W. I., " Wawokye Camp." An Experiment in Group Adjustment, *Proceedings of the American Sociological Society*, vol. 25, 1930. Cf. also III 1 d in the Bibliography.

classification of social controls and for the constant over-lapping. The controls have an objective existence but they appear to us under different aspects—aspects which vary with our own position in the general scheme. A mountain range is a real formation with a structure of its own, but the shape it assumes for the onlooker depends on where he is standing. In social affairs, our standpoint is determined not merely by passive observation but by the direction in which our attention is turned. The nature of our common activities decides which social mechanisms shall be treated as a single unit ; the nature of our intervention in social affairs defines the radius of our action, and this in its turn defines the configuration of events which is likely to be perceived as a single unity. Any new type of control reveals hidden relationships between facts—relationships which formerly passed unnoticed. Thus the active mind penetrates more deeply into the nature of the object than the contemplative one, which very often clings to units which are not really units at all, and only seem to be such because they are observed on an artificial plane. Here we have an analogy in modern physiology. In this field such compact organs as the liver, the spleen, the heart were formerly regarded as organic units. After a more penetrating analysis, it soon became obvious that for certain purposes, such as the production of sugar, partial units which were widely separated (parts of the spleen, the heart, the nervous system), were co-ordinated as a single unit, and that in point of fact it was not the tangible large organs which formed this functional unit, although at first sight they appeared to be the only real entities. The kind of factors which form a single configuration depends to a certain extent on our methods of influencing society and on the nature and depth of our penetration.

Here again we see the truth of our former statement that very often the nature of a profession, the way in which an object is handled, determines the section one is able to grasp. A judge or a diplomat would tend to think in terms of situations, because it is his profession to settle individual conflicts, but a legislator would tend to think in terms of mechanisms and field structures and to co-ordinate social affairs from the main key positions. In short, the categories into which the social structure can be divided depend on the social controls which are possible in our age. As social technique changes, men will intervene from other strategic points and formulate the whole process in terms of other units.

V

THE LAWS OF TRANSMUTATION IN THE FIELD OF SOCIAL CONTROL

The study of social control and its connection with the social process is significant in many different ways. First of all it shows that the present controls need not be regarded as final and unalterable. Secondly, it disabuses us of the idea that only rigid controls, such as regimentation and organization, exist and that control must necessarily make for uniformity. Thirdly, analysis has shown that progress in the technique of control consists in making it less mechanical and in compensating for its inhuman detachment.[1] If life is mastered by real intelligence, which understands the meaning of dynamic control, it need not become stereotyped as it is when left to the half-hearted regulation so widespread in our age. In replacing harmful controls by beneficial ones, we have first to realize how a free society works. We learn that even in an unplanned society there is always the problem of substituting one form of control for another, but here these changes take place involuntarily, through the accumulation of circumstances.

After describing social controls, the next problem is therefore to study the laws of transmutation which govern the substitution of one control for another. At bottom, the transformation of the behaviour and social character of individuals has largely been due to a change in the methods of control. However, the controls have of course been switched over unconsciously, without any clear purpose in mind and without realizing the wider consequences of the change.

There are as many ways of switching over the controls

---

[1] On Social Techniques and Dehumanization, cf. also in the Bibliography II and IV.

as there are possibilities of passing from one form of direct or indirect influence to another. It is obvious that a complete description would require a volume to itself. Most of these methods, too, are open to further observation. Here we can only indicate, by a few examples, the nature and problems of the process of transmutation.

1. *Transmutation of Controls from Direct to Indirect Influence*

The most important forms of transmutation naturally take place when we exchange the broad category of direct influence for indirect influence. In other words, there is an important development in the power to influence mankind, when instead of some form of inculcation, we choose a form of influence where society itself, through its patterns and relationships, urges an individual to alter his behaviour. Far too extensive a use is made of direct methods of inculcation, such as brow-beating, suggestion, emotional appeals, preaching, agitation, and even education in the older sense of the word. These are very often merely provisional solutions adopted by a society which has not had the opportunity of using indirect methods of social influence as a means of training. The clumsier and less adaptable an education is, the more it will try to stamp its effects directly on the pupil's mind, instead of leaving him to make his own reactions. In this sense Dewey and others were right in their belief that experimental education, that is to say, encouraging the child to make his own adjustments, is essential to modern democracy.[1] In the same way, a modern society based on natural adjustment will allow its citizens to learn by experience as much as possible and will avoid, among other things, the unnecessary use of shock methods.

Here is another instance which shows that those who maintain that increased planning is taking us further and further from the natural state of affairs are wholly in the wrong. A society which has been planned on sound principles will be far more natural in its methods of adjustment than a comparatively primitive society that has bungled its social techniques. Any partially managed society will

---

[1] Cf. in the Bibliography, III 7 b.

always stick half-way; it cannot afford to do what a planned society can do—give the individual a natural taste for experiment, where this is desirable for the sake of society as a whole, and only resort to direct methods within strict limits and in the absence of other alternatives.

In what follows I should like to give a few examples in order to indicate that, at a later state of development, rationalization leads to a more natural existence and consciously tends to counteract the dehumanizing effects of exaggerated regulation. The Victorian age for instance with its primitive knowledge of the nature of industrialized society, fostered a cult of the unnatural, while modern mass society, in spite of its greater organization, tends to encourage its citizens to return to nature by means of systematic physical culture, sport,[1] and fresh air. Here it looks as though the early monstrosities, which were the first-fruits of industrialism and urbanization, were only due to the sudden growth of new conditions for which no palliative had been found. In these fields at least more planning and a greater use of social technique have led to more natural conditions. The following instance shows, in another context, how planning, combined with the right scientific insight, can free the suppressed and natural instincts.

Modern psychology and psychiatry have observed that neuroses are very often due to the fact that the child's natural ability to learn from trial and error is paralysed by a rush of inhibitions. We allow a baby to experiment with his body in a variety of situations. In the beginning we are

[1] On the other hand one has to realize that sport in itself may be based on many different psychological gratifications. It may, for instance, deteriorate from a social game with an agreeable sense of team work into a mania for records. These are psychological processes of degeneration which are common in a mass society and which can be set right if one consciously teaches people to enjoy the genuine pleasures of community pastimes. For the different meanings of sport and its psychological implications, cf. Marie Kloeren, *Sport und Rekord* (Kölner Anglistische Arbeiten, vol. 23, ed. by Herbert Schoeffler), Leipzig, 1935 ; and Herbert Schoeffler, *England, das Land des Sports* (Hefte zur Englandkunde, vol. 9), Leipzig, 1935). The former volume contains a historical bibliography. The following works contain some suggestions : Karl Peters, *Psychologie des Sports*, Leipzig, 1927 ; and Risse, *Soziologie des Sports*, Berlin, 1921 ; Fritz Hammer, *Der Massensport : Versuch einer soziologischen Analyse seiner Bedingungen und Erscheinungsweise*, Heidelberg, Ph.D., diss., 1933 ; Ernst Krafft, *Vom Kampfrekord zum Massensport*, Berlin, 1925 ; Gulick, L., "Athletics and Civilization," *The Child*, vol. i, 17, 1911.

all in favour of spontaneous experience. Only when the child's intelligence develops and it is able to ask questions do we interrupt the natural growth of the experimental attitude by intellectual taboos. Among others, we cover up for the child the problem of sex and procreation with artificial ideologies, and later, masculinity, femininity, the fact of death, the question of money and success in life, are all treated in a spirit which tends to arouse both in the child and in the adolescent a lifelong distrust of his powers of independent judgment. This can lead not merely to a thwarted development, but to deep-rooted feelings of anxiety as well, so that he cannot to his life's end get these problems off his mind. Often only the removal of this fear by analysis and re-education will give him power to make his own decisions and assimilate knowledge by experimenting with life.[1] Here it is evident that our more sophisticated knowledge helps to restore the original capacities of mankind by freeing the natural powers of adjustment.

But let us turn to other instances which prove that a more skilful use of indirect influence would lighten the tasks of direct influence. Take, for instance, the habits of the consumer. A society cannot be made to work unless it shows a certain foresight with regard to these habits. At a primitive stage, this would take the form of inculcating certain types of consumption. The formation of taste would be subjected to moral control, the individual would be brought up to observe certain manners and customs in order to prescribe the range of his desires. These desires could be satisfied by household economy or any of its variations, such as town economy. But the advent of capitalist society often brought about a change in the methods employed to control the habits of the consumer. As industrial economy spread, former habits of consumption altered and desires ran riot. The more anarchic individual competition became, with its artificial stimulation of new cravings, the harder it was to foresee the uncontrolled fluctuations in the consumer's choice, and to adjust the market through the price mechanism. One of the reasons for disorganization in

[1] Schilder, P., "The Analysis of Ideologies as a Psycho-Therapeutic Method, especially in Group Treatment," *American Journal of Psychiatry*, vol. 93, 1936, and his article on "The Relation between Social and Personal Disorganization" in the *American Journal of Sociology*, vol. 42, 1937.

the free system of industrial economy was that an absolute freedom of consumer's choice made it difficult to co-ordinate production and consumption.

Even at the present stage of capitalism there is a tendency to pass beyond the temporary chaos created by unlimited choice. Large industrial concerns and department stores are both equally interested in standardizing demand, and produce a type of advertisement which instead of encouraging an endless variety of choice, persuades customers to want only a few carefully considered models. One has only to think of current advertisements for cars, gas, wireless, and electricity. This method of stimulating demand is exactly what a planned but unregimented society should aim at : inducing conformity not by authority or inculcation, but by skilful guidance, which allows the individual every opportunity for making his own decisions. A planned society would direct investment, and by means of efficient advertisement, statistically controlled, would do everything in its power to guide the consumer's choice towards co-ordinated production.

Another field where the change from direct to indirect methods of influence can be observed is that of the motives which induce people to work. The amazing thing is that even our most intimate experiences such as our motives, are constantly exposed to social and psychological manipulation. Modern society has not, of course, invented the manipulation of motives, but has only made it more conscious.

Thus Max Weber had already observed that in a free society the motives which induced people to work varied with the different social classes. Thus the proletariat works mainly in order to earn a living, while the middle classes, once their primary wants have been supplied and their need for security satisfied, work mainly for the sake of increased power and prestige. The introduction of this new motive is largely responsible for the characteristic outlook of the middle class. The group we call the intelligentsia is actuated mainly by motives of its own. A member of this group is only happy when he has work which is in keeping with his special interests and qualifications. While an unskilled labourer wants any work that will remove his insecurity, a man who is specialized by academic training is specialized not only in his knowledge but in his choice of a career, and in his striving for the psychological rewards which go with a certain kind of self-respect.

In this sense, there is normally a graduated scale of motives, by which men from different social classes are driven to work. Whenever a man rises to a higher class, from unskilled labourer to skilled labourer, from small tradesman to large-scale entrepreneur, from petty officialdom to a learned profession, once in the ranks of the élite he switches over from one set of motives to another.

Now this transition from one set of motives to another and the gradual sublimation of impulses which goes with it, will form one of the problems with which a planned society will have to deal. It will be forced not merely to direct this transformation of the motives which impel men to work, but to guide the citizen in the use of his leisure and of the surplus energy which remains when the day's work is done. When wealth has been more evenly distributed, and the ups and downs of the trade cycle have disappeared, the man in the street will cease to feel the immediate pressure of circumstances forcing him to work, and his mind may develop along new paths, just as was formerly the case only in the leisured classes.

This development can never be due to the external situation alone. Whether surplus energy can be guided into socially useful channels of sublimation will largely depend on the educational forces operating in society and on the guidance of élites who set an example of the finer uses of the spirit.[1]

[1] Cf. on the psychological implications of the various forms of the use of leisure, Patrick, G. T. V., *The Psychology of Relaxation*, Boston, 1916 ; Spitz, R., " Wiederholung, Rhythmus, Langweile," *Imago*. Zeitschr, für psychoanalytische Psychologie, vol. 23, 1937 ; Fenichel, O., *Psychologie der Langweile*, *Imago*, vol. 20, 1934 ; Winterstein, A., " Angst vor dem Neuen," *Neugier und Langweile*, vol. 2, 1930 ; Groos, K., " Das Spiel als Katharsis," *Zeitschr. f. päd. Psychol. u. Exper. Pädagogik. Dez*. 7, 1908 ; T. Dashiell Stoops, " The ' Inner Life ' as a Suppressed Ideal of Conduct," *Intern. Journ. of Ethics*, vol. 30, 1919–1920 ; Stewart, H. L., " The Ethics of Luxury and Leisure," *Amer. Journ. of Sociol.*, vol. 24, 1918–19 ; Hahn, K., *Education for Leisure*, Oxford, 1938. For the problem of the sociological implications of leisure, cf. Lundberg, G. A., Komarowsky, M., McIverny, M. A., *Leisure, a Suburban Study*, New York, 1934 ; Chase, St., *Leisure in the Machine Age* ; Franke, P. T., *Machine-made Leisure*, 1932 ; Walker, L. C., *Distributed Leisure*, N.Y. and London, 1931 ; Spizer, J. P., *The Commercialization of Leisure*, 1917 ; Blumer, K., *Movies and Conduct*, N.Y., 1933 :

The problem of discovering the social conditions which govern the sublimation of surplus energy will probably become a universal one, for not only the small élites but every class will be faced with the question of what the psycho-analysts call a libido economy. Comparative studies in the use of leisure show at first glance that a higher position, larger income, and increased security do not necessarily lead to culture. Unless material advancement is combined with personal example and the persuasion exercised by the presence of intelligent standards for the use of leisure, it may end in boredom, neurosis, and general decadence. Sublimation and cultivation are processes which have to be taught. The average citizen is unable to invent new uses for his leisure. If the old methods have broken down and tradition cannot develop others by a process of trial and error, chaos and barbarism will follow. This has been corroborated by recent experiences. When the slum-dweller is transplanted into modern flats he is apt to suffer from depression, unless some effort is made to adjust his whole way of living to changed conditions. The suburban housewife becomes neurotic because of the intolerable boredom of her existence and the lack of any form of community life.

One cannot hand down techniques of sublimation through education and personal influence, if there is no universal security on which to base them. On the other hand, security alone is no guarantee that surplus energies will be turned in any particular direction, unless they are guided by personal influence and education. Security and freedom from anxiety leave open many channels through which surplus human energy can flow.

Even hermits and monks can only sublimate and develop what one may call the inner life when they have a minimum of security, whether from natural wealth, or income from the land. The mendicant order in the late Middle Ages was based on the principle that in an agrarian community, begging

cf. also the whole series " Motion Picture and Youth ", The Payne Fund, Chairman, W. W. Charters ; Spurr, F. C., *The Christian Use of Leisure*, 1928 ; Burns, D., *Leisure in the Modern World* ; Durant, H. W., *The Problems of Leisure*, London, 1938 ; Boyd, W., Ogilvie, V., *The Challenge of Leisure*, London (New Education Fellowship), 1935 ; Sternheim, A., " Leisure in the Totalitarian State," *Soc. Review*, vol. 30, 1938.

can be successful in the country towns. But security or even a good standard of life in itself are not sufficient for the development of contemplation. The real force obstructing the latter is conflict and competition. This is the reason why the church allowed monks to engage in any sort of activities except commercial ones. Even begging, as we have seen, was considered compatible with the contemplative life. In a natural economy, alms could be trusted to supply a sure source of income, and although these alms provided only a modest livelihood they spelt security and made it possible to avoid the mechanisms of competition and struggle and their effects on the spiritual life.

But society does not merely demand that certain motives should be sublimated, but also, at times, that certain sublimations should be destroyed. Thus Freud, in an impressive study, has shown that it is usually war which causes the rejection of a certain type of sublimation and regression to the naked drive.[1] According to him, the sympathy we generally feel under civilized conditions for the sufferings and the death of others is the result of sublimation and identification. But this only works under the peaceful conditions of civilian life. In order to survive in war-time we are bound to revert to the more primitive state of mind in which we withdraw our identification from our fellow beings and in our primitive self-assertion remain unmoved by other people's distress. If we look at this process of sublimation and de-sublimation of motives from the standpoint of our problem of social control, we see that its success depends on co-ordinating the methods of direct and indirect influence.

Society in the past regulated such delicate changes as sublimation only through direct influence. Under present conditions this process is only efficient if it works on the two levels of direct and indirect influence at the same time; in our example producing the general preconditions for sublimation through indirect control (creating wealth, security, etc.), and providing concrete models for desirable forms of sublimation from examples near at hand.

[1] Freud, S., *Reflections*, authorized English translation by Brill, A. A., and Kuttner, B., from " Zeitgemäszes über Krieg und Tod " extracted from *Sammlung Kleiner Schriften zur Neurosenlehre*, New York, 1922.

2. *The Transmutation of Controls within the Sphere of Indirect Influence*

We must now study this law of the transmutation of controls in the sphere of indirect influence. Some of the problems in this sphere are : How and when can crowd behaviour be transformed into co-ordinated group behaviour? How much can be done by replacing the influence of the primary groups and communities by organized behaviour or *vice versa* ? The new possibilities of organized control and the tendency towards a new kind of bureaucracy are especially important here. But similar problems arise in spheres which are controlled, not by bureaucracy, but by situations, field structures, and mechanisms. When should control by situation be replaced by control through field structure or social mechanism ? From this variety of problems a few can be selected which seem to be essential from the standpoint of a new kind of planning, that does not rely mainly on direct pressure. Just as we had first to prove that the deliberate guidance of psychological influences would not necessarily lead to greater mechanization and artificiality, so it seems to be equally important to realize that the conscious management of indirect controls, especially of organization in terms of centralization and decentralization and the institution of bureaucracy, could, if rightly guided, prevent dehumanization, and guarantee the maintenance of certain attitudes. This is the reason why I shall now, out of all the possibilities of organization, deal solely with the two problems of decentralization and a new form of bureaucracy. I hope in this way to show how fruitful the planned manipulation of distant controls can be in this sphere.

As to the problem of decentralization, it is obvious that the modern nature of social techniques puts a premium on centralization, but this is only true if our sole criterion is to be technical efficiency. If for various reasons, chiefly those concerned with the maintenance of personality, we deliberately wish to decentralize certain activities within certain limits, we can do so. That kind of deliberate decentralization will differ from a purely Romanticist one which indulges in the praise of the golden age of pre-industrial civilization or from the handicraftsman's hostility to the advent of machines. We cannot restore the pre-industrial age of small technical units, but we can deliberately insert, wherever it is feasible, relatively autonomous units into the whole industrial system. Here we shall succeed as soon as we begin to explore some of the neglected possibilities of the new industrial techniques. For instance, it is well known that the discovery of electricity encouraged centralization at first owing to the power centres which served several industrial units and thus acted as a centralizing agency. But the discovery of the small motor provides a new chance that in the future in the industrial sphere local centres may develop independently of a regional power centre. In these cases, it depends rather on the decision of the planning groups whether we use the technical amenities in one direction or the other. In the same way, once centralization of the main issues is guaranteed, there is always the possibility of a kind of secondary decentralization, and perhaps we only attribute such great importance to centralized means of influencing human beings—radio, propaganda, mass meetings, sports, cinema, etc.—because we are still in the first period of transition into a mass society, and emotional integration on a large scale and with immediate success is of extreme importance to us. It is, however, also possible that as in former examples, as soon as the most elementary conditions of conformity and co-operation have been assured, we shall again give the local influences a chance to reassert themselves, to create scope for individuality without in any way disturbing the process of planning from key positions.

But decentralization is not the only antidote to the dangers of centralization, mechanization, and dehumanization ; another alternative is to enliven bureaucracy, for however much decentralization is encouraged, planned society will always have to rely upon a very strong centralized bureaucracy.

The problem of an improved bureaucracy falls within the province of the new science of organization, and if rightly conceived, it will include not merely the question of increased efficiency, but the removal of the cold impersonal atmosphere of organization. In order to appreciate this aspect, one has only to remember that even at the transitional stage, half-way between discovery and invention, the task of the new social techniques and institutions was to hand over certain services, formerly rendered by personal contact in the primary groups, to organized management. So we must bear in mind, for instance, that all the duties of state bureaucracy were once carried out by officials who were the servants of their superiors. In the same way, the individual attention of the small tradesman has been replaced by the offices of the great department stores, and the social services have often developed out of private charity. The essential element in the process is that the primary attitudes of love, care, and mutual help, which were originally bound up with primary groups like the family or the neighbours, have become organized. In the first stage of development, we are inclined to regret that this attitude should be transformed from an organic social setting to a more artificial one. The first thing we notice is how markedly impersonal our social relationships have become as a result of that change, how stripped of all emotion. Indeed, it was for the sake of an impersonal efficiency that the methods of social organization were first adopted. It is through the steady growth of new tasks that the king's personal servants, as we have seen, developed into a kind of impersonal bureaucracy, which makes even the personal dependence on the king an impersonal matter, and transforms the activities both of a workshop and of a great business into institutions bent only on efficiency, expediency, and utility, in which the idea of service has not yet developed.

In the intermediate stage of this development, only the negative consequences of this rationalized organization of primary functions were in evidence, and the word bureaucracy betrayed the hostility of the public to this new method of managing people as though they were things. But this early antipathy to bureaucracy was counteracted by some of the more obvious advantages of the new system. First, the broad masses could be served more effectively, and the arbitrariness of the older methods could be replaced by a more calculated efficiency. Secondly, the new bureaucracy brought with it a new objectivity in human affairs. There is something about bureaucratic procedure which helps to neutralize the original leanings towards patronage, nepotism, and personal domination. This tendency towards objectivity may, in favourable cases, become so strong that the element of class consciousness, still present in a bureaucracy which is chosen mainly from the ranks of the ruling classes, can be almost completely superseded by the desire for justice and impartiality.

We must not forget that until the advent of bureaucracy the idea of an impersonal and classless justice could not even arise, since freedom in a hierarchic society was defined in terms of " liberties ", the graded privileges of the various estates. The growth of this new objectivity did not necessarily mean, however, as at first sight it appeared, that human relationships must become impersonal and unemotional. The new conception of objective justice can be developed in such a way that the emotion becomes attached to the handling of the case and not to the individual who is helped. Objectivity and emotion are combined, instead of being mutually exclusive.   Assistance has become institutional, and as a result a modern man prefers to have his rights and duties clearly defined, rather than to receive a personal favour. We prefer a hospital nurse who shows her sympathy by her personal care to one who is too intimate and motherly. Thus the rise of bureaucracy created a demand which had never before been known—the demand that many of our personal affairs should be treated impersonally.

The analysis of these cases teaches us that new blends of feeling and emotion are often produced, not so much by the isolated experiences of the individual, as by comprehensive social processes in which the functions of one group are gradually transferred to another.

The fact that modern society has produced a bureaucracy which is forced to take over many of the tasks of the primary groups, has given rise to some curious syntheses of feeling, such as the combination of emotion and detachment. The actual blends of emotion may vary widely in the different countries, according to the nature of their social development.   In this connection it is interesting to notice that although the department store has made its appearance in every industrial society, in each country it has been built up and organized in a very different spirit. While in England and Germany the customer receives a rather impersonal service, in France the personal type of service is preferred. The assistant will accompany the customer to the cash desk and often to the door, for France is still the land of the small shopkeeper, and the department store has inherited an attitude of mind which would otherwise be alien to its impersonal organization.

This kaleidoscopic blending of attitudes corresponds to the changing functions of our activities. It makes for greater elasticity, and gives us grounds for hope that the immediate defects of an institution may later be removed by a fresh combination of factors, giving rise to new attitudes of mind. As an illustration of a creative combination of attitudes, we may refer to a previous example.

Modern communal bureaucracy has proved that capacity for organization can be combined with executive business ability, that rivalry and commercial efficiency can be stimulated without personal greed for profit. Moreover, commercial life has shown that the spirit of service can be incorporated in big business.

In a more comprehensive study of human attitudes and their transformation through social influences, England would deserve a chapter to itself. Perhaps nowhere else is " kindness ", which in itself is highly personal, treated so objectively. This objective kindness was probably the result of mutual co-operation in the primitive community, where there is a natural obligation existing between neighbours. Owing to the gradual expansion of society, this attitude could be extended to one's fellow-countrymen or even to foreigners resident in the country. The personal element was transformed, but did not lose its genuine qualities. The sense of neighbourliness remained, but without a trace of intimacy or even the thought of a deeper obligation. This impersonal kindness is nevertheless a virtue, and its new function is to compensate for the unbearable abstractness of the relationships which play so large a part in modern society.

Finally, this blending of attitudes to meet the needs of new institutions can be seen in the development of our modern social services. One has only to think of that unusual psychological type, the social worker, who has on the one hand to do material, administrative work, and on the other to practise a new form of charity. These new social services are rapidly supplanting the simple, material conception of charity, and are tending to become more and more psychological. The social worker gives not merely material help but spiritual healing. He adds a touch of emotion and vitality to ordinary intercourse without becoming personally committed or attached. In all these new forms of organized social service, which have definite functions to perform, there is an almost conscious manipulation of the emotional element in the relationship.

This again shows how elastic organized activity can be, and how a higher principle of organization produces new attitudes of mind. If the new type of social work is to be a success, the following social processes must be at work. Activities which were once widely separated must now be combined, official bureaucracy must be tempered with the charity of the primary groups. In addition, adequate training must be provided, the personnel should be wisely selected from classes which are not yet dehumanized and from sects and smaller groups in which affection and certain kinds of reserve are not felt to be mutually exclusive.[1] Apart from that, a preference should be shown for the emotional type of human being who will do only work which has a purpose.

In all these new forms of organized social service, which have definite functions to perform, there is an almost conscious manipulation of the emotional element in the relationship. Our age, at its present stage of development in which a civil servant is steadily developing into a social servant, has learnt something that would have seemed impossible in the age of small groups : that this emotional element lies, up to a point, within the control of the individual, and is often allied to objectivity and distance. To a member of the older generation, the psycho-analytic relationship between patient and analyst must seem wholly unnatural, and an almost absurd manipulation of libidinous attitudes. To him, it must seem a contradiction in terms that anyone should publicly offer services for which " transference " is essential. Transference, without which no cure can be achieved, appears to be something which can only develop in intimate relationships ; while, as it actually occurs, it is a strange combination of intimacy and objectivity, nearness and distance, attraction and repulsion, friendship

---

[1] On my suggestion a thesis was written on these problems. Cf. Truhel, K., *Sozialbeamte*. Ein Beitrag zur Sozioanalyse der Bürokratie. Thesis, Frankfurt/Main. Sagan (Benjamin Krause Hofbuchdruckerei), 1934. Cf. also III 6 in the Bibliography.

and estrangement. It gives help without explicit guidance. The sociology of psycho-analysis will have to discover whether a ready acceptance of this curious mixture of personal and impersonal elements could be conceivable without previous social developments, which have made it possible to blend emotion and detachment in such entirely new combinations.

All these examples show that the universal alarm at the growth of bureaucracy is only justified as long as the public clings to the old belief that institutions and organizations are perfectly rigid, and incapable of developing new attitudes of mind.

The evil lies not in bureaucracy itself, but in an inadequate conception of the new possibilities which are already being realized here and there. The discussion of bureaucracy is apt to take two different roads. Either one regards bureaucracy as an evil in itself or one has grasped its possibilities. A good Liberal, who is the sworn enemy of all bureaucracy, would like to replace universal bureaucratic control by mutual control, in order that completely free individuals might maintain the balance between them. This system would obviously lead to such radical decentralization that it would be unworkable at the present stage of social technique. But there is still another difficulty. Where, as a result of large-scale industry, almost every transaction, economic or otherwise, takes on a social character (for every flaw in the working of large-scale industry injures the community), it becomes more and more necessary to curb the desire for private profit in the common interest and in the interests of planning. To-day it is still an open question which tendency is most likely to succeed—whether it is better gradually to restrain the excesses of capitalism by central regulation or to enliven the bureaucratic tradition by creating opportunities for competition and by promoting a more human organization within its framework.

I believe that this antagonism, however invincible it may seem to-day, will be swept away by the course of events, for the democracies, if they are to keep pace with the dictatorships, will have to subject their industries to a certain amount of control. This will automatically lead to an alliance between the capitalist and state socialist traditions : a process in which even the Civil Service will develop new possibilities. This development will probably take place through an amalgamation of the two principles of administration and competition, varying in degree with the type of problem that has to be faced. But the essential question is, which of these principles is to provide the framework in which the other is to be incorporated ? Is the planned society to be the framework, and the mechanism of competition to be set to work in certain places, or are the basic relationships to be determined by conflict and competition, and administration to take place within the enclave ? In our opinion, the solution lies in the former direction, although it is possible that during the transition, evolution will begin with the latter, as in the United States. There competition still predominates, but planned intervention is increasing.

Much depends in this respect on whether resolutions and wars speed up the development towards planning ; in which case the central bureaucratic element will tend to prevail.

But the vital question is whether the state, as a controlling and co-ordinating agency can itself be controlled : that is, whether the principle of planning can be reconciled with freedom and democracy. The history of parliamentarianism is in this respect the history of the control of control. From our standpoint the history of government must be re-interpreted as the history of a special social technique by which the control of human beings is subjected once more to human control.

If one takes a comprehensive view, it is mere chance that this technique is only clearly apparent in the sphere of state organization. Once the principle of the control of control has been discovered, the scope and the nature of its action can be prescribed to a large extent by the government as well as its relation to the remaining controls. In this setting, it is certainly a political problem, but one which must also be discussed in its social and technical aspects. One can go even further and say that it is impossible to frame a political problem properly, until its technical implications have been thought out.

The history of constitutional development is really nothing but a widespread concentration of once independent centres of control. This concentration forces the rival units which are struggling for power to give up their partial aims in favour of a centralized authority with a new and unified outlook. The significance of sovereignty is that it decides in which direction the concentrated power shall move, so that it hardly matters, from this point of view, whether the sovereign be a king, the people and their representatives, or even a leader. The original focuses of social control—territorial powers such as the prince and the city states, or functional class units such as nobility, clergy, and commons —grew up haphazard. The next thing to decide was whether these controls should be concentrated and whether there should be a redistribution of power based on purely objective grounds.

VI

THE HISTORY OF PARLIAMENTARY AND DEMOCRATIC GOVERNMENT AS THE HISTORY OF SOCIAL CONTROL

1. *Three Stages in the Development of the Control of Controls*

If we study democratic government as a chapter in the concentration of control and a history of the technique of controlling controls, we are again confronted with the three stages of chance discovery, invention, and planning. There is no need to emphasize the fact that the structural changes involved in these successive stages do not always coincide with the current phases of constitutional history. Nevertheless we believe that this typology will help to explain the essential factors in political change.[1]

While the controls are still amorphous we remain at the stage of chance discovery. As long as a group has no specific organization for carrying on the functions of government, the controls are diffused throughout society. They make an appearance whenever they are required to deal with different aspects of behaviour, such as labour regulations, the organization of religious festivals, or the rules governing

[1] Bibliography on Constitutional Government at the end of the book. Cf. in the Bibliography III 4 *c*; V 1, and the article on Government by Shepard, W. J., in the *Encyclopaedia of the Social Sciences*, which I found helpful when arranging the material in this chapter.

the relationship between the different sexes and generations. At this amorphous stage the controls are still spontaneous. There are no special officials with powers of compulsion and no definite authorities for the officials to represent. The customs which express the spontaneous, irrational moral sense of the community determine the boundaries of right and wrong. These standards of behaviour are enforced by the direct pressure of the community. Regulation by custom is both totalitarian and, broadly speaking, democratic. Thus it reaches the ideal at which modern society is aiming, not by deliberate calculation but by intuitive consent. Customs are totalitarian in that they govern what we should now call private relationships as well as public affairs, for at this stage these two spheres are merged in one. Thus there is no freedom in the modern sense—no power to evade this totalitarian regulation, but this naturally does not mean that there are no conflicts and no individual divergencies. At the same time customary law is democratic in the sense that everyone more or less approves of it and helped to create it, for its rules are the result of a gradual process of selection and many generations have felt them to be sound. Its solutions have a dignity of their own, for they are the collective discovery of the group. The whole community takes part in this discovery and the rules are gradually altered a little by individuals who are faced with new situations. Thus subordination and authority, freedom and pressure, consensus and change exist side by side.

The stage of invention has been reached when a special institutional organization is set up, with express authority to govern, enforced by sanctions. Owing to the new principle which entails a division of social functions, its once united elements are now divorced from one another.

(a) There is no longer any unanimous consensus of opinion, but under a democratic system agreement must again be reached, or it will be replaced by authority—a king, an oligarchy, or so on.

(b) Rationalized law gradually becomes distinct from custom and sooner or later there is a cleavage between fundamental law and ordinary law. This process of rationalization may be carried so far that in a modern constitution fundamental law may determine the basic principles of organization governing the legal framework of society, while individual laws are deduced from it, or some attempt is made to reconcile the two. Here we have reached the stage of invention, for the framework of social adjustment has been deliberately thought out, and organized to form an institution ; but we have not yet reached the stage of planning, as this type of system still tolerates the existence of many other spheres of human behaviour beyond its jurisdiction. This is precisely the principle on which the liberal constitution is based ; it is the clearest example of government at the stage of invention, for apart from certain basic relationships, which are constitutionally determined, regulation has been abandoned in favour of *laissez-faire*. This, of course, does not mean that everything is in a state of chaos but merely that other forms of regulation and control pour into the breach, and these are often quite independent of the government and its rationalized system of law.

Thus these amorphous controls which we call customs are preserved in a rationalized form and determine the greater part of human behaviour, just as they did at the stage of chance discovery. Liberal legislation leaves the power of the mores and customs almost untouched, using it merely as a ferment to arouse that fundamental consensus which rational law implies but does not produce.

At this stage in the regulation of behaviour, competition, particularly in the economic field, gives rise to a special form of action ; striving for profit by means of free adjustment. This behaviour is neither a product of former customs nor of modern rationalized legal and administrative procedure, as the liberal state deliberately refrains from interfering within those spheres. The process of adjustment is not, of course, completely without control but is guided by the mechanisms of competition and by the field structure called the world of trade. Thus a commercial system is created with the economic man as its ideal. Although the trade mechanism together with its special economic laws and systematic pressure only worked if certain moral obligations such as fair play, and certain legal regulations such as those governing the sacredness of private property and contract, were observed, it acted nevertheless as an automatic device for securing mutual control, and remained outside the province of the other two systems we have mentioned. If we look at the liberal system from the standpoint of government we may say that it contained two systems which escaped its control, traditional habits and customs on the one hand, and the field structure of independent markets on the other. These are the spheres which will be later absorbed by the modern system of co-ordinated planning.

The great achievement of the liberal age (to which, of course, former centuries contributed) was the institution of parliamentary control over the legal framework of society. As we have already pointed out, it was the discovery of the control of controls by democratic methods. But this discovery could not be applied to every control since many of them, such as the customs and the laws of the market, as we have just seen, were outside the radius of centralized government. Central control over customs had failed—partly because it was too closely bound up with the techniques of local and direct influence, and partly because the combined sciences of sociology and psychology were still too immature to influence them in a conscious and rational way. This sphere was left to the anonymous power of tradition. The church made some attempt at central guidance but was not yet efficient enough really to control the course of events. Nor could the economic process be influenced, owing to the lack of a strong centralized technique and of the knowledge required for thinking out structural connections on a large scale, and for realizing their social implications. It is only in our age that we have reached the stage of planning the sphere of government, so that here, too, centralized intervention becomes theoretically possible, and the technique of the democratic control of control has to be extended to cover every field.

This does not mean—as we must constantly repeat—that every control which has not de facto come under centralized authority must be governed from the centre ; but merely that the central control can interfere more frequently, and when it does not do so it is deliberately renouncing the use of its powers. Our next problem is to consider the essential processes governing this mechanism of control, and the difficulties of transferring it to a planned society.

2. *Analysis of the Essential Social Techniques which keep the Parliamentary and Democratic System in Working Order.*

(1) The first step was to establish the sovereignty of the state, and this was effected in the age of absolutism. It consisted of withdrawing the ultimate power of decision in questions of law and authority from local and limited authorities. This involved a widespread integration and co-ordination of existing social controls, although as we have seen, it left many of them untouched. In terms of social technique, state sovereignty in the realm of law and order corresponds to the simultaneous creation of a royal army and bureaucracy —the visible representatives of this new centralization. Without these, the other elements of sovereignty could not have been centralized. The state now strove to create a financial system which could maintain its military and bureaucratic machinery. But this is where absolutism failed. First, money could only be obtained through the new industries and their exports, but these could not be centralized because of their limited economic techniques. Mercantilism tried to establish state-owned businesses and to exercise state control, but during this period of manufacture economic technique was so rudimentary that only a few large concerns were run at a profit. Moreover, economy was passing through a period of expansion in which new inventions and newly-conquered economic regions at home and abroad constituted the immediate problem, and in themselves required a great number of independent minds, a whole class of pioneering élites. This is the main reason why absolutism had to give the bourgeoisie a clear field as far as economics were concerned, and the centralization which had been achieved in the army and bureaucracy could not be transferred to the economic sphere.

Apart from these a democratic control of sovereignty became more and more possible. Looking at it from that angle the principle of liberalism developed two forms of freedom : the one which expressed itself in the existence of a sphere where mutual controls prevailed (in the field of trade and of custom), the second, which admitted centralization but tried democratically to control it. In the present situation, where the economic sphere because of its new technique is becoming as centralized as the military and bureaucratic sections, freedom is faced with the problem of applying the centralized democratic control also to the first sphere. It need not be emphasized that this democracy was at that time, of course, a fairly extensive oligarchy, but even in this form its achievement was to produce the new pattern of democratic control.

(2) Democratic control achieved two important things. First, it provided a guarantee that the new representatives of sovereign authority would not abuse their power and develop into irresponsible dictators. This was achieved by the subjection of the administration to the power of the legislature or in the most extreme case by the separation of powers which forced the legislature, the executive, and the judiciary to carry on their work in water-tight compartments. It is the old trick of guaranteeing freedom by playing off each power against the others, but whereas before the establishment of sovereignty it was the local authorities who kept the balance between them, it is now the functional units who checkmate each other—the legislature, the executive, and the judiciary.

(3) The democratic and parliamentary régime was also anxious to maintain the balance of power between the controlling groups represented in Parliament, and to prevent any one of the parties or any extra-Parliamentary group becoming so strong that it could overthrow Parliament by a *coup d'état*. This is why the system implied that it was dangerous to organize any class or profession as a political unit, and ultimately appealed to the isolated individual, who, alone and unfettered, found that his interests were represented sometimes by one party, sometimes by another. Every class or professional organization held the individual in its grip once and for all, and thus accumulated power in a way which endangered state sovereignty. At the present stage of capitalism this danger has increased, for as a result of the centralizing tendencies of social technique, large associations like cartels, trusts, and trade unions exercise an authority of their own outside Parliament, and in times of crisis threaten the balance of power.

(4) A further problem is to replace the once spontaneous consensus between opposing groups by rational manipulation. A series of compromises between conflicting interests

maintains dynamic balance in the system. Thus Parliament can be regarded as a new technique for reconciling conflicts. It is a method of removing intellectual and psychological differences, for discussion acts as a cathartic. At one time only a real trial of strength could create a momentary respite between unending feuds; now Parliament has restored the balance of power, so that it has rightly been said that heads are counted instead of being cut off. Differences in power are no longer put to the test of action but are revealed by a kind of calculation, expressed in voting. As in bargaining, the opposing parties are willing to reduce their maximum claims to a point where agreement can be reached.

(5) The particular merit of the parliamentary system is that it separates the vacillating and conflicting motives which are present in any process of bargaining. Whenever two people or groups are engaged in bargaining, in both, the motive of getting the most out of it and the motive of securing the bargain as such are continuously fluctuating. But parliamentary institutions could be considered as a psychological invention for the purpose of separating these two sets of motives completely. On the one hand the function of the election is to strengthen and to integrate those motives which are interested in the maintenance of the bargain. The voter, by electing a government, commits himself in advance to the completion of the bargain and to the maintenance of the basic social relationships in the state. On the other hand, through the Parliamentary forum a public platform has been established to express private interests within Parliament itself. In simple barter or in the private contracts which were so characteristic of feudalism there was always a conflict of interests. Both parties were in most cases determined to have it all their own way or, failing that, to risk the failure of the contract and the destruction of existing institutions. In contrast with that, although different interests are represented in parliament the desire for agreement can be taken for granted. Party bargaining and the public representation of sectional interests are carried out in a way which leaves no shadow of doubt as to the fundamental desire for agreement behind the process of legislation. Economic exchange is also a democratic form of bargaining and the price represents that unstable point of

equilibrium at which both parties abandon part of their claims in order to secure the bargain. When the question of an economic price is raised the whole social act is potentially at stake, for if there were the smallest divergence this social act would not take place. The parliamentary compromise is likewise the expression of an equilibrium, but it is more solid because it prevents the danger of disagreement going so far that the performance of the social act is brought into question. To-day we realize more acutely than ever how greatly the cleavage between this desire for agreement and the institutional representation of sectional interests has slackened the tensions of conflict. This psychological aspect of the parliamentary system becomes even more apparent if one compares it with a person who is driven by ambivalent feelings and is vacillating between the two extremes of love and hatred. A skilful psychologist would create an opportunity for working out the hatred at one time and the love at another. That would at least enable him to show consistency during limited periods of his life. Whether such skilful separation of an individual's vacillating attitudes is possible is beside the point here, but strange as it may seem, it is achieved on a large scale by parliamentary institutions, which make long range action and co-operation possible by this very technique of separating agreement and disagreement, and giving them opportunities for self-expression by means of institutions.

By distributing these two types of motives over longer periods of time, parliamentary institutions do not merely create the possibility of long range action but lessen emotional tension, as they allow for expression of resentment. Only when we have seen how dictatorships, both of the Right and of the Left, are suffering from the fact that feelings of opposition can neither be canalized nor transformed into constructive criticism, can we realize the full achievement of parliamentary technique. Sabotage from below and purges from above are poor substitutes for parliamentary institutions.

(6) The parliamentary system also guarantees the selection and rotation of the leading élites, at least in the political sphere. Elections help to control the advancement of those who are to exercise power, and what is more, they provide a rational and peaceful method of removing those who have

abused their prestige or pursued a policy which is not in accordance with topical needs. Thus both continuity and elasticity are secured.

(7) Democratic control must guard against another danger: mass psychology. We have frequently seen in other parts of this book that growing numbers in themselves are not a danger to democracy. For when we meet a vast number of individuals, not simply as a mass but organized in groups, and actuated either by enlightened self-interest or by an idea, we find that they are no longer merely emotional but rational in their dealings. The danger of mass democracy only arises when unorganized masses are exposed to incalculable waves of emotion, especially in times of crisis. The more the rhythm of the trade cycle threatens the security of the masses in times of depression the more suggestible they become, and under certain conditions they will even surrender their highest privileges, particularly their right to democracy, in a passion of excitement. The fathers of democracy had this danger constantly in mind, and usually made it difficult to change the constitution itself, providing acid tests to prevent the alteration of the system under stress of an emotional mood or of momentary propaganda. There is another influence at work which serves the same purpose and which W. Lippmann [1] has brilliantly described as " the many faceted electorate ". This means that the same elector belongs to many different groups; he is a member of a nation, of a district, of a professional organization, and so on. Here we have the profound sociological discovery that the motives and desires of a single man may vary with the groups in which they are expressed. But there are other methods of neutralizing mass suggestibility and weakening psychotic reactions, and these include a sifting of opinion by experts or the reference of important problems to committees or to Parliament.

3. *The Growing Similarity between the Liberal-Democratic and the Totalitarian States*

The extraordinarily subtle machinery of democratic control is completely at the disposal of a planned society and could prevent it from degenerating into a dictatorship. The only

[1] Lippmann, *The Good Society*, London, 1938, p. 254.

real problem as far as social techniques are concerned is to combine democratic responsibility with rational planning. We cannot decide whether democratic machinery will work in a planned society until we realize the difference between liberal government at the stage of invention and totalitarian government at the stage of planning. Nor is it only in Fascist and Communist states that the government is totalitarian, in the sense that it tries to get all the controls into its own hands. The Western democracies at their present stage of development are gradually transforming the liberal conception of government into a social one. This is chiefly because the state no longer confines its attention to the three spheres of legislation, administration, and jurisdiction, but is changing into a social service state. This change is being rapidly accelerated by the universal preparations for war.

The essence of the change is from the negative safe-guarding of freedom and property to the exertion of a positive influence on the process of production and the distribution of wealth, as exemplified by the social services.

The tradition of non-intervention in the Liberal sense was abandoned when the state undertook social reforms, and indirectly, through taxation, tried to bring about a growing equality in income and to transfer property from the rich to the poor. Thus every step in the direction of social insurance is a breach of the former principle that every man should look after his own interests. Social insurance is a tremendous advance towards the positive conception of the state. This tendency is strengthened every time the state attempts either to direct the trade cycle from the centre or to counteract its ill effects. The various forms of subsidy or public assistance after the collapse of great industries or banks, the different types of currency manipulation, together with the encouragement of public works, the widening conception of public utility, and the rise of the social worker, are symptoms of the transformation of the constitutional state into a state based on social service. In addition the democratic states, like the totalitarian ones, are exploiting every psychological technique according to plan. Propaganda, wireless, and recreation are becoming a matter of public concern with which the state cannot refrain from dealing. The institution of broadcasting is a typical example of an opportunity for centralized propaganda. However democratically a programme is planned in the B.B.C. it has an influence on the leisure of the masses. The mere selection of what will be produced and what suppressed will have its effect upon the tastes and conditions of the people. Owing to the high costs of radio programmes, film industries, and recreation centres, the organization of leisure passes more and more into the hands either of the state or of business concerns. We seem to have the choice simply between commercialized or state controlled leisure. In this sense a structural change is taking place in all countries and unless new possibilities in the use of this centralized influence are invented the quality of leisure will be reduced to the lowest common denominator of the guides and the guided. Compared with the Liberal State the modern state, whether one likes it or not, has an almost complete power of control and it depends almost entirely on its own good pleasure whether it intends to take advantage of it and transform its activities into public service. During this process the power of the State is bound to increase until the State becomes nearly identical with society. It is not society which is absorbing the State but just the other way around. The State is absorbing society. If the present trends remain unchecked, the State instead of withering away, becomes more and more ambitious and powerful.

While Parliament regarded its institutions merely as a canalization of the forces of social change, the modern state will itself regulate the current of these forces. Former states did not manipulate the economic and social processes which brought about the change, but the problem of the trade cycle involves an attempt at this kind of management. For the Liberal state the trade cycle with all its effects is still an inexorable force of nature—at most one could build dams here and there and dig trenches to divert the flow— but for the modern state it is a field for experiment. As soon as the Western states have taken up this fundamental problem of universal security—the management of the trade cycle—they will gradually be forced to manipulate all social control, as the dictatorships have done from the start. They will have to influence the social advancement and decline of different classes and individuals and concern themselves with the psychological effects of unemployment. It is not merely a question of providing credit for ruined industries and building houses for settlements, but of including the psychological condition of the people concerned in their cycle of problems.

4. *Is a Democratic Control of Sovereignty Possible in a State which is becoming Totalitarian? The Divergence between the Social and Technical and the Political and Practical Points of View*

If anyone is unconvinced by these arguments, let him remember that the existence of totalitarian states leads to preparations for war.[1] The next war will be a totalitarian war in which every state which refuses to make use of the technique of co-ordination will collapse. Competition with these states compels the democracies to make use of some, at least, of their methods. This again shows us from another angle that the modern semi-totalitarian democracies have the same basic structure as the manifestly totalitarian states. For there is a basic pattern in modern society which is altering its very structure. Political organizations are more or less efficient experiments for coping with the problems presented by the changing structure. Thus the process of becoming totalitarian is only accelerated but is not initiated by the universal preparations for war.

The more manifest this common structural tendency becomes, the more essential is it to ask : is democratic control of the modern state possible now that it has been transformed into an organ of social service, exercising a totalitarian supervision over every kind of social control? Or does a totalitarian sovereignty necessarily involve dictatorship?

Contrary to the theory current in England, that democracy and planning are mutually exclusive, we believe that democratic control is possible. Out of the growing concentration of social control which is taking place in every state without distinction, a democratic guidance of this control could evolve if we had a clear theoretical understanding of the fields where intervention will be necessary, and are ready to create a favourable public opinion.

[1] Cf. in the Bibliography III 2 *c, d.*

There is nothing in the nature of planning or of democratic machinery which makes them inconsistent with each other. The parliamentary democratic system has worked out a method for the concentration of sovereignty which combines it with the idea of public control. Thus the wisest tactics for democracy and for the defenders of freedom would be, not to obstruct planning, but to try to evolve a type of planning in which democratic control could be maintained by institutional safeguards. This cannot, of course, be achieved in terms of the obsolete formula of *laissez-faire*, but only by an ever more conscious management of techniques, with a view to creating and preserving a scope for freedom and self-determination within the framework of the plan.

I am far from denying that both the right moment to establish these safeguards and their ultimate chances of success are not merely questions of social technique but largely depend on social and political factors. If invincible antagonism between the classes should render such safeguards worthless, then no technical knowledge will help us. But on the other hand it should also not be forgotten that even the most absolute power is useless if we have not the technical knowledge to show us how it could be most wholesomely applied in the interest of the entire community.

The political theory that we are living in an age of class warfare and that social and technical considerations are therefore of no importance has delayed the rational discussion of the problem whether planning and democracy are compatible. In response to this attitude we must insist that the technical problems of society cannot be solved by tactics and class warfare alone.[1] There is a terrible destiny in store for generations who are brought up to believe in the false alternatives democracy or planning, no synthesis on the plane of theoretical analysis being possible. Thus it is essential that in a theoretical analysis like our own, the problem of technical feasibility should be clearly distinguished from political and tactical considerations. Because of the instability of our epoch, a combination of factors may always arise which may make something politically possible which to-day does not seem so. The variety of tactical situations is enormous, and owing to these incalculable factors it would be a mistake to leave the public

[1] See further. pp. 341 ff.

under the delusion that planning is only possible if it is carried out on dictatorial lines.

In the following section I shall make a sharp distinction between political and tactical considerations and social and technical ones, and shall try to prove that, in view of the essential criteria of democratic control we have already discussed, these social and technical factors are compatible with planning.

5. *The Political and Technical Analysis of the Criteria of Democratic Control in Relation to the Possibility of Achieving them in a Planned Society. Discussion of some aspects of War and Class War in this connection.*

Almost every control we have described [1] could, with modifications, be carried over into a planned society.

To begin with the first criterion, the establishment of *sovereignty*, it is obvious that in a planned state, which *eo ipso* implies a concentration of control, it is easier to establish the sovereignty of the state than in a social order where some of the key positions have not been controlled. It is not the mere existence of sovereignty which creates the difficulty, but the question of democratic control and of securing the rotation of leading groups. Once this problem is peacefully solved, any mistaken policy can be corrected by a change in the popular representatives.

There is in theory no reason why a form of democratic control should not be transferred to a planned society. The only way in which a planned society differs from that of the nineteenth century is that more and more spheres of social life, and ultimately each and all of them, are subjected to state control. But if a few controls can be held in check by parliamentary sovereignty, so can many. It is a question of recasting the machinery, rather than of replacing it altogether. For instance, the principle of the separation of powers on functional lines can more easily be applied to a planned society than to a liberal democratic one. The fact that in a planned society the various spheres of planning are interdependent, does not vitiate this principle. In other words there is no necessary reason why, in a planned society, sovereignty should take the form of a dictatorship.

Of course this functional balance, which guarantees that

[1] On pages 331–335.

no department shall remain independent and go its own way, must be subjected to still stronger authority: the sovereign powers which direct this co-ordination. In a democratic state, sovereignty can be boundlessly strengthened by plenary powers without renouncing democratic control. If the liberal theorists persist in believing that planning implies the omnipotence of a dictator, and are therefore opposed to any type of planning, they are just as much on the wrong track as the commonsense observers who, seeing that all the existing planned societies are dictatorial, conclude that planning and dictatorship are necessarily inseparable. There is no discussion more barren than one which argues in terms of *post hoc, ergo propter hoc*. Facts in themselves prove nothing, unless a functional analysis throws light upon their meaning. Only a functional analysis of the compatibility or incompatibility of democracy and planning can illuminate existing experiments. But we block the way to such an analysis from the very beginning if we start with the hypothesis that social reality is a system based upon a single principle. Successful social systems have always been of the mixed type. And although party dictatorship does in fact prevail in the existing planned states, it does not do so for functional reasons. On the contrary, it can be shown that this party dictatorship owes its origin and stability to political factors, and not to the functional impossibility of giving the government wide powers of action, without a loss of democratic control.

There are two arguments which tell against the contention that parliamentary machinery can continue to evolve in an age of reconstruction. The first is the existence of the class war and the likelihood of international wars. According to the first theory, the parliamentary system has only been successful so far because the class antagonism between the ruling groups has never gone really deep ; their conflicts were only a sham. But now that a genuine antagonism has developed, the limitations of the democratic parliamentary system will become only too clear. I wish to emphasize that this is the most serious argument against the possibility of maintaining the democratic system and my discussion of it does not aim at proving that there is no real chance of the class war becoming stronger than any other consideration. But what I wish to stress once more is that this chance, although a very strong one, is only one alternative, and that none of the existing classes, given its impressions of the working of dictatorship in the last decades, would really be anxious to pay the price of a dictatorial system for its absolute victory. If we realize that once a dictatorship is established the hope of removing it under the present conditions of social technique is very remote, except after a war, in the countries which have lost, we shall all have a genuine interest in looking more favourably on alternative possibilities. In this sense I should like to limit the absoluteness of the statement that the class war is bound to counteract the development of planning on a democratic basis.

First of all, it is underrating the significance of former conflicts to say that the class struggle has so far been merely a sham. There have been situations in which the same issue which was fought out by revolutionary means in some countries, was achieved in others in the course of an evolutionary transformation, and whether or not this happens depends not only on the economic wealth of the country but also on many other psychological factors, among which the belief that things can be settled through reform is at least an important one.

Secondly, from the sociological point of view, there are no absolute class antagonisms and the Marxist theory takes the marginal situation of an absolute clash as the normal one. Classes which in one configuration seem to be irreconcilable may march together in another situation. Whether they co-operate, or whether they prefer revolutionary methods, will depend, among other factors, on future chances and past experiences. And in this context it will gradually become a serious issue for discussion whether the losses which might accrue from a revolution and subsequent dictatorship do not outweigh the possible disadvantages of a slower parliamentary adjustment. In such a context it is once more useful to know that there is no real incompatibility between dynamic change, brought about by class antagonism, and parliamentary adjustment. As to the argument that in times of international war or afterwards only the revolutionary seizure of power is likely to be successful, notice must be taken of the changed social and military techniques operating during and after the war. If such a war were to end in a general disorganization of society there would be little difference between winners and losers, it is possible that the suppressed classes might succeed in carrying through a revolution. But it is also possible that in a state of general chaos military bands controlling part of the war machine would establish their power. Should the war end in stalemate or should some nations remain completely integrated, then the diagnosis would take a different form. The planning necessary in war time would very likely be maintained after the war. Certainly there would be no hope of a return to a *laissez-faire* order. In view of this any war time strategy should concentrate, first on maintaining consistency from the standpoint of planning, and secondly on seeing that parliamentary control is not seriously diminished. All of which proves once more that we have good reasons to watch continuously the chances of the evolutionary method at any stage, and our attention is once more directed to the purely technical analysis of the possibility of transferring the method of democratic control to a planned society.

From the technical point of view the next instance to be discussed, the possibility of guarding against a *coup d'état* in a planned society, or against the use of extra parliamentary powers, is considerably simplified in a state where governmental techniques have already been co-ordinated. The state must be strong enough to defend the parliamentary machinery against attack or overthrow. In every society, even in the dictatorships, bargaining and compromise are the basis of decision, and care is taken to see that the arbitrator stands above the parties. It is doubtful whether in the long run, the more primitive and inorganic method of representing different interests by gathering them in cliques around the dictator, and the forcible cutting of the Gordian knot, are any more compatible with a rational and completely organized society than the highly balanced system of parliamentary government.

The institutional separation of consensus from vacillating and selfish group interests and the sublimation of hostility into constructive criticism by the parliamentary system are likely to encourage the growth of rational behaviour in modern society. Again, it is not the functional incompatibility of planning and democracy which makes the solution so difficult to find, but the political and tactical element.

Further, where planning is concerned with processes which were once completely unregulated, such as the manipulation of the trade cycle, the disposition of public works, the re-education of men and women, the regulation of social advancement and the co-ordination of the social services, there is a natural tendency in modern society to enforce co-ordination and control, and this does not in the least imply the discarding of democratic responsibility.

Finally, the great danger in democracy, which is perhaps the strongest impediment to its smooth development, is the uncontrolled eruption of crowd behaviour. But even that can be averted to a great extent, when we have a greater knowledge of mass behaviour and when a greater co-ordination between institutions and psychological influencing has been reached—a possibility which did not exist in previous societies.

To sum up, it is much more plausible to say that the parliamentary machinery ceases to work, not because the class war and other social maladjustments exist, but because the will and the ability to reform is lacking. That is to say, we do not provide the social and economic machinery for the broader changes in society and we allow social institutions and class interests to clash, until these unfettered maladjustments become so strong that the political framework of democracy and parliamentarism is too weak to hold such a society together. Where controls are rationally co-ordinated, the control of controls must sooner or later be run on rationalized lines. The democratic parliamentary machinery clearly forms part of this process of rationalizing social controls. There is no reason therefore why a form of the control of control, which is able to deal successfully with a limited number of key positions in the democratic parliamentary state, should not be applied to a greater number of controls in a manipulated mass society.

6. *The Discussion of some Social and Technical Difficulties in Transferring Democratic, Parliamentary Controls to a Planned Society.*

Our optimism with regard to the theoretical consistency of

democracy and planning should not blind us to the difficulties which arise if the whole machinery of society has to be democratically controlled.

Here I am not speaking of the political and tactical difficulties we have already mentioned, which are always apt to arise during the transition to a new social order, but of the purely technical and functional difficulties, which result from transferring these controls to much wider fields of society. We shall, of course, deal only with a few of these difficulties ; and this, not in the hope of reaching a final solution, but from the conviction that the new task of the sociologist at least is to discover the fundamental principles which govern social organization. Once these principles have been discovered, further thought and experiment have as good a chance of success as in any other province of technique. Technical inventions are always the result of the concrete application of elementary principles. If the principles clash it is very likely that the corresponding empirical processes will clash too. Thus it will now perhaps be useful to discuss the difficulties on the basis of principles.

(a) Can the Ultimate Aim of a Planned Society be Democratically Determined ?

It has often been observed that the greatest obstacle to totalitarian planning on democratic lines is that the ultimate aim of the whole plan must be determined in advance. From the theoretical and philosophic point of view, those who think that it is almost impossible to achieve any ultimate purpose in a modern society based on democratic principles, are perfectly right. Our age is far too individualistic and far too strongly differentiated into groups and sects, each aiming at absolutism, to be reduced to a single common denominator. Liberal society which corresponded to the stage of invention could escape this problem in so far as it refrained from determining ultimate aims by official regulation. This is the meaning of its tolerance in all questions of religion and philosophy of life. This too is the reason for the formalization of most moral issues in the representative thought of the epoch, understanding by formalization that kind of thought which tries to avoid any decision about the content of moral rules and makes the criterion of moral right the idea of formal consistency. Thus, for instance, in the ethics of the age of Enlightenment the inner nature of freedom is purposely left undefined. No answer is given to the simple question : " freedom for what ? " Instead, freedom is described in negative terms as the non-intervention of the state in the private life of the individual, or in the form of maxims which merely limit its range, as in the dictum that individual freedom of action is only restricted as far as is necessary to prevent it encroaching on the freedom of others. All these methods imply that the liberal state leaves both the aims of social dynamics and the differences of outlook they involve to the social process and so evades the responsibility of taking important decisions itself.

In the dictatorial and totalitarian states the situation is very different. There the dictators, with the help of a small band of storm troopers, miraculously restored to the path of uniformity nations which were threatening to drift into chaos through their lack of unified purpose. This miracle was brought about, of course, by means of concentration camps, standardization, violence, and propaganda. Now it is natural for those who value freedom and humanity to feel that too high a price has been paid for this method of creating a single purpose. We must, therefore, ask ourselves whether it is not possible to find the mean between the two extremes of the absolute indeterminateness of social aims and the dictatorial imposition of a closed system of dogmas. These dogmas are often merely the scurrilous ideologies of the dictator, or of some semi-educated intellectuals among his followers, who before their accession to power were known as cranks.

It has often been said that the one case where planning would be possible in the democratic states is the case of war. Then—so runs the argument—in a time of crisis with victory as the goal it would be easy to obtain public recognition of a single purpose and an ultimate value. The question is : Cannot a planned society, especially in the present period of transition, work out a number of vital purposes that are clearly determined by necessity, without the need for war ? Thus a problem which may be quite insoluble on the theoretical plane, where all values —at least at the present moment—seem to be relative, can be instantly solved in practice. The philosophical dilemma is considerably simplified by the fact that our whole society finds itself in an almost military state of emergency.

The more obvious the upheavals in the trade cycle become, the sooner the incalculable desires of groups and individuals will be fused in the demand for security. It is very likely that the slogan of a future state will be " security and justice first and foremost ", and those who can promise security and greater justice will have the proletariat and after the recent negative experiences with Fascism, the middle classes and the reasonable elements among the organizing élites on their side.

(b)   *Hierarchy of the Basic Aims to be determined by Practical Experience.*

If the craving for security springs from a long series of misfortunes (notably those caused by the booms and slumps of the trade cycle), reinforced by a continual dread of war, we already have some indications to guide us in drafting the simplest regulations concerning these things. The manipulation of the trade cycle has definite implications in the economic as well as in the sociological sense, and these involve a hierarchy for organizing the necessary action.

Everything connected with the reorganization of industry, and the encouragement and discouragement of investment, will take precedence, for the effect on the whole cycle is more important than the satisfaction of individual desires. If military preparations are included in the scheme, the scale of needs will be determined by the supremacy of military achievement. It is unfortunate, but this will probably be one of the factors compelling the democracies to set up a compulsory hierarchy of requirements. The same basic situation will result in a revision of opinion on two further counts, to which we turn in the next paragraphs. People will learn that consumer's choice is not sacred, and the entrepreneur will find that he has more control over his business, if he can be guided in his investments by a central plan.

(c)   *The Limitation of Consumer's Choice.*

This double manipulation of economic machinery will probably be accomplished by degrees under pressure of circumstances without much fuss or propaganda.

The renunciation of absolute freedom of choice—if it

should become necessary—will not weigh too heavily on the consumer; mainly because the greater part of the population has never had this freedom of choice and has been forced by poverty to buy standardized goods. There is all the difference in the world between those technical inventions which mark a genuine scientific advance and those which merely satisfy the craving for variety. These luxuries are always making it necessary to reorganize our technical equipment and they will probably have to be restricted in some way. The impossibility of predicting these constant changes in the public taste is at least partly responsible for the difficulty of co-ordinating production and consumption, and is thus a vital source of maladjustment. To create a comparative uniformity of taste will involve considerable sacrifices, but these will not seem too great, if they can provide greater social security.

Moreover in a democratic society this reduction in the incalculable variety of future consumption, as we have seen,[1] might be attained by means of an advertising campaign, provided that it was carefully co-ordinated with production. This is merely to invent a new means of promoting conformity in our basic needs, a conformity which only declined in the age of liberalism. Traditionalist ages have always understood how to induce people through habits and customs to enjoy conformity in dress, food, and housing as more dignified than an aimless change. This unbridled craving for variety is not ingrained in human nature but is the product of the constant stimulation aroused by anarchic competition. In order to make additional profits one has to create new wants so that existing fashions soon become obsolete. According to the dogmas of liberal theorists, consumer's choice is inviolably sacred and on it all progress depends. Nothing could be more erroneous. Freedom of thought in intellectual production is prefectly compatible with the standardization of our primary needs. Lippmann has wittily compared the position of the consumer in the Liberal age to a customer in a restaurant who can dine *à la carte*, whereas in a planned society he would be forced to put up with a *table d'hôte* menu. But there is a possible compromise. In an

---

[1] Cf. p. 315, where we discuss certain aspects of the same problem as they concern the transmutation of direct into indirect controls.

intelligently planned society a whole series of menus could be provided in every sphere of custom. This avoids the chaotic uncertainty of individual idiosyncrasies, and yet allows for a relative amount of variation in the different types of demand. Events are tending to follow this pattern, without attracting much attention. Mass society brings mass production in its train, as far as housing, food, and clothing are concerned, without necessarily producing any spiritual impoverishment. We must not lose sight of the vital principle that in a democratically planned society it is quite possible to draw a dividing line between the spheres which must be standardized for the sake of planning, and those in which individual freedom may be permitted without upsetting the whole plan. It is quite easy to live in a standardized house, possess a standardized wireless, and drive a standardized car without becoming intellectually standardized as well. In the same way a university which is housed in standardized buildings, and has an administration which works like clockwork, may still be entirely individual and unstereotyped in its teachings. It is true that whenever anything is too carefully planned and organized in a society, there is an abstract tendency for this standardization to become all-embracing. But this only applies when we are completely powerless in the grip of these forces. As soon as we decide on the limits of our planning, there are always ways and means of holding such tendencies in check. But people will ask, " Where is the impulse for improvement to come from, if not from competition for the goodwill of the buying public ? Until now public opinion has expressed itself in terms of prices and this is the ultimate spur to new invention, and to the production of goods which are more in accordance with the general taste."

I believe this problem, like many others which seem to be theoretically insoluble, can be solved by a wise combination of techniques. I believe that there exist at least two social and technical innovations which, when combined, will allow the public to decide the future trend of production, as far as consumable goods are concerned, without running the risk of injudicious investment on a large scale.

To-day we have the Industries Fair. It would be possible to invent something similar, where the inventor and the contractor could place their new models on show, and a jury of experts, combined with a scientifically conducted public ballot, could decide which products should be mass produced. Statistics with their improved methods of sampling have shown that the examination of a relatively small number of well-chosen samples rightly reflects the opinions and desires of a large number of people.[1]

Public opinion must help to determine the departments in which production should be developed. It should be guided by a committee of experts—not unlike a guild—which would only sanction models which were artistic and technically perfect, and its judgment could be checked by the democratic ballot we have just described.

Here we come to the point where central control over capital will inevitably increase, and certain rights possessed by the entrepreneur will be curtailed. These tendencies are reflected in the slow transformation of the conception of property in modern society.

(d) *Modern Transformation of the Conception of Property.*

The old conception of property as the unrestricted use of a thing dates from Roman Law, and was maintained until recent times, but is now undergoing a gradual transformation.[2] It is becoming more and more obvious that the enjoyment of income and interest and the right to dispose of capital are two very different things. It is possible that in the future things will so develop that by appropriate taxation and compulsory charity this unrestricted use could be curtailed, and the disposition of capital could be guided from the centre by credit control. Foreign credit could eventually be controlled as well. If invested capital can gradually be directed from the centre into the right channels, much can be achieved without resorting to expropriation. Fascism is making unwillingly an interesting experiment in its unacknowledged expropriation of the capitalists. It has managed to socialize the power of disposition without ejecting the former industrial élite from their posts.

Transformation of the original form of capitalism does not consist in abolishing the claims of private property, but in withdrawing certain functions of the ownership of capital from the competence of the capitalists. The

---

[1] *The American and British Institute of Public Opinion Analysis* successfully prophesied the results of coming elections.

[2] Cf. in the Bibliography I 3 *c*.

entrepreneur may still retain his organizing function, have a relatively higher income, and keep his social prestige, but he will be deprived of his power just as the feudal lord was deprived of his political power at Louis XIV's court. The main difference will be that, whereas in the French king's court the nobility were compensated for the loss of power by the greatness of their prestige, according to recent trends of development the entrepreneur will be compensated by the new administrative tasks he will have to fulfil. Remembering the Russian experiences, where the extinction of the older élites and of indispensable experts was largely responsible for the general lowering of cultural standards and of the quality of production, the progressive groups might try to win over rather than to alienate the technical and organizing élites.

(e) Planned Social Advancement and the Extension of the Social Services

On the other hand, should such a development take place, it is to be expected that the rising classes will only agree to retain parts of the former ruling élite, if constitutional guarantees and effective safeguards are provided against the creation of an oligarchy, and planning ensures that the ablest men rise to the top ; so that within a reasonable space of time (if possible in the next generation) the chief positions will be allotted solely according to merit. This means that wider opportunities must be given for acquiring the necessary education, and that professions must be planned on the basis of supply and demand, so as to prevent the growth of an intellectual proletariat. A *numerus clausus* could be introduced in overcrowded professions, provided that it was based not on discrimination against certain groups, but on high qualifications and aptitude for the work.

Parallel with the guarantee for the advancement of the ablest and best qualified men, assurance must also be given that there will be a minimum standard of living for everybody. Pensions, health, and unemployment insurance must be the first tasks which planning undertakes. This would seem to be quite possible once the *laissez-faire* economy has been corrected. For the latter is responsible, in the distorted form in which it exists in the age of trusts and cartels, for the maladjustments in the economic order. Apart from the guarantee that the careers will be open to the talents and that fundamental security will be provided, the extension of the social services is the very essence of planning, in an age in which highly developed social techniques replace the older forms of neighbourly help.

The social services can be called a form of rational adjustment. Their object is to bring about the readjustment of groups and individuals who have lost their way in the wilderness of modern society. This readjustment was, in the first period of the industrial age, purely external, confined to material help, but it is now being extended to cover psychological help as well. It is here that modern society shows a growing tendency to interfere with the mental activities of the citizen and to proceed from economic to psychological guidance.

(f) Can Freedom in the Intellectual Sphere be Combined with Compulsion as to the Basic Conditions of Social Life?

Dogmatic thinkers tend to answer this question in terms of " one thing or the other ". They think that the first step towards a planned society means complete interference. We, on the other hand, believe that the planner can decide where to stop.[1] We believe that psychological freedom is impossible until fundamental social relationships have been organized. Now there are certain basic virtues which are essential to the maintenance of a planned society and it is necessary that we should use all the resources of our education to create them. These basic virtues are not very different from those which the ethics of all world religions, among others Christianity, have held to be vital : co-operation, brotherly help, and decency. This education is primarily needed to destroy the psychological anarchy of liberal capitalism, which is based on the artificial cultivation of certain exaggerated attitudes. One of these is the mania for competition, which springs not from the desire for objective

[1] This argument is partly analogous to what we have discussed under the heading " Limitation of Consumer's Choice " (pp. 347 *seqq.*). But whereas there the argument is concerned with the problem of minimum conformity necessary in the sphere of economic production, we are dealing now with the intellectual sphere as such, in which a certain amount of basic conformity seems to be not incompatible with freedom on a higher plane.

achievement and community service, but from sheer self-centredness or very often from neurotic anxiety. A democratically planned society must thoroughly develop the new forms of freedom, but once developed it must defend them with the same zeal that any society shows in the defence of its fundamental principles. Democracy ought to instruct its citizens in its own values instead of feebly· waiting until its system is wrecked by private armies from within. Tolerance does not mean tolerating the intolerant. Once integration and equilibrium have been achieved in the sphere of elementary human relationships, there must be very far-reaching liberty on the higher planes of our spiritual life, especially freedom for intellectual discussion. But freedom of thought will not be established merely because it is a virtue in itself but because the unhampered exchange of opinion is the only guarantee of social progress. It is essential to intellectual production that its freedom of action should be preserved in planning. It is necessary to go even further. Since research needs considerable financial support, there is a tendency for it to be monopolized by a few institutions, which can always exert a certain pressure on the course of its development. This inevitably puts the independent thinker at a disadvantage, and it is all the more essential to encourage free lance activities by stipends. These stipends should be allotted by a mixed jury, including a reasonable percentage of jurors who do not represent the views of official institutions, but do justice to changes in intellectual life which escape these large and self-contained bodies. Only those who have worked their way alone unsheltered by institutions, and have thus developed a sense of the new needs and currents in social life are able to develop the new approach which is needed, and to produce the really creative incentives. The great institutions which control all the instruments of research and have access to the material would profit by this stimulation, for they are always in danger of reacting in terms of vested interests, of becoming self-sufficient and ultimately rigid. In the same way vanguard groups ·of amateurs can do valuable work experimenting with new ideas and their effect upon the public in such fields as the cinema or wireless where the amount of capital invested or the nature of the technique involved makes the central monopoly of control extremely probable. One of the greatest merits of a free and democratic civilization is its readiness to draw on the resources of public talent. These devices can easily be incorporated into the framework of a planned society. Adult education has made it easy to arouse larger and larger sections of the working classes and to encourage them to educate themselves.

Self-education is no longer merely intellectual but also religious and artistic.[1] Settlements and colonies where artists and labourers mix are likely to find new forms of self-expression. As a result of this unusual kind of community life, a new valuation of work and leisure [2] will emerge. Once fundamental social conformity has been assured, it is doubly necessary to provide for plasticity, foresight, enterprise, vitality, and a new sense of reality. Planning of this constructive type, which deliberately creates fresh opportunities and incentives, is not a contradiction in terms, but the only genuine form of planning which exists. In this context one is reminded of the ancient Brahmins who laid great stress on a punctilious observance of ritual, but were very tolerant of philosophic doctrines—even atheistic sects were sanctioned. The sociological explanation is that once a society has become united on the plane of ritual or on any other matter which creates basic conformity, it is all the easier to allow freedom and plasticity on a higher level. Now philosophically speaking, the frontiers which divide the province of this conformity from the province where freedom and initiative are essential can never be really drawn. I am the last to underrate the difficulty of exactly defining these borderlines or to be oblivious of the questions which immediately arise. Once we try to single out these basic virtues we have to decide upon our attitudes toward problems like these. Should a society have the right to impose ascetic laws upon its members or are ascetic virtues only linked up with particular religions? Are military virtues to be encouraged or should all citizens be brought up in the spirit of a brotherly pacifism? Even if we agree that issues such as these present very grave difficulties, it is extremely dangerous to remain as we do completely inarticulate about them. Modern society will

---

[1] Beck, Maximilian, *Philosophie und Politik* (Zürich, 1938, Europa Verlag).
[2] Cf. in the Bibliography III 7 d and IV 2, 5.

have to make up its mind upon these points if it is not to drift into chaos. Fortunately such problems can usually be solved more readily in practice than in theory. It must be remembered that even in the liberal order schools and churches were forced to decide these points and never failed to reach a decision. Why should not a planned society make its own decisions when it has expert advice at its disposal and when the social services are there to inform it about the effects of its regulations on individuals? In borderline cases it may be accepted as a general rule that functional considerations should prevail [1]—that is to say decisions should be based on principles which estimate the value of moral regulations by the contribution they make to the maintenance of the social order. If war is threatening, heroic virtues will be needed. If consumption outstrips production, restrictions, even ascetic restrictions, will be needed. And we should not forget that the basic virtues are generally a matter of habit and only rarely involve careful deliberation and decision in the individual.

(g) *The Necessity for Separating Long Range Policy from Temporary Issues and for Introducing the Principle of Leadership where Rapid Decisions are Essential.*

Although it may not be easy we must make a clear distinction between those institutions and programmes which refer to the very structure of society and involve a long range policy, and those which reflect merely temporary and fluctuating changes. The former must be safeguarded by constitutional guarantees, so that they will not be exposed to passing moods or reversed by a mere plebiscite. The various departments of social affairs should be graded according to their importance and plasticity. The issues which have a bearing on long range policy should be clearly separated from those which help to bring about adjustments to fluctuating needs. This is the meaning of consciously planning social change in a society in which not even the dynamic elements are left uncontrolled.

This sharp division between the minimum amount of organization which is necessary for the working of a planned society, and spheres where freedom and variety must prevail,

[1] My article, " Mass Education and Group Analysis," in *Educating for Democracy*, edited by J. Cohen and R. M. W. Travers, London, 1939.

is all the more necessary because it is the only way of competing with the more conscious policy of the totalitarian states and their swifter powers of decision. For this reason the principle of leadership should be adopted in certain places and in dealing with certain types of affairs. There is nothing wrong with the principle of leadership in itself ; on the contrary, it is the right method to adopt in dealing with the new groups which arise when the older institutions have decayed, or in coming to a lightning decision in an emergency. It only becomes an evil when it operates without democratic sanction or responsibility, or when it seizes the opportunity of becoming absolute and irremovable.

(h) Plebiscites in the Age of Mass Society. The Problem of the Education of Emotions.

We must be determined to adapt the genuine principles of democracy to mass society, instead of regarding certain democratic devices as sacrosanct in themselves. If we consider the plebiscitary element in democracy, we are justified in saying, after the experiences of the last epoch, that of all democratic institutions, it has made the largest contribution to the destruction of the system. The plebiscitary principle drives people towards what we have described as crowd psychology. This crowd psychology is one of the chief evils to be feared, a precipice before which democracy stands. The mobilization of the entire populace to hold a plebiscite in circumstances which are more characteristic of a farce than of a turning-point in the national destiny, is one of those democratic customs which are apt to become meaningless, once the social background and the social techniques have changed. The referendum was only reasonable when it applied to the citizens of a small community. Now since it appears in the guise first given it by Napoleon III, that of a managed display of mass emotion, it no longer has an honest part to play in democratic society. A modern plebiscite treats the individual as a spectator, whereas in the smaller democratic groups he was an active and co-operative member of the commune.[1] The spectator is known to be

---

[1] Lindsay, A. D., *The Essentials of Democracy* (William J. Cooper Foundation Lectures), London, 1935, gives a most illuminating analysis of the social conditions under which democracy originally used to work.

completely irresponsible [1]; he is simply there to see the show, and has no intention of weighing the facts or grasping the implications of the spectacle. The plebiscite has lost its original function ; it no longer appeals to individuals living in concrete groups, or draws their attention to concrete problems, but is addressed to members of an indefinite and emotional mass. The purpose of democracy is not to play on the emotions of the masses, but to prevent the vacillating reactions of popular feeling from frustrating the rational and considered opinions of the nation.

In discussing the merits and faults of the plebiscite the new science of democratic institutions should not be too dogmatic. Rather it should be thoroughly realistic and discuss the changing meaning of democratic principles in relation to the new sociological and psychological background of a changed society.

It will then be obvious that the function of the plebiscite in the context of a mass society has been completely reversed. For it no longer interprets the general will as the expression of the considered intentions of the citizens, but is rather the result of skilful agitation and a powerful propaganda machine. It follows that the democratic principle in mass society must be reformed in two directions. On the one hand we must surpass the limits of the age of Enlightenment and rationalism in so far as we must rediscover the integrating significance of emotions in mass society. On the other, we must co-ordinate emotion and reason on a new level. As to the function of emotion in the new society the democracies must learn from the totalitarian states that the emotional integration of mass society cannot be effected by techniques which were adapted to the democracy of little communities, or the democracy of the eighteenth and nineteenth centuries which was restricted to the upper classes. But the acceptance of the role that emotion must play in modern society will not lead us to accept the spirit in which the modern totalitarian techniques are used. For that spirit merely utilizes the lowest common denominator in the moods of the masses, and confines the co-operation of the citizen to fluctuating emotional reactions. For us the significance of emotion must be rediscovered in a new

[1] Cf. on the psychology of the spectator in A. Vierkandt's *Gesellschaftslehre*, Stuttgart, 1923, part 5, § 45.

sense and greater emphasis laid on the appreciation of those basic issues which ultimately integrate groups, and on those fundamental values which are the products of the historical life of the community, and on new ideals which aim at the just reconstruction of society.

Fascism is a form of group integration which is mainly effective in the emotional sphere. There is no attempt to direct this stream of emotion into channels where it could join forces with reason, judgment, and responsible action. Instead of exploiting these emotions in this way so as to choke the development of the intellectual faculties, modern democratic education should regard the emotional element as a necessary preliminary in the re-education of the masses.[1] Far from being over-intellectual in outlook as was the age of Enlightenment, the modern theory of thought acknowledges the significance of emotion in the process of discovery and reasoning, and still more in the field of group education.

To-day we know that without a certain amount of enthusiasm no knowledge can be assimilated, that the significance of certain issues can only be realized in the context of collective processes, which ultimately have their origin in the unconscious strivings of the group. This, of course, does not mean that emotion is an end in itself or a touchstone of truth, or that group education is nothing but an appeal to the emotions. Skilfully handled, emotions do not obstruct the evolution of the higher faculties of the mind ; their function in group education is ultimately to pave the way for reasoned judgment. If our educational institutions are co-ordinated and planned they will gradually advance from the emotional stage to a mastery of the emotions. The education of the masses, if it is democratically planned, does not involve the inculcation of a creed, but starts with certain issues where there is complete emotional agreement, and gradually passes on to a more individual level of critical self-control.

But it is only possible to start from the emotional conformity of primary groups in those democratic countries where the disintegration of the groups, and their traditional life, has not gone too far. If it has the task of bringing about basic conformity, educational planning will obviously be even more difficult. A conscious attempt at community reorganization and the readjustment of disintegrated personalities will be needed.[1]

Only when that basic integration is achieved will it be possible to turn to the task of creating opportunities for the growth of personality, and differentiating attitudes. Only against such a background will it be successful.   In the process of that primary conscious reintegration propaganda may play a valuable role.   For propaganda, if rightly understood, does not necessarily mean the inculcation of false creeds, but the most successful way of dealing with impulses and desires which are not yet embodied in the groups in which we live.   It is at once the simplest and most superficial form of reintegration.   But whereas in fascism the spirit of propaganda imposes itself on all other institutions, in a modern planned democracy it should represent merely a phase in the hierarchy of educational influences.   Its aim should be to capture disorganized groups and individuals, in order to reorganize them as quickly as possible, even on the most superficial emotional level.   But as democracy means the gradual education of the people, and the cultivation of judgment and refinement, the primary integration should gradually be transferred to other educational agencies ;   and their various grades should be carefully worked out : not in order to inculcate the same doctrine on different planes, but so as to educate the individual out of his dependence on mass emotion.   Once such a re-education has been carried out on a large scale, the plebiscite might once more have a real function in democratic society.

(i) Certain Tendencies towards Objectivism and the Decrease of the Political Element in Modern Society.

The recent emphasis upon the plebiscitary element in mass society reflects a universal paradox of our age which we have already met within another context.   The growth of organization and the general interdependence of institutions make for an increase in rationality and detachment.   On the other hand, mass emotions tend to sweep away all traces of foresight and calculation.

[1] Cf. in Bibliography III 6, III 7d, IV 5.

Vital as it is for a democracy that people should make their own contribution to the direction of public affairs, it is equally important that these contributions should merely serve as an indication to the Government, but should not in their crude state be immediately put into practice. Much depends on whether our new social techniques are capable of sublimating and incorporating these genuine impulses of the community in the social order. The disastrous effect of the interference of mob emotions with governmental work presents a problem also to the dictatorial societies and they have dealt with it in two different ways. They either try to neutralize the desire to take part in the decision by making use of every technique for diverting public opinion by pageantry and sport, or else they stage " spontaneous " demonstrations after the decision has been made.

Fortunately, modern society has other mechanisms at its disposal if only it will use them. For elections may well be regarded as a guide only, as an ultimate indication to the consulting bodies who have to carry out the public's wishes. In this way only the ultimate direction of public affairs is to be treated as a political matter and would remain an emotional issue, whereas as a general rule the translation of this policy into practice would gradually become a purely technical matter.

The reduction of the political element is essential for any form of planning, as the continuous flash of emotions and group valuations hinders the execution of the plan. Thus it is worth while watching all those factors in our society which tend to make most subjects non-political, once the essential major decisions have been taken. This applies particularly to the manipulation of the trade cycle. The task of straightening out its booms and slumps and repairing the damage it has done, is only partly a political problem ; it is largely a matter of science and technique. It is clear that any intervention from the key positions is of political importance in so far as the support lent to some groups injures others, and any compensation for these injuries has still further repercussions. Yet once a compromise has been reached on the main questions of policy, the problem is far more exclusively confined to its scientific and technical aspects than it was in the age of free competition ; for then society was composed of warring atoms and social machinery could not be adapted to the real needs of the case.

Another consequence of the manipulation of the trade cycle will be the spread of bureaucracy and the planning of professional promotion, which, in its turn, means a decrease of the political element.

The more the trade cycle makes unemployment (both of intellectual and manual labour) the most important issue, the more the solution of the problem will depend on the allocation of existing posts according to certain principles, rather than natural mechanism of competition.

It is very likely that, owing to the growth of the social services, sooner or later appointment boards and vocational guidance bureaux will dominate the field. Such institutions will not merely be charged with the registration of candidates but also with their selection, re-education, and training. If these tendencies are not to develop into a new form of spoil-system, distributing all the best opportunities among party members, much must be done to improve objective methods of testing. The demand that the distribution should be on the basis of an objective examination of candidates must become an important political issue for democracy. The old democratic principle of equality of opportunity and the selection of the fittest will be even more important in the future, because in our age the just distribution of the existing jobs is even more important than in the past. To-day the fear of unemployment can be used to blackmail every citizen into a complete dependence either on the party machine, or on the state. The prevention of such a spoil-system is necessary not only because it is unjust in itself, but because by pushing achievement into the background it must lead to social decay. England is well on the way towards a planned system of promotion, for here at least an attempt has been made to redress the plutocratic principle by endowing scholarships and by filling at least some important vacancies by means of competitive examinations. This system could be extended. But if promotion were regulated by objective criteria, such as talent and achievement, one of the most important provinces of our common life would have ceased to be political. If the regulation of the trade cycle were gradually to become non-political as well, it would be possible to maintain that it is only in the first stages of planning that everything seems to become more political, and that subsequently more and more spheres of life are governed by purely functional standards.

The reason seems to be that in the first phase of planning these spheres are political, because all parties are seeking for an absolute monopoly of power, using existing arrangements solely for the satisfaction of their own limited interests. They are willing to plan, but only in order to secure their own advantage. There is nothing new in that kind of group egotism, it has always existed in the past, for people have always wanted to increase their share of the spoil. What is new is that every group now craves for an absolute monopoly, and can only achieve its aim by thinking in terms of the social machine as a whole. Although at the beginning the new trend is completely disastrous, since all sections aim at the complete extinction of their enemies, there is a faint hope that the inner contradictions inherent in it will lead to a solution.

First of all, the absolutism which makes all parties struggle for a monopoly may end in a new balance of power, for any marked advance by any one group in that direction mobilizes the rest of the population and forces it to co-operate. Then the fact that even the dictatorial group has to learn to think in terms of the whole social machine makes for the growth of the type of mind which—even perhaps after a long period of conflict—realizes that in the long run planning can only work smoothly after the more blatant differences in wealth and opportunity have been abolished. Such a tendency would ultimately transform a class war into a legitimate struggle for different schemes of reform. Again, this development is not a necessary one, but it is possible. Thus it is all the more important to reinforce every tendency which is working in that direction.

If this theory is correct, the second phase of planning would gradually diminish the number of purely political issues and matter of fact solutions would prevail. In the past this process has already taken place on a smaller scale. With the growth of the state—as we have seen—many local and sectarian interests were subordinated to the advantage of a larger whole. With the growth of a coherent and co-ordinated system of social techniques it soon became clear that many petty decisions which once seemed to be a question of opinion and aim, were largely dependent on the solution of a technical problem of co-ordination. But politics have not yet disappeared from view ; they are now concerned with the key positions rather than with the texture of everyday life.

A hygienic or sanitary problem is usually solved by non-political means ; it is a question of the best scientific methods to employ, and political differences are inconceivable. In the same way scientific planning tends to regard a growing number of problems as non-political. But hygienic questions were once also regarded from a non-technical standpoint, in an age in which the rational treatment of disease and the avoidance of infection were outlawed owing to certain philosophical and superstitious beliefs. It was impossible to come to an agreement as long as any deviations from traditional attitudes were treated as heresies. Once it could be proved with scientific exactitude that certain processes could avert the danger of infection, only the question of values remained—whether life was worth saving —and on this question agreement could be reached without much difficulty. There is no doubt that the values involved in hygienic questions are much simpler than those of the social sciences, where political and philosophical implications are more closely intertwined with the pure facts than anywhere else.[1] But it could be shown that the apparent impossibility of reconciling this conflict of values is ultimately rooted in politics ; and politics—in our age at least—are to a great extent connected with the unequal distribution of scarce commodities.

This point of contention will vanish as soon as the whole population is provided for and security is regarded as a fundamental right, a universal claim on the social services, so that everyone is entitled to a fair place in the social scheme, according to his merits. The necessity of preventing politics from clogging the wheels of planning is one of the factors which, in the long run, makes for equality of opportunity in a planned society. Planning, therefore, ultimately leads to the spread of democracy in the sense of a fundamental

[1] Cf. with reference to the question of the nature of valuations in the natural and social sciences. Kingsley Davis, " The Application of Social Science to Personal Relations," *Am. Soc. Rev.*, Ap., 1936.

equality. Thus planning tends to counteract a danger it has itself partly created—the dictatorial monopoly of key positions. Both tendencies are inherent in planning, and it is a question of policy which should be strengthened. This tendency towards equality does not prevent anyone planning an unequal distribution of property and power. Society can be planned in the form of a hierarchy as well as in the form of a democracy. But planning based on the inequality of classes or estates probably cannot last long, because these inequalities will create so great a tension in society that it will be impossible to establish even that minimum of tacit consent which is the *conditio sine qua non* of the functioning of a system.

If we sum up these tendencies we find that in spite of considerable difficulties, there is always the possibility of adjusting the old principle of social organization to the new. We may venture to say that in this process it is utterly impossible to compromise between the old principle of *laissez-faire* liberalism and planning, whereas planning and democracy are not merely compatible but even complementary. From the wreckage of liberalism nothing can be saved but its values, among others, the belief in a free personality. But its technique, which is based on the principle of *laissez-faire,* is gone for ever. It is impossible to take over a social technique which bases its hopes solely on spontaneous adjustment between the social forces, for our society has left the atomistic stage of small units far behind. Thus the old ideal of freedom can only be attained by the technique of planning for freedom.

Freedom and democracy can no longer be preserved through the idle praise of abstract principles by men who are entirely ignorant of the social techniques which could render them effective, and of the political and tactical methods by which they are to be put into practice. If in this book we have said more about techniques than about tactical issues, it is because, as far as social conditions and social techniques are concerned, there is a real chance for sociology to make a creative contribution to the reconstruction of our society. But in the field of political tactics it is extremely difficult for the scientist to make any valid forecast or to give any sound advice, for tactics deal with everchanging configurations in the struggle for political power. One can give a valid analysis of the compatibility of different social systems and techniques, and of their probable effects : but even if there is agreement as to aims, one can give tactical advice only for a limited period, that is, as long as the relative positions of groups and classes remain constant. Which groups would and should co-operate in the class struggle and in the seizure or maintenance of power in the international field cannot, as we have seen, be absolutely stated, since this will depend on the nature of the enemy and the source of the attack. No theoretical considerations could indicate what form alliances in a future war would take, whereas it *is* possible rationally to analyse the technical issues in the reconstruction of our society.

The difficulty of theorizing on tactical issues sometimes persuades people to become irrational in the sphere of politics. They are too ready to assume that politics are merely a question of power. They sometimes say, " Wait till we are in power—the rest will come of itself." Yet our experiences with Fascism have taught us that power without sociological knowledge is blind and ends by making society a prison for the citizen or by involving us in chaos. If we are going to learn anything at all in the decades to come it must be that power in itself does not suffice unless it be linked up with a scientific as well as a human understanding of the social situation. If anything creative emerges from the general disillusionment of an age which has witnessed the practical deterioration of the ideals of Liberalism, Communism, and Fascism, it can only be a new experimental attitude in social affairs, a readiness to learn from all the lessons of history.

But one can only learn if one has belief in the power of reason. For a time it was healthy to see the limitations of the ratio, especially in social affairs. It was healthy to realize that thinking is not powerful if it is severed from the social context and ideas are only strong if they have their social backing, that it is useless to spread ideas which have no real function and are not woven into the social fabric. But this sociological interpretation of ideas may also lead to complete despair, discouraging the individual from thinking about issues which will definitely become the concern of the day. This discouragement of the intelligentsia which may lead them to too quick a resignation of their proper function as the thinkers and forerunners of a new society, may become even more disastrous in a social setting where more depends on what the leading élites may have in mind than in other periods of history. The theory that thought is socially conditioned and changes at different periods in history is only instructive, if its implications are fully realized and applied to our own age.

In an age of fully developed techniques the opinions of the élite are of less significance, though this may cut both ways. The ideas of the suppressed minorities will automatically lose in relevance but the power of the ideas held by the leading élites will be increased in their efficiency. For the nature of communism in Russia it was not a matter of minor importance which ideas were held by Lenin or later by Stalin. Similarly in Germany the ideas of paganism or anti-semitism do not spring in their present dimension directly from the actual circumstances of society, but depend to a very large extent on ideas previously held by the smaller or larger groups now risen to power. This fact means, if we apply it to ourselves, that the conclusions we arrive at in the period of transformation under the existing conditions of free investigation and research, will be of greatest significance for the period to come, in which the planning of society will be carried out by people who have been moulded by the main trends of our age. It is true that even to-day ideas can create no new worlds by themselves, but it is decisive for future events whether or not sound thinking goes on to-day and whether it reaches the ruling élites. These considerations tend to make it even more desirable in the present period of reconstruction to consider what is the best form of planning and how far it is practicable to combine planning with elements of freedom. After a long search for abstract principles the time must come when more people will realize, even if they have to learn it from their own distress, that the reconstruction of society is a matter of life and death for every citizen, and that most of our calamities can only be removed once we have understood that politics form a set of problems which can never be solved by prejudice, but only by a gradual and conscientious study of society.

PART VI

FREEDOM ON THE LEVEL OF PLANNING

Planning raises the fundamental philosophical question : " Is not an ideally planned society a prison, a strait-jacket, even compared with the almost intolerable life led by many classes in an unplanned society ? In the latter many people may be threatened with insecurity, but the individual is still (potentially at least) a free agent and can cope with his difficulties himself. Does not the continual development of social technique lead to the complete enslavement of the individual ? " The question is only too justified, and if a human solution of our present problems is to be possible at all, an answer must be found.

It is all the more necessary to consider the possibility of freedom in an age of highly developed social technique, as a conception of freedom modelled on the preceding age is an obstacle to any real understanding of our problems and hinders the transition to a new type of action. Both the man in the street and the practical politician have vague conceptions of freedom, so that a historical and sociological explanation of the term is no barren speculation but the prelude to action.

We are gradually coming to realize that the contemporary forces which have led to the development of social technique express the desire of the human mind to control, not merely its environment but also, through the latter, itself. Half-hearted techniques lead to the enslavement of mankind ; fully considered techniques to a higher level of freedom.

It is by no means an accident that the problem of freedom has been one of the most recurrent in the history of religion and the philosophy of man. In spite of all the efforts which have been made to solve it during the course of history, it seems to us that the problem of determinism and free will has always been couched in too abstract a form. The philosophies of the past in so far as they deal with the subjective aspects of the problem have penetrated into the deepest levels of the self. But the same cannot be said about the objective aspects. The question " Is man free ? " in relation to the outside world can only become concrete if one does not think of the universe as a whole but becomes aware of the fact that the forms of freedom can only be formulated in reference to a given society and to the social techniques existing in it. The type of freedom which is possible in one society cannot be reasonably demanded in another, which may have other forms of freedom at its command. In short the actual form depends to a large extent on the level of social technique and is also determined by the following factors :

1. The control which can be exercised over social affairs within the framework of the existing social structure.

2. The type of foresight which is possible in a given social pattern.

3. The strength of the desire for a science of government at the present stage of development ; by which I mean the eagerness of the ruling élites to avail themselves of any existing or potential knowledge as to the fairest and most efficient methods of conducting social affairs.

To the abstract approach of a naïve mind which conceives of freedom in general terms without reference to the concrete historical situation, freedom corresponds to the strength of human initiative, the desire to influence social conditions which are as yet uncontrolled or uncontrollable. This definition is vague, so that the question how far and in which form initiative is possible in a given society, can receive many different answers according to the nature of the social structure. It is equally indeterminate with regard to another question : How far can a definite type of social environment be changed and where are the best points to intervene ? The answer to these inquiries will again depend on the nature of the historical situation.

I should like to give two simple examples to prove that the possible types of freedom vary in different societies. In friendship I call myself free if I always have the opportunity of opposing my partner's wishes. If it were necessary to compromise I should still feel free, provided I agreed to this compromise of my own accord. But I should no longer feel free if my partner got his way by physical force or by psychological compulsion, for instance by hypnosis. Thus in a fairly simple social relationship such as friendship, freedom is expressed in the continual opportunity for resistance, in the continual possibility of taking the initiative, in the continual process of voluntary compromise with the wishes of one's partner. On the same level, coercion would correspond to permanent subjection, a permanent sacrifice of initiative.

The situation is quite different if we imagine a small organized group. It would be senseless to believe that its freedom consisted in all its members exerting their free will and demanding that every step which was taken by the group should always be an unstable compromise between different impulses. An organized group can only act collectively if, when organized action is necessary, individuals obey the prescribed rules. And yet one does not feel that in joining an organization a man necessarily renounces all initiative and free will, but rather that in spite of the sacrifice of unlimited individual freedom, the distinction between free and authoritarian organization can be seen in the methods of regulating collective action. In the former, freedom consists in a clear definition of the spheres where complete freedom of action is possible, and of democratic control over the rules governing the regulated spheres. But we should no longer call an organization free if it made continuous efforts to regulate every sphere of action, allowing individual members no say in the aim and organization of its activities, while its officials were not elected but dictatorially appointed from above. This example will suffice to show how senseless it is to translate one social relationship in terms of another, and to speak of lack of freedom in the abstract instead of thinking what form of freedom is possible in a given social setting.

In our next example we shall deal with another aspect of freedom. Here too we shall study the problem at different stages of group formation and in different social settings. But this time we shall understand by freedom, not so much freedom of action but the possibility of self-expression. We should scarcely call a friendship free, if the stronger partner would never allow the other to express his feelings spontaneously but forced him to act the hypocrite. We should say freedom of self-expression existed if there were a continual give and take of emotion, an emotional harmony based on a common outlook ; the result of a spontaneous discussion of situations and events.

In an organization emotional freedom of this kind is out of the question. An organized group can only function if its members have become accustomed to certain institutional attitudes from the outset. Obedience to orders is not enough, emotions must be subject to control, at least in certain spheres. Instead of the complete freedom of self-expression to be found in the first example, education and training have produced certain permanent attitudes of mind, and therefore in some directions at any rate, have suppressed this freedom.

At the second stage social relationships have grown so complex that institutions are essential, though they can still be democratically controlled. But the same principle applies, and we can still decide whether an organization is wantonly depriving its members of their humanity and turning them into robots, and whether emotional control has been established by authority or by consent.

When character building has reached this stage, not every influence is regarded as a tyranny, but only those which are imposed by a minority without the consent of the group, or which interfere with self-expression to an unwarranted degree, considering the real needs of that particular environment. In any case freedom of self-expression cannot be measured by standards which are transferred from one social setting to another. Freedom in the family is one thing and freedom in the playground is another ; the freedom of a religious sect differs from that of a political party, and the social guarantees of freedom must vary in conception accordingly.

But these sociological variations in the conception of freedom only become significant when we consider the problem, not merely in relation to the different groups and settings in any given society, but from the standpoint of the three stages in the development of social technique, which we have already discussed.

At the stage of chance discovery, of trial and error, freedom expresses itself in direct action on and reaction to the stimuli of the surroundings. Lack of freedom is felt if one is prevented from taking the necessary steps to satisfy one's wishes as they arise. At this stage, not unlike an animal which feels hampered when it is prevented from using its body as it wishes, man feels his freedom at stake when he is not allowed to handle things or people as he hoped to do. The immediateness with which freedom expresses itself at this stage is not essentially changed when man has learnt to use the simple tools. The difference is only that by identification with these tools he will feel frustrated when he is denied their use or possession just as though they were an extension of his body. Although the use of the simple tools does not surpass the stage of chance discovery, it marks an advance, for the process of adjustment is becoming more active. The equilibrium between man, his desires and his environment is now brought about by altering part of the surroundings instead of snatching at any pleasure which offers itself. Any obstacle to the occasional alteration of these surroundings is regarded as a threat to freedom.

In the process of this active adjustment to the surroundings we pass to the second stage—that of invention. Owing to an accumulated knowledge of tools and their combined uses we can set more and more intermediate ends and means between ourselves and some ultimate goal which might still be very vague. At the stage of invention we learn to make ourselves more and more independent of natural conditions as they happen to occur, so that this increased command over intermediate aims becomes the most vital expression of our freedom. An employer, a man of property, a bureaucrat and a general have greater freedom than their subordinates because they can determine both the aims of an enterprise and the methods of achieving them. Apart from freedom to decide one's own destiny and dispose of one's own property, freedom will depend on the influence one is able to exert in determining the aims which are to be realized by collective action.

Technique, while freeing us from the tyranny of nature, gives rise to two new forms of dependence. All progress in technique is bound up with additional social organization. If I use better weapons in a hunting expedition or irrigate the soil to make it more fertile, the necessary preliminaries such as the production of the weapons or the construction of canals can only be completed by means of a collective division of labour. Thus no sooner has technique made me independent of nature than it subjects me in the same measure to the inevitable social coercion which co-operation entails.

But there is another reason why technique is apt to produce a new form of determinism. It has an unintentional effect upon the choice of ends, and ultimately on the psychology of mankind. The first step towards the technical alteration of the surroundings, the first impulse which led a man for instance to collect leaves in order to make a comfortable bed, instead of going to sleep on the bare ground or in the nearest cave, had immediate reactions. Man has begun a series of actions which have made him more delicate and this process of civilization has changed him. When we consider the fact that every invention has helped to change mankind, it soon becomes clear that our own age is not the first in which man, in changing his environment, has changed himself. He has always done it quite unconsciously in the past. The more we consider the history of this process the more obvious it becomes that the formation of character, even in the past, was in no way exclusively dependent on the inner development of the individual. The cumulative effect of civilization alters, not merely our relationship to nature, but our own character as well.

At the second stage (that of invention), a far more complicated " second nature " replaces the first. This " second nature " is technique—and the organized relationships which the mastery of technique demands. The more technique frees us from the arbitrary force of circumstance, the more we are entangled in the network of social relationships we have ourselves created. From the human point of view this " second nature " is no less chaotic and menacing than the first, as long as these relationships cannot be grasped in their totality and therefore controlled. It is immaterial whether man be destroyed by hunger and earthquake, or by social maladjustments leading to war and revolution ; the effect is just the same, although the original calamity was due in the first case to natural, and in the second to social, causes. The course of events as a whole is unpredictable, just as natural events were unpredictable before they had been studied. We are free to produce and manipulate individual tools, or to devise certain organizations and then work them out in detail, but we are powerless at this stage both theoretically and practically to master the cumulative effects of mass psychology or of the trade cycle, or of maladjusted institutions.

In this context too it is clear that the meaning of freedom varies with the situation and that freedom in man's direct struggle with nature is something entirely different from freedom in his struggle with " second nature ". At the level of the first man is free if he can adapt himself immediately to a given situation. He is in full possession of his freedom as long as he is confronted by absolutely chance conditions, but if anyone prevents him carrying out his own experiments with the situation he feels thwarted.

This direct sense of freedom, of not being thwarted in making one's adjustments, can still be maintained when further stages in the development of social technique produce new forms of determinism and also of freedom. This primary freedom will remain, in spite of a more complicated social structure, as long as men are bent on carrying out their immediate wishes and on finding spontaneous forms of self-expression. At the stage of invention the test of freedom is not mere spontaneity, but the desire to create conditions where social adjustment is possible instead of simply accepting things as they are. One feels free when one can make or choose one's own material or set up an organization with certain definite aims in view or at least take part in its administration ; in short, when one is free to invent. For the sake of this freedom men are willing to forgo their primary liberty of action. They do not feel frustrated if they have to take the necessary mechanical steps to make an institution work or give up certain forms of self-expression, provided that they have a right to determine the aims in view or to have a voice in determining them. They allow educational and religious institutions to exercise a deliberate influence over the character and systematically to inculcate habits and ideals which are not the result either of trial and error or of a process of spontaneous growth. Of course there is nothing new in letting oneself be formed by institutions, for mankind has always been moulded by customs and habits, but in the past this has been due to the irresponsible and invisible hand of history. The decisive factor at the present time is that isolated institutions such as schools and training colleges are deliberately established for a purpose. But the regulation of this vast interplay of institutions has never been attempted and at the second stage would be regarded as sheer audacity.

Although this unregulated mass of institutions is as impenetrable and as uncontrollable as nature itself (if on a different plane) men accept this determinism with the same resignation as they accepted the impossibility of controlling natural forces at an earlier stage. If men who had been moulded by the educational tendencies prevailing at the stage of invention had been told that by co-ordinating social institutions they could bring order out of chaos, they would have felt that this was not merely a foolhardy suggestion but an attack upon the freedom of mankind.

Although the blind play of social forces is destroying humanity they regard this destruction as part and parcel of their freedom, simply because it is anonymous and directed by the invisible hand of history. At an earlier date complete subjection to the caprices of nature was regarded as essential to individual freedom. Uncivilized man feels that his freedom is threatened when a doctor saves him from the blind forces of an epidemic by inoculation. It cost a tremendous effort to convince men at the stage of chance discovery that they could be free if they would make full use of technical devices to challenge the powers of nature ; and it will require a thorough re-education to convince them that to combat the blindness of the social forces by the help of human regulation will make man freer than he has been before. The new forms of freedom will always be rejected until men have been spiritually prepared for them, and cease to think in terms of an earlier phase of social existence.

The new conception of freedom creates the desire to control the effects of the social surroundings as far as possible. This is no mere daydream, it is based on the fact that enormous advances in social technique allow us to influence the conduct of social affairs from the key positions, according to a definite plan. Once we have realized this, our outlook on life will change, and we shall feel that while this chaotic tangle of institutions continues we are no longer free. In order to clear up this confusion we must be willing to forgo our former liberties, just as we were in passing from the first stage to the second ; provided that in doing so we gain control of the entire social environment. In many spheres we have abandoned those forms of freedom which allowed the individual to use his inventive powers as a means to his own ends, without considering the consequences for society as a whole. The sacrifice of this primary form of freedom will lead to our complete enslavement unless we are willing to accept the further implication of it and thus strive to regulate the entire social network : that is, to regulate all social relationships so as to secure the collective freedom of the group in accordance with a democratically recognized plan. From now on men will find a higher form of freedom in allowing many aspects of their individual lives to be determined by the social order laid down by the group, provided that it is an order which they themselves have chosen.

At the stage we have just reached, it seems to be greater slavery to be able to do as we like in an unjust or badly organized society, than to accept the claims of planning in a healthy society which we ourselves have chosen. The realization that fair and democratic planning does not involve the surrender of our freedom is the mainspring of those arguments which show that an unplanned capitalist society is not the basis of the highest form of liberty.

It has rightly been pointed out that the " liberties " of liberal capitalist society are often only available to the rich, and that the " have-nots " are forced to submit to the pressure of circumstances. The real representative of this society would be the free workman, who had the right to sell his labour in a " free " market, or if he preferred, to give up the struggle and starve. What is the use of freedom in teaching and learning to a poor man who has neither the time nor the means to acquire the necessary education ? What use is the freedom to choose our own philosophy of life, to form our own opinions, if the sociological mechanisms of our society create insecurity, anxiety, neuroses, which prevent us from making sound and rational decisions ?

Those who cling to the forms of freedom which were current at the stage of invention retort : " What use is the best social order if it is simply imposed on the individual and he cannot escape from it ? What use are the wisest of institutions if I am not free to live my own life ? I would rather work out my own solution, however inadequate, to a difficult state of affairs, than be forced into the mould of a situation, however skilfully designed."

This antagonism clearly shows that the question is only insoluble because the concept of freedom of the second stage has been applied to the third. It is just as impossible to want a rational and planned society without foregoing the luxury of arbitrary interference, as it was for the individual at the stage of invention to preserve his desire for an absolute spontaneity of adjustment.

The guarantees of freedom are entirely different at the three stages. At the first stage freedom is really equivalent to freedom to escape. The possibilities of fleeing from a tyrant, of taking one's head out of the noose, of escaping direct pressure, these are the most obvious marks of freedom. At the second stage where an increasing number of isolated institutions fill up the framework of society and where each is allowed, broadly speaking, to go its own way, the most vital guarantee of freedom consists in playing off these institutions against each other. This is reflected in the political theory of checks and balances. At this stage the balance of power seems to be guaranteed by the mutual supervision and control of individual institutions. Where there is no higher authority to which all lesser powers are subject, freedom can only be guaranteed by a balance of more or less subordinate authorities.

At the third stage, that of planning, freedom cannot consist in the mutual control of individual institutions, for this can never lead to planned co-operation. At the highest stage freedom can only exist when it is secured by planning. It cannot consist in restricting the powers of the planner, but in a conception of planning which guarantees the existence of essential forms of freedom through the plan itself. For every restriction imposed by limited authorities would destroy the unity of the plan, so that society would regress to the former stage of competition and mutual control. As we have said, at the stage of planning freedom can only be guaranteed if the planning authority incorporates it in the plan itself. Whether the sovereign authority be an individual or a group or a popular assembly, it must be compelled by democratic control to allow full scope for freedom in its plan. Once all the instruments of influencing human behaviour have been co-ordinated, planning for freedom is the only logical form of freedom which remains.

This must be carefully considered, for it would be easy to adopt the wrong tactics if we continued to think that freedom could be guaranteed by limiting the unity of the plan, instead of insisting that constitutional guarantees of freedom should be included in the plan itself, and that real political safeguards should be established for its maintenance. Where the key points of a society have already been determined, freedom can only be secured by strategic direction from the key points and not by their destruction.

As soon as the problem of freedom—as opposed to *laisser-faire*—is seen to consist in the creation of free zones within the planned structure, the whole question becomes more detailed. Instead of the unified and abstract conception, concrete issues arise. The various historical interpretations of freedom, freedom of movement, freedom of expression, freedom of opinion, freedom of association, freedom from caprice and tolerance are all special obligations which must be met by the new society. For naturally the advent of planned freedom does not mean that all earlier forms of freedom must be abolished. We saw in the former parts of the book that an advance to a higher social level does not exclude the preservation of former types of action, thought and freedom. On the contrary, the planned retention of ancient liberties is a guarantee against exaggerated dogmatism in planning. We have learnt to realize that even when society has passed to a new stage in many spheres of its existence, some of the old forms of adjustment could still continue. Wherever it is possible and the plan is not endangered every effort must be made to maintain the primary form of freedom—freedom for individual adjustment. This was legitimately retained at the stage of invention, and in spite of an increasing mechanization, it helped to preserve vitality and strengthen initiative. Thus one of the guarantees of freedom in a planned society will be the maintenance of the individual capacity for adjustment. In the same way the freedom achieved at the second stage of invention must be retained in a planned society wherever possible. Constitutional provision must be made for the creation of new institutions through the initiative of small groups, in order to supply the needs of local circles rather than those of the centralized bureaucracy. It is one of the greatest advantages of the Anglo-Saxon tradition that most public institutions, such as hospitals, schools, and universities, are not maintained by the state but are forced as a rule to be self-supporting in order to prove the necessity for their existence. This principle of corporate initiative, these conceptions of the responsibilities and risks which must be borne by small groups, are characteristic of the stage of invention and are genuinely sound. They may mitigate exaggerated tendencies towards centralization, for this technique is a safeguard against bureaucracy and helps to keep the planning authorities in touch with actual conditions. Of course once society has reached the stage of planning separatism and local autonomy cannot be allowed to have the last word as at the stage of invention. Although even in the future corporations must take the initiative in suggesting new institutions, centralized control is essential, in order to criticize any tendencies which are likely to clash with the plan as a whole. This criticism might easily lead once more to an arbitrary bureaucracy, which under cover of objective criticism would oppose the natural growth of these institutions.

But this can only happen if there is no power greater than bureaucracy, for the problem of the democratic constitution of a planned society mainly consists in avoiding bureaucratic absolutism.

It all depends on whether we can find ways of transferring democratic, parliamentary control to a planned society. If this control is destroyed in the effort to establish a planned society, planning will be a disaster, not a cure. On the other hand, planning under communal control, incorporating safeguards of the new freedom, is the only solution possible at the present stage of social technique. The chances of achieving this new society, to be sure, are limited. It is not absolutely predetermined. But this is just where our new freedom begins. We have seen that the quality of freedom varies not only with the ages, but within the boundaries of a single society which gives different scopes to liberty of action. Our present society provides for one kind of freedom within the network of established relationships. But it offers us freedom of another degree outside them—in those spheres where our world is still in the making.

Within the framework of established relationships we can only gradually alter small details, burdened as we are by the pressure of that interdependent system which too often gives our acts only the scope of the mason replacing old bricks in a wall that is already built. But there is a space round the wall where new things have to be done, where new activity from key positions is required. Here as much spontaneity is demanded of our actions as in the first stage where primary freedom reigned. Here is scope for the pioneer, for in face of future possibilities each of us must choose what he would strengthen, what he would overthrow. Thus human freedom is not extinguished when we reach the stage of mass society ; on the contrary, this is where its genuine vigour is needed. If we are only willing to contemplate that sector of life in which it is required, we shall see that the man of to-day has far more freedom in the determination of his destiny than the unsociological ethics of the past would have us believe. Why search the past with a romantic longing for a freedom that is lost, when that freedom is now ready to come into its own if we only have the courage to see what must be seen, to say what must be said, to do what must be done ? Rightly understood, recent tendencies towards a mass society, and our ever increasing awareness of the determinism of sociological factors do not release us from responsibility for the future ; responsibility increases with every advance in the course of history, and has never been greater than it is to-day.

FINIS

BIBLIOGRAPHY *

I. THE MEANING OF PLANNING.

(1) *Theory of Social Control.*

AMERICAN ACADEMY OF POLITICAL AND SOCIAL SCIENCE : Education for Social Control. Annals for 1933.

AMERICAN SOCIOLOGICAL SOCIETY. *Social Control : Publications of the American Sociological Society*, vol. 12. Chicago, 1908.

BERNARD, L. L. *The Transition to an Objective Standard of Social Control.* Chicago, 1911.

—— *Social Control.* New York, 1937.

BRIFFAULT, R. " Taboos on Human Nature " in *The New Generation* (Ed. by Calverton, V. F. and Schmalhausen, S. D.). London, 1930.

BRUNO, F. J. " The Dynamic Aspects of Liberty and Control ": in *Family Life Today* (Ed. by Rich, H. E.). Boston, 1928.

CALVERT, I. R. *The Lawbreaker. A Critical Study of the Modern Treatment of Crime.* London, 1933.

CASE, C. M. " Some Sociological Aspects of Coercion " : *Publications of the Amer. Sociological Society*, 1922, vol. 17, pp. 75–88.

COOLEY, C. H. *Human Nature and the Social Order.* New York, 1902.

—— *Social Organization. A Study of the Larger Mind.* New York, 1912.

—— *Social Process.* New York, 1918.

DEWEY, J. " Social Science and Social Control " : *New Republic*, vol. 18, 29th July, 1931.

DOWD, J. *Control in Human Societies.* New York, 1936.

FARIS, E. Origin of Punishment : *Intern. Journ. of Ethics*, vol. 25, 1915.

GUIGNEBERT, Ch. *L'évolution des dogmes.* Bibl. de philos. scientific. Paris, 1910.

* A synopsis of this bibliography can be found in the table of contents (pp. xviii–xix). The numbers at the end of each part refer to other parts of the bibliography having some bearing on the same subject. Certain important items were repeated in order to facilitate fluent reading. As this bibliography was completed after the outbreak of war the difficulty of access to libraries made the checking of some references impossible.

The bibliography is purely personal : it neither aims at completion, nor does it claim to give the best possible selection. Its attempt at orientation in these vast fields is guided by the author's personal interests and by the subject matter of the book.

HARVARD TERCENTENARY PUBLICATIONS. *Authority and the Individual.* Contributions by Mitchell, W. C., Robertson, D. H., Copland, D. B., Rappard, W. E., Chapham, J. H., McIver, R. M., McLean, Andrews Ch., Dewey, J., Corwin, E. S., Kelsen, H., Jaeger, W., Gine, C., Meinecke, F., Hazard, P., Jones, H. M., Dent, E. J. Cambridge (Mass.), 1937.

HERRICK, C. J. " Self-control and Social Control " in *The Child, the Clinic, and the Court,* 1925.

HOBHOUSE, L. T. *Morals in Evolution. A Study in Comparative Ethics.* 2 vols. London, 1906.

JONES, A. J. *Principles of Guidance.* 2nd ed., New York–London, 1934.

KELSEY, C. " War as a Crisis in Social Control " : *Publications of the Amer. Sociological Society,* vol. 12, 1918.

KNIGHT, M. M., PETERS, L. L., and BLANCHARD, P. *Taboo and Genetics.* London and New York, 1920.

LEWIS, Wyndham P. *The Art of Being Ruled,* esp. Part II. London, 1926.

LUMLEY, F. E. *Means of Social Control.* New York, 1925.

MALINOWSKI, B. *Crime and Custom in Savage Society.* New York, 1926.

MANNHEIM, H. *The Dilemma of Penal Reform.* London, 1939.

MARGOLD, C. W. *Sex Freedom and Social Control.* Chicago, 1926.

MAUSS, M. " La réligion et les origines du droit pénal " : *Révue de l'histoire des réligions,* vol. xxxiv, 1896.

MAY, Geoffrey. *Social Control of Sex Expression.* London, 1930.

MEAD, G. H. " The Psychology of Punitive Justice " : *Amer. Journ. of Sociol.,* vol. 23, 1918.

—— " The Genesis of the Self and Social Control " : *International Journ. of Ethics,* vol. 35, 1925.

MERRIAM, C. E. *New Aspects of Politics.* Chicago, 1925.

—— *The Making of Citizens : A Comparative Study of Methods of Civic Training.* Chicago, 1931

—— (ed.) *Studies in the Making of Citizens.* Series including 10 volumes. Chicago, 1929–1933.

—— *The Rôle of Politics in Social Change.* Chap. 5 : Strategic Controls. New York University Press, 1936.

PRASANTA-KUMARA-SENA. *From Punishment to Prevention.* London, 1932.

ROSS, E. A. Social Control. *A Survey of the Foundations of Order.* New York, 1901.

—— *Sin and Society : An Analysis of Latter-Day Iniquity.* Boston-New York, 1907.

RUSCHE, G. and KIRCHHEIMER, O. *Punishment and Social Structure.* Publications of the International Institute of Social Research, New York City, New York, 1939.

SADLER, G. T. *The Relation of Custom to Law.* London, 1919.

SMITH, W. R. "School Discipline as Training for the Larger Social Control": *Publications of the Amer. Sociological Society,* 1923, vol. 17.

SNEDDEN, David. *Educational Sociology,* esp. Chap. XVI. London, 1923.

SUMNER, W. G. *Folkways : A Study of the Sociological Importance of Usages, Customs, Mores and Morals.* Boston, 1907.

THOMAS, W. I. *Sex and Society. Studies in the Social Psychology of Sex.* Esp. Chap. 2 : "Sex and Primitive Social Control." London, 1907.

—— "Crisis and Social Control": *Source Book for Social Origins.* Chicago, 1909.

UNWIN, J. D. *Sexual Regulations and Human Behaviour.* London, 1933.

WALLAS, G. *Our Social Heritage.* London, 1921.

WESTERMARCK, E. *The Origin and Development of the Moral Ideas.* 2 vols. London, 1906–8.

V. also I, 2 ; III, 1, *a–c* ; III, 2, *a–b* ; III, 7 ; III, 7, *a–e*.

(2) *Planning v. Competition and Conflict.*

ADDAMS, L. *Social Consequences of Business Depressions.* Chicago, 1931.

AMERICAN ACADEMY OF POLITICAL AND SOCIAL SCIENCE : *National and World Planning.* Philadelphia, Annals for 1932.

—— *Government Expansion in the Economic Sphere. A Review of the Increasing Economic Functions of Government.* Philadelphia, Annals for 1939.

AMERICAN SOCIOLOGICAL SOCIETY. Social Conflict, vol. xxv of the *Proceedings of the* Chicago, 1931.

ALLEN, B. W. "Is Planning Compatible with Democracy ? " : *Amer. Journ. of Sociology,* vol. 42, June, 1937, pp. 510 seqq.

BALOGH, T. "The National Economy of Germany " : *The Economic Journal,* 1938.

BASTER, A. S. I. *The Twilight of American Capitalism.* London, 1937.

BRAUNTHAL, A. "Types of Adjustment in Relation to Types of Economic Structure": *Social Research,* vol. 2, No. 1, February, 1935.

BROOKS, E. O. and L. M. "A Decade of Planning Literature " : *Social Forces,* 1934.

BRUCK, H. F. *The Road to Planned Economy : Capitalism and Socialism in Germany's Development.* Cardiff, 1934.

BRUTSKUS, B. *Economic Planning in Soviet Russia.* (Translated from the German by Gilbert Gardiner.) London, 1935.

BROWDER, E. R. *Is Planning Possible under Capitalism ?* New York, 1933.

BURNS, A. R. *The Decline of Competition. A Study of the Evolution of American Industry.* New York–London, 1936.

CLARK, C. *A Critique of Russian Statistics.* New York, 1939.

CLARK, J. M. *The Social Control of Business.* Chicago, 1926.

COLM, G. " Is Planning Compatible with Democracy ? " in *Political and Economic Democracy.* Ed. by Ascoli, M., and Lehmann, F. New York, 1937.

CONGRÈS DES ÉCONOMISTES DE LA LANGUE FRANÇAISE. *La reprise allemande.* Paris, 1938.

COOLEY, C. H. " Personal Competition. Its Place in the Social Order and Effect upon Individuals " : *Amer. Economic Association, Economic Studies,* vol. 4. New York, 1899.

DEUTSCHES INSTITUT FUER BANKWISSENSCHAFT UND BANKWESEN (ed.). *Probleme des deutschen Wirtschaftslebens. Erstrebtes und Erreichtes.* Berlin-Leipzig, 1937.

DOBB, M. " Economic Theory and Socialist Economy. A Reply," with a Rejoinder by Lerner, A. P. *The Review of Economic Studies,* vol. 2, No. 2, 1934–5.

FRANCK, L. R. *L'experience Roosevelt et le milieu social américain.* Paris (Alcan), 1937.

FREYER, Hans. *Herrschaft und Planung.* Hamburg, 1933.

GUILLEBAUD, C. W. *The Economic Recovery of Germany.* London, 1939.

HALL, R. L. *The Economic System in a Socialist State.* London, 1937.

HAYEK, F. A. von, et al. *Collectivist Economic Planning.* London, 1935.

HEIMANN, E. *Mehrwert und Gemeinwirtschaft.* Berlin, 1922.

—— " Types and Potentialities of Economic Planning " : *Social Research,* vol. 2, 1935.

HEKSCHER, E. F. *Planned Economy Past and Present.* Stockholm, 1934.

HEYER, F. *Das neue England. Volkswohlfahrt und Volkswirtschaft im Umbau.* Jena, 1936.

HOLCOMBE, A. N. *Government in a Planned Democracy.* New York, 1935.

HOMAN, P. T. " Economic Planning : The Proposals and the Literature " : *Quarterly Journ. of Economics,* vol. 47, 1933.

KEYNES, J. M. *The End of Laissez Faire.* London, 1926.

KNIGHT, F. H. *The Ethics of Competition and Other Essays.* New York, 1935.

LANDAUER, C. *Planwirtschaft und Verkehrswirtschaft.* München, 1931.

LANGE, O. " Marxian Economics and Modern Economic Theory " : *The Review of Economic Studies*, vol. 2, 1934–5.

—— " On the Economic Theory of Socialism " : *The Review of Economic Studies*, vol. 4, 1936–7.

LAUFENBURGER, H. *L'Intervention de l'état en matière économique.* Paris, 1939.

LAWLEY, F. E. *The Growth of Collective Economy.* Vol. I : The Growth of National Collective Economy. Vol. II : The Growth of International Collective Economy. London, 1938.

LEAGUE OF NATIONS. *The Course and Phases of the World Economic Depression.* Revised ed. 1932.

—— *World Economic Survey.* (Yearly Publication. 8th ed. 1938–9.) Geneva, 1939.

LEDERER, Emil. " National Planning " in *The Encyclopedia of the Social Sciences* New York, 1933.

LERNER, A. P. " Economic Theory and Socialist Economy " : *The Review of Economic Studies*, vol. 2, 1934.

—— " A Note on Socialist Economics " : *The Review of Economic Studies*, vol. 4, 1936–7.

LIPPMANN, W. *The Good Society.* London, 1938.

LÖWE, A. " Economic Analysis and Social Structure " : *Manchester School*, vol. 7, 1936.

MACKENZIE, F. *Planned Society, Yesterday, To-day, To-morrow.* New York, 1937.

McNAMARA, K. *Bibliography of Planning, 1928–1935.* Harvard University Press, Cambridge, 1936.

MANDELBAUM, K., and MEYER, G. " Zur Theorie der Planwirtschaft " : *Zeitschrift für Sozialforschung*, vol. 3, 1932, p. 4.

MAY, Mark A. " A Research Note on Co-operative and Competitive Behavior " : *Amer. Journ. of Sociol.*, vol. 42, 1937.

—— and DOOB, Leonard. *Research on Competition and Co-operation. Social Science Research Council, Bull. 25.* New York, 1937.

MEAD, M. (ed.). *Co-operation and Competition among Primitive Peoples.* New York, London, 1937.

MERRIAM, C. E. " Planning Agencies in America " : *American Political Science Review*, vol. 29, pp. 197–212. 1935.

MISES, L. VON. *Socialism.* Translated by J. Kahane. London, 1936.

NORTH, C. C. *Social Problems and Social Planning.* New York, 1932.

OGBURN, W. F., and THOMAS, D. S. " The Influence of the Business Cycle on Social Factors " : *Journal of the American Statistical Assoc.*, vol. 18, 1932.

Opie, R. " The Webbs on Soviet Communism : A New Civilization ? " *The Quarterly Journ. of Economics,* vol. I, 1937.

Pigou, A. C. *Socialism versus Capitalism.* London, 1935.

Pirou, G. La crise du capitalisme, etc. 2nd ed. Paris (Sirey), 1936.

—— *Essais sur le corporatisme.* Paris, 1938.

Political, Economic Planning. *Planning. A Broadsheet issued by P. E. P.* London.

Poole, K. E. *German Financial Policies, 1932–38.* Cambridge (Mass.), 1939.

Robbins, C. L. *Economic Planning and International Order.* London, 1937.

Rogin, L. " The New Deal : A Survey of the Literature " : *The Quarterly Journ. of Economics,* 1935.

Roos, Ch. F. *N.R.A. Economic Planning.* Bloomington, Indiana, 1937.

Rosenstock-Franck, L. *L'économie corporative fasciste en doctrine et en fait.* Paris, 1934.

Schumpeter, J. A. *Business Cycles. A Theoretical, Historical and Statistical Analysis of the Capitalistic Process,* vols. i–ii. New York, 1939.

Social Science Research Council. *Research Memorandum on Social Aspects of Consumption in the Depression,* by Vaile, R. S. New York.

Soudek, J. *Die sozialen Auswirkungen der Konjunkturschwankungen.* Bonn, 1929.

Soule, G. H. *A Planned Society.* New York, 1932.

Speier, Hans. " Freedom and Social Planning." *Amer. Journ. of Sociol.,* vol. 42, Jan., 1937.

Stamp, Sir Josiah Ch. *The Science of Social Adjustment.* London, 1937.

Tillmann, A. *L'organisation économique et sociale du IIIᵉ Reich.* Paris (Sirey), 1935.

Thomas, D. S. *Social Aspects of the Business Cycle.* London-New York, 1925.

Tugwell, R. G. " Experimental Control in Russian Industry." *Political Science Quart.,* vol. 44, 1928.

—— *The Trend of Economics.* New York, 1928.

Weil, F. " Neuere Literatur zum ' New Deal ' " : *Zeitschrift für Sozialforschung,* vol. 5, 1936.

Welk, W. G. *Fascist Economic Policy. An Analysis of Italy's Economic Experience.* Cambridge (Mass.), 1938.

Wootton, Barbara. *Plan or no Plan ? A Comparison of Existing Socialist and Capitalist Economic Systems,* London, 1934.

V. also III, 1, *g* ; III, 2, *c* ; III, 7, *e* ; IV, 5 ; V, 1–3 ; V, 4.

II. SOCIAL TECHNIQUES.

The Significance of Techniques.

BERNARD, L. L. " Invention and Social Progress " : *Amer. Journ. of Sociology*, vol. 29, 1923.

BOISSONNADE, P. *Life and Work in Medieval Europe.* Fifth to Fifteenth Century. Transl. by Power, E. London, 1927.

DIEHLS, H. *Antike Technik*, 3rd ed. Leipzig and Berlin, 1924.

DURKHEIM, E. *On the Division of Labour in Society.* Transl. by Simpson, G. New York, 1933.

ENGELHARD, V. *Weltanschauung und Technik.* Leipzig, 1922.

ESPINAS, A. *Les Origines de la Technologie.* Paris, 1899.

FOURGEAUD, A. *La rationalisation, États Unis-Allemagne.* Paris (Payot), 1929.

FRENCH, Ch. *Origines et évolution des outils.* Paris, 1913.

FRIEDMANN, G. *Problèmes du machinisme en U.S.S.R. et dans les pays capitalists.* Paris, 1934.

GERHARDT, J. *Arbeitsrationalisierung und persönliche Abhängigkeit.* Tübingen, 1925.

GIESE, F. *Bildungsideale im Maschinenzeitalter.* Halle a.d.S., 1931.

GILFILLAN, S. C. *The Sociology of Invention.* Chicago, 1935.

GLOTZ, G. *Le travail dans la Grèce ancienne.* Paris, 1920.

GOLDSTEIN, J. " Zur Soziologie der Technik " : *Aus dem Vermächtnis des XIX. Jahrhunderts.* Berlin, 1922.

—— " Die Technik," vol. 40 of *Die Gesellschaft.* Frankfurt, 1912.

KLATT, F. *Die geistige Wendung des Maschinenzeitalters.* Potsdam, 1930.

MERTON, R. K. " Fluctuations in the Rate of Industrial Invention " : *Quarterly Journal of Economics*, vol. 49, 1935.

—— " Science, Technology and Society in Seventeenth Century England " : *Ôsiris*, vol. iv, pp. 360–632, 1938.

MUMFORD, Lewis. *Technics and Civilization. On the Social Influence of Machinery.* London, 1934.

NATIONAL RESOURCES COMMITTEE. *Technological Trends and National Policy. Including the Social Implications of New Inventions.* Report of the Sub-committee on Technology to the National Resources Committee, June, 1937. Washington, D.C., 1937.

OGBURN, W. F. " The Influence of Inventions on American Social Institutions in the Future " : *Amer. Journ. of Sociology*, vol. 43, 1937.

—— " Technology and Society " : *Social Forces*, vol. 17, No. 1, 1938.

PARK, R. E. "Cultural Trends and Technique." *Publications of the Amer. Sociol. Society*, vol. 19, 1924.

PAULHAN, F. *Psychologie de l'invention.* Paris (Alcan), 1901.

RANDALL, J. H. *Our Changing Civilization. How Science and the Machine are Reconstructing Modern Life.* London, 1929.

RUGG, H. O. *The Great Technology ; Social Chaos and the Public Mind.* New York, 1933.

SALTER, T. A. *Modern Mechanization and its Effects on the Structure of Society.* London, 1933.

SCHUHL, Pierre Maxime. *Machinisme et philosophie.* Paris (Alcan), 1938.

SCHUMACHER, F. *Schöpferwille und Rationalisierung.* Hamburg, 1932.

—— *Der Fluch der Technik.* Hamburg, 1935.

SCOTT, H. et al. *Introduction to Technocracy.* New York, 1922.

USHER, A. P. *A History of Mechanical Inventions.* New York, London, 1929.

VEBLEN, Th. B. *The Instinct of Workmanship and the State of Industrial Arts.* New York, 1914.

VIERENDEEL, A. *Esquisse d'une Histoire de la technique.* Bruxelles and Paris, 1921.

WEILLER, J. " La crise et les controverses sur le progrès technique " : *Annales du droit et des sciences sociales,* vol. I.

WEINREICH, H. *Bildungswerte der Technik.* Berlin, 1928.

WELLS, H. G. *The Work, Wealth, Happiness of Mankind.* 3rd ed. London, 1934.

WENDT, A. *Die Technik als Kulturmacht.* Berlin, 1906.

WYER, Samuel S. *Man's Shift from Muscle to Mechanical Power.* Columbus, 1930.

ZSCHIMMER, E. *Deutsche Philosophen der Technik.* Stuttgart, 1937.

V. also IV, I.

III. I. THE SCIENCE OF INFLUENCING HUMAN BEHAVIOUR.

(a) *Behaviour.*

ALLPORT, F. H. *Institutional Behavior.* Essays toward a Re-interpreting of Contemporary Social Organization. University of North Carolina Press, Chapel Hill, 1933.

ANDERSON, J. E. " The Genesis of Social Reaction in the Young Child " in *The Unconscious,* ed. by Dummer, E. New York, 1927.

BERNARD, L. L. *Instinct : A Study in Social Psychology.* London, 1925.

BURROW, T. *The Biology of Human Conflict. An Anatomy of Human Behavior, Individual and Social.* New York, 1937.

BURROW, T. "Altering Frames of Reference in the Sphere of Human Behavior": *Journ. of Social Philosophy*, vol. 2, No. 2, 1937.

CARREL, Alexis. *Man the Unknown*. New York and London, 1935.

CASE, Clarence Marsh. "Instinctive and Cultural Factors in Group Conflicts": *Amer. Journ. of Sociol.*, vol. 28, July, 1922.

COOLEY, Ch. H. *Human Nature and the Social Order*. New York, 1912.

CRAIG, W. "Appetites and Aversions as Constituants of Instincts": *Biol. Bull.*, vol. 34, 1918.

DEWEY, J. *Human Nature and Conduct. An Introduction to Social Psychology*. London, 1922.

DOUGLAS, A. Th. "Habit Clinics for Children of the Pre-School Age": *Mental Hygiene*, vol. 13, 1929.

—— "Habits, Their Formation, Their Value, Their Danger": *Mental Hygiene*, vol. 16, 1932.

FOSTER, Sybil; STEBBENS, Dorothy. "Problems Presented and Results of Treatment in 150 Cases seen at the Habit Clinic for Pre-school Children in Boston": *Mental Hygiene*, vol. 13, Jan., 1929, No. 1.

GARRETT, H. E. "Personality as Habit Organization": *Journ. of Abnormal Psychol.*, vol. 21, 1926.

GUTHRIE, S. *The Psychology of Human Conflict*. New York and London, 1938.

HARVARD TERCENTENARY PUBLICATIONS. *Factors Determining Human Behavior*, contributions by Adrian, E. D., Collip, J. B., Piaget, J., Jung, Ch. G., Janet, P., Carnop, R., Lowell, A. L., Malinowski, B. Cambridge (Mass.), 1937.

HERRICK, C. J. "Control of Behavior, its Mechanism and Evolution": *Amer. Journ. of Psychiatry*, vol. 93, 1935.

HOCKING, W. E. *Human Nature and its Remaking*. New Haven, 1923.

JENNINGS, H. S. *The Biological Basis of Human Nature*. London, 1930.

KARDINER, A. "The Rôle of Security in the Adaptation of the Individual": *The Family*, Oct., 1936.

—— "Security, Cultural Restraint, Intrasocial Dependencies and Hostilities": *The Family*, Oct., 1937.

LURIA, A. R. *The Nature of Human Conflicts or Emotions, Conflict and Will. An Objective Study of Disorganizations and Control of Human Behaviour*. New York, 1933.

McDOUGALL, R. "Habits and the Social Order": *School and Society*, vol. 3, 1916.

McDOUGALL, W., SHAND, A. F., and STOUT, G. F. "Symposium on Instinct and Emotion": *Proceedings of the Aristotelian Society*, vol. 15.

MASSON-OURSEL, P. " La mâitrise des réflexes selon l'Occident et l'Orient " : *Psychol. et vie*, vol. 5, 1931.

OVERSTREET, H. A. *Influencing Human Behaviour*. London, 1926.

PARMELLE, M. *The Science of Human Behaviour*. New York, 1913.

PATON, S. *Human Behaviour*. New York, 1921.

SAPIR, E. " The Unconscious Patterning of Behaviour in Society " : *The Unconscious : A Symposium*. New York, 1928.

SHERRINGTON, C. S. *The Integrative Action of the Nervous System*. New York, 1906.

STRAUS, E. *Wesen und Vorgang der Suggestion*. Abhandlungen aus der Neurologie, Psychiatrie und ihren Grenzgebieten. Heft, 28, Berlin, 1925.

STREHLE, H. *Analyse des Gebahrens*. (Die Lehre von der praktischen Menschenkenntnis. Ed. by the Psychological Laboratory of the " Reichswehrministerium ".) Berlin, 1935.

THOMAS, W. I. " The Behavior Pattern and the Situation," in *Personality and the Group*, ed. by Burgess, E. W. Chicago, 1929.

—— *Primitive Behavior. An Introduction to the Social Sciences*. New York–London, 1937.

THOULESS, R. H. *The Control of the Mind*, esp. Chapter III : "How Habits May be Formed and Broken." London, 1922.

WATSON, J. B. *Behavior : An Introduction to Comparative Psychology*. London, New York, 1925.

—— *Psychology from the Standpoint of a Behaviorist*. Philadelphia, 1919.

YOUNG, P. C. " A General Review of the Literature on Hypnotism and Suggestion " : *Psychol. Bull.*, vol. 24, 1927 and vol. 28, 1931.

V. also III, 1, *b* ; III, 1, *d*, *e* ; III, 7, *d*.

(b) *Attitudes, Sentiments, Motivations, Wishes, etc.*

ALLPORT, F. H. " Suggestibility with and without Prestige in Children " : *British Journ. of Psychology*, vol. 12, 1931.

ALLPORT, G. W. " Attitudes " in *A Handbook of Social Psychology*, ed. by Murchison, C. Worcester (Mass.), London, 1935.

—— and SCHRANEK, R. L. " Are Attitudes Biological or Cultural in Origin ? " *Character and Personality*, vol. 4, 1936.

BARTLETT, F. C. " The Psychological Process of Sublimation." *Scientia*, vol. 43, 1928.

BRENNER, B. *Effect of Immediate and Delayed Praise and Blame upon Learning and Recall*. A Thesis. Teachers College, Columbia University. New York, 1934.

BRIDGE, J. W. "A Reconciliation of Current Theories of Emotion": *Journ. of Abnorm. Psychol.*, vol. 19, 1924.

CANNON, W. B. "The Significance of the Emotional Level." *The Journ. of the Missouri State Med. Association*, 1934.

CLARK, J. A. "The Structure of Responsibility" Ethics. Vol. xlix, July, 1939, No. 4.

DODGE, R. "Mental Nearness." *Journ. of Abnormal and Social Psychology*, vol. 28 (1933).

DOLLARD, J. "Hostility and Fear in Social Life" (with Discussion). *Social Forces*, vol. 17, No. 1, 1938.

DOLLARD, J., DOOB, L. W., NEAL, E. MILLER, MOWRER, O. H., SEARS, R. R. Frustration and Aggression. Publ. for the Institute of Human Relations by the Yale University, New Haven, 1939.

DROBA, D. D. "Topical Summaries of Current Literature: Social Attitudes": *Amer. Journ. of Sociol.*, vol. 39, 1934.

FARIS, Ellsworth. "Attitudes and Behavior." *Amer. Journ. of Sociol.*, vol. 34, 1928.

—— "The Concept of Social Attitudes." *Journ. of Applied Soc.*, vol. 9, 1925.

FARNSWORTH, P. R., and BEHNER, A. "A Note on the Attitude of Social Conformity." *Journ. of Social Psychol.*, vol. 2, 1931.

FLUEGEL, J. C. "Sexual and Social Sentiments." *British Journal of Medical Psychology*, vol. 4, 1924.

FOLSOM, J. K. "Wish Frustration and Personality Readjustment" in his *Social Psychology*, New York, London, 1931.

FRANK, J. O. "Some Psychological Determinants of the Level of Aspiration": *Amer. Journ. of Psychology*, ovl. 47, 1935.

FRANK, Lawrence K. "The Management of Tensions": *Amer. Journ. of Sociol.*, vol. 33, 1928.

GATES, G. S. "The Effect of Encouragement and of Discouragement upon Performance": *Journ. of Educ. Psychol.*, vol. 14, 1923.

GOODENOUGH, F. L. "The Diagnostic Significance of Children's Wishes." *Mental Hygiene*, vol. 9, 1925.

GUILFORD, I. R., and BRADEY, K. W. "Extroversion and Introversion": *Psychological Bulletin*, vol. 27, 1930.

HARMS, E. "Rural Attitudes and Social Structure." *Social Forces*, vol. 17, No. 4, 1939.

HART, H. "The Transmutation of Motivation." *Amer. Journ. of Sociol.*, vol. 35, 1930.

HARTMANN, G. A. *The Influence of Customs and Traditional Idealism on Social Behavior*. A Master's Thesis, Ohio. 1934.

HARTSHORNE, H., and MAY, Mark E. *Studies in Deceit*. New York, 1928.

HILLER, E. Th. " Social Attitudes and the Social Structure " : in his *Principles of Sociology*, New York, London, 1933.

HOHMAN, L. B. " Formation of Life Patterns " : *Mental Hygiene*, vol. 11, 1927.

JANET, P. " The Fear of Action " : *Journ. of Abnorm. Psychol.*, vol. 16, 1921.

JASTROW, J. *The Psychology of Conviction*. Boston, 1918.

JONES, E. " Rationalization in Everyday Life " : *Journ. of Abnorm. Psychol.*, vol. 3, 1908.

—— " The Significance of Sublimating Processes for Education and Re-education " in his *Papers on Psychoanalysis*, 3rd ed., London, 1923.

—— " The Theory of Symbolism " in *Papers on Psychoanalysis*. London, 1923.

LASKER, Br. *Race Attitudes in Children*. New York, 1929.

EWIN, K. " Experiments on Autocratic and Democratic Atmospheres " : *Social Frontier*, vol. iv, 1938.

LICHTENSTEIN, A. *Can Attitudes be Taught ?* A Thesis. Reprinted from " The John Hopkins Univ. Studies in Education ", No. 21.

LUND, F. H. *Emotions, their Psychological, Physiological and Educational Implications*. New York, 1938.

MALLER, J. B. *Co-operation and Competition : An Experimental Study in Motivation*. Teachers' College Contributions, No. 384 (Columbia University Press), New York, 1929.

MCDOUGALL, W. " Organization of the Affective Life. A Critical Survey " : *Acta Psychologica*, vol. 2, 1937.

MARTIN, A. H. " An Empirical Study of the Factors and Types of Voluntary Choice " : *Archives of Psychology*, vol. 51, 1925.

MERRIAM, C. E. *The Written Constitution and the Unwritten Attitudes. Lectures*. New York, 1936.

MOORE, H. T. " The Comparative Influence of Majority and Expert Opinion " : *Amer. Journ. of Psychol.*, 1921, vol. 32.

PALLISTER, H. " Negative or Withdrawal Attitude " : *Arch. of Psychol.*, No. 151, 1933.

PARK, R. Human Nature, Attitudes and the Mores " in *Social Attitudes*, ed. by Young, K. New York, 1931.

PHILLIPS, M. *The Education of the Emotion*. London, 1937.

PUTNAM, J. J. " Human Motives " in *Mind and Health Series*, ed. by H. A. Bruce. London, 1915.

RAVITCH, J. " Relative Rate of Change of Customs and Beliefs of Modern Jews " : *Publications of the American Sociological Society*, No. 19.

ROOT, W. T. " The Psychology of Radicalism " : *Journ. of Abnormal Psychology and Social Psychology*, vol. 19, 1924.

RYAN, John A. " Intolerance : Causes and Lessons " : *Publications of the American Sociological Society*, vol. 17, 1923.

SAADI, M., and FARNSWORTH, P. R. " The Degrees of Acceptance of Dogmatic Statements and Preferences for their Supposed Makers " : *Journ. of Abn. and Soc. Psychol.*, vol. 29, 1934.

SHAND, A. F. *The Foundations of Character : Being a Study of the Tendencies and Sentiments.* London, 1914.

SHEFFIELD, A. D. " What Happens in Ordering and Forbidding " : the *Inquiry*, June, 1930 (reprinted in *Occasional Papers*).

SHERIF, Muzafer. *The Psychology of Social Norms.* New York, London, 1936.

SOLOMON, M. " The Mechanism of the Emotion " : *British Journ. of Medical Psychology*, vol. 7, 1927.

SWIFT, W. B. " Mental Attitudes in Debates " : *Journ. of Applied Psychology*, vol. 3, 1919.

TESSENBERG-WESIERSKA, F. Wesen und Bedeutung des Zweifelns. Breslau, 1928.

THORNDIKE, E. L. *The Psychology of Wants, Interests, and Attitudes.* New York, 1935.

TROLAND, L. T. *The Fundamentals of Human Motivation.* London, 1938.

TROW, W. C. " The Psychology of Confidence " : *Archives of Psychol.*, No. 151, 1923.

VAUGHAN, W. *The Lure of Superiority. A Study in the Psychology of Motives.* New York, 1928.

WEISS, A. P. " The Biosocial Approach to the Problems of Feeling " in *The Wittenberg Symposium, Feelings and Emotions.* Worcester (Mass.), 1928.

WELLS, F. L. " Mental Regression : Its Conception and Types " : *Psychiatr. Bulletin*, vol. 9, 1916.

—— " Social Maladjustment : Adaptive Regression " in *Handbook of Social Psychology*, ed. by Murchison, C. Worcester (Mass.) and London, 1935.

WHEELER, D. J. H. " Change of Individual Opinion to Accord with Group Opinion " : *Journ. of Abnormal Psychol.*, vol. 24, 1929.

WHITE, R. K. " Democratic and Autocratic Group Atmospheres " (Report at meeting of the American Psychological Association, 9th September, 1938) : *Psychol. Bulletin*, vol. 3, 1938.

WHITE, W. The Unconscious Motives Determining Social Attitudes : *Proceedings, National Conference of Social Work*, 1923.

WOLF, Th. H. *The Effect of Praise and Competition on the Persisting Behavior of Kindergarten Children.* Institute of Child Welfare, Monograph No. 15. Minneapolis, 1938.

WOLFE, A. B. *Conservatism, Radicalism, and Scientific Method. An Essay on Social Attitudes.* New York, 1923.

WOLFF, Werner. " Selbstbeurteilung und Fremd-beurteilung im wissentlichen und unwissentlichen Versuche ": *Psychologische Forschungen*, vol. 16 (1932).

WRIGHT, H. W. " Rational Self-Interest and Social Adjustment ": *Intern. Journ. of Ethics*, vol. 30, 1919–1920.

YOUNG, K. (ed.). *Social Attitudes.* New York, 1931.

YOUNG, P. Th. *Motivations of Behaviour. The Fundamental Determinants of Human and Animal Activity.* New York, 1936.

ZNANIECKI, Fl. *The Laws of Social Psychology,* esp. Chapter IV: " Social Sublimation." Chicago, 1925.

ZUBIN, J. *Some Effects of Incentives. Study of Individual Differences in Rivalry, etc.* A Thesis, Teachers College, Columbia University. New York, 1932.

V. also III, 1, *a–f* ; III, 2, *d* ; III, 3, *b* ; III, 6 ; III, 7, *b* ; III, 7, *d* ; IV, 1, and the bibliography on substitute activities (p. 131, nn. 2–3).

(c) Personality.

ALEXANDER, F. *Psychoanalyse der Gesamtpersönlichkeit.* Leipzig, Wien, Zürich, 1927.

ALLPORT, F. H. " Self-Evaluation: A Problem in Personal Development": *Mental Hygiene,* vol. 11, 1927.

ALLPORT, G. W. *Personality. A Psychological Interpretation.* London, 1938.

AMERICAN PSYCHIATRIC ASSOCIATION COMMITTEE ON RELATIONS WITH THE SOCIAL SCIENCES. *Proceedings of the First Colloquium on Personality Investigation.* Baltimore, 1928.

—— *Proceedings of the Second Colloquium on Personality.* Investigation, 1930.

BINSWANGER, L. " Lebensfunktion und innere Lebensgeschichte ": *Monatsschrift für Psychiatrie und Neurologie,* vol. 48, 1928.

BOISEN, A. T. " Personality Changes and Upheavals Arising out of the Sense of Personal Failure ": *Amer. Journ. of Psychiatry,* vol. 5, 1926.

BOVET, P. " Les conditions de l'obligation de conscience ": *L'Année Psychologique.* 1912.

BURGESS, E. W. " The Family and the Person ": *Publications of the American Sociological Society,* vol. 22, 1927.

—— " The Cultural Approach to the Study of Personality ": *Mental Hygiene,* vol. 14, 1930.

—— *Personality and the Social Group.* Chicago, 1929.

CARPENTER, J., and EISENBERG, P. " Some Relations between Family Background and Personality ": *Journal of Psychology,* vol. 6, 1938.

DOLLARD, J. *Criteria for the Life History.* Institute of Human Relations, Yale University, New Haven, 1935.

ELSENHANS, Th. *Wesen und Entstehung des Gewissens.* Leipzig, 1894.

FAUCONNET, P. *La responsabilité. Étude sociologique.* Paris (Alcan), 1920. ·

FREUD, Anna. *The Ego and the Mechanisms of Defence.* (Translated by Cecil Baines.) London, 1937.

GOODENOUGH, F. L., and HEALY, A. M. " The Effect of Certain Family Relationships upon the Development of Personality " : *Pedagogical Seminary*, 1927.

GROVES, E. R. *Personality and Social Adjustment*, 2nd ed., New York, 1931.

HABERLIN, P. *Der Character*, especially Chapter III. Basel, 1925.

HARTMANN, H. " Ich-Psychologie und Anpassungsproblem " : *Intern. Zeitschr. für Psychoanalyse*, 1939.

HARTSHORNE, H., MAY, Mark A., and SHUTTLEWORTH, J. K. *Studies in the Nature of Character.* New York, 1930.

HARTSHORNE, Hugh. *Character in Human Relations.* New York–London, 1932.

HEALY, W. *Personality in Formation and Action.* London, 1938.

HEATH, A. G. *The Moral and Social Significance of the Conception of Personality.* Oxford, 1921.

HOUSE, F. N. " Development in the Theory of the Social Personality " : *Social Forces*, vol. 6, 1927–8.

HUGHES, E. C. " Personality Types and the Division of Labour " : *Amer. Journ. of Sociol.*, vol. 33, 1928.
—— " Institutional Office and the Person " : *Amer. Journ. of Sociol.*, vol. 43, 1937–8.

JOHNSTON, J. C. *Biography—The Literature of Personality.* New York, 1927.

KERRIS, F. *Integration und Disintegration der Persönlichkeit bei Janet und McDougall.* (Aus dem Psychol. Institut der Universität Bonn), Wuerzburg, 1938.

KRUEGER, E. T. " Personality and Life History Documents " : *Publications of the American Sociological Society*, vol. 19, 1924.

LICHTENBERG, J. P. " The Social Significance of Mental Levels " : *Publications of the Amer. Sociol. Society*, vol. 15, 1920.

MEAD, G. H. " The Social Self " : *Journ. of Philosophy, Psychology, and Scientific Method*, vol. 10, 1913.

MURRAY, H. A. *Explorations in Personality.* Oxford University Press, 1938.

PARK, R. " Personality and Cultural Conflict " : *Publications of the Amer. Sociol. Society*, vol. 26, 1931.

PLANT, J. S. " Social Factors in Personality Integration " : *Amer. Journ. of Psychiatry*, vol. 9, 1929.
—— *Personality and the Cultural Pattern.* New York, 1937.

RICE, St. " Stereotypes : a Source of Error in Judging Human Character " : *Journal of Personnel Research*, vol. 45, 1926.

ROBACK, A. A. *A Bibliography of Character and Personality.* Cambridge (Mass.), 1927.

RUNDQUIST, E. A., and STETTO, R. F. *Personality in the Depression.* (Univ. of Minnesota Press), Minneapolis, 1936.

SCHETTLER, C. " Topical Summaries of Current Literature : Personality Traits " : *Amer. Journ. of Sociol.,* vol. 45, 1939.

STOKER, H. G. *Das Gewissen.* Bonn, 1929. .

SYMONDS, P. M. *Diagnosing Personality and Conduct.* New York, 1931.

WHITE, A. K., and MACBEATH, A. *The Moral Self, Its Nature and Development.* 1923.

WOODARD, J. W. " The Relation of Personality Structure to the Structure of Culture " : *American Sociol. Review,* vol. 3, No. 5, 1938.

WOODWARD, W. E. *Relations of Religious Training and Life Patterning to the Adult's Religious Life.* Teachers' College, Columbia University, New York, 1932.

WIRTH, L. " Some Jewish Types of Personality " : *Publications of the Amer. Sociol. Society,* vol. 20, 1926.

YOUNG, K. " The Integration of Personality " : *Pedagogical Seminary,* vol. 30, 1923.

—— " Topical Summary of Current Literature on Personality " : *Amer. Journ. of Sociol.,* vol. 43, 1926–7.

V. also III, 7, *b* ; III, 7, *d* ; and the bibliography on personality disorganization, pp. 118–19 n.

(d) Behaviour in Social Groups.

ALLPORT, F. H. " The Influences of the Group upon Association and Thought " : *Journ. of Experimental Psychol.,* vol. 3, 1920.

BALDERSTONE, C. C. *Group Incentives.* Ed. by University of Pennsylvania Press, 1930.

BARTLETT, F. C. " Group Organization and Social Behaviour " : *Intern. Journ. of Ethics,* vol. 35, 1924–5.

BLONDEL, C. *Introduction à la psychologie collective.* Paris, 1928.

BROWN, B. W. *Social Groups.* Chicago, 1926.

BUSCH, H. M. *Leadership in Group Work.* New York, 1934.

CHRISTENSEN, A. E. *Politics and Crowd Morality : a Study in Philosophy of Politics,* translated from the Danish by A. Cecil Curtis. New York, 1915.

COYLE, G. L. *Social Process in Organized Groups.* New York, 1930.

—— (ed.). *Studies in Group Behavior.* New York, 1937.

DEANES, W. " The Methods and Presuppositions of Group Psychology " ; *University of California Publications in Philosophy,* vol. 6, No. 1. Univ. of California Press, Berkeley, California, 1924.

DEWEY, F. A. *Some Aspects of Behavior in Social Groups.* New York, 1915 (Thesis Columbia Univ.).

ELLIOT, Thomas D. " A Psychoanalytic Interpretation of Group Formation and Behavior " : *Amer. Journ. of Sociol.,* vol. 26, 1920, 333–352.

GEIGER, Theodor. *Die Masse und ihre Aktion.* Stuttgart, 1928.

KORNHOUSE, Arthur W. " Attitudes of Economic Groups " : *Public Opinion Quarterly,* vol. 2, 1938, p. 260.

MADGE, Ch., and HARRISON, T. (ed.). *First Year's Work, 1937–38, by Mass Observation.* With an essay on A Nation-Wide Intelligence Service, by Malinowski, B. London, 1938.

—— *Britain by Mass Observation.* London, 1939.

MALINOWSKI, B. " The Group and the Individual in Functional Analysis " : *Amer. Journ. of Sociology,* vol. 44, No. 6, 1939.

MANNHEIM, K. " Mass Education and Group Analysis " in *Educating for Democracy,* ed. by Cohen, J. I. and Travers, R. M. W. London, 1939.

MARSH, C. L. " Group Psychotherapy in Psychiatric Clinic " : *Journ. of Nervous and Mental Diseases,* vol. 82, 1935.

MICHELS, R. " Psychologie der antikapitalistischen Massenbewegungen " : *Grundriss der Sozialökonomik,* ix, Tübingen, 1926.

MOEDE, W. *Experimentelle Massenpsychologie. Beiträge zur Experimentalpsychologie der Gruppe.* Leipzig, 1920.

—— " Die Massen- und Sozialpsychologie im kritischen Ueberblick " : *Zeitschr. f. päd. Psychol.,* vol. 10, 1915.

NEWSTETTER, W. I. " Wawokye Camp: An Experiment in Group Adjustment " : *Proceedings of the American Sociological Society,* vol. 25, 1930.

NEWSTETTER, W. I., FELDSTEIN, M. J., and NEWCOMB, T. M. *Group Adjustment: A Study in Experimental Sociology.* Cleveland Western Reserve University, 1938.

PALANTI, G. " L'esprit de corps. Remarques sociologiques " : *Revue Philosophique,* vol. 48, 1899.

PARK, R. E. " Human Nature and Collective Behavior " : *Amer. Journ. of Sociol.,* vol. 32, pp. 733–741, 1927.

REANEY, M. J. " The Psychology of the Organized Group Game, with Special Reference to its Place and its Educational Value " (Thesis, London) : *The British Journal of Psychology, Monogr. Supplement,* No. 4, 1916.

SIMMEL, G. " Exkurs über die Negativität kollektiver Verhaltungsweisen " in *Soziologie* (Leipz., 1908).

THIE, T. M. " The Efficiency of the Group Method " : *English Journ.,* vol. 14, 1925.

THRASHER, F. M. *The Gang. A Study of 1,313 Gangs in Chicago.* New ed. Chicago, 1937.

VAERTING, M. " Der Korpsgeist bei Herrschenden und Beherrschten " : *Archiv für system. Philos. und Soziologie*, vol. 31, 1928.

VINCENT, G. E. " The Rivalry of Social Groups " : *Amer. Journal of Sociology*, vol. 16, 1910.

WHITEMORE, J. C. " The Corporative Consciousness " : *Journ. of Abnorm. Psychol*, vol. 20, 1925.

WIRTH, L. " Social Interaction : The Problem of the Individual and the Group " : *Amer. Journ. of Sociol.*, vol. 44, May, 1939, No. 6.

V. also III, 1, *f* ; III, 2, *b* ; III, 2, *d* ; III, 7, *d* ; bibliographies on crowd behaviour (pp. 60 and 107). On group disintegration and its effect on personality, cf. also the bibliography on pp. 118–19 n.

(e) The Different Psychologies.

ACHILLES, P. S. (ed.). *Psychology at Work*. New York, 1932.

ADLER, A. *Practice and Theory of Individual Psychology* (Translated by Radin, P.). London, 1924.

ARNOLD, V. *La psychologie de Réaction en Amerique*. Paris (Guillon), 1926.

BARTLETT, F. H. *Sigmund Freud*. A Marxian Study. London, 1938.

BIBRING, E. " Versuch einer allgemeinen Theorie der Heilung." Part of a Symposium on Therapeutic Results : *Intern. Zeitsch. für Psychoanalyse*, vol. 18, 1937.

CHILD, C. M., KOFFKA, K., ANDERSON, J. E., WATSON, J. B., SAPIR, E., THOMAS, W. I., KENWORTHY, M. E., WELLS, F. L., WHITE, A. W., and DUMMER, Ethel S. (ed.). *The Unconscious. A Symposium*. New York (Knopf), 1927.

DEWEY, J. *Human Nature and Conduct. An Introduction to Social Psychology*. London, 1922.

ELLIS, Willis (Ed.). *A Source Book of Gestalt Psychology*. London, 1938.

FERENCZI, S., and RANK, O. *Development of Psychoanalysis*. New York, Washington, 1925.

FREUD, S. *A General Selection from the Works of Sigmund Freud*, ed. by Rickman, J. London, 1937.

—— *Introductory Lectures on Psychoanalysis*. Translated by Rivière, J. London, 1922.

—— *New Introductory Lectures*. Translated by Sprott, W. J. H. London, 1937.

FRENCH, T. M. " Interrelations between Psychoanalysis and the Experimental Work of Pavlov " : *Amer. Journ. of Psychiatry*, vol. 12, 1933.

GOLDSTEIN, K. " Die Beziehungen der Psychoanalyse zur Biologie " : *Bericht über den II. Allgemeinen ärztlichen Kongress für Psychotherapie in Bad Nauheim*, 27–30. April, 1929.

GOLDSTEIN, K. Die ganzheitliche Betrachtung in der Medizin. Einheitsbestrebungen in der Medizin. Dresden, Leipzig, 1933.
—— Der Aufbau des Organismus. Haag, 1934.
HEALY, A., BRONNER, A. F., BOWERS, A. M. The Structure and Meaning of Psychoanalysis as Related to Personality and Behavior. New York, 1930.
HEIDBREDER, E. Seven Psychologies. New York, 1933.
HORNEY, Karen. New Ways of Psychoanalysis. New York, 1939.
JUNG, C. G. Psychological Types : or the Psychology of Individuation. Transl. by Baynes, H. G. New York, 1923.
—— Psychology of the Unconscious. Translated by Hinkel, B. 2nd ed. London, 1916.
KARPF, F. American Social Psychology ; Its Origins, Development, and European Background. New York, 1932.
KOFFKA, K. Principles of " Gestalt " Psychology. New York, 1935.
KRONFELD, A. Das Wesen der Psychiatrischen Erkenntnis. Beiträge zur allg. Psychiatrie. Berlin, 1920.
KUBIE, L. S. " Die Beziehung des bedingten Reflexes zur psychoanalytischen Technik " : Intern. Zeitschrift für Psychoanalyse, vol. 19, 1933.
LASSWELL, H. D: "Psychoanalyse und Sozialanalyse " : Imago, vol. 19. 1933.
LEWIN, K. A Dynamic Theory of Personality. Selected Papers. New York–London, 1935.
—— Principles of Topological Psychology. New York, 1936.
LEWIS, C. I. The Pragmatic Element in Knowledge. Berkeley, 1926.
LOVEJOY, A. D. " The Thirteen Pragmatisms " : Journ. of Philosophy, 1908.
LURIA, A. R. " Die moderne russische Psychologie und die Psychoanalyse " : Intern. Zeitschrift für Psychoanalyse, vol. 12, 1929, pp. 40–53.
McDOUGALL, W. An Introduction to Social Psychology. 2nd ed. 1926.
McDOUGALL, W. W., MURCHISON, C., TUFTS, J. H., and HOUSE, F. N. " A Symposium on Pareto's Significance " : Journal of Social Philosophy, vol. 1, 1935–6.
MEAD, G. H. Mind, Self and Society. Chicago, 1934.
—— The Philosophy of the Act. Chicago, 1938.
MILLER, E. Modern Psychotherapy. London, 1930.
MEYER, Adolf. Genetisch-dynamische Psychologie versus Nosologie " : Zeitschrift für die Gesamte Neurologie und Psychiatrie, 1926, vol. 101, pp. 406–427.
MURCHISON, C. Psychologies of 1925. 1st ed., Worcester (Mass.), 1925 ; 2nd ed., Worcester (Mass.), 1927 ; 3rd ed., Worcester (Mass.), 1928.

MURCHISON, C. (ed.) *Psychologies of 1930.* Worcester (Mass.), 1930.
—— *The Psychological Register.* (A list of Psychologists and their Work.) Worcester (Mass.), 1929.
MURPHY, G. *A Historical Introduction to Modern Psychology.* New York, 1932.
PARETO, V. *The Mind and Society.* Translated by Bongiorno, A., and Livingston, A. 4 vols. New York, 1938.
PAVLOV, I. P. *Lectures on Conditioned Reflexes.* London, 1928.
PRINZHORN, H. (Ed.). *Auswirkungen der Psychoanalyse in Wissenschaft und Leben.* Leipzig, 1928.
PFISTER, Oscar. *Psychoanalysis in the Service of Education.* (Trans. by Dr. Charles Rockwell Payne and F. Gschwind, revised by Barbara Low.) London, 1922.
RANK, O. and SACHS, H. *Die Bedeutung der Psychoanalyse für die Geisteswissenschaften.* Wiesbaden, 1913.
REUTER, E. B. " Relation of Biology and Sociology " : *Amer. Journ. of Sociol.,* vol. 32, 1926.
RICKMAN, John. " Index Psychoanalyticus " (1893–1926) in *International Psychoanalytical Library,* vol. 14. London, 1928.
RILEY, I. W. *American Thought from Puritanism and Beyond.* New York, 1935.
SCHILDER, P. *Introduction to a Psychoanalytic Psychiatry.* Nervous and Mental Disease Pub. Co., Mon. Series No. 50. New York–Washington, 1928.
—— " Psychoanalysis and Conditioned Reflexes " : *The Psychoanalytic Review,* vol. 24, No. 1. Jan., 1937.
—— *Psychotherapy.* London, 1938.
STEVENS, S. S. " The Operational Definition of Psychological Concepts " : *Psychol. Review,* 1935, vol. 42.
SWISHER, W. S. *Religion and the New Psychology.* London, 1920.
WEXBERG, Erwin. *Individual Psychology.* London, 1930.
WHEELER, W. M. " Present Tendencies in Biological Theory " : *Scientific Monthly,* vol. 28, 1929.
WOODWORTH, R. S. *Contemporary Schools of Psychology.* New York, 1931.
YOUNG, K. *Social Psychology.* New York, 1930.
V. also III, 1, *f*; III, 7, *a*, and the bibliographies on psychology and biology (pp. 127, n. 1–2 ; 131, n.).

(*f*) *The Sociological Aspects of Psychology.*

ALEXANDER, F. " The Sociological and Biological Orientations of Psychoanalysis." *Mental Hygiene,* vol. 20, 1936, pp. 232–248.
ALLPOERT, F. H. " Psychology in Relation to Social and Political Problems " in *Psychology at Work,* ed. by Achilles, P. S. New York, 1932.

ANDERSON, J. E. "The Development of Social Behaviour ": *Amer. Journ. of Sociol.*, vol. 44, 1938–9.
—— (Chairman). *The Young Child in the Home: A Survey of Three Thousand American Families.* (Report of the Committee on the Infant and Preschool Child, White House Conference on Child Health and Protection.) New York, 1936.

BAIN, R. "Sociology and Psychoanalysis." *Amer. Sociol. Review,* vol. 1, No. 2, 1936.

BARTLETT, F. C., GINSBERG, M., LINDGREN, E. J., THOULESS, R. H. (ed.). *The Study of Society.* London, 1939.

BERNARD, L. L. "A Classification of Environments ": *Amer. Journ. of Sociol.,* vol. 31, 1925–6.

BIRNBAUM, K. *Soziologie der Neurosen. Die nervösen Störungen in ihre Beziehungen zum Gemeinschafts- und Kulturleben.* Berlin, 1933.
—— *Grundzüge der Kultur-psychopathologie.* Berlin, 1924.

BROWN, J. F. *Psychology and the Social Order.* New York, 936.

BROWN, Mabel Webster, WILLIAMS, F. E. *Neuropsychiatry and the War. A Bibliography with Abstracts.* New York, 1918.

BURROW, T. *The Social Basis of Consciousness.* London, 1927.

DAVIES, A. E. "Social Implications of Psychiatry ": *British Journal of Psychol.,* vol. 12, 1932.

DUNN, M. "Psychiatric Treatment of the Effects of the Depression. Its Possibilities and Limitations ": *Mental Hygiene,* vol. 18, 1934.

EDMAN, Irwin. *Human Traits and their Social Significance.* Boston, 1920.

ELIOT, TH. D. "The Use of Psychoanalytic Classification in the Analysis of Social Behaviour ": *Proceedings of the American Sociological Society,* vol. 21, 1927.
—— "Psychiatrische Soziologie und soziologische Psychiatrie ": *Kölner Vierteljahrshefte für Soziologie,* vol. 9, 1930.

ELLWOOD, C. A. *Sociology in its Psychological Aspects.* New York, 1912.

ESSERTIER, D. "Psychologie et sociologie. Essai de bibliographie critique": *Publications du Centre de Documentation Sociale.* Paris, 1927.

FARIS, E. L. "Standpoints and Methods of Sociology in the Study of Personality and Social Growth ": *Fourth Conference on Research in Child Development,* 1933 (Appendix).

FARIS, E. L., and DUNHAM, H. W. *Mental Disorder in Urban Areas. An Ecological Study of Schizophrenia and Other Psychoses.* Chicago, 1939.

FLUGEL, J. C. *The Psychoanalytic Study of the Family*. London, 1921.

FRANK, L. K. "Physiological Tensions and Social Structure": *Publications of the American Sociological Society*, vol. 22, 1928.

FRENCH, Th. M. Social Conflict and Psychic Conflict. (Read before the Chicago Society for Personality Study as a part of a Symposium on *Psycho-Analysis and Sociology*, 22nd February, 1939. Chicago, 1939.

FREUD, S. *Group Psychology and the Analysis of the Ego*. Translated by Strachey, J. London, New York, 1932.

FROMM, E. "Die Gesellschaftliche Bedingtheit der psychoanalytischen Therapie": *Zeitschr. f. Sozialforschung*, vol. 4, 1935.

GECK, L. H. A. "Social Psychology in Germany: A Bibliographical Introduction." Translated by Norovkin, B. V. *Sociology and Social Science*, July and November, 1929.

—— *Sozialpsychologie im Auslande*. Berlin, 1928.

GINSBERG, M. *The Psychology of Society*. London, 1921.

—— "Psychology and Sociology": *Further Papers on the Social Sciences*, ed. by Dugdale, J. E. London, Le Play House Press, 1937.

GLOVER, E. "Psychology and the Social Sciences": *Further Papers on the Social Sciences*, ed. by Dugdale, J. E. London (Le Play House Press), 1937.

HELLPACH, W. *Nervenleben und Weltanschauung*. Wiesbaden, 1906.

HOPKINS, Pryns. *The Psychology of Social Movements*. A Psychoanalytic View of Society. London, 1938.

ISAACS, S. *Social Development in Young Children*. London, 1933.

JANET, Pierre. "Les sentiments sociaux dans le délire de persécution": *Journal de psychologie normale et pathologique*, Nos. 3–4, 5–6, 1932.

JONES, E. "Social Aspects of Psycho-Analysis": *Lectures Delivered under the Auspices of the Sociological Society*. London, 1924.

KORNILOW, R. N. "Psychology in the Light of Dialectic Materialism" in *Psychologies of 1930*, ed. by Murchison, C., Worcester (Mass.), 1930.

KUNZ, H. "Die Psychoanalyse als Symptom einer Wandlung im Selbstverständnis des Menschen." *Zentralblatt für Psychotherapie und ihre Grenzgebiete*, vol. 4.

LASSWELL, H. D. *Psychopathology and Politics*. Chicago, 1930.

—— "What Psychiatrists and Political Scientists can Learn from one Another": *Psychiatry: a Journal of the Biology and Pathology of Interpersonal Relationships*, vol. 1, No. 1, 1932.

LASSWELL, H. D. "Selected References on Social Psychiatry": *Amer. Journ. of Sociology*, vol. 42, 1937.

MALAMUD, J. T. "Psychological Approach to the Study of Social Crises": *Amer. Journ. of Sociol.*, vol. 43, 1937-8.

MALINOWSKI, B. "Psychoanalysis and Anthropology": *Nature*, vol. 92, No. 2818, 1923.

MANNHEIM, K. "The Sociology of Human Valuations: the Psychological and Sociological Approach": *Further Papers on the Social Sciences, Their Relations in Theory and in Teaching*, ed. by Dugdale, J. E. London (Le Play House Press), 1937.

MORENO, TH. *Who Shall Survive?* Washington, D.C., 1934.

MUELLER BRAUNSCHWEIG. "Psychoanalytische Gesichtspunkte zur Genese der Moral, insbesondere des moralischen Aktes": *Imago*, 1921.

MURCHISON, C. *A Handbook of Social Psychology*. Worcester (Mass.), 1935.

MURPHY, L. B., and MURPHY, G. *Experimental Social Psychology. An Interpretation of Research upon the Socialization of the Individual*. Revised ed. New York, 1937.

OSBORN, R. *Freud and Marx*. London, 1937.

PLANT, J. S. "Sociological Factors Challenging the Practice of Psychiatry in a Metropolitan Community": *Journ. for Psychiatry*, vol. 8, 1939.

REINER. Bericht über die bisherigen Ergebnisse der Gemeinschaftsarbeit zwischen Psychotherapeuten und Sozialfürsorgern. *Z. für Wohlfahrtspflege*, 1933.

ROBINSON, Virginia P. *A Changing Psychology in Social Case Work*. (Univ. of North Carolina Press), 1930.

SAPIR, E. "The Contribution of Psychiatry to an Understanding of Behaviour in Society": *Amer. Journ. of Sociol.*, vol. 42, 1937.

SOSSETT, Mariette. "Les Influences sociales dans les nouvelles méthodes psychopathologiques": *Révue de l'Institut de Sociologie*, 1933, No. 1.

STRATTON, G. M. *Social Psychology of Internal Conduct*. New York, 1929.

SYZ, H. "The Social Neurosis": *Amer. Journ. of Sociol.*, vol. 42, 1937.

TAFT, Jessie. *The Dynamics of Therapy in a Controlled Relationship*. New York, 1933.

WAELDER, R. "Die Bedeutung des Werkes Sigmund Freud's für die Sozial- und Rechtswissenschaften": (*Révue Internationale de la Théorie du Droit*), Année x, 1936, No. 2.

—— "Aetiologie und Verlauf der Massenpsychose": *Imago*, vol. 21, 1935.

WALLAS, G. *Human Nature in Politics*. 3rd ed., London, 1924.

WEIZSACKER, W. von. *Soziale Krankheit und Soziale Gesundung.* Berlin, 1930.

WETZEL. Soziologie der Schizophrenie Bumkes Handbuch der Geisteskrankheiten, vol. 9.

WHITE, W. A. " Some Suggestions Regarding Practical Contacts between Sociology and Psychoanalysis " : *Publ. of the Amer. Sociol. Society,* vol. 16, 1920.

—— *Twentieth Century Psychiatry. Its Contribution to Man's Knowledge of Himself.* London, 1936.

WILLIAMS, F. E. *Some Social Aspects of Mental Hygiene.* Philadelphia, 1930.

WILLIAMS, J. W. *Principles of Social Psychology.* New York, 1930.

WIRTH, L. " Some Characteristics of the Sociological Approach to Personality " : *Fourth Conference on Research in Child Development,* 1933.

WOLFE, W. B. " Psychoanalysing the Depression " : *Forum,* 87, April, 1932.

YOUNG, K. " Contributions of Psychiatry to the Study of Group Conflict " in *Group Conflict Papers Presented at the 28th Meeting of the American Sociological Society,* vol. 25, 1930.

Cf. also III, 1, *d* ; III, 2, *d* ; III, 6 ; III, 7 ; IV, 1, and the bibliographies on unemployment (p. 220 n.) and psychology and biology (pp. 127, n. 1–2, 131, n. 1), and the psychological implications of leisure (316 n.).

(g) *Psychological and Sociological Elements in Economics.*

CLARK, J. M. " Economics and Modern Psychology " : *Journ. Pol. Econ.,* vol. 26, 1918.

DICKINSON, Z. C. *Economic motives. A Study in the Psychological Foundations of Economic Theory.* Harvard Economic Studies, vol. 24. Cambridge (Mass.), 1922.

FLORENCE, P. S. *Economics and Human Behaviour. A Rejoinder to Social Psychologists.* (Psyche Miniatures.)

HANEY, L. H. " The Social Point of View in Economics " : *Quarterly Journ. of Econ.,* vol. 28, 1913

HASBACH, W. *Die allgemeinen philosophischen Grundlagen der von Fr. Quesney und A. Smith begründeten politischen Oekonomie.* Leipzig, 1890.

—— *Untersuchungen über Adam Smith und die Entwicklung der politischen Oekonomie.* Leipzig, 1891.

KNIGHT, F. H. *Ethics of Competition.* New York, 1935.

LOEWE, A. *Economics and Sociology. A Plea for Co-operation in the Social Sciences.* London, 1935.

—— " Economic Analysis and Social Structure " : *Manchester School,* vol. vii.

MANNHEIM, K. " Ueber das Wesen und die Bedeutung des wirtschaftlichen Erfolgsstrebens " : *Archiv für Sozialwissenschaft,* vol. 63, 1930.

MITCHELL, W. C. "The Rationality of Economic Activity": *Journ. of Polit. Econ.*, vol. 18, 1910.

—— "Human Behavior and Economics: A Survey of Recent Literature": *Quarterly Journal of Economics*, vol. 29, 1914–15.

PARKER, C. H. "Motives in Economic Life": *Amer. Econ. Review*, vol. 8. Suppl., March, 1918.

PARSONS, T. "Wants and Activities in Marshall": *Quarterly Journ. of Econom.*, vol. 46, 1931–2.

—— "Economics and Sociology: Marshall in Relation to the Thought of his Time": *Quarterly Journ. of Economics*, vol. 46, 1931–2.

—— Some Reflections on "The Nature and Significance of Economics": *Quarterly Journ. of Economics*, vol. 48, 1933–4.

—— "Sociological Elements in Economic Thought. I, Historical; II, The Analytical Factor View": *Quarterly Journal of Economics*, vol. 49, 1934–5.

ROCHE-AGUSSOL, M. *La psychologie economique chez les Anglo-Americains*. Montpellier, Paris, 1918.

—— *Études bibliographiques des sources de la psychologie économique chez les Anglo-Americains*. Montpellier, Paris, 1919.

TARDE, G. *Psychologie économique*. 2 vols. Paris (Alcan), 1902.

VEBLEN, Th. B. "The Preconceptions of Economic Science" in *The Place of Science in Modern Civilization*. New York, 1919.

WEBER, M. "Soziologische Grundkategorien des Wirtschaftens" in his Wirtschaft und Gesellschaft. Vol. 3 of the *Grundriss der Sozialökonomik*. Tübingen, 1925.

ZEYSS, R. Adam Smith und der Eigennutz. Thesis. Tübingen, 1899.

Cf. also I, 2 ; III, 3, *b* ; III, 3, *c* ; III, 4, *a–b* ; V, 1–3.

III. 2. MILITARY METHODS AND THE APPLICATION OF POWER AS SOCIAL TECHNIQUES.

(a) *The Principle of Power.*

BECKER, C. *Progress and Power*. Stanford Univ. Press, Stanford University, 1936.

CASE, C. M. "Some Social Patterns of Coercion": *Proceedings of the American Sociological Society*, vol. 17, 1922.

DEWEY, J. "Force and Coercion": *Intern. Journ. of Ethics*, vol. 26, 1916.

GOLDHAMER, H., and SHILS, E. A. "Types of Power and Status": *Amer. Journ. of Sociology*, vol. 45, 1939.

HADFIELD, J. A. *The Psychology of Power*. London, 1933.

KRAUS, O. *Der Machtgedanke und die Friedensidee in der Philosophie der Engländer*. Leipzig, 1926.

LEWIN, J. *Power Ethics*. New York, 1931.

MACPHERSON, W. *The Psychology of Persuasion*. Especially Chapter 3 : Group Pressure and the Source of Power. London, 1920.

MENZEL, A. " Kallikles : Eine Studie zur Geschichte der Lehre vom Rechte des Stärkeren " : *Zeitschrift für Öffentliches Recht.*, vol. 3.

MERRIAM, C. E. *Political Power*. New York, 1934.

MILLER, H. A. *Races, Nations, and Classes. The Psychology of Domination and Freedom*. Philadelphia, 1924.

NEELY, I. E. " Sources of Political Power " : *Amer. Journ. of Sociol.*, vol. 33, 1927, 1928.

MURCHISON, C. *Social Psychology. The Psychology of Political Domination*. (International University Series in Psychology). Worcester (Mass.), 1929.

PARSONS, E. C. *Social Rule : A Study of Will to Power*. New York, 1916.

PARSONS, T. *The Structure of Social Action. A Study in Social Theory with Special Reference to a Group of Recent European Writers*. New York–London, 1937.

RUSSELL, B. *Power. A New Social Analysis*. London, 1938.

VAERTING, M. *Soziologie und Psychologie der Macht*. I : Die Macht der Massen. Berlin, 1928.

VIERKANDT, A. " Machtverhältnis und Machtmoral " : *Philosophische Vorträge in der Kantgesellschaft*, No. 13, Berlin, 1916.

WEBER, M. " Die Typen der Herrschaft " in his Wirtschaft und Gesellschaft. *Grundriss der Sozialökonomik*, vol. 3. Tübingen, 1925.

Cf. also III, 1, *b* ; III, 2, *b–d*.

(b) *Some Concrete Forms of Social Pressure.*

BENTLEY, A. F. *The Process of Government. A Study of Social Pressure*. Chicago, 1908.

BOURGIN, G. " Blanqui's Anweisungen für den Strassenkampf " : *Grünbergs Archiv für die Geschichte des Sozialismus*, vol. 15, 1930.

FOSTER, W. Z. *Strike Strategy*. (Trade Union Education League.) Chicago, 1924.

GREER, D. *The Incidence of Terror During the French Revolution*. Cambridge (Mass.), 1935.

GUMBEL, E. J. *Verschwörer. Bieträge zur Geschichte und Soziologie der deutschen nationalistischen Geheimbünde*. Wien, 1924.

HILLER, E. T. *The Strike. A Study in Collective Action*. Chicago, 1928.

KALLEN, H. M. " Persecution " : *Encyclopedia of the Social Sciences*.

—— " Radicalism " : *Encyclopedia of the Social Sciences*.

LASSWELL, H. L. " Bribery." *Encyclopedia of the Social Sciences.*

LIMAN, P. *Der politische Mord im Wandel der Geschichte. Eine historisch-psychologische Studie.* Berlin, 1912.

McIVER, R. M. " Social Pressures ": *Encyclopedia of the Social Sciences.*

MASCHKE, R. *Boycott, Sperre und Aussperrung.* Jena, 1911.

MUSTE, A. J. " Factional Fights in Trade Unions " in *American Labour Dynamics,* ed. by Hardman, J. B. S. New York, 1928.

POUGET, E. *Sabotage.* Chicago, 1913.

Cf. also I, 1 ; III, 2, *a* ; III, 2, *c–d* ; V, 4.

(c) Modern Warfare and the Totalitarian War.

BELLI DE PINO, A. von. *Der Krieg der Zukunft im Urteil des Auslandes.* Preussische Jahrbücher, Schriftenreihe, No. 28, 1936.

BELLOC, H. *A General Sketch of the European War.* London, 1915.

CASPARY, A. *Wirtschaftsstrategie und Kriegsführung.* Berlin, 1932.

CLAREMORIS, M. *Lo Spirito della guerra moderna.* Cremona, 1935.

DELBRUECK, H. *Geschichte der Kriegskunst im Rahmen der politischen Geschichte.* Fortgesetzt von Emil Daniels und Otto Haintz, 6 vols. Berlin, 1900–1936.

DEMETER, K. *Das deutsche Offizierskorps in seinen historisch-soziologischen Grundlagen.* Berlin, 1930.

DOUHET, Giulio. *La Guerra integrale.* Rome, 1936.

FOERTSCH, H. *Kriegskunst Heute und Morgen.* Berlin, 1939.

FRANKE, H. (ed.). *Handbuch der neuzeitlichen Wehrwissenschaften.* Berlin (W. de Gruyter), 1936–9.

FULLER, J. F. Ch. *War and Western Civilization, 1832-1932. A Study of War as a Political Instrument and the Expression of Mass Democracy.* London, 1932.

HALDANE, J. B. S. *A.R.P.* London, 1938.

KÄHLER, A., and SPEIER, H. *War in our Time.* New York, 1939.

KENWORTHY, J. M. (Lord Strabolgi). *The Real Navy.* London, 1927.

—— *New Wars, New Weapons.* London, 1930.

LAMPE, A. Allgemeine Wehrwirtschaftslehre. Jena, 1938.

LIDDELL HART, B. H. " An International Force ": *International Affairs,* vol. 12, 1933.

—— *Europe in Arms.* London, 1938.

—— *The Defence of Britain and of the West.* London, 1939.

LUDENDORFF, E. *Der totale Krieg.* München, 1935.

—— *The Nation at War,* trans. by Dr. A. S. Rappoport. London, 1936.

MATHIAS, W. Die staatliche Organisation der Kriegswirtschaft in Frankreich, Grossbritannien, Italien, Tschechoslowakei und den Vereinigten Staaten von Amerika. Berlin, 1937.

MAURIN, L. F. T. L'armée moderne. Paris, 1938.

MERTON, R. K. " Science and Military Technique " : The Scientific Monthly, vol. 41, 1935.

PIATIER, A. Economie de la guerre. Paris, 1939.

POSSONY, S. T. To-morrow's War : Its Planning, Management and Cost. London, 1938.

ROSINSKI, H. " The Past and Future of Warfare " : Round Table, 1938.

—— " Command of the Sea " : Brassey's Naval Annual, 1939.

—— The German Army. London, 1939.

SCHMITT, C. " Totaler Feind, totaler Staat " : Voelkerbund und Voelkerrecht, vol. 4, No. 3, 1937.

SCHWERTFEGER, Bernhard. Das Weltkriegsende. Gedanken über die deutsche Kriegsführung, 1918. Potsdam, 1937.

VOGT, Alfred. History of Militarism. New York, 1937.

WEHBERG, H. Theory and Practice of International Policing, London, 1935.

WEIL, F. " Neuere Literatur zur deutschen Wehrwirtschaft " : Zeitschrift für Sozialforschung. Vol. 7, 1938.

WINTRINGHAM, T. H. How to Reform the Army. London, 1939.

Cf. also III, 2, a ; III, 2, b ; III, 2, d ; III, 4, b ; V, 4, and the bibliography On war (p. 124 n.).

(d) *Psychological Aspects of Modern Militarism. Morale.*

BARTLETT, F. C. Psychology and the Soldier. Cambridge (England), 1937.

BROUSSEAU, A. Essai sur la peur aux armées, 1914–18. Paris (Alcan), 1926.

CAMPANEO, Essai de psychologie militaire individuelle et collective. Paris, 1902.

DEMETER, K. Das deutsche Offizierskorps in seinen historisch-soziologischen Grundlagen. Berlin, 1930.

ELERT, W. Zur Geschichte des Kriegerischen Ethos, 1928.

ENDRES, F. C. " Soziologische Struktur und dazugehörige Ideologie des Offizierskorps vor dem Weltkrieg " : Archiv für Sozialwissenschaft, vol. 58, 1927.

FULLER, J. F. Ch. Training Soldiers for War. London, 1914.

—— Generalship : its Diseases and their Cure. A Study of the Personal Factor in Command. London, 1933.

GODDARD, Harold. Morale. New York, 1918.

HALL, G. Stanley. Morale. New York, 1920.

JUENGER, E. (ed.). Krieg und Krieger. Berlin, 1930.

KEHR, E. "Zur Genese des preussischen Reserve-offiziers": *Die Gesellschaft*, 1929.

LASSWELL, H. D. "Morale": *Enc. of the Social Sciences*.

MONCEAU, Emile (Emile Mayer). *La Psychologie du Commandement*. Paris, 1923.

MUNSON, E. L. *The Management of Men. A Handbook on the Systematic Development of Morale and the Control of Human Behavior*. London, New York, 1921.

PINTSCHOVIUS, C. *Die seelische Widerstandskraft im modernen Kriege*. Oldenburg, Berlin, 1936.

PLAUT, P. "Psychographie des Kriegers": Beiheft zur *Angewandten Psychologie*, vol. 21. Leipzig, 1920.

PSYCHOLOGISCHES LABORATORIUM DES REICHSKRIEGS-MINISTERIUMS, BERLIN (ed.). *Abhandlungen zur Wehrpsychologie*. Vorträge aus einem Fortbildungs-kurs beim P.L.d.R–K–M., Berlin, 1936. Berlin–Leipzig, 1936.

SUMNER, W. G. Discipline, and Other Essays (Purposes and Consequences, Power and Progress, Liberty and Responsibility), from the Collected Works of W. G. Sumner. Yale University, New Haven, 1923.

WARDLE, M. K. "Note on Fear in War." *Army Quarterly*, vol. 4, 1922.

WAELDER, R. "Psychological Aspects of War and Peace": *Geneva Studies*, vol. 10, No. 2, Geneva, 1939.

Cf. also III, 1, *b*; III, 1, *d*; III, 4, *b*; IV, 1; IV, 4; V, 6, and also the bibliographies on fear, aggressiveness, anxiety (p. 122 n.).

III. 3. LAW, PROPERTY AS MEANS OF SOCIAL TECHNIQUE.

(*a*) *Legal Institutions : Their Sociology, Main Trends.*

ALLEN, C. K. *Law in the Making*. 2nd ed. Oxford, 1930.

CAIRNS, H. *Law and the Social Sciences*. New York, 1935.

CARDOZO, Benj. *The Nature of the Judicial Process*. Yale University Press, (Storr Lectures) London, 1921.
—— *The Growth of the Law*. New Haven, London, 1924.

COHEN, M. *Law and the Social Order*. New York, 1933.

COMMONS, J. R. *The Legal Foundations of Capitalism*. New York, 1924.

DARMSTADTER, F. *Das Wirtschaftsrecht in seiner soziolo-gischen Struktur*. Berlin, 1928.

DICEY, A. V. *Lectures on the Relation between Law and Public Opinion in England during the Nineteenth Century*. 2nd edition. London, 1914.

DUGUIT, L. *Le droit social, le droit individuel et la trans-formation de l'état*. Paris (Alcan), 1911.
—— Les transformations generelles du droit prive depuis le Code Napoleon. Paris, 1912.

DUGUIT, L. *Law in the Modern State*. With an Introduction by H. Laski. Translated by F. and H. Laski. New York, 1919.

EHRLICH, E. *Fundamental Principles of the Sociology of Law*. Translated by Moll, W. L. Cambridge (Mass.), 1936.

FRAENKEL, E. *Zur Soziologie der Klassenjustiz*. Berlin, 1927.

GURVITCH, G. *Le Temps Présent et l'Idée du Droit Social*. Paris, 1931.

HARVARD TERCENTENARY PUBLICATIONS. *The Future of the Common Law*. Cambridge (Mass.), 1937.

HUBER, M. *Beiträge zur Kenntnis der soziologischen Grundlagen des Völkerrechts und der Staatengesellschaft*, 1928.

KANTOROWICZ, H. U. *Rechtswissenschaft und Soziologie*, 1911.

KEETON, G. W., and SCHWARZENBERGER, G. *Making International Law Work*. London, 1939.

KELSEN, H. *Der soziologische und juristische Staatsbegriff*. Tübingen, 1922.

LASKI, H. J. "The Judicial Functions": *Politica*, vol. 2, 1936.

LEVY-ULLMANN, G. L. *The English Legal Tradition, its Sources, its History*. Translated by Mitchell, H. London, 1935.

LONDON SCHOOL OF ECONOMICS AND POLITICAL SCIENCE (Univ. London). (ed.) *Modern Theories of Law*. London, 1933.

MCMILLAN, H. P. *Two Ways of Thinking. A Comparison of the English Type of Legal and Political System with those Derived from the Roman System* (The Rede Lecture.) Cambridge, 1934.

MAINE, Sir H. J. S. *Ancient Law*. London, 1931.

MENGER, A. *Das bürgerliche Recht und die besitzlosen Klassen*. 5th ed. Tübingen, 1927.

MORIN, G. Le Sens des transformations contemporaines du droit : *Rev. de métaph et morale*, 34, 2.

NEUMANN, F. "Der Funktionswandel des Gesetzes im Recht der bürgerlichen Gesellschaft": *Zeitschrift für Sozialforschung*, vol. 6, 1937.

POUND, R. "Scope and Purpose of Sociological Jurisprudence": *Harvard Law Review*, vols. 24–5, 1911–12.

RADBRUCH, G. *Der Mensch im Recht*, Tübingen, 1927.

RENNER, K. *Die Rechtsinstitute des Privatrechts und ihre soziale Funktion*. Tübingen, 1929.

SINZHEIMER, H. *Diesoziologischen Methoden in der Privatrechtswissenschaft*. 1909.

TIMASHEFF, N. S. "The Sociological Place of Law (with a Discussion)": *Amer. Journ. of Sociol.*, vol. 44, 1938, No. 2.

VINOGRADOFF, P. *Historical Jurisprudence.* Oxford, 1920.

WEBER, M. " Rechtssoziologie " in his " Wirtschaft und Gesellschaft " : *Grundriss der Sozialökonomik,* vol. 3. Tübingen, 1925.
Cf. also III, 3, *b–c* ; III, 4, *c.*

(b) *Property.*

ARON, R., OBOLENSKI-OSSINSKY, V. V., FRANCK, L.-R., VAUCHER, P., POLIN, R., PRACHE, G., LEFRANC, G., DEAT, M. *Inventaires II. L'Économique et le politique.* Introduction by Bougle, Ch. Paris (Alcan).

BEAGLEHOLE, E. *Property : A Study in Social Psychology.* London, 1931.

BERLE, A. A., and MEANS, G. C. *The Modern Corporation and Private Property.* New York, 1933.

BOWLEY, A. L., and HOHG, M. H. *Has Poverty Diminished ?* London, 1925.

CLARK, C. *National Income and Outlay.* London, 1937.

ELY, R. T. *Property and Contract in Their Relation to the Distribution of Wealth,* 2 vols. London, 1914.

FRIEDMANN, G. *De la Sainte Russie à l'U.R.S.S.,* chap. IV, Niveaux de vie. Paris (Gallimard), 1938.

HIRSH, F. W. *Economic Freedom and Private Property.* London, 1935.

HOBSON, J. A. *Property and Improperty.* London, 1937.

LAIDLER, Harry W. " The Trend Towards Public Ownership " in Page, Kirby, *A New Economic Order.* New York, 1930.

LARKIN, P. *Property in the Eighteenth Century with Special Reference to England and Locke.* Dublin, 1930.

LAVERGNECT, HENRY. *La Richesse de la France, fortune et revenus privés.* Paris, 1908.

LECARPENTIER. " Revenus et fortunes privées en France et en Grande-Bretagne " : *Revue Politique et Parlementaire.* October, 1937.

NOYES, G. R. *The Institution of Property.* New York, 1936.

ORTH, S. P. (ed.). Readings on the Relation of Government to Property and Industry. Boston, New York City, 1915.

Property : Its Duties and Rights. Essays by various authors. London, 1915.

ROBSON, W. A. (ed.). *Public Enterprise. Developments in Social Ownership and Control in Great Britain.* London, 1937. (New Fabian Research Bureau.)

SCHMIDT, W. *Das Eigentum auf den ältesten Stufen der Menschheit.* Vol. 1 : Das Eigentum und Volkskultur. Münster i. W., 1937.

STAMP, Sir Josiah. *The National Income and other Statistical Studies.* London, 1937.

Statistical Abstract of the United States. Washington, 1938.

TUGWELL, R. G., and HILL, H. C. *Our Economic Society and its Problems. Study of American Levels of Living and how to improve them.* N.Y., 1934.

VEBLEN, K. *Absentee Ownership and Business Enterprise in Recent Times.* New York, 1936.

VILLE-CHARBOLLE. " La concentration des entreprises en France depuis la guerre " : *Bulletin de la statistique générale.* Avril, 1933.

WEDGWOOD, J. *The Economics of Inheritance.* London, 1939.

Cf. also I, 2 ; III, 3, *a* ; III, 3, *c.*

(c) Social Classes and Their Psychology.

ARON, R., HALBWACHS, M., VERMEIL, E., FRANCK, L.-R., VAUCHER, P., MARJOLIN, R., POLIN, R., GRAVIER, R., YOVANOVITCH, D., FELDMAN, V., MOUGIN, H. *Inventaires III Classes Moyennes.* Paris (Alcan), 1939.

AYNARD, J. *La bourgeoisie française. Essay de psychologie.* Paris (Perrin), 1934.

BEARD, Ch. et M. R. *The Rise of American Civilization.* N.Y., 1930.

BOUTON, A. *La fin des rentiers. Histoire des fortunes privées en France depuis 1914.* Paris (M. P. Trémois), 1932.

CARR-SAUNDERS, A. M., and JONES, D. Caradog. *A Survey of the Social Structure of England and Wales.* London (Oxford University Press), 1927.

COLE, G. D. H. and M. I. *The Condition of Britain.* London, 1937.

COREY, L. *The Crisis of the Middle Class.* New York, 1935.

—— *The Decline of American Capitalism.* London, 1935.

DESCAMPES, P. *La hierarchie des classes en Angleterre.* Bibl. de la Science Sociale, 1911.

DOLLARD, J. *Caste and Class in a Southern Town.* New Haven, 1937.

DREYFUSS, C. *Beruf und Ideologie der Angestellten.* Tübingen, 1925.

FAHLBECK, P. E. *Die Klassen und die Gesellschaft : eine geschichtlich-soziologische Studie über Entstehung, Entwicklung und Bedeutung des Klassenwesens.* Jena, 1922.

FERRÉ, L. M. *Les classes sociales dans la France contemporaine.* Paris, 1934.

GEIGER, Th. *Die soziale Schichtung des deutschen Volkes.* Stuttgart, 1932.

GREAVES, H. R. G. *Reactionary England.* London, 1936.

GRETTON, R. H. *The English Middle Class.* London, 1917.

GROETHUYSEN, B. *Les origines de l'esprit Bourgeois en France.* Paris (Gallimard), 1927.

Grundriss der Sozialökonomik, vol. ix (on Social Classes). Tübingen, 1929.

HALBWACHS, M. *Les Classes Sociales*. Paris (Alcan), 1937.

HOBSON, J. A. *The Evolution of Modern Capitalism*. London, Felling-on-Tyne, New York, 1926.

MARSCHAK, J. "Zur Modernen Interessendifferenzierung" in *Soziologische Studien zur Politik, Wirtschaft und Kultur der Gegenwart. Festschrift Alfred Weber gewidmet*. Potsdam, 1930.

MARSHALL, T. H. (ed.). *Class Conflict and Social Stratification*. Third Conference on the Social Sciences. London (Le Play House Press), 1939.

MEUSEL, A. "Proletariat" : *Encyclopedia of the Social Sciences*.

MITGAU, F. *Familienschicksal und soziale Rangordnung*. Leipzig, 1928.

—— "Grundlagen des sozialen Aufstieges" in *Alfred Weber Festschrift*. Potsdam, 1930.

NIETZ, J. A. "The Depression and the Social Status of Occupations" : *Elementary School Journal*. vol. 35, 1935.

PALM, F. C. *The Middle Classes, Then and Now*. New York, 1935.

RANULF, S. *Moral Indignation and Middle Class Psychology*. Copenhagen, 1938.

SOMBART, W. *The Quintessence of Capitalism : A Study of the History and Psychology of the Modern Business Man*. Translated by Epstein, M. London, 1915.

SOROKIN, P. *Social Mobility*. New York–London, 1927.

SPOHN, M. Erich. *Zur Grundlegung einer Theorie des sozialen Aufstiegs*. Rost. Phil. Diss. Rostock, 1934.

TAWNEY, R. H. *Acquisitive Society*. London, 1921.

—— *Religion and the Rise of Capitalism*. London, 1938.

TOBIS, A. *Das Mittelstandsproblem der Nachkriegszeit und seine statistische Erfassung*. Leipzig, 1932.

WARNOTTE, D. "Les vertues bourgeoises, leurs origines, leur signification" : *Revue de l'institut sociologique*, Bruxelles, 1939.

WEBER, M. "Klassen, Stand Parteien" in his "Wirtschaft und Gesellschaft", vol. iii of *Grundriss der Sozialökonomik*. Tübingen, 1925.

—— *The Protestant Ethic and the Spirit of Capitalism*. Translated by Parsons, T. London, 1930.

Cf. also I, 2 ; III, 1, *a–b* ; III, 1, *d* ; III, 1, *f* ; III, 7, *c* ; IV, 1 ; IV, 5 ; V.

III. 4. THE SCIENCE OF SOCIAL ORGANIZATION AS A MEANS OF SOCIAL TECHNIQUE.

(a) *Industrial Organization and Business Management.*

BAUMGARTEN, Fr. *Psychologie der Menschenbehandlung im Betriebe*. Halle, 1930.

BAUMGARTEN, Fr. "Der Fayolismus" in *Industrielle Psychotechnik*, vol. 4, 1927.

BECKERATH, H. V. *Modern Industrial Organization.* New York, 1933.

BRIEFS, G. "Betriebssoziologie," Art. in *Handwörter-buch der Soziologie*, ed. by Vierkandt, A. Stuttgart, 1931.

DUBREUIL, H. *A Chacun sa chance. L'organization du travail fondée sur la liberté.* Paris, 1935.

FAYOL, H. *Industrial and General Administration.* Translated by J. A. Conbrough. London, 1930.

FLORENCE, Ph. S. *Economics of Fatigue and Unrest and the Efficiency of Labour in English and American Industry.* London–New York, 1924.

—— *The Logic of Industrial Organization.* London, 1933.

GABLENTZ, G. H. von der. "Industrieburokratie." *Schmollers Jahrbücher* 50. Jahrg., 1926.

GIDE, Ch. *Les colonies communistes et coopératives.* Assoc. pour l'enseignement de la coopération. Paris, 1930.

HILDAGE, H. T., MARPLE, T. G., and MEYENBERG, F. L. *The New Management.* London, 1938.

HOBSON, J. A. *Incentives in the New Industrial Order.* London, 1922.

HUNT, E. E. *Scientific Management Since Taylor.* New York, 1924.

INTERNATIONAL LABOUR OFFICE. *Social Aspects of Rationalisation.* Geneva, 1931.

JOST, W. *Das Sozialleben des industriellen Betriebes. Eine Analyse des sozialen Prozesses im Betrieb.* Schrift-enreihe des Instituts für Betriebssoziologie, vol. 2. Berlin, 1932.

JOVANOVIĆ, D. *Le rendement optimum du travail ouvrier. Étude sur les stimulants modernes de l'activité ouvrière.* Paris, 1923.

KIMBALL, D. S. *Industrial Economics.* New York, 1929.

MAN, H. de. *Joy in Work.* (Translated by Paul, E. and C.) London, 1929.

MAYO, E. *The Human Problems of an Industrial Civiliza-tion.* New York, 1933.

MEANS, G. C. "The Distribution of Control and Responsi-bility in a Modern Economy": *Political Science Quarterly*, vol. i, No. 1, March, 1935.

METCALF, H. C. *The Psychological Foundations of Management.* Chicago, New York, 1927.

MILES, G. H. *The Problem of Incentives in Industry.* London, 1932.

MODLIN, G. M., and McISAAC, A. M. *Social Control of Industry.* Boston, 1938.

PALEWSKI, J. P. *Le rôle du chef d'entreprise dans la grande industrie. Étude de psychologie economique.* Paris (Les Presses Universitaires), 1924.

PATTERSON, S. H. *Social Aspects of Industry.* New York, 1929.

REUTER, F. *Handbuch der Rationalisierung.* Berlin, 1930.

ROBERTSON, D. H. *The Control of Industry.* Cambridge, 1936.

ROETHLISBERGER, F. J., and DICKSON, W. J. *Management and the Worker. Technical versus Social Organization in an Industrial Plant.* Harvard School of Business Administration Studies in Industrial Research. Boston, 1934.

ROSENSTOCK, E. *Werkstattaussiedlung. Untersuchungen über den Lebensraum des Industriearbeiters.* Berlin, 1922.

TAYLOR, F. W. *The Principles of Scientific Management.* New York–London, 1911.

TODD, A. J. *Industry and Society.* New York, 1933.

TUGWELL, R. G. *The Industrial Discipline and the Governmental Arts.* University of Colorado Press (Boulder), 1933.

TEAD, O. *Instincts in Industry.* Boston, 1918.

VEBLEN, Th. B. *The Theory of Business Enterprise.* New York, 1904.

WARE, C. T., MEANS, Gardner C. *The Modern Economy in Action.* New York, 1936.

WARD, H. F. *In Place of Profit.* New York, London, 1933.

WHITEHEAD, J. N. *Leadership in a Free Society.* Cambridge, 1936.

WOLDT, R. *Die Lebenswelt des Industriearbeiters.* Leipzig, 1926.

YOVANOVITCH, D. *Das grossindustrielle Beamtentum.* Stuttgart, 1911.

Cf. also I, 2 ; II ; III, 4, *b* ; IV, 1.

(b) *General Social Organization, Administration. The Problems of Bureaucratization.*

ALLEN, C. K. *Bureaucracy Triumphant.* London, 1931.

BARKER, Ernest. *The Development of Administration, Conscription, Taxation, Social Services, and Education.* Vol. 5 of *European Civilization*, ed. by Eyre, E. London, 1937.

BARTHLÉMY, H. " Comparaison des principes du droit administratif français aux pratiques administratives des pays anglosaxons " : *Bulletins de la société de législation comparée*, vol. 51, 1931.

BEARDS, Charles and William. " The Case for Bureaucracy " : *Scribner's Magazine*, vol. 93, April, 1933.

BOGDANOW, A. *Allgemeine Organisationslehre.* Berlin, 1926.

BUSHEE, F. A. *Social Organization.* New York, 1930.

DESSAUER, Fr. *Recht, Richtertum und Ministerialbürokratie.* Mannheim, Berlin, Leipzig, 1928.

DICKINSON, John. *Administrative Justice and the Supremacy of Law in the United States.* Cambridge (Mass.), 1927.

DICKINSON, John. "The Perennial Cry of Bureaucracy": *Yale Review*, Spring, 1935.

—— Administrative Law and the Fear of Bureaucracy, Parts I and II: *American Bar Association Journal*, Oct., Nov., 1928.

GOOCH, R. K. *Regionalism in France.* University of Virginia, Institute for Research in the Social Sciences, Institute Monograph No. 12. New York, 1931.

GRABOWSKY, A. *Die Reform des deutschen Beamtentums.* Gotha, 1917.

FINER, H. The Civil Service in the Modern State: *American Political Science Review*, vol. 19, 1925.

FRIEDRICH, C. J., COLE, Taylor. *Responsible Bureaucracy. A Study of the Swiss Civil Service.* Harvard University Press, Cambridge, 1932.

GALLOWAY, L. *Organization and Management.* New York, 1913.

GOEBEL, Otto. *Taylorismus in der Verwaltung.* Hannover, 1925.

GOODNOW, F. J. *Politics and Administration.* New York, 1900.

GOWIN, E. B. *The Executive and His Control by Men.* New York, 1915.

HART, J. K. *Community Organization.* New York, London, 1935.

HERRING, E. P. *Public Administration and the Public Interest.* London, 1936.

HILL, N. L. *International Administration.* New York, 1931.

KOETTGEN, A. *Das deutsche Berufsbeamtentum und die parlamentarische Demokratie.* Berlin, Leipzig, 1928.

LAFEUILLADE, J. *Les grandes lois de l'organisation. Le XVIII⁰ siècle. L'évolution militaire organique.* Paris, 1937.

LAIRD, D. M. *The Psychology of Selecting Men.* New York, 1925.

LASKI, H. J. *The Limitations of the Expert.* (Fabian Tract No. 235.) London, 1931.

—— "Bureaucracy": *Enc. of the Social Sciences.*

—— "The Problem of Administrative Areas": *Smith College Studies on History.* Northampton, 1918.

LINDSAY, A. D. "The Organization of Labour in the Army in France during the War and its Lessons" in his *Christianity and Economics*, London, 1933.

LINDSELL, W. G. *Military Organization and Administration.* 16th ed. Aldershot, 1936.

MOSHER, W. E., and KINGSLEY, J. D. *Public Personnel Administration.* New York, London, 1936.

NATIONAL INSTITUTE OF PUBLIC ADMINISTRATION. *A Bibliography of Public Administration*, ed. by Greer, S. New York, London, 1926.

NORTON, H. K. *Foreign Office Organization. A Comparison of the British, French, German, and Italian Foreign Office Organizations with that of the Department of State of the United States of America.* (*Annals of the Amer. Acad. of Political and Social Science*, vol. 143, Suppl.). Philadelphia, 1929.

POTTER, P. B. "International Organization": *Enc. of the Social Sciences.*

—— *An Introduction to the Study of International Organization.* 4th ed. New York, 1932.

ROBSON, W. A. *From Patronage to Proficiency in the Public Service. An Inquiry into Professional Qualifications and Methods of Recruitment in the Civil Service and in the Municipal Service.* The Fabian Society, London, 1922.

SHARP, W. R. *The French Civil Service : Bureaucracy in Transition.* New York, 1930.

SHELDON, O. *The Philosophy of Management.* London, 1923.

SIMON, Sir Ernest D. *A City Council from Within.* With a preface by Graham Wallas. London, 1926.

WALKER, Harvey. *Training Public Employees in Great Britain.* Commission of Inquiry on Public Service Personnel, Monograph 6. New York, London, 1935.

WEBER, A. "Der Beamte" in his *Ideen zur Staats- und Kultursoziologie.* pp. 81–102. Karlsruhe, 1927.

WEBER, G. A. "Organized Efforts for the Improvement of Methods of Administration in the United States": *Institute for Government Research, Studies in Administration.* New York, 1919.

WEBER, M. "Bürokratie" in his Wirtschaft und Gesellschaft in *Grundriss der Sozialökonomik*, vol. iii. Tübingen, 1925.

WHITE, L. *Introduction to the Study of Public Administration.* New York, 1926.

—— BLAND, Ch. H., COSTBERG, F., and Others. *The Civil Service in the Modern State* (*Great Britain, Canada, France, Germany, Australia, Japan, etc.*). Chicago, 1930.

—— "Trends on Public Administration": *Recent Social Trends Monographs.* New York, 1933.

—— *The Prestige Value of Public Employment.* Chicago, 1929.

WILLOUGHBY, W. F. *Principles of Public Administration.* Baltimore, 1927.

WIDENFELD, Kurt. *Kapitalismus und Beamtentum.* Berlin, Leipzig, 1932.

Cf. also I, 2 ; III, 2, *c* ; III, 4, *a* ; III, 6 ; IV, 1 ; IV, 5.

(*c*) *Constitution and Government.*

ARNOLD, T. W. *The Symbols of Government.* Yale Univ. Press, New Haven, 1935.

BAGEHOT, W.   *The English Constitution.*   Oxford, 1928.

BARTHELEMY, J.   *Le rôle du pouvoir executif dans les républiques modernes.*   Paris, 1906.

BEARD, Ch. A.   *An Economic Interpretation of the Constitution.*   New York, 1913.

BECKERATH, V. H.   " Politische und Wirtschaftsverfassung " in *Festgabe für Werner Sombart.*   München, 1933.

BONNARD, R., D'HAUCOURT, G., COUZINET, P., WALINE, M., ROUSSEAU, C., MOUSKHELI, M., DELPECH, H., LEDUC, G., WEÏLLER, J., PRADELLE, P. de la.   "La Réforme de l'état."   *Annales du droit et des sciences sociales,* 1934.

DARESTE DE LA CHAVANNE, F. R.   *Les constitutions modernes.*   5 vols.   Paris, 1928–1931.

FINER, H.   *The Theory and Practice of Modern Government.*   London, 1932.

FOLLETT, M. P.   *The New State.   Group Organization the Solution of Popular Government.*   New York, 1918.

FRIEDRICH, C. J.   *Constitutional Government and Politics. Nature and Development.*   New York, London, 1937.

GAUS, J. M., WHITE, L. D., DEMOCK, M. E.   *The Frontiers of Public Administration.*   Chicago, 1936.

GOOCH, R. K.   " The French Parliamentary Committee System."   *Publications of the University of Virginia Institute for Research in the Social Sciences.*   Institute Monograph No. 21.   New York, London, 1935.

HINTZE, O.   " Weltgeschichtliche Bedingungen der Repräsentativverfassung " :   *Historische Zeitschrift,* vol. 143, 1939.

HOLCOMBE, A. N.   *State Government in the United States.*   3rd edition.   New York, 1931.

JENNINGS, W. I.   *The Law and the Constitution.*   2nd ed. Revised and enlarged.   London, 1938.

LASKI, H. J.   " The British Cabinet ; a Study of its Personnel, 1801–1924 " :   *Fabian Tracts,* No. 223. London, 1928.

—— *A Grammar of Politics,* 2nd edition.   London, 1929.

—— *Parliamentary Government in England.* London, 1938.

LOWELL, A. L.   *Public Opinion and Popular Government.*   New edition.   New York, 1916.

MCIVER, R. M.   *The Modern State.*   Oxford, 1926.

MITRANY, D.   *The Progress of International Government.*   London, 1933.

MONZIE, A. de.   *L'état Moderne.   L'encyclopédie Française,* vol. x.   Paris, 1935.

OGG, F. A.   *European Governments and Politics.*   New York, 1934.

ROBSON, W. A.   *Justice and Administrative Law.   A Study of the British Constitution.*   London, 1928.

SCHINDLER, E.   *Verfassung und soziale Struktur.*   Zürich, 1932.

WILLOUGHBY, W. F. *An Introduction to the Study of the Government of Modern States.* New York, 1919.

ZIMMERN, A. E. *Nationality and Government.* London, 1918.

Cf. also V, 1–3 ; VI.

III. 5. THE GUIDANCE OF PUBLIC OPINION, PRESS, AND PROPAGANDA AS SOCIAL TECHNIQUES.

AMERICAN SOCIETY OF NEWSPAPER EDITORS. " Problems of Journalism " : *Proceedings,* published annually, 1925.

ANGELL, Sir Norman. *The Press and the Organization of Society.* London, 1922.

BERNEYS, E. *Propaganda.* New York, 1928–1936.

BERTKAU, F. " Tendencies Toward Financial Concentration in the International Newspaper Field " : *Journalism Quarterly,* June, 1933.

BIDDLE, W. W. " A Psychological Definition of Propaganda " : *Journ. of Abnorm. Psychol. and Social Psychol.,* vol. 26, 1931.

—— *Propaganda and Education.* New York, 1932.

BOEMER, K. *Internationale Bibliographie des Zeitungswesens.* Leipzig, 1932.

CHILDS, H. L. *A Reference Guide to the Study of Public Opinion.* Princeton, 1934.

DOOB, L. *Propaganda.* New York, 1935.

HANDBUCH DER WELTPRESSE. *Eine Darstellung des Zeitungswesens aller Länder.* 3rd ed. Leipzig, Frankfurt a. M., 1937.

INDEPENDENT LABOUR PARTY. *The Capitalist Press : Who Owns It and Why ?*

INSTITUT DE SCIENCE DE LA PRESSE DE L'UNIVERSITÉ DE PARIS (ed.). *Cahiers de la presse.* Paris.

INSTITUTE OF PROPAGANDA ANALYSIS. *The Group Leader's Guide to Propaganda Analysis.* New York, 1938.

—— *Propaganda Techniques of German Fascism.* New York, 1938.

—— *The Fine Art of Propaganda. A Study of Father Coughlin's Speeches* (ed. by Lee, A. M., and Lee, E. E.). New York, 1939.

LASSWELL, H. D. *Propaganda Technique in the World War.* London, 1927.

——, CASEY, R. D., SMITH, B. L. *Propaganda and Promotional Activities. An Annotated Bibliography.* Minneapolis, 1935.

LENIN, V. I. *Agitation und Propaganda.* Ein Sammelband. Wien (Verl. für Literatur und Politik), 1929.

LLOYD, A. H. " Newspaper Conscience : A Study in Half Truths " : *Amer. Journ. of Sociol.,* vol. 27, 1921.

LUEDDECKE, Th. *Die Tageszeitung als Mittel der Staatsführung.* Hamburg, 1933.

LUMLEY, F. E. *The Propaganda Menace.* New York, London, 1933.

MACPHERSON, W. *The Psychology of Persuasion.* London, 1920.

MARX, F. M. " Propaganda and Dictatorship " : *Annals of the American Academy of Political and Social Science,* vol. 179, May, 1935.

RASSACK, J. *Psychology de l'opinion et de la propagande politique.* Paris, 1927.

ROSENSTOCK, E. *Abbau der politischen Lüge.* 1924.

RUEHLMANN, P. *Kulturpropaganda : Grundsätzliche Darlegungen und Auslandsbeobachtungen.* Charlottenburg, 1919.

SCHOENEMANN, F. *Die Kunst der Massenbeeinflussung in den Vereinigten Staaten von Amerika.* Berlin–Leipzig, 1924.

SCHULER, E. " Recent Works on Propaganda " : *Social Forces,* vol. 15, No. 2, Dec., 1936.

STERN-RUBARTH, E. *Die Propaganda als politisches Instrument.* Berlin, 1921.

STRONG, E. K. " Control of Propaganda as a Psychological Problem " : *Scientific Monthly,* vol. 14, 1922.

WILHELM, Donald. " The Lobby in Washington " in *Readings in Public Opinion,* ed. by Graves, W. Brooke, New York, 1928.

WILLEY, M. M. *The Country Newspaper. A Study of Socialization and Newspaper Content.* London, 1926.

ZIMMERMANN, W. *Die Englische Presse zum Ausbruch des Weltkrieges.* Berlin, 1928.

YOUNG, K. and LAWRENCE, D. Bibliography on Censorship and Propaganda. (Univ. of Oregon Journalism Series, vol. 1, No. 1.) Eugene, 1928.

Cf. also 7, *c* ; V, 1–3.

III. 6. SOCIAL WORK AS A SOCIAL TECHNIQUE.

ACHINGER, H. " Fürsorge und Weltanschauung " : *Zentralblatt für Jugendrecht,* 1930–1.

CHAPIN, F. S. " Research Memorandum on Social Work in the Depression " : *Studies in the Social Aspects of the Depression.* Social Science Research Council. New York.

CLEMENT-BROWN, S. " The Methods of Social Case Workers " in *The Study of Society,* ed. by F. C. Bartlett *et al.* London, 1939.

FARIS, E., LAUNE, F., TODD, A. J. (ed.). *Intelligent Philanthropy.*

HAINES, A. J. *Health Work in Soviet Russia.* New York, 1928.

INSTITUTE FOR JUVENILE RESEARCH, Staff of. *Child Guidance Procedures. Methods and Techniques Employed at the Institute for Juvenile Research.* New York, London, 1937.

INTERNATIONAL LABOUR OFFICE. *International Survey of the Social Services*, vol. 1. Geneva, 1936.

KARPF, M. J. *The Scientific Basis of Social Work*. New York, 1928.

KLOPFER, B. *Bibliographische Einführung in die Heilpadagogik*. Erfurt, 1930.

KOESTERS, H. *Die Wandlungstendenzen der deutschen und englischen Wohlfahrtspolitik seit der Jahrhundertswende*. A Thesis. Emsdetten, 1935.

LEE, P. R. *Social Work as Cause and Function; and Other Papers*. New York School of Social Work Publication. New York, 1937.

MCIVER, R. M. *The Contribution of Sociology to Social Work*. (The Forbes Lectures of the New School of Social Work.) Oxford University Press, London, 1931.

MARCUS, Grace. " How Case Work Training can be Adapted to meet the Worker's Personal Problems " : *Mental Hygiene*, vol. 11, No. 3, July, 1927.

MYRICK, H. L. " The Non Verbal Elements in the Interview " : *Social Forces*, vol. 6, 1927–8.

NEWSHOLME, A. *Evolution of Preventive Medicine*. Baltimore, 1927.

ODENCRANTZ, L. C. *The Social Worker in Family, Medical, and Psychiatric Social Work*. New York–London.

QUEEN, S. *Social Work in the Light of History*. Philadelphia, 1922.

—— " Social Interaction in the Interview. An Experiment " : *Social Forces*, vol. 6, 1928.

RICHMOND, Mary. *Social Diagnosis*. New York, 1917.

ROBINSON, V. " Some Difficulties in Analysing Social Interaction in the Interview " : *Social Forces*, vol. 6, 1927–8.

—— *A Changing Psychology in Social Case Work*. Social Study Series. University of North Carolina. 1930.

RUSHMORE, E. M. *Social Workers Guide to the Serial Publications of Representative Social Agencies*. New York, 1911.

SCHERPNER, H. *Fürsorge und Politik*. Berlin, 1933.

SHEFFIELD, A. D. *The Social Case History : Its Construction and Content*. New York, 1920.

—— " What Is the Case Worker Really Doing ? " : *Journal of Social Forces*, vol. 1, 1924.

—— *Social Insight in Case Situations*, in *The Social Worker's Library*, ed. by J. L. Gillin. New York, 1937.

SIMON, H. *Aufgaben und Ziele der neuzeitlichen Wohlfahrtspflege*. Berlin, 1922.

TAFT, Jessie. " The Use of Transfer within the Limits of the Office Interview " : *The Family*, vol. 5, Oct., 1924.

TRUHEL, K. *Sozialbeamte. Ein Beitrag zur Sozio-analyse der Bürokratie.* A Thesis. Frankfurt a. Main, 1933. Sagan (Benjamin Krause), 1934.

WELLS, F. L. "The Systematic Observation of the Personality": *Psychological Review*, vol. 21, 1914.

WICKWAR, W. H. *The Social Services. A Historical Survey.* London, 1936.

WILLIAMSON, M. A. *The Social Worker in Group Work.* New York, London, 1929.

WINSLOW, C. E. A. *The Evolution and Significance of the Modern Public Health Campaign.* New Haven, 1923.

WRONSKY, S. and KRONFELDT, A. *Sozialtherapie und Psychotherapie in den Methoden der Fürsorge.* Berlin, 1932.

—— and MUTHESIUS. *Methoden individualisierender Fürsorge in Deutschland. Vorbericht zur Intern. Konferenz für Wohlfahrtspflege und Sozialpolitik in Paris* 9–13, Juli, 1928. *Dritte Sektion.*

YOUNG, P. V. *Interviewing in Social Work.* New York, London, 1935.

Cf. also III, 1, *d–f*; III, 7, *d*; IV, 5.

III. 7. EDUCATION AS A MEANS OF SOCIAL TECHNIQUE.

(a) *Sociology of Education.*

ADAMS, Sir John. *Modern Developments in Educational Practice.* London, 1922.

ANSPACH, C. L., and CONGDON, W. H. *Problems of Educational Sociology.* New York, 1935.

ASHBY, A. W. *The Sociological Background of Adult Education in Rural Districts.* London, 1935.

BEAR, R. M. *The Social Functions of Education.* New York, 1937.

BUSEMANN, A. *Handbuch der pädagogischen Milieu-kunde.* Halle a.d.S., 1932.

CERTAIN, C. C. "Some Practical Applications of Sociology to Education": *Publications of the American Sociological Society*, vol. 17, 1923.

CHILDS, J. L. *Education and the Philosophy of Experimentation.* New York, London, 1931.

COUNTS, G. S. *The American Road to Culture. A Social Interpretation of Education in the United States.* 2nd ed., New York, 1930.

—— *Secondary Education and Industrialism (The Inglis Lecture.)* Cambridge (Mass.). Harvard University Press, 1929.

—— *The Social Foundation of Education. (Report of the Commission on the Social Studies*, Part IX.) New York, 1934.

COUNTS, G. S. and BEARD, C. H. *Education in the Industrial Age*: Report of the Commission on the Social Studies. American Historical Association.

CUBBERLEY, E. P. *Changing Conceptions of Education.* Boston, 1909.

CURRY, W. B. *The School and a Changing Civilization.* London, 1934.

CURTI, M. E. *The Social Ideas of American Educators. Report of the Commission on the Social Studies,* Part X. New York (Scribner), 1935.

DEWEY, J. *The School and Society.* Chicago, 1910.

DOBBS, A. F. *Education and Social Movements, 1700–1850.* London, 1919.

DOERING, W. O. *Psychologie der Schulklasse. Eine empirische Untersuchung.* Osterwick am Harz, (A. W. Zickfeldt, Verl.,) 1927.

DURKHEIM, E. *Education et sociologie.* Paris, 1922.

EVANS, J. M. *Social and Psychological Aspects of Primitive Education.* London, 1932.

FINNEY, R. L. *A Sociological Philosophy of Education.* New York, 1928.

FOSTER, R. G. " Family Life Education in Democratic Society " : *Social Forces,* vol. 17, 1939.

GOOD, A. *Sociology and Education.* New York, London.

JACKS, M. L. *Education as a Social Factor.* London, 1937.

JUDD, Ch. H. *Education and Social Progress.* New York, 1934.

HOYLER, A. *Gentleman Ideal und Gentleman Erziehung vornehmlich in der Renaissance.* München, 1938.

KARSEN, F. " Neue Literatur über Gesellschaft und Erziehung " : *Zeitschrift für Sozialforschung,* vol. i, 1934, pp. 82–6.

—— " Neue amerikanische Literatur über Gesellschaft und Erziehung " : *Zeitschrift für Sozialforschung,* vol. 8, 1939.

KILPATRICK, W. H. *The Teacher and Society. First Yearbook of the John Dewey Society.* New York, London, 1937.

—— *Education and the Social Crisis.* New York, 1932.

KRUCKENBERG, A. Die Schulklasse als Lebensform : *Zeitschrift für pädag. Psychol. und experimentelle Pädagogik,* vol. 25, 1924.

—— *Die Schulklasse.* Leipzig, 1926.

LANDFORD, H. D. *Education and the Social Conflict :* New York, 1936.

LECHTENBERG, P. *Deutsche Einflüsse auf die Englische Pädagogik.* Osterwick am Harz, 1930.

LESER, H. *Das pädagogische Problem in der Geistesgeschichte der Neuzeit.* München, Berlin, 1925.

LINDEMAN, E. C. *Social Education.* New York, 1933.

LOWNDES, G. A. N. *The Silent Social Revolution. An Account of the Expansion of Public Education in England and Wales, 1895–1935.* London, 1937.

NEWLON, J. H. *Educational Administration as Social Policy. Report of the Commission on the Social Studies*, Part VIII. New York, 1934.

NOHL, H. and PALLAT, L. *Handbuch der Pädagogik*, esp. vol. 2, chapter 3 : " Die soziologischen Grundlagen der Erziehung." Langensalza, Berlin, Leipzig, 1929.

PATTERSON, S. H., CHOATE, E. A., and PRUNNER, E. de S. *The School in American Society*. (Intern. Textbook Company), Scranton, 1936.

PETERS, C. C. *Foundations of Educational Sociology*. New York, 1927.

PETERS, Charles. " Sociological Bases of Education for Culture " : *Publications of the Amer. Sociological Society*, vol. 17, 1924.

PIAGET, J. *Social Evolution and the New Education*. (*Education To-morrow*.) London, 1933.

RIPPE, F. *Die Pädagogik Deweys*. A Thesis. Breslau, 1934.

RUGG, H. O. " The Problems of Contemporary Life as a Basis for Curriculum Making " : *Twenty-second Yearbook of The National Society for the Study of Education*, Part II. Bloomingyon, Illinois, 1923.

—— *Culture and Education in America*. New York, 1931.

—— *Changing Governments, Changing Cultures*, 1934.

—— *American Life and the School Curriculum. Next Step towards School of Living*. Boston, New York, ed. 1936.

RUSSELL, B. *Education and the Social Order*. London, 1932.

SCHAIRER, R. *Education and the Social Crisis in Europe*. 1937.

SCHMIDT, T. Hartefeld. *Das Erziehungsziel als Ausdruck des soziales Lebens*. 1931.

SCHROEDER, H. *Soziologie der Volksschulklasse. Vom Gemeinschaftsleben der Volksschulkinder*. Halle, 1928.

SNEDDEN, D. *Educational Sociology*. London, 1923.

—— " Sociology a Basic Science to Education " : *Publications of the Amer. Sociological Society*, vol. 17, 1923.

—— *Sociological Determination of Objectives in Education*. Philadelphia, London, 1921.

YOUNG, K. Primitive Social Norms in Present Day Education : *Social Forces*, 5th July, 1927.

WALLER, W. *The Sociology of Teaching*. New York, 1932.

WEIL, H. *Die Entstehung des deutschen Bildungsprinzips*. Schriften zur Philosophie und Soziologie. Ed. by Mannheim, K., Bonn, 1930.

WHITEHOUSE, J. H. *The English Public School*. (*A Symposium with a Bibliography*.) London, 1919.

Cf. also III, 1, *a-f* ; III, 7, *b-e* ; IV, 3-5 ; V, 1-6 ; IV.

(b) *Psychology of Education.*

ALLEN, A. B., in collaboration with WILLIAMS, E. H. *The Psychology of Punishment : The New School Discipline.* London, 1936.

ANDERSON, V. Y., and KENNEDY, W. M. *Psychiatry in Education.* New York, London, 1932.

COHEN, J. I. and TRAVERS, R. M. W. " Psychology and Modern Education " in *Educating for Democracy,* ed. by the same authors. London, 1939.

DEWEY, J. *Moral Principles in Education.* Boston, 1909.

GATES, A. Y. " Recent Advances in Educational Psychology." At the Request of the American Association for the Advancement of Science : *School and Society,* vol. 29, 1929.

GRAY, J. S. *Psychological Foundations of Education.* New York, 1935.

HUTCHINS, R. M. " Ideals in Education " : *Amer. Journ. of Sociol.,* vol. 43, 1937.

JENNINGS, H. S., WATSON, J. B., MEYER, A., THOMAS, I. *Suggestions of Modern Science Concerning Education.* New York, 1918.

LEIGHTON, J. A. *Individuality and Education.* New York, London, 1928.

LEWIN, Kurt. " Psycho-Sociological Problems of a University Group " : *Character and Personality,* vol. 3, 1935.

NUNN, T. P. *Education : Its Data and First Principles.* 2nd ed. London, 1930.

OTIS, W. Caldwell, SKINNER, C. L. E., TIETZ, J. W. *Biological Foundations of Education.* Boston, 1931.

POWERS, F. F., and UHL, W. L. *Psychological Principles of Education.* New York, London, 1933.

PRESSEY, S. L. *Psychology and the New Education.* New York, London, 1933.

RICKMAN, J. *Bringing Up Children. A Symposium by Five Psychoanalysts.* New York, 1936.

ROWE, St. *Habit Formation and the Science of Teaching.* New York, 1909.

SCHMIDT, V. *Psychoanalytische Erziehung in Soviet-Russland. Bericht über das Kinderheim Laboratorium in Moskau.* Leipzig, Wien, Zürich, 1924.

STORMZAND, M. J. *Progressive Methods of Teaching.* Boston, 1924.

THOMAS, R. " The New Psychology at Work in the School " : *New Era,* July–August, 1936.

THORNDIKE, E. L. *Educational Psychology,* 3 vols. Teachers' College, Columbia University, New York, 1913–14.

TROW, E. *Character Education in Soviet Russia.* Michigan, 1934.

ULICH, R. " Psychology and Education " : *Mental Hygiene,* vol. 19, 1935.

VALENTINE, C. W. " Educational Psychology in the United Kingdom " in *A Review of Educational Thought, etc.* University of London, Institute of Education, London, 1936.

VARIOUS AUTHORS. " The Making of the Free Personality " : *New Era*, vol. 17, No. 8, 1936.

VOELKER, I. F. *The Function of Ideals and Attitudes in Social Education.* An experimental Study. A Thesis. Teachers' College, Columbia University, New York, 1921.

Cf. also III, 1, *a–f* ; III, 2, *d* ; III, 6 ; III, 7, *a* ; III, 7, *c–e* ; IV, 4.

(c) Education and Politics.

AMERICAN ACADEMY OF POLITICAL AND SOCIAL SCIENCE. *Education for Social Control.* Annals for 1933.

AMERICAN HISTORICAL ASSOCIATION. *Conclusions and Recommendations of the Commission on the Social Studies.* New York, 1934.

BIDDLE, W. W. *Propaganda and Education.* Teachers' College, Contribution to Education, No. 521. Columbia Univ., New York, 1932.

CAMPAGNAC, E. T. *Education in its Relation to the Common Purposes of Humanity.* London, 1925.

CLARKE, F. *Essays in the Politics of Education.* Cape Town and Johannesburg, 1923.

DEWEY, John. *Democracy and Education.* New York, 1916.

DUBOIS, M. *L'aspiration ouvrière vers la culture et les loisirs des travailleurs.* Paris, 1937.

ELLIS, E. (ed.). *Education Against Propaganda.* National Council for the Social Studies Yearbook. Publ. by the Council of Harvard University, Cambridge (Mass.), 1937.

HANS, N. A. *Educational Traditions in the English Speaking Countries.* London, 1938.

—— *The Principles of Educational Policy.* 2nd ed. London, 1933.

HANSEN, A. O. *Liberalism and American Education in the Eighteenth Century.* New York, 1926.

HART, J. K. *Democracy in Education. A Social Interpretation of the History of Education.* New York (Century Co.), 1918.

HESSEN, S. Das kommunistische Bildungsideal und seine Wandlungen. *Neue Jahrbücher für Wissenschaft und Jugendbildung.* 1930.

HOERNLE, E. *Grundfragen der proletarischen Erziehung.* Berlin (Verlag der Jugendinternationale), 1929.

LUNARTSCHARSKY, A. *Die Kulturaufgaben der Arbeiterklasse. Allgemeinmenschliche Kultur und Klassenkultur.* Berlin, Wilmersdorf, 1919.

MACMURRAY, J. " The Christian Movement in Education " in *Problems of Modern Education*, ed. by Laborde, E. D. Cambridge, 1939.

NATIONAL COUNCIL FOR THE SOCIAL STUDIES. *Education Against Propaganda* (ed. by Ellis, E., published by the Council of Harvard Univ.). Cambridge (Mass.), 1937.

NORWOOD, C. *The English Educational System*. London, 1928.

PRING, Beryl. *Education, Capitalist and Socialist*. London, 1937.

REISNER, E. H. *Nationalism and Education Since 1789*. New York, 1922.

SIMON, E. D., HUBBARD, Eva M. *School Systems. Training for Citizenship*. Oxford University Press, London, 1935.

SPRANGER, E. " Der Zusammenhang von Politik und Pädagogik in der Neuzeit " : *Deutsche Schule*. 1914–16.

STURM, K. F. *Deutsche Erziehung. Von der pädagogischen Reformbewegung zur völkischen und politischen Erziehung*. 4th ed. Berlin, 1938.

WORLD ASSOCIATION FOR ADULT EDUCATION. International Handbook of Adult Education. London.

ZINSSER, H. " What is Liberal Education ? " : *School and Society*, vol. 45, 1937.

Cf. also III, 2, *d* ; III, 7, *a* ; III, 7, *e* ; V, 1–3 ; V, 6 ; VI.

(d) Education, Re-education, Post-education.

ANDREWS, R. and PEABODY, M. E. *Parent Child Relationship*. New York, 1930.

BAZELEY, E. T. *Homer Lane and the Little Commonwealth*. London.

BEYER, R. " Menschliche Reife und Unreife in ihrer Beziehung zum Konkreten " : *Die Erziehung*, vol. 6, 1931.

BLANCHARD, Ph. and PAYNTER. " Changing the Child's Behavior by Direct Methods " : *Journ. of Applied Sociology*, vol. 9, 1924–5.

BLUM, E. *Arbeiterbildung als existentielle Bildung*. Bern, Leipzig, 1935.

BOEKE, K. *The Children's Workshop Community at Bilthoven*. Ilford, Essex.

BOVET, P. *Vingt ans de vie. L'Institut Jean Jacques Rousseau de 1912 à 1932*. Paris, 1932.

BOYD, W. (ed.). *Towards a New Education*. A record and Synthesis of the discussions on the New Psychology and the Curriculum at the Fifth World Conference of the New Education Fellowship held at Elsinore, Denmark, in Aug., 1929. London and New York, 1930.

BRITISH INSTITUTE OF ADULT EDUCATION. *Adult Education in Great Britain and the U.S.A.* A Symposium arranged by Williams, W. E. London, 1938.

BURGER, E. W. *Arbeitspädagogik. Geschichte-Kritik-Wegweisung.* Leipzig, Berlin, 1914.

BURT, C. *The Young Delinquent.* New York, 1925.

—— *The Backward Child :* University of London Press, London, 1937.

CAMERON, A. M. " The Lincoln Experiment " in *Civilization and the Unemployed.* 2nd ed. London, 1935.

COLE, L. *Psychology of Adolescence.* New York, 1936.

DUBOIS, M. *L'aspiration ouvrière vers la culture et les loisirs des travailleurs.* Paris, 1937.

FERRIÈRE, A. *La liberté de l'enfant à l'école nouvelle.* Bruxelles, 1928.

—— *The Activity School.* New York, 1928.

The Francis W. Parker School Yearbooks. New York.

FREINET, C. " L'imprimerie à l'école " : *L'Ere Nouvelle,* Oct., 1936.

GOLDSTEIN, J. " Das Irrationale und die Volksbildung," in his *Aus dem Vermächtnis des Neunzehnten Jahrhunderts.* Berlin, 1922.

GLUECK, B. " Significance of Parental Attitudes for the Destiny of the Individual " : *Mental Hygiene,* vol. xii, 1928.

HÄBERLIN, P. *Wege und Irrwege der Erziehung.* Basel, 1918.

HAMAÏDE, A. *La méthode Decroly.* (Délacheaux and Niestle.) Neuchatel–Paris, 1922.

—— *The Decroly Class. A Contribution to Elementary Education.* London, Toronto, 1925.

HARTMANN, G., and SHUMAKER, A. *Creative Expression. The Development of Children in Art, Music, Literature and Dramatics* : ed. for the Progressive Education Association. New York, 1932.

HEALY, Wm., BRUNNER, A. F., BAYLOR, E. M. H., and MURPHY, J. P. *Reconstructing Behavior in Youth.* New York, 1931.

HEIM, W. *Die Kollektiverziehung.* Berlin, 1931.

HERMES, Gertrud. *Die geistige Gestalt des marxistischen Arbeiters und die Arbeiterbildungsfrage.* Tuebingen, 1926.

HONIGSHEIM, P. *Menschenbildung und Industriepädagogik.* Mannheim, Berlin, Leipzig, 1930.

ICHHEISER, G. " Zur Psychologie des Nichtkönnens " : *Archiv für die Gesamte Psychologie,* vol. 92, 1934.

JACOBY, H. " Die Befreiung der schöpferischen Kräfte dargestellt am Beispiel der Musik " : *Das Werdende Zeitalter,* vol. 4, No. 4 (L. Klotz), Gotha, 1925.

JONES, E. "The Significance of Sublimating Processes for Education and Re-education " in his *Papers on Psychoanalysis,* 3rd ed., London, 1923.

KANITZ, O. F. *Das proletarische Kind in der bürgerlichen Gesellschaft.* Jena (Diederichs), 1925.

KELLEY, T. Oddities in the Mental Make-Up: *School and Society*, vol. 24, 1926.

KILPATRICK, W. H. *Montessori Examined.* London, 1915.
—— *Froebel's Kindergarten Principles Critically Examined.* New York, 1916.
—— (ed.). *The Educational Frontier.* New York, London, 1933.

KLEISLER, M. E. " The Behaviour of Young Children in Failure : An Experimental Attempt to Discover and to Modify Undesirable Responses of Pre-school Children to Failure " : *University of Iowa Studies*, vol. 14, 1937.

LANDAUER, K. " Intellektuelle Hemmungen ": *Zeitschrift für Psychoanalytische Pädagogik*, No. 11–12, 1930.
—— Psychosexuelle Genese der Dummheit. *Zeitschr. für Sexualwissenschaft*, 1929.

LINDEMANN, E. C. *The Meaning of Adult Education.* New York, 1926.

MACMILLAN, M. *The Nursery School.* London, Toronto, New York, 1919.

MEARNS, H. *Creative Youth.* New York, 1925.

MILLER, E. " Education for Parenthood " in *Educating for Democracy*, ed. by Cohen, J. I. and Travers, R. M. W. London, 1939.

MUNRO, Th. " Fr. Cizek and the Free Expression Method " : *Journ. of the Barnes Foundation*, vol. i, Oct., 1925.

NEILL, A. S. *The Problem Child.* London, 1934.
—— *That Dreadful School.* London, 1937.

OJEMANN, R. H. *et al.* Researches in Parent Education. *University of Iowa Studies*, New Series, No. 270, 1934. Iowa City, Iowa, 1934.

REUTER, E. B. " The Sociology of Adolescence " : *Amer. Journ. of Sociol.*, vol. 43, 1937.

REUTER, E. B., MEAD, M., FOSTER, R. G. " Sociological Research in Adolescence " : *Amer. Journ. of Sociol.*, vol. 42, 1936.

ROMAN, F. W. *The New Education in Europe.* London, 1930.

RUEHLE, Otto. *Das proletarische Kind.* München, 1911.

RUGG, H. O., and SHUMAKER, A. *The Child Centered School. An Appraisal of the New Education.* London, 1928.

SCHMALHAUSEN, S. (ed.) *Why We Misbehave.* New York, 1928.

SCHWARZENBERGER, S. *Die Bedeutung der modernen Erziehungswissenschaft für das juristische Strafproblem.* Heidelberg, 1933.

THURSTON, F. M. *A Bibliography of Family Relationships.* New York (National Council of Parent Education), 1932.

WASHBUNE, C., and MEARNS, M. *New Schools in the Old World.* New York, 1926.

WHEELER, O. *The Psychological Bases of Adult Education.* National Union of Teachers, London, 1938.

WILSON, L. L. " Experimental Schools " : *School and Society*, vol. 31, No. 809, 1930.

Cf. also III, 1, *a–f* ; III, 6 ; IV, 2 ; IV, 3 ; IV, 5.

(e) Educational Planning.

BEARD, Ch. A. " A Charter for the Social Sciences. (Report of the Commission on the Social Studies.)" : *American Historical Association.* New York, 1932.

BETTS, G. L., FRAZIER, B. W., and GANBLE, G. L. Selected Bibliography on the Education of Teachers. National Survey on the Education of Teachers. Bulletin 1933, No. 10. Washington, 1932.

BOARD OF EDUCATION. Reports. London.

BODE, Boyd. " Education and Social Change " : *Progressive Education.* 1934.

BRAND, H. W. " Equality of Opportunity " : *Adult Educational Quarterly*, June, 1935.

BUREAU INTERNATIONAL D'EDUCATION, Geneva. Monthly Bulletins.

CHAPIN, S. (ed.). " Symposium on Educational Planning " : *Journ. of Educat. Sociology*, vol. vii, No. 4, Dec., 1934.

CHAPMAN, J. C., and COUNTS, G. S. *Principles of Education.* Boston, 1924.

CLARK, H. F. Economic Theory and Correct Occupational Distribution. New York, Teachers' College, Columbia Univ., 1931.

CLARKE, F., and Others. *A Review of Educational Thought.* London, 1936.

COHEN, J. I., and TRAVERS, R. M. (ed.). *Educating for Democracy.* London, 1939.

COOK, K. M., and REYNOLDS, F. E. The Education of Native and Minority Groups. A Bibliography, 1923–1932. Washington (U.S. Government Printing Office), 1933. U.S.A. Department of the Interior, Office of Education Bulletin, 1933.

COUNTS, G. S. " Education in Soviet Russia " in *Soviet Russia in the 2nd Decade* (ed. by Stuart Chase and others). London, 1928.

EDUCATIONAL POLICIES COMMISSION. *A Bibliography on Education in the Depression.* Social Science Research Council, New York, 1937.

—— *Research Memorandum on Education in the Depression.* Social Science Research Council, New York, 1937.

GRAY, J. L., and MOSHINSKY, P. " Ability and Opportunity in English Education " : *The Sociological Review*, vol. 39, Apr., 1935.

—— " The Measurements of Educational Opportunity " : *Adult Educational Quarterly*, Sept., 1935.

GRAY, R. A. Bibliography of Research Studies in Education Bulletins. United States Department of the Interior. Office of Education. H. L. Ickes, Secretary, J. W. Studebaker, Commissioner. U.S. Government Printing Office, Washington, 1935.

HAMLEY, H. R. "Education and Research" in *Educating for Democracy*, ed. by Cohen, J. I. and Travers, R. M. V. London, 1939.

HANS, N. A., and GESSEN, S. I. *Educational Policy in Soviet Russia.* London, 1930.

HARTOG, Sir Philip. "The Place of Examinations in the Social System" in *Educating for Democracy*, ed. by J. I. Cohen and R. M. V. Travers. London, 1939.

—— and RHODES, E. C. An Examination of Examinations. International Institute Examination Inquiry. London, 1935.

H.M. STATIONERY OFFICE. *Education of the Consumer.* London, 1935.

INSTITUTE OF EDUCATION OF THE UNIVERSITY OF LONDON. *Year Book of Education.*

INTERNATIONAL INSTITUTE OF TEACHERS COLLEGE, Columbia Univ. *Educational Yearbook.*

JONES, E. J. *Some Aspects of Adult Education in Italy.* London, 1934.

KANDEL, I. L. *Comparative Education.* Boston, 1933.

—— *Conflicting Theories of Education.* New York, 1938.

—— *The Making of Nazis.* New York, 1936.

—— "Comparative Education" in *Educating for Democracy*, ed. by Cohen, J. I. and Travers, R. M. V. London, 1939.

KELLER, F. J., and VITELES, M. S. *Vocational Guidance throughout the World : A Comparative Survey.* New York, 1937.

KELLY, F. J. "The Place of Education in Social–Economic Planning": *School and Society*, vol. 36, 1932.

KILPATRICK, W. H. *Education for a Changing Civilization.* Three lectures, etc. New York (McMillan), 1926.

KING, B. *Changing Man : The Education System of the U.S.S.R.* London, 1936.

KOTSCHNIG, W. M. *Unemployment in the Learned Professions. An International Study of Occupational and Educational Planning.* London, 1937.

KOTSCHNIG, W. M., and PRYS, E. *The University in a Changing World.* London, 1932.

LABORDE, E. D. (ed.). *Problems in Modern Education.* Cambridge, 1939.

LEEUW, J. J. *The Task of Educating in a World Crisis.* New Education Fellowship. London, 1932.

LINDSAY, K. *Social Progress and Educational Waste.* London, 1926.

MARRARO, H. R. The New Education in Italy. Current History, vol. 38. 1933.

NATIONAL RESOURCES COMMITTEE. Research—a National Resource, I : Relation of the Federal Government to Research. Washington, 1938.

PINKEVICH, A. P. The New Education in the Soviet Republic. New York, 1929.

—— Science and Education in the U.S.S.R. London, 1935.

SANDIFORD, P. M. (ed.). Comparative Education Studies of the Educational Systems of Six Modern Nations. London, Toronto, 1918.

SIEMSEN, A. Beruf und Erziehung. Berlin, 1926.

TAWNEY, R. H. Education : the Socialist Policy. London (Independent Labour Party), 1924.

—— Some Thought on the Economics of Public Education. (L. T. Hobhouse Memorial Trust Lectures.) London, 1938.

—— The School Leaving Age and Exemptions. 1936.

—— (ed.) Secondary Education for All. London, 1922.

TUROSIENSKI, S. K. Foreign and Comparative Education. A List of References. Foreign and Comparative Education, Bulletin No. 10, 1934. United States Dept. of the Interior. Washington, 1934.

U.S.A. DEPARTMENT OF THE INTERIOR—OFFICE OF EDUCATION (Pamphlet No. 37). Religious Education. Bibliography, Jan.–Dec., 1932. Washington, U.S. Government Printing Office.

Cf. also I, 1–2 ; V, 1–3 ; VI.

IV. SOME PROBLEMS OF SOCIAL RECONSTRUCTION.

(1) Effects of Civilization, Dehumanization, Social Isolation. Changing Attitudes toward God, the World of Nature and Man.

ADORNO, T. W. Über den Fetischcharakter in der Musik und die Regression des Hörens. Zeitschrift für Sozialforschung, vol. 7, 1938.

ARNOLD, M. Culture and Anarchy. London, 1869.

BAERWALD, R. Psychologische Faktoren des modernen Zeitgeistes. Schriften der Gesellschaft für psychologische Forschung. Leipzig, 1905.

BAIN, R. " Our Schizoid Culture " : Sociology and Social Research, vol. xix, 1935.

BELL, C. Civilization. London, 1938.

BENJAMIN, W. " L'œuvre d'art à l'époque de sa reproduction mecanisée " in Zeitschrift für Sozialforschung, vol. 5, 1930.

BIESE, A. Das Naturgefühl im Wandel der Zeiten. Leipzig, 1926.

BLACK, H. Culture and Restraint. 5th ed. London, 1909.

BUISSON, F. " Le fond religieux de la morale laïque " : Revue Pedagoguique, 1907.

BURROW, Tr. "Our Mass Neurosis": *Psychological Bulletin*, vol. 23, 1926.

CHADWICK, W. E. *Social Relationships in the Light of Christianity.* London, 1910.

CANAT, R. *Une forme du mal du siècle. Du sentiment de la solitude morale chez les romantiques et les parnassiens.* Paris, 1904.

CURTIS, L. *Civitas Dei.* London, 1938.

DILTHEY, W. "Weltanschauung und Analyse des Menschen seit der Renaissance und Reformation": *Gesammelte Schriften*, vol. 2. Leipzig, Berlin, 1914.

DOUGLASS, P. F. (ed.). *Crisis Personality and its Weltanschauung.* Poultney, 1938.

DYCKMANS, W. *Das mittelalterliche Gemeinschaftsdenken unter dem Gesichtspunkt der Totalität. Eine rechtsphilosophische Untersuchung.* Goerres Gesellschaft. Sektion für Rechts- und Staatswissenschaft. Bonn, 1937.

ELIAS, N. *Über den Prozess der Zivilisation. Soziogenetische und psychogenetische Untersuchungen.* Vol. I: *Wandlungen des Verhaltens in den weltlichen Oberschichten des Abendlandes.* Vol. 2: *Wandlungen der Gesellschaft. Entwurf zu einer Theorie der Zivilisation.* Basel, 1937–8.

FLEMMING, W. *Der Wandel des deutschen Naturgefühls vom 15. zum 18. Jahrhundert.* 1931.

FREUD, S. *Civilization and its Discontents.* London, 1930.
—— *Modern Sexual Morality and Modern Nervousness.* Translated by W. J. Robinson. New York, 1933.
—— *Civilization, War and Death.* Selection from three works, ed. by Rickmann, J. London, 1939.

FRIEDLÄNDER, L. *Ueber die Entstehung und Entwicklung des Gefühls für das Romantische in der Natur.* Leipzig, 1873.

FROMM, E. "Zum Gefühl der Ohnmacht": *Zeitschrift für Sozialforschung*, vol. 6, 1937.

GLOVER, E. G. *The Danger of Being Human. On Psychoanalysis and Social Order.* London, 1936.

HARDMAN, O. *The Ideals of Asceticism.* London, 1924.

HAZARD, R. *La crise de la conscience européenne.* 3 vols. Paris (Boivin), 1934.

HEARNSHAW, F. J. C. *Medieval Contributions to Modern Civilization.* London, 1921.

HELLWEG, M. *Der Begriff des Gewissens bei Jean Jacques Rousseau. Beitrag zu einer Kritik der politischen Demokratie.* Marburger Beiträge zur Romanischen Philologie. Heft 20.

HOFFMANN-KRAYER, E. "Entwicklung des Naturgefühls in der deutschen Dichtung und Kunst": *Studien zur vergleichenden Literaturgeschichte.* Heft 1.

HOFFMANN, P. Th. *Der mittelalterliche Mensch.* Gotha, 1922.

HORNEY, Karen. *The Neurotic Personality of Our Time.* London, 1937.

HUGHES, E. R. (ed.). *The Individual in East and West.* London, 1937.

JAN, E. von. *Die Landschaft des französischen Menschen dargestellt im französischen Schrifttum vom Mittelalter bis zum Ausgang des 18. Jahrhunderts.* " Literatur und Leben " Series, vol. 6. Weimar, 1935.

KAUTZSCH, R. *Die bildende Kunst und das Jenseits.* Jena-Leipzig, 1905.

KARDINER, A. " Security and Cultural Restraints." *The Family,* Oct., 1937.

KOWALEWSKI, A. " Studien zur Psychologie des Pessimismus " : *Grenzfragen des Nerven- und Seelenlebens,* No. 24. Wiesbaden.

LAFORGUE, R. *Libido, Angst und Zivilisation.* Wien, 1932.

LASSWELL, H. *World Politics and Personal Insecurity.* New York–London, 1935.

LOCHORE, R. A. *History of the Idea of Civilization in France, 1830–1870.* Bonn, 1935.

LOVEJOY, A. O. *A Documentary History of Primitivism and Related Ideas.* The John Hopkins University. Baltimore, 1935.

MANZ, L. Der Ordo-Gedanke. Ein Beitrag zur Frage des mittelalterlichen Staatsgedankens. *Vierteljahrsschrift für Sozial- und Wirtschaftsgeschichte.* Beiheft 53. Stuttgart, Berlin, 1937.

MARITAIN, J. *Religion and Culture.* London, 1931.

MARTIN, A. von. *Soziologie der Renaissance.* Stuttgart, 1932.

MAUS, M. " Les civilisations, éléments et formes " in *Civilisation, le mot et l'idée.* Ière semaine internationale de synthèse. 2me fasc. Paris (Renaissance du Livre), 1930.

MAUTHNER, F. *Der Atheismus und seine Geschichte im Abendlande.* 2 vols. Stuttgart, Berlin, 1920.

MISCH, G. *Geschichte der Autobiographie,* vol. 1. Leipzig, 1907.

PARK, R. E. " Magic Mentality and City Life " : *Publications of the Amer. Sociol. Society,* vol. 18, 1923.

RAINACH, Th. *et al. Religions et Sociétés,* 1905.

ROBERTSON, J. M. *A Short History of Freethought.* 2nd ed. 2 vols. London, 1906.

ROBSON, W. A. *Socialism and the Standardised Life.* (Fabian Tract, No. 219). London, 1926.

ROESSLE, W. (ed.). *Romantische Naturphilosophie.* Jena, 1926.

ROSENHAUPT, H. W. *Der deutsche Dichter um die Jahrhundertwende und seine Abgelöstheit von der Gesellschaft.* Bern–Leipzig, 1939.

ROTTWEILER, Hektor. Über Jazz. *Zeitschr. f. Sozialforschung,* vol. 5, 1936.

ROUTH, H. V. *Money, Morals and Manner as Revealed in Modern Literature.* London, 1935.

SACHS, H. *Über Naturgefühl.* Imago, 1902.

SCHEUNERT, . " Kultur und Neurose im Ausgang des 17. Jahrhunderts " : *Cyclos,* vol. 3.

SCHILDER, P. " The Analysis of Ideologies as a Psychotherapeutic Method, especially in Group Treatment " : *Amer. Journ. of Psychiatry,* vol. 93, 1936.

SCHNEIDER, H. W. *The Puritan Mind.* New York, 1930.

STRICH, W. *Der Irrationale Mensch. Studium zur Systematik der Geschichte.* Berlin, 1928.

SCHULTZE, S. *Die Entwicklung des Naturgefühls in der deutschen Literatur des XIX. Jahrhunderts.* Halle a. d. S., 1907.

—— *Das Naturgefühl der Romantik.* 2nd ed., 1911.

SIMMEL, G. *Die Philosophie des Geldes.* 2nd ed. Leipzig, 1907.

SODDY, Frederick. *Money versus Man.* London, 1931.

STEFFES, J. P. *Religion und Politik. Eine religions- und kulturwissenschaftliche Studie.* Freiburg i. B., 1929.

STEINHAUSEN, G. *Der Wandel des Gefühlslebens seit dem Mittelalter.* Hamburg, 1896.

STEINHAUSEN, S. " Fachmenschentum und Arbeitsmenschentum als Geistige Typen des letzten Herscheralters." Preussische Jahrbücher, vol. 204, Heft 3.

SUMNER, W. G. " Religion and the Mores " : *Papers and Proceedings of the Amer. Sociol. Society,* vol. 4, 1909.

THRUM, G. *Der Typ des Zerissenen. Ein Vergleich mit dem romantischen Problematiker.* " Von deutscher Poeterey " Series, vol. 10. Leipzig, 1931.

TOYNBEE, A. J. *A Study of History.* 6 vols. so far. London, 1935–1939.

TROELTSCH, E. *Social Teachings of the Christian Churches.* Transl. by Wyon, O. New York, London, 1931.

VIATLE, A. *Les sources occultes du romantisme : Illusiomisme. Theosophie.* 1928.

WEBER, A. *Kulturgeschichte als Kultursoziologie.* Leiden, 1935.

WIESER, M. *Der sentimentale Mensch.* Gotha-Stuttgart, 1924.

WILLE, W. *Studien zur Dekadenz in Romanen um die Jahrhundertwende.* Dissertation, Greifswald, 1929.

WOOLF, L. *After The Deluge.* A Study of Communal Psychology. London, 1937.

Cf. also II ; III, 1, *b–c* ; III, 1, *f* ; III, 2, *c* ; V, 5.

(2) *The Use of Leisure.*

BOYD, W. and OGILVIE, V. *The Challenge of Leisure.* (New Education Fellowship), London, 1936.

CANTRELL, H., and ALLPORT, G. W. The Psychology of Radio. New York, 1935.

DURANT, H. W. The Problems of Leisure. London, 1938.

GROOS, K. "Das Spiel als Katharsis": Zeitschr. f. Päd. Psychol. u. Exper. Pädagogik, 7th Dec., 1908.

GULICK, Luther. "Play and Democracy." Charities and the Commons, vol. 18, 1907.

HAHN, K. Education for Leisure. Oxford University Press, Oxford, 1938.

HARAP, H. "Planning the Curriculum for Leisure": Journ. of Educational Sociology, vol. 7, 1934.

LEAVIS, Q. D. Fiction and the Reading Public. London, 1932.

LONDON COUNTY COUNCIL; EDUCATIONAL COMMITTEE. School Children and the Cinema. London, 1932.

LUNDBERG, George A., KOMAROWSKY, M., McINERNY, M. A. Leisure, a Suburban Study. New York, 1934.

LYON, H. "Training for Leisure": Spectator, 20th January, 1933.

KING, C. L., and TICHENOV, F. A. The Motion Picture in its Economic and Social Aspect. Philadelphia, 1926.

PANGBURN, W. "The Worker's Leisure and His Individuality": Amer. Journ. of Sociology, vol. 27, 1921–2.

THE PAYNE FUND (Chairman: Charters, N.W.). Motion Pictures and Youth. A Series. New York.

POSTGATE, R. What to do with the B.B.C. London, 1935.

SEANBURY, W. M. The Public and the Motion Picture Industry. New York, 1926.

SOCIAL SCIENCE RESEARCH COUNCIL. "Research Memorandum on Recreation in the Depression": Studies in the Social Aspects of the Depression, by Steiner, J. F. New York.

—— "Research Memorandum on Social Aspects of Reading in the Depression": Studies in the Social Aspects of the Depression, by Waples, D. New York.

SOMBART, W. Luxus und Kapitalismus. München, Leipzig, 1922.

STEINER, J. F. Americans at Play. Recent Trends in Recreation and Leisure-Time Activities. New York, London, 1933.

STERNHEIM, A. "Leisure in the Totalitarian State": The Soc. Review, vol. 30, 1938.

STEWART, H. "The Ethics of Luxury and Leisure": Amer. Journ. of Sociology, vol. 24, 1918–19.

THOMSON, D. C. Radio is Changing Us. London, 1937.

VEBLEN, Th. B. The Theory of the Leisure Class. New York, 1912.

Cf. also IV, 1; IV, 3; IV, 5; V, and the bibliographies on sport (p. 313 n.), and on the psychological implications of the use of leisure (p. 316 n.).

(3) *Youth and Youth Movements.*

BELL, E. H. " Age Group Conflict and Our Changing Culture " : *Social Forces*, vol. 12, 1933.

BERNFED, S. *Trieb und Tradition im Jugendalter.* Leipzig, 1937.

COMMITTEE ON YOUTH PROBLEMS. *Youth—a Contemporary Bibliography with Annotations*, by Exton, E. U.S. Office of Education, Circular No. 152. Washington, 1935.

FRANK, Lawrence K. Childhood and Youth. *Recent Social Trends in United States*, vol. ii, chap. xv. New York–London, 1933.

HARTMANN, H. *Die junge Generation in Europa.* Berlin, 1930.

JUNGMANN, F. " Autorität und Sexualmoral in der freien bürgerlichen Jugendbewegung " : *Studien über Autorität und Familie*, ed. by Horkheimer, M. Paris (Alcan), 1936.

LINDSEY, B. B., and EVANS, W. *The Revolt of Modern Youth.* London, 1928.

LUETTKENS, Ch. *Die deutsche Jugendbewegung. Ein soziologischer Versuch.* Frankfurt, 1925.

MEHNERT, K. *Youth in Soviet Russia* (translated by M. Davidsohn). London, 1933.

MESSER, A. *Die freideutsche Jugendbewegung.* 5th ed. Langensalza, 1915.

REUTER, E. B., MEAD, M., FOSTER, R. G. *et al.* " Sociological Research in Adolescence " : *Amer. Journ. of Sociol.*, vol. 43, 1936.

SCHAIRER, R. *Not, Kampf, Zeil der Jugend in sieben Ländern.* Frankfurt, 1935.

THURNWALD, R. (ed.). *Die Neue Jugend.* Vol. v of *Forschungen zur Völkerpsychologie und Soziologie.* Leipzig, 1927.

WINSLOW, T. *Youth—A World Problem.* Washington, 1937.

Cf. also III, 6 ; III, 7, *d* ; IV, 1 ; IV, 4–5.

(4) *Leadership and the Sociology of Prestige and Fame.*

BOGARDUS, E. S. *Leaders and Leadership.* New York, 1934.

BOSCH, B. " Massenführer und Gruppenführer " : *Zeitschrift für Pädagog. Psychol.*, vol 30, No. 6, 1929.

BURR, W. *Community Leadership.* New York, 1924.

BUSCH, Henry M. *Leadership in Group Work*, especially Chapter 5 : " Types of Group Leadership." New York Association Press, 1934.

CHAMPERNOWNE, H. *The Boss : An Essay upon the Art of Governing American Cities.* New York, 1894.

CLARKE, E. L. " The Recruitment of the Nation's Leaders. Part I. Historical : A Study of Motives. Part II : The Way to the University." *Sociological Review*, vol. 28, 1936.

COOLEY, Ch. H. Genius, Fame and a Comparison of the Races. *Annals of the Amer. Academy of Political and Social Sciences.*

DAVIS, Jerome. " A Study of One Hundred and Sixty-three Outstanding Communist Leaders " : *Proceedings of the American Sociological Society*, 1930, vol. 25.

DONHAM, W. B. " Training for Leadership in a Democracy " : *Harvard Business Review*, vol. xiv, No. 3, Spring, 1936.

EICHLER, G. A., and MERRIL, R. R. " Can Social Leadership Be Improved by Instruction in its Techniques " : *Journal of Educational Sociology*, vol. 17, 1933.

FUELOP-MILLER, René. *Leaders, Dreamers, and Rebels.* New York, 1935.

GRABO, C. H. " Education for Democratic Leadership " : *Amer. Journ. of Sociol.*, vol. 23, 1918.

HIRSCH, J. *Die Genesis des Ruhmes.* Leipzig, 1914.

KLUCKHOHN, P. " Berufungsbewusstsein und Gemeinschaftsdienst des deutschen Dichters im Wandel der Zeiten " : *Deutsche Vierteljahrsschr. für Literatur, Wissenschaft, und Geistesgeschichte*, vol. 14, 1936.

LEOPOLD, L. *Prestige : A Psychological Study of Social Estimates.* London, 1913.

LUITHLEN, W. F. " Zur Psychologie der Initiative und der Führereigenschaften " : *Zeitschrift für angewandte Psychologie*, vol. 39, 1931.

MAAS, Fritz. " Ueber die Herkunftsbedingungen der geistigen Führer " : *Arch. f. Sozialwissenschaft und Sozialpolitik*, vol. 41, 1916.

MAN, Hendrik de. *Massen und Führer.* Potsdam, 1932.

MILLER, A. H. *Leadership.* New York, 1920.

MORGAN, E. L. " The Professional Training of Rural Leaders " : *Publications of the Amer. Sociological Society*, vol. 17, 1923.

MUMFORD, E. *The Origins of Leadership. Amer. Journ. of Sociol.*, vol. 12, 1927.

NICHOLSON, H. " The Meaning of Prestige " : *The Rede Lecture*, 1937. Cambridge University Press, 1937.

PARTRIDGE, E. de Alton. *Leadership Among Adolescent Boys, etc.* A Thesis. Teachers' College, Columbia University, New York, 1934.

PIGORS, P. *Leadership or Domination.* London, 1936.

PRINZHORN, H. *Das Problem der Führung und die Psychoanalyse.* Akademie Gemeinnütziger Wissenschaften zu Erfurt. Abt. für Erziehungswissenschaft und Jugendkunde. No. 14. Erfurt, 1928.

RATCLIFFE, S. C. " Social Structure and Status " : *Sociol. and Social Research*, vol. 14, 1929–1930.

ROCHESTER, Anna. *Rulers of America.* New York, 1935.

RUSSELL, B. " The Role of the Intellectual in the Modern World " : *Amer Journ. of Sociol* , vol. 44, No. 4, 1939.

SARTRE, V. *Georges Sorel : Élites syndicalistes et révolution proletarienne.* Paris, 1937.

SCHMIDT, Richard. "Leadership" in *Encyclopedia of the Social Sciences.*

SCHNEIDER, J. "Social Class, Historical Circumstances and Fame " : *Amer. Journ. of Sociology,* vol. 43, 1937.

SHEFFIELD, A. D. *Training for Group Experience ; a syllabus of materials from a laboratory concise for group leaders given at Columbia University, 1927.* New York, 1929.

SIKORSKI, Hans. Die Auswahl und soziale Zusammensetzung des Führernachwuchses : *Volk und Reich* 8 (2), 1932.

SMITH, H. L., and KRUEGER, L. M. "A Brief Summary of the Literature on Leadership " : *Bull. of the School of Education (Bureau of Co-operative Research), Indiana University,* vol ix, No. 4, Bloomington, Indiana, Sept., 1933.

SPEIER, H. "Honor and Social Structure " : *Social Research,* vol. 2, 1935.

TAUSSIG, F. W., and JOSLYN, C. S. *American Business Leaders. A Study in Social Origins and Social Stratification.* New York, 1932.

TEAD, Ordway. *The Art of Leadership.* New York, 1935.

THORNDIKE, E. L. "The Relation Between Intellect and Morality in Rulers " : *Amer. Journ. of Sociol.,* vol. 42, 1936.

WITTIG, P. A., and LEHMAN, H. C. Nervous Instability and Genius, Military and Political Leaders : *Journ. of Soc. Psychol.,* 1932, vol. 3.

YARROS, V. "Representation and Leadership in Democracies " : *Amer. Journ. of Sociol.,* vol. 23, 1917–18.

ZILSEL, E. *Die Entstehung des Geniebegriffes.* Tübingen, 1926.

ZINK, H. "City Bosses in the United States. A Study of Twenty Municipal Leaders " : *Duke University Public.* Durham, North Carolina, 1930.

Cf. also IV, 3 ; V, 1–3 ; V, 5 ; V, 6, and the bibliographies on intelligentsia and leadership (pp. 82 n., 88 n., 91 n., 92 n., 99 n., 101, 103).

(5) *Rural and Urban Life. Community Organization and Disorganization. Regionalism.*

ABERCROMBIE, P. *Town and Country Planning.* London, 1933.

ADDAMS, J. "A Function of the Social Settlement " : *Annals of the Amer. Acad. of Political and Social Science,* vol. 13, 1899.

BOARD OF EDUCATION, JUVENILE ORGANIZATIONS COMMITTEE. *Report on the Need for Youth Community Centres on New Housing Estates.* London, 1935.

BURGESS, E., W., (ed.). "The Urban Community": *Selected Papers from the Proceedings of the American Sociological Society*, 1925. Chicago, 1925.

CREUTZBURG, N. *Kultur im Spiegel des Landschaft.* Leipzig, 1930.

DURANT, R. *Watling : A Social Survey of a New Housing Estate.* London, 1939.

GRAS, N. B. S. "The Rise of the Metropolitan Community": *Publications of the American Sociological Society.*, vol. 20, 1925.

HANSEN, G. *Die drei Bevölkerungsstufen.* München, 1889.

HINTZE, H. (Guggenheimer). "Regionalism." Article in the *Encyclopedia of the Social Sciences.*

JONES, D. Caradog and Others (ed.). *The Social Survey of Merseyside.* Liverpool, 1934.

LE CORBUSIER, J. *The City of To-morrow and its Planning.* London, 1929.

—— *Towards a New Architecture.* London, 1931.

LINDEMANN, E. C. *Community : An Introduction to the Study of Community, Leadership, and Organization.* New York, 1920.

LYND, R. S., and LYND, H. M. *Middletown. A Study in Contemporary American Culture.* London, 1929.

—— —— *Middletown in Transition. A Study in Cultural Conflicts.* London, 1937.

MARQUAND, H. A. *South Wales Needs a Plan.* London, 1936.

McIVER, R. M. *Community.* 3rd edition. London, 1924.

MESS, H. A. *Industrial Tyneside.* London, 1928.

MUMFORD, L. *The Culture of Cities.* New York, 1938.

NATIONAL COUNCIL OF SOCIAL SERVICE, New Estates Committee : *New Housing Estates and their Social Problems.* London, 1936.

The New Survey of London Life and Labour. London, 1930.

NEW YORK STATE HOUSING AND REGIONAL PLANNING COMMISSION. *Final Report.*

NORMANN, D., FRANK, W., ROSENFELD, P., and MUMFORD, L. *The Metropolitan Milieu.* New York, 1934.

PARK, R. E., and BURGESS, E. W. (ed.). *The City.* Chicago, 1925.

PEAKE, H. J. E. *The English Village.* London, 1922.

PERRY, C. "The Neighborhood Unit": *Regional Service of New York*, vol. 7, *Neighborhood and Community Planning.* New York, 1929.

SCHIMBERG, M. E. "An Investigation into the Validity of Norms with Special Reference to Urban and Rural Groups": *Archives of Psychology*, vol. xvi, No. 104 (1928–9).

SCHMIEDLER, E. *The Industrial Revolution and the Home.* A Thesis. Catholic Univ. of America, 1927.

SIMMEL, G. " Die Grosstädte und Geistesleben " :
Die Grosstadt, ed. by Petermann, Th. Dresden, 1903.
SOCIAL SCIENCE RESEARCH COUNCIL. *Research Memorandum on the Family in the Depression.* By Stouffer,
S. A., and Lazarsfeld, P. F. Bulletin 39. New York,
1937.
—— *Research Memorandum on Religion in the Depression. Studies in the Social Aspects of the Depression.*
By Kincheloe, S. C. New York.
—— *Research Memorandum on Rural Life in the Depression.* By Sanderson, D. *Studies in the Social Aspects.*
New York.
SOROKIN, P. A. and ZIMMERMANN, C. C. *Principles of
Rural-Urban Sociology.* New York, 1929.
—— —— and GALPIN, C. J. *A Systematic Sourcebook
in Rural Sociology.* Minneapolis, 1930.
THOMAS, W. I. " The Problem of Personality in the
Urban Environment " : *The Urban Community,* ed.
by Burgess, E. W. Chicago, 1925.
WARD, E. J. *The Social Centre.* New York and London,
1913.
WILLIAMS, J. M. *Our Rural Heritage.* New York, 1925.
WIRTH, L. " Localism, Regionalism and Centralization " : *Amer. Journal of Sociology,* 1937.
—— " Urbanism as a Way of Life " : *American
Journ. of Sociology,* vol. 44, no. 1, 1938.
WOODS, R. A. The Neighborhood in Social Reconstruction. *Publications of the Amer. Sociol. Society,*
vol. 8, 1913.
WOOLF, L. *After the Deluge. A Study of Communal
Psychology.* London, 1937.
WOOLSTON, H. " The Urban Habit of the Mind " :
Amer. Journal of Sociology.
WRIGHT, F. L. *Modern Architecture.* Princeton, 1931.
Cf. also III, *d* ; III, 1, *f* ; III, 7, *a* ; III, 7, d ; IV, 1–4, and
the bibliography on unemployment (pp. 220–1 n.).

V. SOME GENERAL PRINCIPLES OF SOCIAL
RECONSTRUCTION.

(1) *Democracy and Liberalism.*

AMERICAN HISTORICAL ASSOCIATION. *Certain Early
Reactions against Laissez Faire.* By Hall, W. P. Annual
Report for the Year 1913, I ; Washington, 1915.
ARNOLD, Th. W. *The Folklore of Capitalism.* New
Haven—Yale Univ. Press, 1937.
ASCOLL, M. F., LERNER, F. (editors). *Political and
Economic Democracy.* New York, 1937.
BARTHOLEMY, J. *La crise de la démocratie contemporaine.*
Paris (Sirey), 1931.
BOUGLÉ, C. *Les idées égalitaires.* Étude sociologique.
Paris (Alcan), 1925.
BRYCE, James. *Modern Democracies.* London, 1921.

CLARK, R. T. *The Fall of the German Republic. A Political Study*. London, 1935.

CRIPPS, Sir Stafford. *Democracy Up To Date*. London, 1939.

DELAISI, F. *La démocratie et les financiers*. Paris, 1910.

DRUCKER, P. *End of Economic Man*. London, 1939.

DURBIN, E. F. M. *et al. War and Democracy*. London, 1938.

FULTON, J. S. and MORRIS, C. R. *The Defence of Democracy*. London, 1935.

HANKINS, F. H. " Individual Differences and Democratic Theory " : *Political Science Quarterly*, vol. 38, 1923.

HEIMANN, E. *Communism, Fascism or Democracy*. New York, 1938.

HERMENS, F. A. *Demokratie und Kapitalismus*. München, 1931.

HOBHOUSE, L. T. *Liberalism*. London, 1911.

HOBSON, J. A. *Democracy and a Changing Civilization*. London, 1934.

HOLCOMBE, A. N. *Government in a Planned Democracy*. New York (Norton), 1935.

HUGHES, E. R. (ed.). *The Individual in East and West*. London.

ILBERT, Sir Courtenay. *Parliament, its History, Constitution, and Practice*. London–New York, 1911.

KANDEL, J. L. *The Dilemma of Democracy*. The Inglis Lecture, 1934. Cambridge, Mass., Harv. Univ. Press, 1934.

LANDAUER, C. " Die Wege zur Eroberung des demokratischen Staates durch die Wirtschaftsleiter " : *Erinnerungsgabe für Max Weber*. München, Leipzig, 1923.

LASKI, H. J. *Democracy in Crisis*. London, 1933.

LINDSAY, A. D. " Individualism." Article in the *Encyclopedia of the Social Sciences*.

—— *The Essentials of Democracy* (*William J. Cooper Foundation Lectures*). London (Oxford Univ. Press), 1935.

LIPPMANN, Walter. *The Good Society*. London, 1938.

MANN, T. *The Coming Triumph of Democracy*. New York, 1938.

McKINLEY, S. B. *Democracy and Military Power*. New York, 1934

MARCUSE, H. " Der Kampfgegen den Liberalismus in der totalitären Staatsauffassung " : *Zeitschrift für Sozialforschung*, vol. 3, 1934.

MARTIN, K. *The French Liberal Tradition in the Eighteenth Century*. London, 1929.

MICHELS, R. *Political Parties : A Sociological Study of the Oligarchic Tendencies of Modern Democracy*. New York, 1925.

MIDDLETON MURRY, J. *The Defence of Democracy*. London, 1939.

Mises, L. *Liberalismus*. Jena, 1927.

Oncken, A. *Die Maxime laissez faire und laissez passer, ihr Ursprung, ihr Werden*. Berner Beiträge zur Geschichte der Nationalökonomie. No. II, 1886.

Ostrogorsky, M. L. *Democracy and the Organisation of Political Parties*. Trans. by Clarke, F., London, 1902.

Pirou,G. *Néo-libéralisme, néo-corporatisme, néo-socialisme*. Paris (Gallimard), 1939.

Rosenberg, A. *The Birth of the German Republic, 1871–1918* (trans. by I. F. D. Morrow). London, 1931.
—— *Demokratie und Sozialismus. Zur Geschichte der letzten 150 Jahre*. Amsterdam, 1938.

Ruggiero, G. de. *History of Liberalism in Europe*. Transl. by Collingwood, R. G. London, 1927.

Schatz, A. *L'individualisme économique et social*. Paris (Colin), 1907.

Schmitt, C. *Die geistesgeschichtliche Lage des heutigen Parlamentarismus*. 2nd ed. München, Leipzig, 1926.

Tawney, R. H. *Equality*. (Halley Stewart Lectures.) London, 1929.

Tocqueville, A. de. *Democracy in America*, 2 vols. London, 1889.

Zürcher, A. J. *The Experiment with Democracy in Central Europe*. New York, 1933.

Cf. also III, 3, *a–c* ; III, 4, *c* ; III, 7, *c* ; III, 7, *e*.

(2) *Fascism. National Socialism.*

Abel, Th. *Why Hitler came into Power. An Answer based on the Original Life Histories of Six Hundred of his Followers*. New York, 1938.

Beckerath, E. von. *Wesen und Werden des fascistischen Staates*. Berlin, 1927.

Beuze, R. *Wegweiser ins Dritte Reich. Published by the National Socialist, Lehrerbund*. 2nd ed. Braunschweig, 1934.

Bibliographia fascista. Rassegna Mensile (Quindicimale). Rome.

Borgese, G. A. " The Intellectual Origins of Fascism " : *Social Research*, vol. 1. New York, 1934.

Bottai, G., Arias, G., Masci, G., Papi, G. V., Fanno, M., etc. Articles on Corporative System in Jahrbücher f. Nationalökonomie und Statistik 1938.

Brady, Robert A. *The Spirit and Structure of German Fascism*. New York and London, 1937.

Dreyer, E. A. *Deutsche Kultur im Neuen Reich. Wesen, Ziele und Aufgaben der Reichskulturkammer*. Unter Mitarbeit der Präsidenten und der Präsidialratsmitglieder der Kammern. Berlin, 1934.

Finer, H. *Mussolini's Italy*. London, 1935.

Gentile, G. *Origini e dottrina del fascisimo*. Rome, 1929.

Goad, H. E. and Currey, M. *The Working of a Corporative State. A Study of National Cooperation*. London, 1934.

HAIDER, C. *Capital and Labour under Fascism.* New York, 1936.

HAYES, C. J. H. *The Historical Evolution of Modern Nationalism.* New York, 1931.

HEIDEN, Conrad. *A History of National Socialism.* London, 1934.

KLAGGES, D. *Idee und System. Vorträge an der deutschen Hochschule für Politik über Grundfragen national-sozialistischer Weltanschauung.* Leipzig, 1934.

LARSON, C. " The German Press Chamber " : *Public Opinion Quarterly,* vol. 1, Oct., 1937.

LESCURE, J. *Le nouveau régime corporative italien.* Paris, 1934.

LEUD, E. *The Underground Struggle in Germany.* London, 1938.

MANOILESCO, M. *Le siècle du corporatisme. Doctrine du corporatisme integral et pur.* Paris, 1938.

MARSCHAK, J. " Der korporative und der hierarchische Gedanke im Fascismus " : *Archiv f. Socialwissenschaft und Socialpolitik.* 1924 und 1925.

MARX, Z. M. *Government in the Third Reich.* New York, 1936.

MUELLER, W. *Das soziale Leben im neuen Deutschland unter besonderer Berücksichtigung der Deutschen Arbeits-front.* Berlin, 1938.

POLLOCK, T. K., and HENEMANN, H. T. The Hitler Decrees. Ann Arbor, 1934.

RAUSCHNING, H. *Germany's Revolution of Destruction.* London, 1939.

SANTANGELO, G. and BROCALE, C. *Guida Bibliographica del Fascismo.* Rome, Liberia del Lettorio, 1928.

SCHUMAN, F. L. *The Nazi Dictatorship.* 2nd ed. New York, 1936.

STEILRECHT, H. *Der deutsche Arbeitslagerdienst,* 2nd ed. Berlin, 1933.

UNGER, E. " Das Schrifttum des Nationalsozialismus, 1919–1934 " : *Forschungsberichte zur Wissenschaft des Nationalsozialismus,* No. 1, Berlin, 1934.

Cf. also I, 2 ; III, 2, *c* ; III, 2, *d* ; III, 5 ; III, 7 ; IV, 2–4 ; V, 6.

(3) *Communism.*

BORKENAU, F. *The Communist International.* London, 1938.

BUKHARIN, N. *Historical Materialism.* New York, 1928.

CURIAN, W. *Bolshevism : Theory and Practice.* Translated by Watkin, E. I. London, 1932.

DUCZINSKA, Hana. " Zum Zerfall der K.P.U." in *Unser Weg,* Berlin, 1922.

HARPER, S. N. *The Government of the Soviet Union,* New York, 1937.

HECKER, J. *Religion and Communism. Religion and Atheism in Soviet Russia.* London, 1933.

LENIN, V. U. " Imperialism. The Highest Stage of Capitalism " in his *Selected Works*. 12 vols. London, 1936.

LYON, Eugene. *Assignment in Utopia*. New York, 1937.

MALEVSKY-MALEVICH, P. (ed.). *Russia—U.S.S.R. A Complete Handbook*. New York, 1933.

MARX, K. *Capital*. Translated from the 4th German Edition by Eden and Cedar Paul. London, Toronto, New York, 1930.

—— *A Contribution to the Critique of Political Economy*. New York, 1904.

—— *Der historische Materialismus. Die Frühschriften*. 2 vols., ed. by Landshut, S. and Mayer, I. P. Leipzig, 1932.

MARX, K., and ENGELS, F. *The Communist Manifesto*, ed. by Ryazanow, D. New York, 1931.

MEHNERT, K. *Die Sowjet Union, 1917–1932*. Berlin, 1933.

PEYREL, H. (ed.). " Bilan du Communisme " in *Cahiers Economiques et Sociaux*. (Librarie Technique et Écono-mique.) Paris, 1937.

ROSENBERG, A. *A History of Bolshevism. From Marx to the First Five Years Plan*. Translated by Morrow, E. F. D. London, 1934.

SCHLESINGER, R. " Neue sowjetrussische Literatur zur Sozialforschung I–III " : *Zeitschrift für Sozialforschung*, vol. 7–8, 1938–9.

SIMON, E. D., *et al*. *Moscow in the Making*. New York, 1937.

SOUVARINE, B. *Stalin : A Critical History of Bolshevism*. London, 1939.

STALIN, J. *Leninism*. 2 vols. London, 1928–1934.

—— *Doctrine de l'U.S.S.R.* Paris (Flammarion), 1938.

TROTSKY, L. *The Revolution Betrayed*. London, 1937.

—— *History of the Russian Revolution*. New York, 1936.

WEBB, Sidney and Beatrice. *Soviet Communism*. London, New York, 1936.

WILLIAMS, A. R. *The Soviets*. New York, 1937.

Cf. also I, 2 ; III, 2, *a–d* ; III, 3, *c* ; III, 5 ; III, 6 ; III, 7, *e* ; IV, 2–4 ; V, 4–6.

(4) *Forms of Social Change.*

ADAMS, Brook. *The Theory of Social Revolutions*. New York, 1913.

BAIN, R. " Cultural Integration and Social Con-flict " : *Amer. Journ. of Sociol.*, vol. 44, 1939.

BERNARD, J. B. *Sociology and the Study of International Relations*. Washington. University Studies, New Series, Social and Philosophical Sciences, N. 4. St. Louis, 1907.

BERTH, E. *Du " Capital " aux " Reflexions sur la violence "*. Paris, 1932.

BURGESS, E. W. *The Function of Socialization in Social Evolution*. Chicago, 1916.

BURY, J. B. *The Idea of Progress. An Inquiry into Its Origin and Growth.* London, 1921.

BUTLER, N. M. *The Family of Nations, its Needs and its Problems.* Essays and addresses. New York, London, 1938.

CARR, E. H. " Honour Among Nations : A Problem of International Cant " : *The Fortnightly*, 1939.

CHANG, Duck Soo. *British Methods of Industrial Peace : A Study of Democracy in Relation to Labour Disputes.* New York, 1936.

CHAPIN, F. S. *Cultural Change.* New York, London, 1928.

COLTON, E. *Four Patterns of Revolution.* New York, 1935.

CRUTTWELL, C. R. M. F. *A History of Peaceful Change in the Modern World.* London, 1937.

DEWEY, J. " Authority and Resistance to Social Change." *School and Society*, Oct., 1936.

DUPRAT, G. L. " Prévision Sociologique et structures sociales." Rapport présenté au XIᵉ congrès de l'Institut International de Sociologie. *Archives de Sociologie*, 1933

EASTMAN, M. *Marx, Lenin, and the Science of Revolution.* New York, 1927.

ELLIOT, W. Y. *The Pragmatic Revolt in Politics. Syndicalism, Fascism and the Constitutional State.* New York, 1928.

ELLIOTT, M. A., and MERRILL, F. E. *Social Disorganization.* New York, London, 1934.

FREYER, Hans. *Revolution von Rechts.* Jena, 1931.

GOTTSCHALK, L. " Leon Trotsky and the Natural History of Revolutions " : *Amer. Journ. of Sociol.*, vol. 44, No. 3, 1938.

GREAT BRITAIN FOREIGN OFFICE HISTORICAL SECTION. *Schemes for Maintaining General Peace.* Handbook. London, 1920.

HAMEL, Joos A. van. " Federating as a Motive Power Towards Peace " : *Transactions of the Grotius Society*, vol. 23, 1938.

HANDMAN, M. " The Bureaucratic Culture Pattern and Political Revolutions " : *Amer. Journ. of Sociol.*, vol. 39, 1933.

HARVARD TERCENTENARY PUBLICATIONS. *Independence, Convergence, and Borrowing in Institutions, Thought, and Art.* Contributions by Childe, V. G., Merrill, E. D., Rostowitzeff, M. I., Norden, E., Wenger, L., Maunier, R., Ginzberg, L., Dodd, Ch. H., Lowicke, F. M., Taylor, H. O., Goldschmidt, A., Bédier, J., Gilson, E., Shi Hu, Añesaki, Marsham, Pelliot, Paul. Cambridge (Mass.), 1937.

HOBHOUSE, L. T. *Social Development.* London, 1924.

HYNDMANN, H. M. *The Evolution of Revolution.* London, 1920.

JEVONS, W. S. *Methods of Social Reform. And Other Papers.* London, 1883.

JOINT LEGISLATIVE COMMITTEE INVESTIGATING SEDITIOUS ACTIVITIES. *Revolutionary Radicalism, Its History, Purpose and Tactics.* A Report. Albany, 1920.

KROPOTKIN, P. *Mutual Aid. A Factor of Evolution.* London, 1902.

LASSWELL, H. D. " The Strategy of Revolutionary and War Propaganda " in *Public Opinion and World Politics,* ed. by Quincey Wright. Chicago, 1035.

LEAGUE OF NATIONS, Secretariat. *Ten Years of World Co-operation.* Geneva, 1930.

LENIN, N. *Preparing for Revolt.* London, 1929.

LENZ, J. *Proletarische Politik im Zeitalter des Imperialismus und der sozialistischen Revolution,* Part I : *Grundbegriffe der Marxistisch Leninistischen Strategie und Taktik.* Berlin (Intern. Verlag), 1931.

LOEWENSTEIN, K. *Control legislatif de l'extremisme politique dans les democraties Européennes.* Paris, 1939.

MACDONALD, J. R. *Parliament and Revolution.* New York, 1920.

McIVER, R. M. *Society : A Textbook of Sociology.* (Book 3 : " Social Change "). New York, 1937.

MALAPARTE, C. *Technique du Coup d'État* (trans. by Juliette Bertrand). Paris, 1931.

MANNING, C. A. W. (ed.). *Peaceful Change. An International Problem.* London, 1937.

MAYREDER, R. *Der typische Verlauf sozialer Bewegungen.* 2nd ed. Wien, 1926.

MERRIAM, Ch. E. *The Rôle of Politics in Social Change.* New York, 1936.

MEUSEL, A " Revolution and Counter-Revolution " : *Enc. Soc. Sc.*

OGBURN, W. F. " Stationary and Changing Societies " : *Amer. Journ. of Sociol.,* vol. 42, 1936.

—— *Social Change.* New York, 1922.

PATRICK, G. T. W. *The Psychology of Social Reconstruction.* Boston, 1920.

PEARSON, K. *Social Problems. Their Treatment, Past, Present and Future.* London, 1912.

POSTGATE, R. *How to Make a Revolution.* New York, 1933.

POTTER, P. B. *The Relations of Order and Progress in International Security.* Chicago.

RAPPARD, W. E. *The Geneva Experiment.* London, 1931.

REEVE, S. A. *The Natural Laws of Social Convulsion.* New York, 1933.

ROSENSTOCK-HUESSY, E. *Out of Revolution. Autobiography of Western Man.* New York, 1930.

SCHELER, M. *Die Ideen des Friedens und des Pazifismus.* Berlin, 1931.

SEE, H. E. *Evolution and Revolution.* New York, 1935.

SCHUMAN, F. *International Politics*. 1937.

SOMBART, W. " Die Formen des gewaltsamen Kampfes " : *Koelner Vierteljahrshefte für Soziologie*, vol. 4, 1924.

SOREL, G. *Les illusions du progrès*. 2nd ed. Paris, 1911.

SOROKIN, P. A. *The Sociology of Revolution*. Philadelphia, 1925.

—— *Social and Cultural Dynamics*. 3 vols. New York, 1937.

STREIT, C. K. *Union Now*. London, 1939.

SUMNER, W. G. " Reform and Revolution " in his *Folkways*. Boston, 1906.

THORNTON, J. E. (ed.). Science and Social Change. Brookings Institution, Washington, 1939.

TOYNBEE, A. J. Peaceful Change or War ? *Intern. Affairs*. 1936.

VERHANDLUNGEN DES DRITTEN SOZIOLOGENTAGES. *Das Wesen der Revolution*. Lectures given by Wiese, L. v. and Hartmann, L. M. Tübingen, 1923.

VOSSLER, O. " Die Amerikanischen Revolutionsideale in ihrem Verhältnis zu den Europäischen " : *Hist. Zeitschrift Supplement No. 17*, Berlin, 1929.

Cf. also I, 2 ; III, 2, *b* ; III, 3, *c* ; IV, 5 ; V, 1–3.

(5) *New Developments in Cultural Life.*

BACHELARD, G. *Le nouvel esprit scientifique*. Paris, 1934.

BARBUSSE, H. *Manifeste aux intellectuels*. Paris, 1927.

BARTH, K. *Theologische Existenz heute*. München, 1933.

BAUER, O. *Die illegale Partei* (Aus dem unveröffentlichten Nachlass). Schriftenreihe des Sozialistischen Kampf, N. 1. Paris (Edition La Lutte Socialiste), 1939.

BEARD, Ch. and M. *America in Mid Passage*. New York, 1939.

BELGION, M. *Our Present Philosophy of Life*. (On Shaw, S. Freud, etc.) London, 1938.

BENDA, Julien. La fin de l'étérnel. Paris, 1929.

—— *The Great Betrayal* (trans. by R. Aldington). London, 1928.

BENN, Gottfried. *Der Neue Staat und die Intellektuellen*. Stuttgart, Berlin, 1933.

BERDYAEV, N. *The End of Our Time*. London, 1933.

BLOCH, E. *Erbschaft dieser Zeit*. Zürich, 1935.

BOAS, G. *Our New Ways of Thinking*. New York, London, 1930.

BRIFFAULT, R. *Breakdown : The Collapse of Traditional Civilization*. London, 1935.

BUREAU, P. *La crise morale des temps nouveaux*. Paris, 1907.

BURKE, K. *Permanence and Change. An Anatomy of Purpose*. New York, 1935.

CHURCH, COMMUNITY AND STATE. *The Churches Survey Their Task* (Series). Reports of the Conference at Oxford. London, 1937–8.

CARR, E. H. *The Twenty Years' Crisis* (1919–1939). London, 1939.

CHAMBERLAIN, John. *Farewell to Reform. The Rise, Life, and Decay of the Progressive Mind in America.* New York, 1933.

DAWSON, Ch. *Beyond Politics.* London, 1939.

DEARMER, P. (ed.). *Christianity and the Crisis.* London, 1933.

DELAISI, F. *Les contradictions du monde moderne.* Paris, 1925.

DÖBLIN, A. Wissen und Verändern. Berlin, 1931.

EASTMAN, M. Artists in Uniform. A Study of Literature and Bureaucratism. New York, 1934.

EINSTEIN, Albert, *et al. Living Philosophies.* New York, 1931.

ELIOT, T. S. *The Idea of a Christian Society.* London, 1939.

ERNST, P. *Der Zusammenbruch des Idealismus.* München, 1919.

Esprit (Periodical), Paris.

FRAENKEL, A. M. *Die seelische Situation der Gegenwart. Probleme der Lebensgestaltung.* Erlenbach, Leipzig, 1935.

FRIEDMANN, G. *La crise du progrès. Esquisse d'histoire des idées 1895–1935.* Paris, 1935.

FRIEDMANN, W. The Disintegration of European Civilization and the Future of International Law. *Modern Law Review*, vol. 2, 1938.

GENTILE, G. *Der aktuale Idealismus.* Tübingen, 1932.

GOEBBELS, J. *Wird die Kunst untergehen?* Berlin, 1933.

GROETHUISEN, B. *Introduction à la pensée philosophique allemande depuis Nietzsche.* Paris (Stock), 1926.

HALÉVY, E., ARON, R., FRIEDMANN, G., BERNARD, E., MARJOLIN, R., DENNERY, E., BOUGLÉ, C. *Inventaires I. La Crise Sociale et les idéologies nationales.* Avant-propos by Bouglé, Ch. Paris (Alcan).

HAUER, W., HEIM, K., ADAM, K. *Germany's New Religion. The German Faith Movement.* Trans. by F. T. S. K. Scott-Craig and R. E. Davies. London, 1937.

HINDUS, M. *Humanity Uprooted.* 2nd ed. London, 1931.

HORKHEIMER, M. " Egoismus und Freiheitsbewegung. Zur Anthropologie des bürgerlichen Zeitalters " in *Zeitschrift für Sozialforschung*, vol. 5, 1936.

HUIZINGA, J. *In the Shadow of To-morrow.* Translated by Huizinga, J. H. Toronto, 1936.

HUXLEY, A. *Ends and Means. An Inquiry into the Nature of Ideals and into the Methods Employed for their Realization.* London, 1937.

INTERNATIONAL LITERATURE (Periodical). Moscow.

JASPERS, C. *Man in the Modern World*, trans. by Eden and Cedar Paul. London, 1933.

KIRCHWEY, F. (ed.). *Our Changing Morality*. London, 1925.

LEE, Porter R. " Changes in Social Thought and Standards which Affect the Family " in Reuter, E., Band, J. S., Runner, J. R., *The Family*. New York, 1931.

LINDQUIST, R. *The Family in the Present Social Order*. Chapel Hill, 1931.

MANNHEIM, K. *Ideology and Utopia*. An introduction to the Sociology of Knowledge. Trans by Wirth, L. and Shils. E. London, 1936.

MARITAIN, J. *Le Crépuscule de la Civilisation*. Paris, 1939.

—— *True Humanism*. London, 1938.

MARTIN, J. L., and GABO, N. (ed.). " Circle " : *International Survey of Constructive Art*. A Yearbook. London.

MAURRAS, Ch. " L'Avenir de l'Intelligence." Paris, 1909.

MONOD, V. *Devalorisation de l'homme*. Études d'histoires et de philosophie religieuse, fasc. 31. Paris, 1936.

MOUNIER, E. *Revolution personaliste et communitaire*. Paris (ed. Montaigne), 1935.

MIDDLETON MURRY, J. *The Price of Leadership*. London, 1939.

NIEBUHR, R. *Moral Man and Immoral Society. A Study in Ethics and Politics*. New York, 1932.

—— *Reflections on the End of an Era*. London, 1934.

NIETZSCHE, F. *Kritik und Zukunft der Kultur*. Ed. and introduced by Mayer, P. Zürich, 1935.

Nouveaux Cahiers (Periodical). Paris.

ORTEGA Y GASSET, J. *Revolt of the Masses*. London, 1932.

PLESSNER, H. *Schicksal des deutschen Geistes am Ausgang seiner bürgerlichen Epoche*. Zürich, 1935.

POHL, G. *Vormarsch ins 20. Jahrhundert. Zerfall und Neubau der Europäischen Gesellschaft im Spiegel der Literatur*. Leipzig, 1932.

POZNER, V. *Panorama de la littérature russe contemporaine*. (With a preface by P. Hazard.) 6th ed. Paris, 1929.

PRESIDENT'S RESEARCH COMMITTEE ON SOCIAL TRENDS. *Recent Social Trends in the United States*. Report. 2 vols. New York, 1933.

RANDALL, J. H., and J. H., Jr. *Religion and the Modern World*. London, 1930.

—— *Our Changing Civilization*. New York, 1929.

READ, H. *Art Now*. 2nd ed. London, 1936.

ROBINSON, J. H. *The Mind in the Making*. London, 1932.

SAZONOVA, J., et BEUCLER, A. " La littérature sovietique. Textes suivis de débats." *Cahiers de la Quinzaine*, 1933.

SCHWEITZER, A. *Verfall und Wiederaufbau der Kultur.* München, 1923.

SOCIÉTÉ DES NATIONS INSTITUT DE COOPERATION INTELLECTUELLE. *L'Avenir de la culture.* Paris, 1934.

STERNBERGER, D. Panorama, oder Ansichten vom 19. Jahrhundert. Hamburg, 1938.

STRASSER, G. *Der Nationalsozialismus, die Weltanschuung des XX. Jahrhunderts.* Berlin, 1931.

WELLS, H. G. *The Open Conspiracy.* London, 1930.

WHITEHEAD, A. N. Science and the Modern World. Cambridge, 1932.

ZIMMERN, Sir Alfred. " The Decline of International Standards " : *International Affairs,* vol. 17, 1938.

—— *Spiritual Values and World Affairs.* London, 1939.

Cf. also IV, 1 ; IV, 3 ; IV, 5.

(6) *Dictatorship and the Principle of Authority.*

ADAMS, D. E. " The Altered Basis of Religious Authority." : *Atlantic Monthly,* vol. 138, 1926, pp. 237–240.

CAMBO, F. I. *Les dictatures.* Paris (Alcan), 1930.

COBBAN, A. *Dictatorship. Its History and Theory.* London, 1939.

DICKINSON, J. " Social Order and Political Authority " : *Amer. Political Science Review,* vol. 23, 1929.

ELLWOOD, Ch. E. " Intolerance " : *Publications of the American Sociological Society.* vol. xix, 1925.

ELKIN, A. *Bibliography of Dictatorship.* Appendix to a Study on *Dictatorship* by Kantorowicz, H. Cambridge, 1935.

FRIEDMANN, W. " The Growth of State Control over the Individual and its Effects upon the Rules of International State Responsibility " : *Brit. Year Book of International Law,* 1938.

FORD, G. S. *Dictatorship in the Modern World.* Minneapolis (University of Minnesota Press), 1936.

HERTZLER, J. O. " Typical Cycle of Dictatorships " : *Social Forces,* vol. 17, No. 3, 1939.

HORKHEIMER, M. (ed.). Studien über Autorität und Familie : *Schriften des Institut für Sozialforschung,* vol. 5, Paris (Alcan), 1936.

KANTOROWICZ, H. *Dictatorships : A Sociological Study.* (Bibliography by Elkin, Alexander). Cambridge, 1935 (also in *Politica,* vol 1, No. 4, Aug., 1935.)

LASKI, H. J. *Authority in the Modern State.* New Haven, 1927.

—— The Foundations of Sovereignty. London, 1922.

LOWENSTEIN, K. " The Dictatorship of Napoleon the First " : *South Atlantic Quarterly,* vol. 35, July, 1936.

OTTO, M. C. " Intolerance " in the *Enc. of the Social Sciences.*

PARRISH, H. " From Authority to Experience " : *Atlantic Monthly*, vol. 138, 1926.

PLANT, J. S. " Human Nature under Authority " : *Proceedings of the National Conference of Social Workers*, 1929. Chicago, 1930.

POLLOCK, F. " Theory of Persecution " in *Essays in Jurisprudence and Ethics*. London, 1882.

RITCHIE, D. G. *The Principles of State Interference*. 3rd ed. London, 1902.

SABATIER, Auguste. *The Religions of Authority and the Religion of the Spirit*. London, 1904.

SCHMITT, C. *Die Diktatur von den Anfängen des modernen Souveränitätsgedankens bis zum proletarischen Klassenkampf*. Berlin, Leipzig, 1921.

STERN, L. " The Sociology of Authority " : *Publication of the Amer. Sociological Society*, vol. 18, 1923.

THURNWALD, R. Despotie in *Reallexikon der Vorgeschichte*.

TINGSTEN, K. *Les pleins pouvoirs l'expansion des pouvoirs gouvernementaux pendant et après la grande guerre*. Transl. by Sönderlink, E. Stock. Paris, 1934.

Cf. also I, 1 ; III, 2, a–d ; III, 5 ; V.

(7)   *The Principle of Freedom.*

ACTON, J. E. *The History of Freedom and Other Essays*. Ed. by John N. Figgis and R. V. Lawrence. London, 1907.

AMERICAN ACADEMY OF POLITICAL AND SOCIAL SCIENCE. " Freedom of Inquiry and Expression " : *Annals*, ed. by Cheyney, E. November, 1938.

BARTHELEMY, J. H. J. B. *Valeur de la liberté et adaptations de la république*. Paris, 1935.

BURGESS, J. W. *The Reconciliation of Government with Liberty*. New York, 1915.

CAUDEL, M. *Nos libertés politiques, origines, évolution, état actuel*. Paris (Colin), 1910.

CLARKE, F. " The Crisis of Freedom in Education " in *Problems in Modern Education*, ed. by Laborde, E. D. Cambridge, 1939.

CURTIS, James. *A Guide to British Liberties*. London, 1937

DEWEY, J. " The Social Significance of Academic Freedom " : *Social Frontier*, vol 2, March, 1936.

DUGUIT, L. *Souveraineté et liberté*. Paris, 1922.

EPHRAIM, F. *Untersuchungen über den Freiheitsbegriff Hegels in seinen Jugendarbeiten*, Part I, in *Philosophische Forschungen*, ed. by Carl Jaspers, vol. 7, Berlin, 1928.

FREUND, M. *Die Idee der Toleranz im England der Grossen Revolution*. Halle, 1927.

HADLEY, A. T. " The Conflict Between Liberty and Equality " : *Raymond F. West Memorial Lectures*. Boston, 1925.

HAYEK, F. V. *Freedom and the Economic System.* Public Policy Pamphlet No. 29. The University of Chicago Press, 1939.

HOBSON, J. A. *Free Thought in the Social Sciences.* London, 1926.

JORDAN, W. K. *The Development of Religious Toleration in England.* London, 1932.

KALLEN, H. M. (ed.). *Freedom in the Modern World.* New York, 1928.

KNIGHT, F. H. " Freedom as a Fact and Criterion " : *Intern. Journ. of Ethics,* vol. 39, 1928-9.

LASKI, H. J. *Liberty in the Modern State.* London, 1930.

LIPPMAN, W. *The Method of Freedom.* London, 1934.

LÖWE, A. *The Price of Liberty. A German on Contemporary Britain.* London, 1937.

MACMURRAY, J. *Freedom in the Modern World.* 2nd ed. London, 1935.

NATIONAL COUNCIL FOR CIVIL LIBERTIES. *Reports of Commissions of Inquiry.* London, 1936.

NATIONAL COUNCIL OF EDUCATION. " Thesis on Freedom in Relation to Culture, Social Planning and Leadership," by G. S. Counts (with a Discussion). February, 1932.

POUND, Roscoe. " The Rejection of Liberalism " : *University of California Chronicle,* vol. 31, 1929.

PRABHU, Datta Sastri. *The Conception of Freedom in Hegel, Bergson, and Indian Philosophy.* Calcutta, 1914.

ROSENZWEIG, F. *Hegel und der Staat.* München and Berlin, 1920.

RUFFINI, Francesco. *Religious Liberty,* transl. by Heyes, J. P. Turin, 1901 (London, 1912).

RUSSELL, B. Roads to Freedom : Socialism, Anarchism, Syndicalism. London, 1918.

WOLFF, A. *Der Toleranzgedanke in der Deutschen Literatur seit Mendelsohn.* Berlin, 1915.

WUNTCH, D. (ed.). *Epoch Making Liberty Documents.* Tyler, 1936.

Cf. also I ; III, 3, *a–c* ; III, 7, *a–e* ; III, 6 ; IV, 1 ; IV, 2 ; V, 1.

INDEX OF SUBJECT MATTER

INDEX OF NAMES